Consuming History

In recent years, history has been described variously as the new rock'n'roll, the new gardening or the new cookery. There is currently a voracious audience for all things historical: cultural histories, celebrity historians, historical novels, star-studded historical films, TV drama, documentaries and reality shows, as well as cultural events and historical re-enactments. Non-academic history – 'public history' – is a complex, dynamic entity which impacts on the popular understanding of the past at all levels.

In *Consuming History*, Jerome de Groot examines how society consumes history and how a reading of this consumption can help us understand popular culture and issues of representation. This book analyses a wide range of cultural entities – from computer games to daytime television, from blockbuster fictional narratives such as *The Da Vinci Code* to DNA genealogical tools – to consider how history works in contemporary popular culture.

Jerome de Groot probes how museums have responded to the heritage debate and the way in which new technologies have brought about a shift in access to history, from online gameplaying to internet genealogy. He discusses the often conflictual relationship between 'public' and academic history, and raises important questions about the theory and practice of history as a discipline.

Consuming History is an important and engaging analysis of the social consumption of history and offers an essential path through the debates for readers interested in history, cultural studies and the media.

Jerome de Groot is Lecturer at the University of Manchester. He is the author of *Royalist Identities* (2004) and numerous articles on popular history, manuscript culture and the English Civil War.

Consuming History

Historians and heritage in contemporary popular culture

Jerome de Groot

Routledge
Taylor & Francis Group

LONDON AND NEW YORK

First published 2009
by Routledge
2 Park Square, Milton Park, Abingdon, Oxon OX14 4RN

Simultaneously published in the USA and Canada
by Routledge
270 Madison Ave, New York, NY 10016

Reprinted 2009 (twice)

Routledge is an imprint of the Taylor & Francis Group, an informa business

© 2009 Jerome de Groot

Typeset in Baskerville by
Taylor & Francis Books
Printed and bound in Great Britain by
CPI Antony Rowe, Chippenham, Wiltshire

British Library Cataloguing in Publication Data
A catalogue record for this book is available from the British Library

Library of Congress Cataloging in Publication Data
De Groot, Jerome, 1975–
    Consuming history : historians and heritage in contemporary popular
    culture / Jerome de Groot.
        p. cm.
    Includes bibliographical references.
    1. Public history. 2. History in popular culture. I. Title.
    D16.163.D4 2008
900–dc22   2008017319

ISBN 978-0-415-39946-3 (hbk)
ISBN 978-0-415-39945-6 (pbk)
ISBN 978-0-203-88900-8 (ebk)

This book is for Sharon Ruston, with all my love

Contents

PART VI
Artefact and interpretation   233

Acknowledgements

I acknowledge support of the British Academy in funding research for sections of this book. The University of Manchester has also been extremely generous in supporting my work.

At Routledge, Philippa Grand and Victoria Peters have been brilliant at all points, and Liz Gooster guided the project through its initial stages. Lizzie Clifford has been extremely helpful and supportive, for which many thanks. Martin L. Davies, Frank Trentmann and an anonymous reviewer were interrogative and generous readers of the project.

I am indebted to the following for information and assistance: Jan Dixon, Rupert Gaze, Bernadette Lynch, Ben Hulme, and Don Henson. In particular, I would like to thank Anke Bernau, Sue Chaplin, Tim Derby, Chris Dixon, Olivia de Groot, Sharon Ruston, and Chris Taylor for their generosity and great help in reading and commenting on sections of the text. Friends in London, Liverpool and Manchester have been wonderful as ever throughout the gestation of this book.

Many people have discussed aspects of this project with me, and it is a pleasure to thank them: Simon Bainbridge, Erin Bell, Louis de Bernières, Michael Bibler, Fred Botting, John Corner, Matthew Creasy, Oliver Daddow, Alex Drace-Francis, Laura Doan, Susannah Dunn, Tobias Ebbrecht, Patrick Finney, Alex Graham, Ann Gray, Crawford Gribben, Amy Holdsworth, Andrew Hoskins, Matt Houlbrook, Tristram Hunt, Ian Jack, Tony Jackson, Emily Keightley, Hari Kunzru, John McAuliffe, Scott McCracken, Robert McFarlane, Emma Mahoney, David Matthews, Kaye Mitchell, Alun Munslow, Daragh O'Reilly, Derek Paget, Guy Redden, Simon Schama, Jackie Stacey, Simon Titley-Bayes, Sarah Waters, and Mark Whitmore. Thanks to Jeremy Maule as ever.

I have presented material at research seminars and conferences in Keele, Lincoln, Liverpool, Manchester, Sheffield, Leeds, Lancaster, and Swansea and I thank all those who invited me to speak at these events and asked questions which made me reconsider my thinking.

I would like to thank the staff of the following libraries for their time and expertise: University of Wales, Bangor; John Rylands, University of Manchester; the British Film Institute and the National Film and Television Archive; the

British Library; Manchester Central Library. Sections of Chapters 8, 9, 10 and 11 appear in 'Empathy and Enfranchisement: Popular Histories', *Rethinking History: The Journal of Theory and Practice*, 10(3), (2006), 391–413, reprinted by permission of the publisher.

Thanks and love to my family.

Introduction

History and popular culture

Why is the professional historian ... seemingly alone in being able to determine the proper answer to the question 'what is history?'?[1]

In his polemic *Refiguring History*, Keith Jenkins portrays professional historians as labouring under illusions and clinging to self-definitions which are foolish and predicated upon falsehoods. He argues that historians access the past by deploying a particular set of 'discursive skills' yet that they are as expert in the studying of 'the before now' as 'anyone': 'journalists, politicians, media commentators, film makers, artists – can and do successfully access "the before now" often in ingenious ways which pay scant regard for the "skills and methods" of the historian'.[2]

Historians, for Jenkins, utilise generic skills to investigate a set of problems that they themselves legitimise as important. Writing that history should be freed from overly deterministic models, Jenkins argues that 'it frees us up from being held in thrall to commonsensical rigid designations if we see that terms like "the past" and "history" are, like other terms, *empty signifiers*'.[3] Jenkins' broadside against the professional historian presents key questions: Who, then, tells the public what 'history' is and what it means? If 'the past' is after all an empty signifier, just what are the semiotic processes involved in constructing, perpetuating and consuming purported meaning – what strategies are in place for pouring sense into such representational aporia?

This book investigates the blurring of the lines Jenkins sees as being drawn between professional historians and others who 'access' the past, in order to discern better what 'History' means: how it is sold, presented, transmitted and experienced. Professional historians have kept much of their traditional legitimacy, but this has been eroded due to shifts in technology, theory and access.[4] History is a set of stories and a range of discursive practices that have been borrowed liberally by popular culture and *Consuming History* looks at the various hybrids that have been the consequence. Ludmilla Jordanova has persuasively argued that 'Public history uses a wide variety of genres, which are different from those of the academic discipline – a fact that shapes the content of the type of history we are designating "public".'[5] She continues, 'If we can identify and reflect upon this generic range, the whole phenomenon, including the means by which publics develop their sense of the past, can be appreciated more fully.'[6] This book considers the interface between History and 'the historical', and illustrates the diffusion of History into multiple 'historicals'. Since the early 1990s, 'History' and genres of the 'historical' have grown exponentially as cultural artefact, discourse, product and focus. While professional historians busied themselves with theoretical argument, 'History' as leisure pursuit boomed. The historical as a cultural trope developed largely unchecked and unconsidered during the late 1990s and early twenty-first century. As a nation, across a bewildering amount of media, the past seems incredibly interesting. Britain is a society fascinated, continually reading, rereading, plotting and conspiring different versions and different timelines. Technological improvements, funding changes, institutional revolutions and political interventions have all impacted on the selling, packaging and presentation of the past over the past two decades.

Through a consideration of a variety of cultural forms and practices this book analyses what has changed regarding the consumption of history, and in particular, what impact new technologies, different experiences and historiographical debates have had on the way that history is consumed, understood and sold. This book analyses these new forms of historical consumption with a view to understanding contemporary culture and nuancing our understanding of the relationship between the public and its history. In particular, attention is paid to the way that new technologies have effected a shift in historical access, from online gameplaying to the uses made of the internet by genealogists. The book particularly looks at historical presentation in mediums which are generally ignored by professional historians, and posits something of a 'virtual turn' in historiography.[7] It considers the ways that the public forms its sense of history, and particularly how this past is fast attaining the attributes of a commodity. How a society consumes its history is crucial to the understanding of contemporary popular culture, the issues at stake in representation itself, and the various means of self- or social construction available. Indeed, it allows us to question the very notion of consumption, too, articulating the concept across a variety of different media and socio-economic models. Consumption practices influence what is packaged as history and work to define how the past manifests itself in society.

Should we look at the way that history is transmitted in culture? Is it possible to understand or conceptualise 'history' as a social or cultural entity? In 1994, Raphael Samuel gave television 'pride of place' among the 'unofficial sources of historical knowledge' that historians should attend to.[8] He posited that in order to understand what history actually was, a 'social form of knowledge', scholars had to look at the often populist and unusual ways that historical knowledge was constructed, transmitted and perpetuated.[9] Since Samuel wrote these words, a flourishing market for cultural histories, celebrity historians, historical novels, films, TV drama, documentaries, and a number of cultural events from the launching of the *History* Channel (US 1994; UK 1996) to the David Irving trial have pushed 'History' into the mainstream in a number of new guises. The various popular historical genres became hugely popular, with an unusually wide profile and unprecedented range and reach. It is crucial that the types of the 'historical' that are being presented and sold are analysed initially to try to understand Samuel's 'social form of knowledge', and thence to begin to conceive of how History as a set of entities and discourses works in contemporary society: what it means, how it means, how it is consumed, and how people might use it.

Samuel's arguments suggest a certain self-awareness about how the past works in society on the part of those who use it. Approaching the same issue, from a different perspective, Vivian Sobchack argued that:

> Popular audiences have become involved in and understand the stakes in historical representation, recognize 'history in the making,' and see themselves not only as spectators of history but also as participants in and adjudicators of it. Current debates around the nature, shape, and narration of history are no longer only the province of academic historians and scholars of film and literature. 'History happens' now in the public sphere where the search for a lost object has led not only to cheap substitutes but, in the process, also to the quickening of a new historical sense and perhaps a more active and reflective historical subject.[10]

Does this self-aware historical subject exist? If so, what is it fed on, and how is it defined and constructed? How have the increased immediacy and multiplicity of historical possibilities and experiences impacted on the ways that the past is viewed and presented? How, why and when does a society 'consume' history? What are the implications for considering history as a *product*? How have non-professional media (TV, drama, film, web) influenced and helped construct cultural memory? How does fictionalised history – the past as cultural production – impact upon the popular imagination? Samuel's privileging of television is fast looking outdated with the advent of digitisation, streaming media, Web 2.0 and specialised niche programming. How do these technologies change the popular perception and understanding of history? Are we able to audit the way that history is understood through considering this evolution of transmission?

This book emerged as an attempt to address these various questions and from a sense that popular engagement with history in the UK had undergone great shifts over the past decade and a half. Two things had gone largely unaudited by academic historians. The first was a shift in access – from reality TV to new curatorial practice to popular history books to Web 2.0 – that allowed the individual to seemingly conceptually and materially circumvent the historical professional and appear to engage with the 'past' in a more direct fashion. There appeared to be something of a crisis of historical legitimacy as a consequence, and a new – if possibly illusory – popular epistemology. Second, and concurrently (and somewhat contradictorily), History was increasingly prevalent as a cultural, social and economic trope and genre. The historical psychology (Sobchak's 'historical sense' and what I occasionally term the historic imaginary) anticipated, addressed and provided for by television producers, curators, novelists, playwrights and film-makers was multiple, prevalent, complex and unstable. History was associated with nationhood, nostalgia, commodity, revelation and knowledge but also personal testimony, experience and revelation; it was at once a deferred, distanced discourse and simultaneously something that the individual could literally at times hold in their hand, change in their own way, or experience in a variety of mediums.

I have attempted, then, to take up Samuel's challenge and look at the 'unofficial' histories available within popular culture. What became clear in the course of my study was that the 'historical' in popular culture and contemporary society is multiple, multiplying, and unstable. The variety of discourses that use history; the complexity of interrogations, uses and responses to that history; and the fracturing of formal, technological and generic systems, all contribute to a dynamic and massively important phenomenon. What this book therefore demonstrates is that culturally the 'historical' is part of an important and complex set of representational practices.

Non-academic or non-professional history – what has been defined as 'public' history – is a complex, dynamic phenomenon. While 'public' history is increasingly attended to by historians, the implications of new ways of engaging with the past have not been thoroughly investigated.[11] This is often the result of professional distaste for the various popular forms of history, emerging from a critique of the popular and a theoretical model of the cultural industries which encourages a binary of high (History) versus low (heritage or 'the historical').[12] In theoretical discussions of the role and nature of history, analyses of the public historian and the impact of popular media on historical understanding have been marginalised. What discussion of history in popular culture there is tends to bemoan its debasing of 'history'.[13] David Lowenthal has bitter words for those who create and imbibe what he calls heritage products:

> Celebrating some bits and forgetting others, heritage reshapes a past made easy to embrace. And just as heritage practitioners take pride in creating artifice, the public enjoys consuming it. Departures from history distress only a handful of highbrows. Most neither seek historical veracity nor mind its absence.[14]

As he argues elsewhere, 'The past ceases to be a foreign country, instead becoming our sanitised own.'[15] Without doubt, the various industries created to sell history – via film, television (drama and documentary), advertising, even pornography – are in the business of creating an artificial relational product which is as interested in deferring as identifying historical otherness. A caveat might be that most of this material is self-conscious, representing and reflecting on its own artificiality in ways which are associated with postmodern tropes and also often due to an historiographic sense of ephemerality and subjectivity. Conversely, the breadth of access to history – either embodied re-enactment, interactive exhibit or actual archival materials (however digitised and virtual) – and the bleeding of genres into each other suggest that, as Raphael Samuel argued, history is a socially and culturally constructed and consumed entity, able at once to hold within itself difference and sameness, to represent otherness and familiarity, and to remind the individual of their distance from the past while enabling them through that difference to understand themselves somehow in a way more complex than hitherto.

In a similar vein to Lowenthal's, Patrick Joyce asserts that: 'History is not commodity' and that the historians must stand firm 'against the market power of the mass, capitalist market'.[16] His thoughtful analysis argues that critical history contains within it a 'critique of present power' that challenges contemporary popular paradigms.[17] Academic history helps 'shape a public that is historically conscious' and should help protect this public from the threats of consumer society.[18] This book responds to Joyce's worries in two ways. First, history has become commodified (or works within a nexus of commodification) irrespective of the actions of historians, and understanding the processes of communication and consumption that are undergone in contemporary popular engagement with the past will afford us a more nuanced perception of this phenomenon. If the historian seeks to protect the historical consciousness of the public, they must first understand how that group is informed and resourced. Second, within most of the practices and forms outlined here is a space of dissidence and possibility, a subjective quality that tends to undermine the broader system. Popular culture is in a state of constant contention and evolution, and the representation of the historical is part of this development. Heritage-consumerism might well be a problematic, potentially destructive force, but, at the same time, these historical products bear within them a potentiality for reading against the grain or introducing new ways of conceptualising the self and social knowledge; and in this they might be valuable for their defiance and dissidence.[19] This book therefore in some ways narrates and illustrates – rather than promulgating – a populist historiography, emphasising the crucial value of studying contemporary cultural-historical practices. It formulates an agenda for further study of the ways that history is presented and engaged with.

Ludmilla Jordanova has little time for those who would 'dismiss public history as "mere" popularisation, entertainment or propaganda', and her contention that 'we need to develop coherent positions on the relationships between academic history, the media, institutions such as museums, and popular culture' provides the broad context for what follows.[20] The novelty of my approach is not just the revelation and investigation of materials underconsidered by historians; scholars from a range of disciplines have called for a synthesised consideration of the ways in which history interfaces with popular culture. In a review essay considering David Cannadine's collection *History and the Media*, Professor of Media Studies John Corner took to task those historians whose 'anxiety level about the integrity of popular mediated history' was so high they considered any such work 'dangerous' or 'simply intolerable'.[21] Corner's point was that rather than bemoaning television history or 'routinely lamenting the crassness of media exposition', professionals from a wide range of disciplines need to look at 'the positioning of popular history in popular culture and the way that the media now resource this'.[22] In particular, he suggested scholars consider the multiple ways that new media forms are impacting upon the popular presentation of history and on traditional documentary style. What is necessary, as Jordanova similarly argued, is what Corner calls an exploration of 'the full stretch and complexity of the historical within the everyday'.[23]

In 1998, Robert Rosenzweig and David Thelen conducted a kind of ethnographic test to see how history impacted on the everyday lives of American citizens.[24] They found, among other things, that 'normal' Americans were generally put off by overly academic history, felt that history was prevalent in their lives nonetheless and would prefer a personal or first-hand account to a narrative being told to them. In articulating the justification for their project, Rosenzweig and Thelen argued that in order to: 'help create a history that would extend beyond the content and practice of elites, we needed to hear a much wider range of people tell us about how (or even whether) the past mattered to them'.[25] While this current book grapples with various models of reception, and only attempts to define the experiences of the history-user in no more than vague terms because of the range and scope of material under analysis, the spirit is the same – the desire to demonstrate that the past works in society and culture in ways that historians rarely comprehend, and the assertion that the ways in which non-academic audiences understand and engage with the past are far more complex than we imagine.

Popular cultural manifestations of history, then, challenge professional historians as they present something of a dissident historiography which embraces this innate multiplicity. The phenomena considered here tell us much about the possible relationships to, and valuing of, historical knowledge. They offer a series of versions of the past that suggest a variety of experience but also a deep sophistication in reading and responding to historical discourse. Popular histories do not represent the standardisation of history as a unified product so much as they reflect the complexity of contemporary cultural and social interface. Reading history allows insight therefore into the ways in which culture works as a whole.

A good – or bad – example of the problematic, insubstantial/significant and high-level manifestation of history in the popular imagination is the *Daily Mirror*'s cover of 24 June 1996. The day before England played Germany in the semi-finals of the European Football Championships, the newspaper led with the headline 'Achtung! Surrender! For you Fritz ze Euro 96 Championship is over' accompanied by images of two English players in soldier's helmets. Such appropriation of war film and war comic vocabulary, tub-thumping jingoism and blatantly aggressive historicised nationalism demonstrated that there are a number of key tropes still loudly resonating within English tabloid culture.[26] The 'Dunkirk' or 'Blitz' spirit is repeatedly invoked in public life, and the use of such ideas draws on folk myth, televisual and film tropes, as well as lazy journalism.[27] This is despite the fact that revisionist history has undermined the heroic narratives of these events.[28] As this demonstrates, History permeates popular culture, and its manifestations are wider than historians often allow for. Popular understanding, use and consumption of 'pastness' are powerful models and paradigms for the ways in which society thinks of history. Three brief examples of how the past works in contemporary popular culture will serve to demonstrate this.

The prizewinning past

One way that historical *knowledge* – both in terms of what is known and how it is modelled – circulates in ways that historians find difficult to account for is its appearance as a category in games. Game shows, pub quiz nights and board games present history as a set of facts which are correct, the right answer. This ludic epistemology introduces 'History' as one of a number of competing discourses mastery of which will lead to cultural capital.[29] Historical 'knowledge' in these manifestations is the command and recall of a set of facts – generally dates, leaders, events or places. In the original *Genus* edition of the multi-million-selling *Trivial Pursuit* (Hasbro, 1982–) 'History' is one of six categories of question. The question, answer and progress format of the game presents knowledge as inquiry-based and rewards the retention and ownership of one-dimensional and discrete facts, despite branding this information 'trivial'.[30] The special editions of the game – *Totally 80s*, *Baby Boomer*, *Silver Screen*, *Bring on the 90s* – often create an entire game around a particular time period. These special editions are aimed at demographic groups and work on a combination of nostalgia and the desire to historicise the recent – and personal – past. Knowledge of biographical history is being tested, to an extent (players have not learnt these facts, they have lived through them). *Trivial Pursuit* is of course now played globally online and has been made into television shows in the USA and the UK.

Television quiz shows – which underwent a boom in the 1990s and became more culturally visible and viable – present history as a category of information, again something subject to personal intellectual recall.[31] It is information which has a purpose – the furthering of one's narrative on the show. In some instances – in shows as diverse as *Are You Smarter than a Fifth Grader?* (Fox 2007, and global) and *University Challenge* (BBC, 1962–87, 1994–) – historical materials are presented within an educational framework. Game shows have, much like documentary, been subject to the generic pressures of reality TV, deregulation, commercialisation and new cultural modes of accessing, valuing and interpreting information. Their systems of knowledge and reward-based dynamic have been undermined by sensationalist exploitation, debased by blame culture, and stimulated by an interest in aggressive group psychology and the entertainment value of 'impoliteness'.[32] Knowledge is still a key part of their systems but the hybridity of formats and the importation of new entertainment motifs mean that the ability to know things is less important than the ability to entertain. At root, gaming is now fundamental in contemporary culture, from the widespread prevalence of *Sudoko* to internet gaming and gambling, through the massive increase in computer game sales to entire game and quiz television channels. This underlying ludicness, then, associated with mediated discourses of knowing, throws history into a complex set of interactions – something that gains the owner credibility, and might enlarge their self-worth or actual worth, but at the same time having little innate value outside of the (game) structure. History's manifestation in games therefore shows that as a category of knowledge it might be considered inflexible, purposeful and something to be retained by the individual to gain them cultural worth and social status.

Selling historically

Raphael Samuel's theory of 'retrochic' considered the ways in which the past bled into the present, making 'room for historicist fantasy in everyday life'.[33] As economic and bodily projections of this retrochic desire-fantasy, advertising and pornography encompass many of the ways that the past is manifested in contemporary culture. They both include within their multifaceted typology the following diverse (contradictory) ways of engaging with the past (amongst many other things): as a mode of nostalgia; as a way of relating to now; as a form of self-knowledge and self-definition; as a set of easily identifiable cultural tropes that are deployed without any real sense of their agency or true 'meaning'; as a set of representational tropes which point to something 'other'; as an economically inflected historiography; as something that is – literally at times – consumed, commodified, and experienced bodily. The complexity of this range of possible – probable – 'meanings' suggests that the psychology of the historical, or the historical imaginary, is a constantly evolving phenomenon. Epistemologically the contemporary historicised subject is multiple.

Advertising has increasingly become part of the cultural furniture.[34] It is important to comprehend the mediated way in which consumers of such texts engage with them, to see 'the interconnectedness of advertising experiences with other aspects of … young adults' lives'.[35] Commercials create and perpetuate brands in the popular imagination and are direct ways in which history is experienced as something to be consumed, albeit tangentially as connected to product rather than commodity itself. Advertising campaigns can be so effective that it becomes difficult to divorce the consumption of the product from the mediated promotion of that item. A key originary example here is the nostalgia associated with the *Hovis* 'Bike Ride' advert (1973; and a series up to 1979), directed by Ridley Scott, which was voted the nation's favourite commercial in 2006 and rescreened during May of that year.[36] The adverts presented an idealised version of Englishness (one was set post-war and emphasised the revelation of having real butter again) with an older voice recounting the experiences of its pictured youthful self in eating Hovis; as Raphael Samuel notes, they made 'soft-focus nostalgia a leitmotiv of TV commercials'.[37] The 'Bike Ride' was set in a cobbled country lane during what appears to be the nineteenth-century (certainly the *mise-en-scène*, which includes thatched cottages, and the costume, appears as such; the advert is also filmed in a kind of sepia). The tagline – a second, more authorial, antidiegetic voiceover – reflected the historicised text: 'It's as good for you today as it's always been'.[38] The original nostalgia of the advert became folded into memory of the text itself and therefore it functions in two ways:

initially with the allying of certain nostalgic tropes (childhood, pastoral England, Dvořák's accompanying music) to the product and thereafter with the commercial itself becoming part of a nostalgic yearning for an idealised past associated with the original experience of the advert (to the extent that the Dorset setting of the text has become a tourist site and the music is now known as the *Hovis* music).

Deploying historical tropes in order to sell goods – from Levi Strauss's use of classic soul music during the 1980s to Stella Artois' parodies of the *Jean de Florette* series of French films (ongoing campaign) – illustrates just how ingrained in the cultural imagination certain versions of the past are, whether they happened or not.[39] The Levi's adverts mainly drew upon recent cultural versions of the 1950s and 1960s (*American Graffiti, Grease!* or *Happy Days*) for their tone, and Stella Artois clearly aligns itself with a sophisticated art-house film source.[40] These adverts also demonstrate the irrelevance of authenticity, insofar as it is the feel and the look of the accepted past – or the ready-made imaginative simulation which has been constructed already – which are being deployed. Advertising, more attuned to the evolving systems of consumer capitalism, has been quick to use pastiche and in doing so to render some artefacts historically inert.

Raphael Samuel suggests that in postmodernism semi-parodic 'retrochic' occurs 'only when history has ceased to matter' and that the 'detachment and ironic distance' of such texts is central to their purpose.[41] These adverts are not authentic or narrative, they are clearly part of an intertextual culture in which history is one of a number of fetishised discourses that can be used to market commodities (the films that Stella Artois echoes are French, the beer is from Belgium, the adverts are shown across Europe). The past, as a set of tropes for advertising product, is often shorthand for a suite of possibilities: authenticity, quality, Englishness, classiness. However, it can just as easily mean dirtiness, ignorance, disease and war. Importantly the past is something which it is assumed the viewer can connect to and consume, quite literally, at an economic level. Using the past to articulate a brand necessarily implies that there is something about that pastness that is marketable and that an ordinary viewer will happily buy into. This notion of connection is demonstrable in such key texts as the Guinness 'Noitulove' campaign (2005) in which three drinkers revert onscreen into mudskippers (the evolution of the perfect pint has taken some time to occur), and the Peugeot 207CC 'Change' advert (2007) in which two lovers get into their car in 1934 and the past develops into the present around them. Both campaigns accentuate continuation and quality. The telescoping of time presents history as something linear in which the constant is the product; the Guinness advert creates a kind of teleology of the commodity (all evolution has been towards the 'good thing' which comes to 'those who wait') whereas the Peugeot suggests that despite the vagaries of history their car is an ever present point of orientation.

Adverts are an integral part of day-to-day cultural life – the estimates of how many an average Western adult sees a day range from 150–3000. Historical adverts take their place as one of a massive range of semi-cultural phenomena and often there is nothing particularly important about their historicity. The viewer is expected to be quite comfortable switching from an advert set in the present day to one set in 1930. Indeed, many adverts move between time periods quite happily, such as the 2006 'Past experience' campaign for Heineken predicated upon a man travelling back to the 1920s; the world around him transforms in front of his eyes, but the beer is reassuringly 'exactly the same' as it is 'unchanged since 1873'. Again, the product is constant and even somehow ahistorical. History becomes background, but also history becomes part of the day-to-day culture – fetishised in some fashion but shorn of its capacity to be other. This is particularly true of the increasingly common adverts in which celebrities are inserted into well-known footage of important historical moments.[42] This began in the 1990s with Heineken's series of adverts intercutting footage of famous film stars, and continued with the 1998 Mercury one2one campaign in which celebrities spoke of the historical figures they would most like to converse with.[43] There is a kind of historiographic model at work in these texts – a march of progress towards the present and a self-conscious citation of canonical and familiar history. However, such debasing and fracturing of the historical record – turning the past essentially into a wish-list for well-known contemporary figures to engage with – emphasise a connection (the desire to communicate with the past in order to understand both it and oneself) and a distance (this is impossible). The celebrity becomes a more rounded person through an appreciation of the past and the audience, through purchasing the brand, connect to them and through them to history – becoming whole via economic transaction. The insertion of the celebrity into the past – often by adding them to footage – flattens history and removes its otherness. It has happened in reverse, too, with archive and older film footage being doctored to include modern products (such as the use of Steve McQueen's (1968) film *Bullitt* to advertise the Ford Puma in 1997, the digital updating of Gene Kelly's performance of 'Singin' in the Rain' for Volkswagen in 2005 with the tagline 'the original, updated', or the use of *The Wizard of Oz* to advertise Federal Express in 2000).[44]

Vintage, nostalgia-led marketing, and retrochic are key parts of a culture which is saturated with historical-ness, a constantly evolving set of (economic) relationships to particular pasts as defined in a multitude of ways. The visual past is part of contemporary (global) consumption practice, one of many parti-cular tropes deployed to encourage brand recognition and subsequent economic investment. History is co-opted here as part of the service industry, encouraging the consumer; it is not commodity itself but part of marketing and commodifi-cation. The phrase and practice of 'Consuming' History in this context, therefore, articulate many things, from the branded association of a product with a time period, to the rendering of the past as just one of many tropes used to represent and sell commodities, and the status of the past within a set of consumption practices that give it a certain power in the nexus of economic desire.

Desiring history

Pornography, which still makes up the most substantial share of internet traffic (*c.* 25 per cent of searches, 8 per cent of emails), is not exempt from the pre-valence of the past – there is a large audience for historic erotica and nostalgia pornography.[45] This very basic deployment of the historical as trope to satisfy primal/acculturated desires, while being sold using the vocabulary of heritage, nostalgia or vintageness, presents the past as just another one of a set of fetish characteristics.[46] It is something recognisable, usable, consumable – in short, an historical body is as much a commodity as that of a modern porn star, a product (which gains some legitimacy from its 'authenticity' and surrounding discourses of nostalgia and historical significance) to be bought, sold, or downloaded. Historical pornography seemingly empowers the gazing viewer, creating a set of (obvious) power relations within a nexus of gender and economics, rendering the historical explicit in its representation and violated in its consumption. Online historical pornography demonstrates the prevalence of historicisation in popular culture, and its manifestation, global reach and increasing significance as a consequence of the expansion of the internet. It also suggests tangentially that the historical is a trope or a set of meanings that is subject to varieties of desire (sexual and economic), which might be an element of self-actualisation and, more grossly, is something to be consumed, experienced and used in physical, material (abject) ways.

Pornography entered the historical mainstream with a six-part documentary on Channel 4 in 1999.[47] Indeed, the collection of historic pornography and vintage erotica is a legitimate enterprise; certainly the age of the materials involved was part of the defence deployed by the actor Paul Reubens in 2003 when arrested on child pornography charges (the charges were dropped when he pleaded guilty to a separate obscenity charge). Events such as the revival of burlesque (sometimes termed 'neo-Burlesque') in the USA and the UK in the late 1990s, the interest surrounding the film documentary *Inside Deep Throat* (Fenton Bailey and Randy Barbato, 2005), and the release of *The Notorious Bettie Page* (Mary Harron, 2005), have combined to make antiquated sex – or the visual tropes associated with it – very much part of the contemporary popular imagination. These examples map on well to some of the key concerns of this book – self-conscious re-enactment and embodiment of an historicised activity (burlesque), historical documentary interest in popular culture (*Deep Throat*), and the increasing hybridity and textual complexity of historical film and drama (*Bettie Page*). Vintage erotica too has much in common with the trope of erotic historical fiction or romance fantasy novels such as those by Bertrice Small or the Black Lace imprint's historical series, in the conscious presentation of familiar practices in an antique setting.[48] This brief set of cultural elements accruing around one particular activity – sex – and its mode of manifestation and representation as an 'historical' or historicised practice in contemporary society demonstrates the complexity and extraordinary reach of the past in the present, illustrating the manifold and often perplexing ways in which the historical has permeated contemporary life.

Historiocopia/historioglossia

As can be seen from these brief examples, the range of the 'historical' is enormous and multivalent. I confess that often in writing this book I was daunted by the range and complexity of materials. How to account for historical films as far apart in intention, audience, marketing, and theme as *La Reine Margot, Revenger's Tragedy* or *The Queen*? How to audit the teeming complexity of popular history books? How might one think about audiences in the UK and the USA, and within those countries, the massive range of genders, races and classes all engaging with the past? Most of the topics covered herein would benefit from book-length or even career-length consideration. Despite this scale, and with the caveat as a consequence of it that this study is in no way exhaustive, *Consuming History* attempts to follow Corner's and Jordanova's stipulation that work bringing together analysis of these multiplying genres is crucial.

The process of writing the book, furthermore, convinced me of the importance of such a broad and multiple approach. For one, the multivalency of signs and the ways in which genres were embedded in a variety of practices were impressed upon me. An example of this might be Philippa Gregory's historical romance novel *The Other Boleyn Girl*. This book, the first in a sequence of four Tudor novels, sold in excess of 800,000 copies worldwide. Its status as a global text is important – despite being very specifically about British history, the book has a reach way beyond an audience for whom that past might be expected to resonate. The genre of the novel is complex: it is a romance (and therefore feeds the fantasy world of the reader); it is historical (and has the apparatus of the form – including an author's note on methodology and context, and endpapers replicating manuscript letters by Anne Boleyn). It is comfortable genre fiction, but at the same time has the inescapable self-consciousness of the historical novel, constantly aware of itself as making something other familiar. Importantly, this otherness and self-reflexivity are necessary and fundamental to the form, and accepted by the readership without complication – suggesting a sophistication of response.[49] It imposes clarity and narrative upon the chaos of history but also rescues women from the margins of a repeatedly told story. Gregory's books meld fact and fiction by weaving a narrative out of historical fact and historical conjecture or, as the dust jackets coyly put it, 'contemporary rumour'. They are populist romance novels, presenting the difficulties for women in the sixteenth century but still wed to models of non-resistance, marriage and family. Independent, strong women in the text – Anne Boleyn particularly – are punished by history and rejected by the novel; conversely, Mary Boleyn, who steps out of history and returns to maternal normality and marriage, is rewarded with a happy ending. Gregory gives the past a fundamental morality; the judgement that Anne is an incestuous witch is that of a vengeful patriarchy on an ambitious woman. The novel has been made into a television series and a Hollywood film. Gregory has a PhD and serves as historical advisor to BBC television's archaeological series *Time Team*; she was also on hand to advise the makers of the film.[50] Gregory's traditional approach, 'realist' style and incipient authority were emphasised in Amazon user-reviews of other Boleyn novels (in this instance of Susannah Dunn's (2004) *Queen of Subtleties*): 'try *The Other Boleyn Girl*, a historically accurate and interesting account that rings true'.[51]

The multiple meanings, manifestations and uses of this one text demonstrate how the modern historical artefact is expressed and articulated in contemporary culture: as part of recognisable but conceptually overlapping genres (historical novel, historical romance fiction, television costume drama, Hollywood film); produced by an author whose legitimacy was originally drawn from numerous sources (institutional, cultural) and concomitantly whose status as an author (and proto-celebrity) ensured that she would become legitimate; an artefact considered accurate in its – obviously fictionalised – stylistic rendering of the past, and through that accuracy granted cultural ascendancy. It is impossible to consider this one text independently; its meanings can only be fully understood through a multi-platform consideration of the text's placement within various discourses. *The Other Boleyn Girl* illustrates cultural 'Historioglossia', a multiplicity of hybrid discourses accruing around a single instance.[52] The historical has multiple meanings, all of which might be simultaneously in operation within culture, and which this book attempts to trace.

As a consequence of this type of cross-genre consideration, I gained a growing awareness of the complexity and range of contemporary cultural engagement and consumption; a sense that one might follow 'history' as a thread through contemporary culture and that it might show anew and in greater depth the consumptive practices of society. The *range* of the historical is the point – professional historians still have yet to investigate the cultural manifestation of the past in anywhere near as much depth as is necessary, and, therefore, the scope of this book attempts to demonstrate the scale of the task in hand. Hence, *Consuming History* describes Historiocopia – overflowing plenty and abundance of meaning. These modes of consumption are extremely varied and incoherently complex; the common user might in the course of one day interface with the past architecturally, through television, art, fiction, game, magazine and advertising. All these practices relate to one another somehow, and form a web of historical meanings and experiences. Comparative study of these different forms and discourses is important in order to gain some small understanding of the multitude and variety of ways in which contemporary society engages with and consumes the past. Much of my concerns in this book is with media, forms and practices that have been rarely considered in any depth, particularly those of genealogy, re-enactment, computer games and the internet; moreover familiar narratives and forms take on fresh relief and nuance when considered side by side with these phenomena.

I have divided *Consuming History* into six relatively discrete parts which each consider key aspects of the contemporary historical: I The popular historian; II Enfranchisement, ownership and consumption; III Performing and playing history; IV History on television; V The 'historical' as cultural genre; and VI Artefact and interpretation. Taken together, they present a detailed and powerful cross-section of contemporary culture and forms of knowledge. The parts demonstrate the teeming diversity, complicated significance, overlapping semiology and sheer frequency of contemporary historical engagement and consumption.

Part I

The popular historian

'Public' history

The following three chapters consider the idea of history in public, civic and cultural life in order to begin to perceive what contributory factors there might be in a construction of understanding of, and engagement with – and consumption of – 'the past'. Ludmilla Jordanova reminds us:

> The past is essentially open-ended, and accounts of it are public property, available for numerous uses. Recognising this should help historians to see their own activities in a wider perspective and to raise broad questions about the practice of history.[1]

Part I as a whole analyses the status and representation of the historian in social interaction and culture in order to conceptualise these various 'uses' made of history.

What can the figure of the media historian – both in terms of their practice and their representation – tell us about contemporary conceptions of the subject? Chapter 1 considers the impact and importance of the 'celebrity' historian. The phenomenon of 'celebrity' is analysed, with a consideration of the impact and importance of the 'celebrity' historian, ranging from authors of cultural history to television presenters. The demands upon such 'public' historians – market, production, audience – affect their work. How does the very public historian present complexity and sell nuance? How does the status of Simon Schama and David Starkey influence their standing as historical authorities? While populist, the celebrity historian is still interested in presenting a 'truth' and in authoring or controlling that truth. It is important to understand how celebrity intersects with historical documentary in order to comprehend the status of these new histories. Historians have become public figures of authority and influence in a way somewhat reminiscent of that accorded to E.P. Thompson, A.J.P. Taylor and Christopher Hill a generation ago, but with multiple new dimensions in this celebrity-craving time. Nationally renowned historians have become somehow abstracted from the academic arena, becoming cultural commentators. Linda Colley and Tristram Hunt write political columns for national newspapers; Richard Holmes canvases for votes in BBC One's *The Big Read*. This chapter, then, considers the new contexts for the historian in public. These contexts include celebrity, cultural representation and the erosion of the authority of the academic expert, before investigating the most famous – or infamous – 'public' historian of the past few decades, David Irving.

It is worth briefly reflecting on the relationship of the professional university historian to the historian in public. The celebritising of the academic profession – the creation of 'star' professors and the increasing commodification associated with this – has been critiqued as a direct consequence of the increasing commercialisation of the university sector.[2] The relationship between 'academic capital' and wider 'cultural capital' is complex but brokered by entrepreneurial universities aimed at increasing their market share and competitiveness. However, as Joe Moran points out, it was generally the case that star academics were little known outside of the university sector. More recently, however, this scholarly membrane has become more permeable, and increasingly high-level appointments are being made in order to boost a department or university's brand recognition. Nearly every 'public' historian included in this book is associated with a university, quite unlike many critics or public cultural figures. This might demonstrate that an academic imprimatur is still necessary to legitimise the historian-presenter, although the independent scholar Dan Snow gains much of his legitimacy from his father, BBC journalist Peter Snow, and David Starkey no longer has a nominal teaching position (although he is associated with Fitzwilliam College, Cambridge). Furthermore, it also suggests that the celebrity-historian model is a poor fit – historians are famous for their work, primarily, and then their fame. In a society in which fame begets fame, the historian has something material to point to in order to justify their existence in the public mind.[3]

Chapter 2 develops Ludmilla Jordanova's idea of 'genre' to consider how 'history' as a textual form is sold – mainly through the consideration of books and magazines – with particular attention paid to the dynamism and complexity of this 'genre'. The chapter considers historical publications. It raises questions relating to evidence, reception and the status of the memorial text as historical artefact. The chapter considers the wide variety of popular historical writing available to the reader, ranging from the first-hand accounts of events found in political diaries to historical biography. The ways in which popular historical writers are constructed by their reception are considered, looking at the case of Richard Holmes.

These chapters argue that there are multiple 'genres' of history in the public cultural imagination, increasingly diverse ways that these genres are presented and serviced, and that they are constantly evolving. History in these public manifestations is incredibly dynamic, and Part I begins the work of attempting to understand and partially map its complex make-up. In order to bring into focus wider questions of the status and representation of the historian, Part I concludes with a consideration of their impact and significance in fiction such as films, novels and games.

1 The public historian, the historian in public

The 'new gardening' and the publicity historian

Historians in the public eye are not new. A.J.P. Taylor's iconic television series ran until 1984, Norman Stone was an advisor of Margaret Thatcher and in the 1980s E.P. Thompson helped revitalise CND. However, increasingly through the 1990s 'History' became part of a media culture less interested in the factual than in narratives and personalities. It was Simon Schama's documentary series *Simon Schama's A History of Britain* (BBC1 2000, 2001) which provided the catalyst to push history from a standard part of television programming to being a media phenomenon, and made the historian into a public figure in an unprecedented way.[1] The series gained a vast audience and provoked wide debate about nationhood and memorialisation (at a time when History as a subject was extremely unpopular at school and university applications went down). With the wide success – in terms of ratings and influence – of Schama's programme and the high profile then accorded to David Starkey, Tristram Hunt and Niall Ferguson, in 2001 History was variously termed the 'new rock'n'roll', the 'new cookery' and the 'new gardening'.[2] The former suggests producers attempting to make the phenomenon fashionable, hip and edgy, whereas the last two descriptions signal history's entrance into lifestyle programming and the world of leisure pursuit. Each phrase suggests the sudden and surprising prevalence of the past in the popular imagination, although in the main this means on television, and each was a reaction to the extraordinary mushrooming of documentary, reality history shows and the associated genealogy boom. These descriptions also insert history into a discourse of individualised or personality/presenter-led television, emphasised, for instance, by Schama and Starkey's titular ownership of their histories and Ferguson's discussion of his own family in his first considerations of Empire.[3] History becomes part of a discourse of leisure, not a professionalised pursuit, and those who present it are personalities and celebrities.[4]

As a consequence of the explosion of interest, the historians involved became a hybrid combination of television personalities, media figures, and cultural gatekeepers.[5] They were abstracted from their disciplinary and academic origins and instead inserted into a set of increasingly complex and problematic social and cultural matrices. The contemporary public intellectual figure is part of a multifarious set of mediated cultural discourses, many of which they do not control.[6] A few examples might demonstrate this teeming complexity: Simon Schama was compared to Bob Barker (host of gameshow *The Price is Right* in the USA); letters were published by the *New York Times* from schoolgirls with 'a bizarre sort of a crush' on him; there are eleven Facebook fan groups devoted to him with hundreds of members worldwide including 'Simon Schama is God'; he and Tony Blair led a podcast-video historical tour of 10 Downing Street on the Prime Minister's office website; he appeared alongside film star Cate Blanchett on Tina Brown's *Topic* chatshow in 2003 to discuss the Prince of Wales's engagement to Camilla Parker-Bowles (characteristically he combined sharp camp with historical perspective: 'The mistress-toting King is the rule, not the exception. He's making an honest women of someone who has been strangely, fragrantly *naughty*').[7] Germaine Greer – literary critic and theorist – similarly found herself trapped within these new and disempowering discourses of communication when she volunteered for Channel 4's *Celebrity Big Brother* in 2005 (she left after five days). Schama 'made history sexy', his style, direct delivery and informal dress (often in a leather jacket) undermining the standard image of a television historian (although his slightly patrician bearing and accent maintain some of this aura).[8] Schama has entered the public imagination and popular culture in a way inconceivable to populist and public historians of the 1980s.

A similarly celebritised historian is David Starkey, who, despite a respected career before television, really made his public reputation outside of history. Starkey's rebarbative and aggressive appearances on the Radio 4 programme *The Moral Maze* in 1992 provoked the *Daily Mail* to ask whether he was the 'rudest man in Britain' and led to a series of articles which created a public image of what he himself calls 'Starkey the Wit'.[9] Starkey certainly had a profile external to his scholarly work, and it was as a consequence of this that he took to making documentaries for Channel 4. The success of these programmes led to Channel 4 in 2002 tying him to a contract in a widely publicised 'golden handcuffs' deal. Starkey has pulling-power and star quality as historian and controversialist with a high profile (standard articles on him are entitled 'The importance of being insolent' and 'The apoplectic academic'). He is also openly gay, right-wing and populist. For all that he appears to satisfy many cultural clichés about historians – gladiatorial, Oxbridge, contemptuous, besuited and bespectacled – he is as much an iconoclast as anything else (accusing the Queen of being a 'philistine' and comparing her to Josef Goebbels, for instance).[10] He slots into a British continuum of controversial and interrogative intellectuals. Similarly Simon Schama has name-brand recognition and a public profile outside of his immediate work. His £3m exclusive contractual deal with the BBC was publicly debated and explicitly contrasted with Starkey's £2m.[11] These kinds of big-money deals designed to tie a presenter to a channel are more commonly thought of in relation to key celebrity figures such as Michael Parkinson or Terry Wogan; they are further evidence of the particularity and peculiarity of these two historians in British popular culture.[12]

In 2004, Schama introduced the programme *Historians of Genius* which presented the historiographical arguments of Macaulay, Gibbon and Carlyle. Their works were read by distinguished actors such as Samuel West, and supported by the usual documents, images and props.[13] *Historians of Genius* celebrated the achievements and innovations of each figure, claiming some kind of transcendence in their work. The series suggested that historians themselves were worthy of documentary study. By 2004, then, the historian's place in the popular imagination was such that television programmes could move away from the facts and focus instead on the practitioners themselves. Granted, this was a minor series on a non-main-stream channel (BBC4), but the entry of historiography into documentary is instructive. The historian is here an independent entity, worthy as much as the scientist or the inventor of introduction. Their ideas and style, rather than any-thing they achieved or created, are central to the films, which focus on a parti-cular book and narrative thread (the French Revolution or the Monmouth Rebellion). However, the series also had polemic value, with Schama using it to attack contemporary academic historical writing: 'History's adventure has become a bit lost … it's not as explosive or exciting as it used to be. What we need to recover is our reckless literary courage.'[14] Here we have the historian as genius, as great writer, as socially and culturally important and wide-reaching in sig-nificance. Schama's evident desire to make the historian important and 'adven-turous' clearly contrasts the style of the popular historian with that of the academic historian. The academic is cautious, has lost the common touch in comparison with the multi-selling reforming populist.[15]

The popularity and influence of these celebrity figures in the mainstream are demonstrated in the repeated representation of Schama and Starkey in popular media. In the opening episode of the Public Relations comedy series *Absolute Power* (BBC1, 2003) the lothario historian Nigel Harting was a cross between Schama and Starkey.[16] Schama also became a staple of the impression show *Dead Ringers* (BBC1, 2002–). For instance, the sketch 'Yet Another History Programme' satirises *A History of Britain* by lampooning some of the presenter's more obvious laconic vocal mannerisms and mocking *A History of Britain*'s recycling of symbolic images to illustrate his clichéd script. The sketch demonstrates the cultural impact that Schama has had; his personality and his visual style are worth joking about and recognisable enough to sustain a sketch. The show also dramatised the rivalry between the 'tyrant' Schama and the 'vile pretender' Starkey in a scene in which they marshalled their film crews together and did battle.[17] This neatly highlights the ambivalent binary competitive relationship that Schama and Starkey enjoy. *Dead Ringers* highlighted Schama's distinctive style of delivery, suggesting that he brought something novel to the presentation of history as well as highlighting the cult of personality associated with the new style of programming. The individual is as important as the information; the styles of Starkey and Schama are so distinct as to be almost a brand. Furthermore, the historian is a cultural figure, as worthy of mockery in their authority as other public figures such as politicians.

Schama and Starkey, then, are culturally- and economically-constructed human commodities, and therefore as such are famous for their fame as much as for their profession. They are quite probably the exceptions in terms of their wide-ranging fame, but there are many historians who are on the fringes. These figures are on the edges of celebrity culture – it would be difficult to define most 'public' historians as celebrities when they are really 'personalities' – although they are obviously also part of the mediated cultural continuum from which celebrity springs.

Personality historians still tend to be male – Linda Colley and Bettany Hughes have a relatively high profile in the UK, as does Lisa Jardine (who is not strictly an historian), but more common might be the press coverage of archaeologist Dorothy King which concentrated more on her figure and her hair than her intellect: she 'breaks the mould of the dusty academic'; is 'A brilliant, glamorous and controversial young archaeologist'; and notably 'Blonde, glamorous and a fearless hunter of treasures'.[18] This last reviewer repeated the fallacious story that she had been asked to pose for *Playboy*, while the second comment is from her own publisher. King writes editorials for the *LA Times* and describes herself as a 'PhDiva', a kind of third wave/post-feminist academic:

> I started the week feeling proud to be one of a new breed of woman – the PhDiva. We wear Manolo Blahniks but we also have doctorates ... We know that a little charm and a little cheek will get us almost anywhere.[19]

King is very clearly interested in disassociating herself from the caricature of the fusty, dowdy scholar. Instead she posits a new type of glamorous, intelligent career women, although unfortunately still reliant on charm and cheek rather than their intellectual credentials. This is scholar as *Sex and the City* character, well-dressed and forthright.

King's public stature is associated with her television and published work, and sustained through her presence in newspapers through her column writing. Other historians who have become abstracted from their institutional origins in this way – writing columns with some 'historical' flavour or inflection – include Tristram Hunt (*Observer*), Linda Colley (the *Guardian*), Niall Ferguson (*LA Times*), Hywel Williams (*Guardian*), Max Hastings (*Daily Mail*); many other historians contribute occasional articles. Ferguson particularly has courted controversy and his columns range far from the historical into politics, economics and particularly US foreign policy (although he is hardly the first conservative historian to do this, with Norman Stone's right-wing views finding particularly high level coverage through his *Sunday Times* column from 1987–92). Their involvement in print media of this type reinforces the sense of historians as possessors of great cultural capital and as having some role as social gatekeepers. Their particular knowledge and insight give them the ability to form important and influential opinions. Being part of newspaper culture in this way distances historians from their institutional roots, ensuring that they become media figures associated with a certain paper rather than part of the academy. They are figures in public political life, commentators as much as critics, shaping and directing national debate.

Hunt is also keenly interested in taking a public role, as is demonstrated by his interest in becoming an MP (although again in this he follows Stone).[20] The well-known public leadership figure who is an historian is not unusual – British Prime Minister Gordon Brown did a History PhD in 1982 – but the perception of the historian as national commentator and leader in contemporary public cultural life seems new, even if precedented. Lynn Cheney also has a PhD in History and has co-authored a book with her husband, US Vice-President Dick Cheney, as well as several historical books for children including *America: A Patriotic Primer* (2002). She also founded the James Madison Book Award to encourage the communication of history to children. This high-level political involvement in particular narrative history demonstrates the clear importance that history-writing can have in contemporary society. Cheney's patriotic work has a clear nationalist agenda which resonates with the Bush administration's expansionist rhetoric: 'One of the important lessons we can learn is that freedom isn't inevitable ... This realization should make the liberty we enjoy all the more important to us, all the more worth defending.'[21]

A History of Britain had in many ways an unashamedly nationalistic-leadership quality as it attempted to explain 'our story'. Schama concluded his series with these stirring words:

> History ought never to be confused with nostalgia. It's written not to revere the dead, but to inspire the living. It's our cultural bloodstream, the secret of who we are. And it tells us to let go of the past even as we honour it, to lament what ought to be lamented, to celebrate what should be celebrated. And if in the end, that history turns out to reveal itself as a patriot, then I think that neither Churchill or Orwell would have minded that that much, and as a matter of fact, neither do I.[22]

This sense of a dynamic, interrogative, instructive history which celebrates and enables nationhood, figures the historian as somehow involved in the process of explaining these materials to the public, as engendering not nostalgia but an active, inspired sense of citizenship. On this model the historian does have a clear public role, but it is one not framed by media outlets – instead it is a clear social duty to lead. Academic historians have expressed disquiet that television history seems to be addressing wider civic questions of nationhood deemed too problematic by the academy, and certainly the allure of the public historian tends to the teleological, explanatory and positivistic (Schama's attempts to tell 'our' story of nation in *A History of Britain* was much criticised for leaving out the Welsh and the Scots).

A significant effect of this populist interest in, and concomitant civic-national importance of, history is found in an unlikely programme. In 2005, BBC's flagship news programme *Newsnight* appointed Greg Neale (then editor of *BBC History*) as its resident historian, employed to make a series of films commenting upon contemporary events and giving an historical perspective. For instance, in April 2005, he contributed films on past elections to demonstrate that issues such as low voter turnout or the impact of new media were not solely concerns of the present; in January of that year he reported on the psychological impact of disasters in history to nuance a special edition of the programme focusing on the Asian Tsunami. This deployment of historical relativism is a useful corrective for news audiences that are generally presented with more positivist models of events as unprecedented; it is also a way of thinking about the contemporary world that suggests a fluid dynamic between then and now. The perspective of history is used in these films to demonstrate the wider causes of events as well as to undermine government and cultural myths of modernisation and progress. Neale added arch comments about the uses of history to his work, particularly within the context of the ongoing situation in Iraq and the way that historical comparison had been used (particularly that of Saddam Hussein with Hitler) in such a shoddy fashion to justify that action. The employment of Neale demonstrates the increased profile of history in public contexts.

History, historians, historiography, and celebrity: *Great Britons*

While the high profile documentary series rely on a figurehead academic figure, these make up a small percentage of historical programming. Most historically-themed programmes eschew an historian altogether, being presented or narrated by a well-known figure with advice from experts. However, the celebrity is generally someone who has something of a cerebral quality, or at least in the public imagination is associated with gravitas (Griff Rhys Jones in *Restoration*) or enthusiasm (Tony Robinson in *Time Team*). Again, it is unusual that this celebrity presenter be female. Even the daytime television shows which feature historical subjects or artefacts tend to be presented by men. The presenter of the historical programme is at once the audience's representative – the enthusiastic amateur – and the director of events. Experts – historians, genealogists, architects, DNA investigators – advise the presenter and the audience, creating a narrative journey of sorts with expert testimony providing the clues as to where to go next.

The semiotics of the presenter-expert are further muddied by the celebrity history book. Comic or satirical 'histories' written by media personalities are standard stocking-filler publications – comedian John O'Farrell's (2007) *An Utterly Impartial History of Britain* is a good example here.[23] Such writing is either narrative with a particular thematic purpose, or a cataloguing, as in the case of Christine Hamilton (wife of the disgraced former MP Neil Hamilton) and her *Bumper Book of British Battleaxes*.[24] This type of popular historical writing figures history as a site of humour and something throwaway and almost trivial. Occasionally public figures write 'proper' histories. MPs often write biography and history, as is the case with former Prime Ministers William Hague and John Major.[25] This conflation of politician with history has an august ancestry – Winston Churchill won the Nobel Prize for Literature in 1953 for his historical work – and suggests that an insight into politics, a kind of career affinity, might inform the writing of history in the public mind. Television presenter and newsreader Jeremy Paxman's *The English: A Portrait of a People* attempts to historicise the question of nationhood: 'I set out to try to discover the roots of the present English anxiety about themselves by travelling back into the past, to the things that created that instantly recognizable ideal Englishman and Englishwoman.'[26] This cross-pollination of celebrity or public figure with historical writer further erodes the authority of the professional historian and renders work about the past part of a suite of intellectual possibilities open to modify the public profile of a semi-intellectual personality. Television gardener Alan Titchmarsh's *England, Our England* attempts an anthology-miscellany of 'everything the Englishman ought to know' including Wordsworth and the rules of cricket.[27] Similarly to Paxman, he struggles for contemporary national definition through historical information and fact. The kind of gifted/gentleman amateur tradition that this work keys into allows the journalist access to the forms of historical writing and explanation. From the 1980s onward, the national paradigm has been inter-rogated within University History by a variety of models from comparative and transnational history, gender history, post-colonial history; however, the popular appeal of national histories demonstrates that the idea of nation is strong in the public imagination. At the point when academic historians ceased for various historiographic and theoretical reasons to describe the state, journalists and popular presenters stepped in to help create and sustain a historicised sense of nationhood.[28]

The confusion over the definition and status of historical gatekeepers was further fostered by *Great Britons*, a national popularity contest broadcast by the BBC in 2002. The show attempted to create a national debate by choosing a shortlist of ten key figures and having a series devoted to showcasing their importance. Each figure had a celebrity-historian avatar advocate who presented an hour-long programme dedicated to demonstrating how *significant* their subject had been. A final 'winner' would be decided by real-time national vote. The voting element of the series was important to the way it presented the programmes as simply part of a wider social debate. This element made the series – and by extension the debate about 'greatness' and nationality – interactive and evaluative, enfranchising the viewer (who was given an investment and an ability to judge). The series' use of Peter Snow, famous psephologist veteran of General Election coverage, helped create an official illusion. The vote was not simply popularity, as viewers rated the figure out of nine for, for instance 'Legacy', 'Genius', 'Leadership', 'Bravery', 'Compassion'. There was therefore a sense of historical evaluation with criteria of particular qualities. The series was extremely popular and controversial: questions were asked in Parliament; papers and television discussed the virtues of the debate; museums devoted exhibition space to it; comedy series mocked it; Channel 4 ran an equivalent show a year later to find the *100 Worst Britons* (Tony Blair won this particular competition). The final round was voted for by 1.5 million people. As an approach, the interactive notion of establishing a national heritage through a vote seems democratic and therefore enfranchises the viewer in the creation of their own national story, even if this national story is dominated by men, politics, and particular 'achievement'.

Great Britons and the majority of the subsequent worldwide versions made use of celebrity advocates. The BBC version deployed a range of documentary styles – reconstruction, archive footage, artefact, texts (letters, manuscripts, books) – but they were strongly individualised according to the personality of the presenter. No other expert speakers appeared and therefore the programmes drew on the hybrid model of historical documentary that Simon Schama's *A History of Britain* had constructed, with one strong personality tying together a range of information into a coherent and mainly polemic piece. These programmes similarly imputed motive to historical figures, used up-to-date comparisons (Victorian engineers were compared to rock stars, for instance), and re-enacted key moments or illustrated important ideas. The rhetoric force of the presenters was key to their success (Isambard Kingdom Brunel, an unfashionable figure, was in the top three at the conclusion of the series mainly due to the forceful pro-gramme fronted by TV personality Jeremy Clarkson). The shows made use of fictional film – in the episode on Churchill, for instance, archive footage was spliced with film of the invasion of Pearl Harbor from the film *Tora! Tora! Tora!* (Richard Fleischer/Kinji Fukasaku, 1970) – although this was never identified. Archive footage and re-enactment was, for many of the advocates, the key ele-ment of the programmes as it allowed the audience to visualise and empathise with the subjects: 'because we have no footage of them [those from centuries ago] they seem very far away and people think they were less sophisticated or less able'; 'it just doesn't seem relevant to people now'.[29]

The purpose of the programmes was to demonstrate the significance of the figure being advocated, both at the time but also subsequently ('We have many local heroes; we only have one world-changer,' claimed Andrew Marr at the opening of his programme on Darwin).[30] Each episode, clearly, was intended to be persuasive and therefore the historiography reflected such bias; but at the same time the notion of 'significance' tied the series together. At odds with this was the biographical element of the programmes which suggested that large achievements came from small events or aspects of a life. There was also an underlying nationalism surrounding the conception of greatness. The debate the programmes intended to provoke was one about nationality and significance, about reasserting the international importance of Britishness by remembering the most important figures in the country's history. The series was clearly biographical in its focus, suggesting that we can understand the figures of history through their lives rather than an analysis of external contexts. For instance, Michael Portillo interpreted Elizabeth I's early imprisonment to mean that 'she had to undergo an extraordinary test. Her imprisonment confirmed her courage, but it also reinforced in her tendency to mercy, moderation, and com-passion.'[31] The focus was individualistic and concerned the significance of particular events in the biography of the individual and the development of the character of the country. There were also assertions for which there is little evi-dence, mainly about character (ordering executions was the part of reigning Elizabeth liked the least, according to Portillo) and the significance this had for their actions.

The point at which *Great Britons* became most obviously about transcendent values emerged during historian Tristram Hunt's programme on Newton:

> As an historian I'm fascinated by the idea of genius. In any given era all of us think along broadly similar lines. We are more or less products of our age. But every now and then along comes someone who can slip the knots of history, who can live outside their time and overturn all established thinking ... such drive and self-belief, such arrogance, how was Newton able to see the world so differently to his peers?[32]

Hunt's presentation of 'genius' takes Newton somehow out of history. On the one hand, there is subtle historiography in the statement that 'We are more or less products of our age'; at the same time the suggestion is that somehow a figure might be – or might make themselves seem to be – external or other in some way and through that difference be able to affect the world more than merely participate in it. Hunt's programme argued that Newton's premature birth influenced him, the fact that he survived demonstrating 'a stubborn resolve, a resolve that was to come to define his character'.[33] Once again, there is a notion of biographical events influencing and creating character and thence organising and changing the world.

The key programme, though, eschewed this notion of masculinised progress and Whiggish 'greatness' in order to consider a more interesting way of thinking about historical significance. Feminist journalist Rosie Boycott's challenge in presenting the episode on Diana, Princess of Wales, was that her subject had actually 'done' very little – indeed, Boycott made this her key virtue. Diana was not part of a male-dominated history of progress and technological innovation, or political domination; Boycott attacked the 'intellectual snobbery' that suggested Diana was 'an insignificant lightweight', arguing instead that 'emotions do count' and that progress and science do not 'always add to the sum of human happiness'.[34] Boycott proposes an emotional significance, and in terms of biography her episode is not interested in the factual elements of a life rather than the more insubstantial aspects. She proposes a sensationalist, anti-statist and non-political way of thinking about nationhood focused through personality: 'power and privilege ... doesn't mean anything when love and passion are on the menu'.[35]

Boycott repeatedly used the comparison of a fairy story, arguing that history is an hegemonic cultural narrative below which the real story is happening. Diana's life was symbolic and metonymic of the nation's desires and distresses, and her death was cathartic insofar as it enabled a national purge and a stumbling into a world of emotion and feeling. A key trope here was that of the life lived through the media and constructed in 'public' forums less accessible to more mainstream figures – the only real historical 'evidence' that Boycott used to buttress her documentary was tabloid pages and news footage. Diana was not defined by her deeds but by the projection of her image; people mourn her without meeting her due to an identification with her mediated self. Diana becomes the unique text for a society obsessed by celebrity and by public becoming. As such, the personalised, emotional, therapy-led, publicly self-revelatory form of thinking about the historical figure keys directly into, indeed, might be argued to have been instrumental in forming, the revelatory nexus of self evidenced in reality television and subsequently throughout media production and in particular historical programming. Boycott's Diana destroys old school historical approaches, eschewing fact and evidence in search of real people, cultural references (particularly to fairy stories, and in particular Bluebeard), emotional understanding and happiness. Greatness is not measured by significance but by an internalised ability to empathise and understand. Diana's significance is exemplified by *Great Britons* itself – while seemingly Whiggish 'great men' history the series was equally informed by a contemporary cult of the individual, by an attempt at understanding the personality of significance – and this obsession with the ethereal rather than the effect of the individual is one of the cultural consequences of Diana's death.

The simplicity of the 'Great' concept ensured that this programme format subsequently ran in Germany, Canada, Holland, America, South Africa, Finland, France, Belgium, Czech Republic, Wales, Bulgaria, New Zealand and Romania. While the concept was generally similar, the shows demonstrated discernible national characteristics. For instance, there were seven Presidents in the top ten Americans (and only one woman, although two African-Americans), and only one cultural figure (Elvis Presley). The Czechs voted for their 'Greatest Villain', too, giving that position to the former Communist Prime Minister Klement Gottwald; they also voted a fictional character (Jára Cimrman) the winner, although he was disqualified.[36] Another former Communist country dealing with their immediate past was Romania. The newspaper *Evenimentul Zilei* ran a poll concurrent with the national *Mari Români* ('Great Romanians') to find the 'Worst Romanian'; surprisingly Nicolae Ceauşescu only came second in this (and was eleventh in the 'Great' poll). The German list was moderated to prevent the appearance of Hitler and the Nazis, and was similar to the British list insofar as it emphasised international achievement and cultural significance (including, for instance, Albert Einstein, Karl Marx, Johann Sebastian Bach and Johannes Gutenberg; although, again similarly to Britain, the 'winner' was a politician of national unity, Konrad Adenauer). The French list was even more lightweight politically, with only the winner, Charles de Gaulle, being a figure from public life; the remainder were writers (Molière, Victor Hugo), scientists (Marie Curie) and cultural figures such as Edith Piaf and Jacques-Yves Cousteau.

Despite the vagaries of fleeting popularity, voter demographic and reception (the American shows were in less depth, for instance, and were broadcast on *The Discovery Channel* rather than national television), these shows demonstrate a clear sense of the importance of personality in national self-definition. The South African edition became part of a wider debate about nationality and the controversy over the inclusion of various figures associated with apartheid or colonialism (Eugene Terre'Blanche, Cecil Rhodes, Hendrik Verwoerd) as well as accusations of bias over voting access (TV and phones are more commonly to be available to white South Africans) led to the cancellation of the show. Similarly, although less divisive, the '100 Welsh Heroes' poll was an obvious response to the perceived 'English' bias in *Great Britons*. Another instance of national fragmentation occurred when 'The Greatest Canadian' was made without Canadian Broadcasting Corporation's French-language company Radio-Canada, ensuring that there were subsequently few figures from that community (the Canadian top ten was all male and unusually included athletes; there was also a great deal of grass-roots campaigning for particular candidates). Belgium held two competing polls, one Flemish (on Canvas) and one Walloon (on RTBF; both called themselves the search for 'the greatest Belgium', and there were overlapping figures).

The very notion of 'greatness' presupposes something about national and international significance, and the reaction to these programmes (both extraneous and the voting itself) suggests a great deal about the way that countries perceive themselves and their histories.[37] The controversies surrounding these programmes demonstrate the way that the debate polarises opinion extremely neatly and quickly; they also show that cultures are keen on the idea of rating themselves, of adjudging who is most fit to represent them. The idea of constructing a country's history through rating its figures – emphasising the individual rather than imagining a shared space – presents a multiple conceptualisation of nation, in some ways the sum of extraordinary parts rather than the slow accretion of significance.

The use of celebrity-historians to apportion significance and to guide the viewer through the story of a life and the measuring of importance reflects a kind of vanishing point where historians become personality-stars and lose their disciplinary definition. While professional historians were involved – Tristram Hunt and Richard Holmes – their subject-specific authority was eroded and blurred by the televisual maelstrom. They were important due to their familiarity as television presenters rather than their expertise. The 'historian-ness' of the television historian started to drain away. For instance, as a consequence of the series, Andrew Marr (who was a political journalist) wrote a short history of journalism and became the presenter of *A History of Modern Britain* (BBC2, 2007).[38] Historical authority is something that can be acquired by the cultural figure or celebrity, and increasingly the *actual* historian is replaced by the famous, the good-looking, the seasoned journalist with gravitas, or a combination of all three.

The David Irving libel trial and aftermath

Further erosion and complication of the historian's standing in public were a consequence of the libel trial conducted between David Irving and Penguin Books in 2000. The trial was the same year as Schama's *A History of Britain*, and in their separate ways these two events provide the keynote for 'public' history during the subsequent years. As previously argued, Schama's documentary series kickstarted a trend for sweeping historical documentary and firmly established the historian in the public imagination; Irving's involvement in a high-profile

libel trial meant that the historian's interpretative methods and archival scholarship were being debated and questioned in public in a way they had not been
since the Hitler diaries fiasco in 1983.[39]

Irving issued a writ in 1997 to the author Deborah Lipstadt and her publisher,
Penguin books, for libel, over suggestions that he was a Holocaust denier and a
discredited historian.[40] These arguments had appeared in her book *Denying the
Holocaust*. Irving countered the allegations that he had distorted and manipulated
information to 'support his contention that the Holocaust did not take place' and
argued that it was 'part of a concerted attempt to ruin his reputation as an historian'.[41] The trial took place in early 2000, and its various outcomes have been
well documented by participants (Richard Evans and Lipstadt), onlookers (D.D.
Guttenplan), and other commentators. The trial was as much about historiography as fact, as is made clear by the eighty-page account of the problems,
misrepresentations and inaccuracies in Irving's approach in the Judge's decision.[42] Yet it was also clearly about actually getting things wrong and actively
misinterpreting. The verdict was that Irving was 'an active Holocaust denier;
that he is anti-semitic and racist'.[43]

The trial gained a huge level of press interest around the world for its four-
month run. It was not just Irving who was in the public eye, as the performance
and credibility of other historians in the trial – namely Evans, Lipstadt and
Robert van Pelt – were subject to public discussion and debate. The event
focused media attention on the key skills and interpretative approaches of historians – their use of evidence, approach to documents, marshalling of argument
and ordering of data. The legal interface with the historiography was complex.
The judge clearly outlined his role in proceedings:

> It is not for me to form, still less to express, a judgement about what happened.
> This is a task for historians. It is important that those reading this judgement
> should bear well in mind the distinction between my judicial role in resol-
> ving the issues arising between these parties and the role of the historian
> seeking to provide an accurate narrative of past events.[44]

Despite this care, Penguin's victory in the case was clearly seen as a judicial triumph
for an historical 'truth', the implication being that despite the complexities of
English libel law, what had won through was right and proper. The idea that
'history was on trial' was prevalent, if erroneous.[45] Historians who balked at the
judgement – including, famously, Sir John Keegan's claim that Irving 'has many
of the qualities of the most creative historians ... he still has much that is interesting
to tell us' – were questioned and wondered at.[46]

The key aspect of the Irving trial, and an interesting issue in terms of how it
relates to historiography, is that it was in the main concerned with falsification
and distortion rather than narrative interpretation. Irving was found to have
ignored and misapprehended evidence. This demonstrated a moral duty to the
truth, a now legalised obligation or responsibility to history. The combination of
evidence and interpretation destroyed the denier's house of cards.[47] Irving was

not a bad historian, he was someone who wrote erroneously: 'in most of the instances cited by the Defendants Irving has significantly misrepresented what the evidence, objectively examined, reveals'.[48] The criticisms of the defendants of Irving's historiography were 'almost invariably well-founded'.[49] Charles Gray, the judge in the case, said in his judgement:

> It is necessary also to consider whether and, if so, to what extent, what Irving has said and written is consistent with or borne out by the available historical evidence. For, as the Defendants accept, there can be no valid criticism of Irving for denying that a particular event occurred unless it is shown that a competent and conscientious historian would appreciate that such a denial is to a greater or lesser extent contrary to the available historical evidence.[50]

Does the judgement mean that legally history has been defined as being something that can illustrate a final truth? The intersection of history and law is very complex – one a disciplining set of rules which demand ordering, one a much more complex set of investigative strategies. Gray here suggests that there is a kind of 'beyond reasonable doubt' element of history at the same time as he demonstrates that the trial was about Irving's fitness as an historian.

The Hitler diaries had embarrassed some high-profile historians, but the issues surrounding them were of straightforward veracity (and they were proved to be fakes, establishing a true/false binary). The Irving trial was something of a watershed – at least in the UK – in terms of the publicising of historiographical issues: it was the first time that ideas of value, moral judgement, historiography, methodology and historical epistemology had been publicly debated; the first time that ideas of historical 'truth' were explicitly considered in a larger public arena. Yet as much of the present book demonstrates, these discussions were already being had – or at least implicitly being addressed and dramatised – throughout a range of cultural modes, media and forms.

Irving has been rendered literally indefensible as a scholar and a public historian, though he still continues to lecture. The UK libel action is a relatively minor aspect of the legal reaction to his work. As a consequence of his views, Irving has been banned from entering Germany, Australia, Italy, Canada and New Zealand (he was deported from Canada in 1992); he cannot enter France unless he agrees to attend court and he has been fined by the German and Austrian governments.[51] In 2005, a 1989 warrant was invoked by Austrian police and he was arrested, charged with trivialising the Holocaust, and jailed for ten months before being ejected and banned from ever entering the country again.

Thus, the most famous 'historian' – or, rather, the historical author with the greatest international public profile – during the late 1990s and early 2000s was someone whose method had been proved to be corrupt and whose bigotry led him to change the course of his research. The complexity of the English libel laws meant that the defendants had to *prove* that Irving was 'wrong': historiographically; in his use of archives; in his moral outlook; and in his scholarship.

Irving's trial became the subject of documentary when the American popular science drama/witness-documentary *Nova* (which itself is part of the discourse of popular history, as it often covers historical discoveries) covered the case in October 2000, with actors re-enacting key events. The massive publicity over the case and the discrediting of Irving gave popular history a troubling profile while at the same time banishing his 'untrue' narrative. This is worrying to historians, and even Deborah Lipstadt has voiced concern over the possible censorship of Irving's historical voice.

Irving now lives in the public imagination as a discredited, foolish man who has been repeatedly found to have lied and misrepresented. As an historian, no matter how wrong-headed or problematic his techniques were, he has been found guilty. The idea that one might interpret a piece of evidence in multiple fashions has seemingly been disowned, as it could lead to moral relativism and denial that horrific events took place. In contrast, then, the virtuous historian surmounts their bias, and does not bend the facts to match a wished-for conclusion. Irving is in some ways the epitome of the public historian – not part of the academy (his website claims he writes 'Real History'), a maverick, looking to a wider public audience rather than a circumscribed elite, a military 'shirtsleeves' historian as Guttenplan calls him.[52] Yet he is also proof of how non-professional history can lose its objectivity, it would seem. As Evans argued, 'The real test of a serious historian was the extent to which he or she was willing or able to subordinate political belief to the demands of historical research.'[53] The 'serious' here is disingenuous. Irving's loss and subsequent fall into penury and prison appeared to be a victory for moral history and a public blow to relativistic and postmodern historiography. It seemed to establish that there *was* a kind of truth that might be established in historical investigation. At the same time the entire event was the semi-tragic narrative of the fall of Irving, the demonstration that, for all his archival talents and populist ability, he had become perverted in his mind and was increasingly losing touch with what actually happened. As Richard Evans stated quite simply after the judgement: 'He fabricates.'[54]

2 Popular history in print

For all their celebrity status, the new generation of historians still rely on books to establish their authority, to develop their profile, and to make money. Popular history in print appeals to, and caters for, a mass audience in a way that is generally unaudited by professional historians. It is also extremely profitable. In 2003, the publishing company Tempus announced a £10 million profit from its local history series, for instance. History authors command large advances and are marketed aggressively. It is also a massively dynamic genre. Popular history publishing encompasses broad sweep analyses of epochs, biographies, military history, local history and particularised cultural histories. Popular history sections in bookshops and libraries are expanding to cater for an increasing desire for accessible narratives about the past. The generic complexity of the mode is vast, ranging from basic introductory texts in branded and familiar series such as *The Idiot's Guide to Ancient Egypt* or *World War II for Dummies* to people's history and BBC-led accounts of nation like *This Sceptred Isle* ('a simply told story of a century that we can all touch').[1] Formats include history in quotations, biography, cultural history, military history, books about anniversaries, memoirs, histories of science, histories of institutions, witness accounts, historical geography, fact books, art history, autobiography, local history of all types, revisionary history, marginal history. The generic range, number of, and sales figures of popular history from tomes on the English Civil War to accounts of the end of the Raj demonstrate the extent to which historical writing is ingrained and embedded in cultural life, and how it is continually evolving. Popular history is written by those in the academy, by journalists and independent scholars, by politicians, comedians and novelists.[2] Popular history is continually added to – but old favourites still continue to be published, so the dynamism of the form is underpinned by the perennials of Antonia Fraser, Eric Hobsbawm, S.R. Gardiner, Stephen Ambrose, Roy Strong, A.J.P. Taylor (even Gibbon is available in paperback). Certain periods are more popular and therefore better served – the Second World War, Egyptology, military history in general, Empire (and these are just British tastes). However, there is still space and a large market for – for instance – a major biography of Robert Hooke, or work on the last rulers of India.[3]

Popular historical books, in their various forms, have a huge audience and sell in massive numbers. In 2003, £32m worth of history books were bought, 3 per cent of all books sold; this was a record, demonstrating the growth of the market share as well as the popularity of the format.[4] Similarly to television, and indeed nearly all historical product, they underwent a market transformation during the 1990s which resulted in huge sales figures and a complexity of genre. Such history has evolved and developed in numerous directions. A working model of the genre of textual 'popular history', then, would have to somehow encompass all these various forms, show an awareness of particularity and singularity (as well as similarity), understand the vagaries of audience, and be aware of the differing cultural values apportioned to each particular publication. Each text has, in some way, to be taken on its own merits but somehow be read back into the wider social and cultural contexts. There is not room enough here to survey in any useful way the plethora of popular history books, to somehow consider Alison Weir in conjunction with A.N. Wilson, or Terry Jones in comparison with Rebecca Fraser or Alan Haynes.[5] Instead this section looks at some of the forms and tropes using brief case-studies – particularly focusing on various phenomena associated with the history of the personal, the individual, and the recounting of experience. These texts range from 'instant memorialisation' books such as the accounts of power by fallen politicians to grander narratives of nationhood and government, from intimate memoirs to traditional biography, from witness testimony to history for children. This chapter, then, illustrates the range of tropes and forms recounting the past available to the reader, and suggests that the dynamism and sheer multiplicity of texts demonstrate a thriving culture of complex engagement with the past. It is organised into two parts: the first considers various tropes of the popular historical genre, the second looks at reception and consumption.

Narrative history

Several notable bestsellers set the trend for the explosion – nationally and internationally – in the production and consumption of popular history. In particular, Dava Sobel's (1995) *Longitude* demonstrated the new market for popular narrative history.[6] It recounted the story of John Harrison, who in the mid-eighteenth century had discovered an accurate way to measure longitude while at sea by using clocks. In doing so he won the British 'Longitude Prize' and solved a problem which had bedevilled navigation for centuries. Being able to measure one's longitude (location on the earth east or west of the Prime Meridian, now taken as Greenwich in London) and latitude (location on the earth north or south of the Equator) is key when sailing long distances and when drawing maps. Harrison, a 'man of simple birth and high intelligence', invented a highly accurate chronometer to allow mariners to calculate their exact position.[7] He managed, against the wishes of the scientific and naval establishments, to prove that his inventions worked, and the consequences of this were immense. Harrison's story is one of obsession and drive, but it also manages to encompass politics, empire and economics; rich with possibility for the talented narrative writer and extremely attractive to an audience hungry for scientific success stories. Written simply and directly, Sobel's book was an astonishing worldwide publishing phenomenon. As such it was widely imitated, inaugurating a new style of popular narrative history and biography which was generally focused upon science or a cultural artefact.

Sobel showed that the public were interested in reading about the untold stories of human progress. *Longitude* also demonstrated the complexity of popular history. Generically it is a history of science book, part of another new movement in publishing. History of science as a sub-genre of popular history demonstrates 'the excitement of discovery, the remarkable nature of the findings, the implications of the ideas for the human condition – in short, the cultural significance of science'.[8] Popular history of science books present science as the province of genius: 'In such works, hagiography and Whiggish approaches to history are alive and well.'[9] In this one relatively minor subsection of popular history, then, we can see a teeming complexity of information, an interest in genius, a desire to celebrate the individual (and particularly the 'ordinary' or poor man), a tendency to positivism and teleology, and the ability to reach a massive audience.

Simon Schama has claimed a 'golden age' of popular narrative history, arguing that there is 'more history which combines scholarship of the highest level with narrative craft' than ever before.[10] The popularity of work by Tristram Hunt, Bettany Hughes, Richard Holmes, David Starkey, Lisa Jardine, Niall Ferguson and David Cannadine (as well as Schama himself) attests to an interest in accessible history written by professional historians (often with related television profiles). This celebration of the narrative and populist suggests a flowering of a particular type of popular history, both technical and accessible. Key to this popular writing is a strong narrative and a 'literary' quality to the writing. This methodology of technically proficient storytelling is clearly reflected in Schama's championing of historians such as Macaulay and Gibbon. The public historian in this model is someone who writes compelling tales, communicating effectively through their personal style and clarity of expression.

Political diaries and witness accounts

In addition to narrative history, there are a number of more immediate ways in which the reader can access the past. Diaries, witness accounts, autobiography and memoir all promise unique and unmediated insight into important lives and events. The political diary has been an important publication for decades. The diary appears to offer the reader unrestricted access to the subject. A similar genre is the letter collection, again promising an immediate and personal insight into important personalities.[11] The diary has built into itself biases and personal animus – and, indeed, these make the format more enthralling to the amateur student of history. Even when edited, they are original documents, and therefore bring the reader closer to 'actual' historical investigation than most popular history books. Labour MP Tony Benn's *Diaries* (multiple volumes, 1963– but published 1988–), dictated nightly before later transcription, have offered personal accounts –

and 'a useful historical perspective' – of key events from the Vietnam War to the Common Market.[12] More salaciously, the scandal associated with the publication of Tory MP and historian Alan Clark's diaries (1955–, pub. 1992–2002) laid bare Thatcherism but also revealed Clark as an arch, vain, rude, indiscreet and priapic figure, combining the personal with the political.[13] They brought Clark sensationalist celebrity following their first publication, as much for his unguarded and robust style in discussing political life as his description of his lavish lifestyle and affairs. Clark's direct and blunt style somehow made him more believable than other diarists (and all politicians) in the public imagination, the unvarnished element of his writing giving his work more value.

A fellow Tory with a chequered public image is the prominent figure of former MP Edwina Currie. Her *Diaries* ('a remarkable insight into politics at the top') includes a prefatory author's note that reflects on their own historicity as well as gesturing towards a deeper significance for Currie's career to be recognised by future generations of scholars: 'The originals will, I hope, eventually be placed with supporting papers in the archives of the Women's Library in London as part of their collection of twentieth-century women in politics.'[14] The disingenuous 'I hope' belies Currie's confidence in the significance of her work and the fact that the publication of the diaries is part of an attempt at self-memorialisation, somehow less self-serving than an autobiography due to the element of immediacy. This sense of the archival importance of the diary, the notion that the reader is holding in their hand an historical document which allows them to comprehend the recent past personally rather than accessing it through the writing of others, is crucial to the appeal of such texts.

Furthermore, published diaries can offer an instant way of clearing oneself from scandal, giving historical perspective to actions. Labour MP David Blunkett published his in 2006, the final entries of November 2005 recounting his fall from grace and eventual resignation from government. Blunkett interpolates comments throughout his diary with insights ranging from 'I still have a bottle they gave me that evening' to 'there was no requirement for me to step down'.[15] The publication of his diaries enabled Blunkett to attempt a public justification and instantly create a legacy for himself ('legacy' being extremely important to members of the Blair Labour government). These four examples briefly illustrate the political diary as an individual account, often enlivened (and certainly sold) by the diarist's personality as much as their significance. They are history in the raw, and this is no doubt part of their appeal, but they are also deeply flawed and particular ways of reordering the recent past. The huge advances that political diaries now command make them ever more needful of raunch and intrigue to justify such investment.

Witness accounts provide a similarly direct – if edited – interface with history. Such accounts often focus on the words and experiences of ordinary people. They invoke pity, particularly accounts relating to hardship and horror. The tyranny of the witness is such that their words are given enormous weight – despite their being biased and sometimes false.[16] Richard Holmes' *The World at War* is an edited selection of the transcripts of *The World at War*, Thames

Television's landmark (1973) series.[17] The documentary collected together a enormous number of interviewees, ranging from Albert Speer to Antony Eden, from the great (Mountbatten) to the obscure (Tsuyako Kii, a Tokyo resident in 1945). While the book works to create a loose narrative of the war, the witness testimonies complicate and nuance to render any sense of an overview redundant. One result of this multiplicity of voices is a new insight into key events from area bombing to Dunkirk to the economics of warfare. Another powerful effect is to give an intimate view of familiar people and occurrences. Laurence Rees' *Their Darkest Hour* is a collection of eye-witness testimony attempts to account for the horrors of the Second World War by asking those who experienced and perpetrated them to explain events.[18] Rees does not always allow their own words to tell the story, often looking for unspoken indications of guilt or complicity. Few stories are heroic or life-affirming; the grind of survival is the most important thing here, as the reminiscences illustrate the banality of horror. Rees' interviewees illustrate the minutiae of the war, accounting for violence and atrocity on all sides, including memories of the British betrayal of Cossacks in 1945, the Nazis' use of human mine detectors in Belarus, human experimentation in Japan and the American fire bombing of Tokyo and Osaka. Rees attempts to understand the psychology of involvement – from the Belgian SS officer to the Polish Sonderkommando at Auschwitz – and the book is intended to nuance understanding of the horrific experience of total war. Collections of witness testimony are part of the wider people's history project – the impulse towards recording everyday lives, although, as Holmes' collection demonstrates, such books can also encompass the recollections of leading figures and prime movers.

Autobiography, personal memoir and biography

The flourishing general market for autobiographies demonstrates a further interest in lives and in instant memorialisation – autobiographies increasingly being commissioned to commemorate a particular event rather than the end of a long life of achievement. Once useful historical documents – evidence of the contemplation of a life, the memoir of a particular period – they have evolved into simple elements of the brand-marketing of a famous figure. This Polaroid–mayfly textualising of the recent past makes it throwaway and personality-led (or at least part of the aura of celebrity). The instant autobiography, written when the subject is in the middle or even at the beginning of their career, demonstrates a desire to capture a key moment (rather than wait for a time for reflection), argues that momentary significance is more important than any notion of wider importance, and illustrates a culture obsessed with contextualising and historicising the immediate rather than a broader contemplation of events. Celebrity autobiographies and memoirs are huge-sellers: those by Robbie Williams, Katie Price, Sheila Hancock and Paul Gascoigne sold a combined 1,232,604 copies in 2005.[19] The popularity and prevalence of celebrity autobiography suggest an interest in the biography of the famous and an obsession with discovering where they came from. It meshes with the genealogical impulse outlined in Chapter 3 to suggest an interest in family pre-history, in the origins and roots of the famous figure; to, in effect, historicise the celebrity. Celebrity autobiographies are singly focussed and interested only in the flowering of the subject (*'my* story') rather than the significance of the life in other contexts.

The biggest-selling autobiography in the UK over the past five years is that of glamour model Katie Price, also known as Jordan. Her *Being Jordan* describes in unvarnished style her career to date. The direct style is part of the honesty of the account, similarly suggesting that the book gives the fan-reader an insight into Price's life. It is disingenuous at points, avoiding explanation at times: 'I don't blame my unsuccessful relationships with men on the fact that my dad left when I was three. Yes, I can be insecure in relationships; I do need constant reassurance … I don't feel any bitterness.'[20] The book has a vanishing point at 'now', attempting to account for Jordan and tell her story. The motivation for the reader is a sensational interest in the minutiae of the lives of the famous, the promise of understanding and explanation, and the hint of possible scandal. The life remembered in these books is done so within the context of present fame; it is a teleology towards the current position of the writer. Additionally there is an element of poignancy and nostalgia that has been added to the format, particularly in semi-autobiographical memoirs of the recent dead by those who knew them (Sheila Hancock's (2005 *The Two of Us*, John Bayley's (2002) *Iris*). Current autobiography, then, is transient and instant, telling the pre-history of subjects who are interesting only for their manifestation now rather than their development then. They are the ephemera of celebrity culture.

One of the biggest industries in the past decade has been that devoted to remembering, accounting for, and narrating the life of Diana, Princess of Wales. When she was alive, there were various biographies (including Andrew Morton's authorised *Diana: Her True Story*) catering to the massive audience keen to discover all they could about her.[21] Since her death in 1997, the publishing industry surrounding her memory has exploded.[22] The conspiracy theories surrounding Diana's life and death, and the scramble for ownership of her memory and the interpretation of her significance, have led to these books being resolutely anti-official 'history', quite consciously locating themselves as contrary to the perceived mainstream position (and offering tantalising insight into the 'truth' of the matter). Foremost has been the work of her former butler, Paul Burrell, whose various books have controversially laid bare her life and personality. Much like the diary and the autobiography, the accounts of the privileged insider promise revelation, key personal details and information left out of 'official' biographies and accounts. In *The Way We Were*, published to coincide with the tenth anniversary of her death, Burrell emphasises her easy charm and appeal when discussing Mario Testino's photographs of the Princess:

> This was the princess I knew, and how I remember her; the princess Mario wanted the world to see, as if each person who viewed those photos was sitting on the sofa chatting to her. As he did. As I did, during ten years of service at her side.[23]

Subtly, Burrell pinpoints Diana's appeal (making people feel loved in a kind of unthreatening way) while at the same time emphasising the fact that most people had not actually sat on a sofa with her. Indeed, this is quite an insight into the strange workings of Diana's celebrity – people thought they knew her, despite the fact that the closest they got was a photograph. Those who have been on that sofa (himself and a celebrity photographer) understand this appeal but also had the 'privilege' of an actual personal relationship with her. Further, Burrell's self-serving title *The Way We Were* (casting himself as Robert Redford to Diana's Barbara Streisand) here illustrates the narcissism involved in this type of text, the placing of the self next to a person of importance and celebrity. The book presents revelation and new evidence, selling itself on promises of rare photographs, letters, personal reminiscences and the tantalising possibility of finding out more about her and her private life. Burrell calls her 'the boss', publishes extracts of her annotated copy of self-help book *The Road Less Travelled*, tells of her plans for secret marriage, describes bringing back her ring from the hospital she was taken to, and relates her personal relationship with him (for instance, how she comforted him after his mother's death). He also attempts to ascribe motive and shape to events – 'it was as if all the tears and suffering had led the princess to that crucial point in her life' – although in the main the book is an account of minutiae and detail.[24]

P.D. Jephson, Diana's Private Secretary, similarly offered intimacy and the promise of a crucial understanding through publication: he presents his book as a necessary corrective to misguided and biased accounts. Due to the efforts of 'the self-appointed guardians of her thoughts, motives and values' it 'seemed to me that history was recording an image which bore little resemblance to the Princess I knew better than most'.[25] Jephson is less hagiographic than Burrell, offering nuance and therefore tempering his account somewhat ('However cynical, manipulative or self-indulgent her motives might sometimes have been for doing some of the good things for which she received such credit, in the *act* of doing them there was no cynicism at all').[26] Yet it is still the personal insight, relationship, and experience that are key here. Even her security detail has got in on the act, with an 'authentic' insider's accounts of her life.[27] Diana is a key example of the way a figure can become abstracted, as a celebrity, from reality. These texts are marketed in a way that promises gritty 'reality' – factual insight – but at the same time simply provide further fuel for the speculative and conspiratorial. They demonstrate a perpetuating interest in royal biography, a desire for personal insight into the lives of the untouchable and famous, and an insatiable need for accounts of intimacy. As with the diary, such books offer the reader a direct relationship with the subject, suggest an insight that official histories might not be interested in or repress. The scrutinising of the ordinariness of lives that such memoirs entail – as well as insider's accounts of key events – means that, similarly to the autobiography, they mix bathos with insight. Readers are interested in the detail of the life as much as in the motivation behind important actions, and the two combine in these accounts.

Historical biography

In contrast to these expressions of personal experience, historical biography has long been self-aware enough to highlight its own subjectivity. Amanda Foreman's *Georgiana, Duchess of Devonshire* won the Whitbread prize for biography in 1998 and was a popular account of a fairly obscure figure. Georgiana Spencer had little to recommend her to readers, most of whom would not have known her. The fact that she was related to Diana, Princess of Wales, was key – Georgiana was the first 'celebrity' woman, queen of high society and fashion:

> She was thrust into public life at the age of sixteen, unprepared for the pressures that quickly followed and unsupported in a cold and loveless marriage. Though most of her contemporaries adored her because she seemed so natural and vibrant, only a few knew how tormented she was by doubt and loneliness.[28]

Her relevance to a society just grappling with what seemed like incipient celebrity culture and the death of a similarly miserable Diana was obvious, and this biography offered insight and understanding. Foreman's work is rigorous, scholarly and extremely engaging. The Diana-parallels were, however, invoked at the time and demonstrate how popular biography can become intertwined with broader issues and different readings. Foreman gestures to a tradition of women biographers – Antonia Fraser and Stella Tillyard – and also recounts her 'Stockholm syndrome', the moment at which she realised that she was identifying with her subject too much. Foreman's self-consciousness as a biographer reflects an understanding of the problems of subjectivity and empathy, although she suggests that it is the process of *research* that is the problem. Writing, she claims, is the corrective:

> Fortunately, the emotional distance required to construct a narrative from an incoherent collection of facts and suppositions provides a powerful counterbalance. By deciding which pieces of the puzzle are the most significant – not always an easy task – the biographer achieves a measure of separation ... the subject gradually diminishes until he or she is contained on the page.[29]

The biography is a collage of well-chosen facts arranged by the writer to create a semblance of order and to 'contain' their subject. A biographer makes sense of incoherence, imposes a framework ('the puzzle' she refers to here is both the confusion of the life and the ordering impetus of a particular, if complex, geometric shape). Foreman's idea that articulation is what creates objectivity is a suggestive one, proposing that it is in the act of formulation that the chaos of history is controlled, focussed, and made understandable. The popular biographer does this for the reader, taking the confusion represented by diary, archival document, letter, image, artefact and historiography and making it into a readable whole. The biographical form is something which fundamentally *contains* a life, attempts to explain, account for and map it out.

The past for children: school and *Horrible Histories*

Another market for historical writing, and one which demonstrates again the flexibility and dynamism of the 'historical' form, is children's writing. Terry Deary's history books for children, *Horrible Histories*, have been published since 1993. They are globally popular, selling 20m copies worldwide in 31 languages; there are around 70 books in the series. The books play on children's fascination with goriness, selling themselves as 'history with the nasty bits left in'. The books are mischievous, irreverent and iconoclastic, appealing to a child audience's desire for silly jokes, presenting history as something tactile and simple. They are illustrated and generally have a section of narrative and then a set of obscure questions which are then answered – the information in the book is generally trivial, silly and often grim. Information is presented in a variety of ways – lists, paragraphs, letters, images, maps – and often will encourage interactivity, for instance, by reprinting recipes or outlining 'what would you do' multiple choice sections. The use of illustration in education is common as a way of presenting complex information, as can be seen in Glenn Thompson's massively successful *For Beginners* comic books which were first published in the mid-1980s.

Horrible Histories are designed to engage and enthuse the reader about the subject while appearing subversive.[30] The books are primarily entertainment, with educative purpose. They are ancillary to school history, offering an iconoclastic and revisionist contrast and implicitly suggesting that the past as taught is not as interesting as what really happened:

> History can be horrible. Horribly hard to learn. The trouble is it keeps on *changing* … In history a 'fact' is sometimes not a fact at all. Really it's just someone's 'opinion'. And opinions can be different for different people … Teachers will try to tell you there are 'right' and 'wrong' answers even if there aren't.[31]

This scepticism about sources is laudable but the animus against teachers militates against this objectivity.[32] The series emphasises period-based chronology and characterises each particular historical epoch (*The Smashing Saxons*; *The Gorgeous Georgians*; *The Barmy British Empire*). They are also mostly about the history of Great Britain, which suggests that their wider popularity is due to their tone and style rather than their content. While their prurience is uppermost, the books are full of information presented in an informal way. The tone of the books is conversational: 'you would be disgusted by his [Ivan the Terrible's] life-story. So I won't tell you. What? You still want to read it? Oh, very well. I'll tell you the story but I'll leave out the gruesome bits.'[33] Their 'deliberate attempt to provide alternative readings' enshrines within their very format a challenge to traditional, institutionalised forms of knowledge as represented by history classes.[34] This is underlined by the regular 'Test your Teacher' sections which encourage students to ask awkward questions, and passages like this: 'Your teachers will tell you all about the legions and what they wore and how they lived. But they don't know everything.'[35] Deary's series suggests that formal education has bowdlerised the past (and taken the nasty bits out). They are interested in the day-to-day experience of particular time periods, in empathy, and develop a pedagogy using humour and offhandness rather than particularity. *Horrible Histories* often read like the flippant *1066 and All That* in their informal style but they are also keenly interested in generating interest and communicating information.[36] They ignore broader historical issues to give a clear sense of particularity about a period or event. However, they still include various familiar and standard elements: time-lines, tests, top facts.

Taught history in British schools is subject to the National Curriculum (NC), a statutory entitlement with a centralised set of targets, aims and pedagogical paradigms (History has been mandatory from 5–14 since 1995, so is no longer compulsory up to the school leaving age of 16). In itself, this collectivised and centralised curriculum is controversial, and it focuses the educational experience of schoolchildren on a small set of foundational periods and texts.[37] This ensures that plurality of historical education is lost. Similarly it means that a generation has been taught a broadly similar and circumscribed set of issues and occurrences; basic historical knowledge, then, is good but limited in scope. The American school system has developed a similar nationwide consensus model expressed in the National Standards for History, enshrined in the GOALS 2000 Educate America Act (1994).[38] In the UK, History has boomed at GCSE and Advanced levels but the lack of specifically-trained teachers at primary and earlier levels, plus the squeeze on time, have led to poorly prepared students and a downturn in interest in the subject; while the number taking AS level increased by 40 per cent between 2001–6, in 2006, two-thirds of students withdrew from the subject after their Key Stage 3 exams (at aged 13–14).

The British NC for History was revised in 1999, in particular focusing on children's ability to 'develop intellectual autonomy'.[39] Terry Haydn illustrates the move in school history teaching away from narratives of national glory and development towards a more objective and interrogative approach; this shift was incorporated to an extent in the NC.[40] This development is an attempt to make history class more relevant to contemporary pupils, instil transferable and vocational skills, as well as to incorporate new historiographical models and encourage a sense of good citizenship. History is increasingly taught as a system of knowledge rather than a set of bare important facts.[41] In primary schools history is rarely taught by historians, and is often (although increasingly less) integrated into schemes which incorporate a number of different disciplinary elements, from geography to environment and literature; it is also taught through numerous methods from drama, museum-based visits, music and dance.[42] Students' sense of coherence and their 'historical literacy' are increasingly threatened in this way.[43] Secondary school classes formalise the teaching of history and begin to differentiate it from other disciplinary subjects, but the downturn in numbers mean that fewer students gain from this increased rigour.

The National Curriculum is predicated upon the idea that History moves and inspires pupils 'with the dilemmas, choices and beliefs of people in the past. The

NC helps pupils develop their own identities through an understanding of history at personal, local, national and international levels.'[44] History 'fires pupils' curiosity and imagination, moving and inspiring them with the dilemmas, choices and beliefs of people in the past ... It helps them to ask and answer questions of the present by engaging with the past.'[45] This model of history as inspiration and as rooted as much in understanding contemporary concerns figures history as a school subject as something to encourage active citizenship through empathy with the 'dilemmas, choices and beliefs' of historically othered people. The key concepts to be communicated are 'Chronological understanding', 'Cultural, ethnic and religious diversity', 'Change and continuity' and 'Cause and consequence'. Local issues are clearly foregrounded, as the curriculum should allow for the investigation of 'aspects of personal, family or local history'; the students should be able to use ICT to research and to present information.[46] Finally, the subject's links with Citizenship are emphasised. History is the major entrée for students to Citizenship as a formal subject, teaching as it does communication and political understanding. A sense of a national narrative is key for citizenship, if potentially problematic – as can be seen in the American school system – but history is also useful here due to its ability to 'record competing stories of identity'.[47]

Crucial to secondary education – at least in terms of framing the subject – is a sense of empathy and of connection:

> History isn't all Dead and buried.
> History isn't all about Kings and dates – it's full of *life-changing events*.
> Just think–
>
> - What would you have done if there was a sudden outburst of bubonic plague?
> - Would you have chosen to fight for the Roundheads or the Cavaliers during the Civil War?
> - Would you have protested to abolish slavery?
>
> These were all decisions ordinary people had to make, and their outcomes *still affect you* today.[48]

However, it is evident from revision guides and curricula that timelines, sources, interpretation of data and key information are still the most important elements – history is not just about 'facts but how to use them'.[49] Indeed, secondary history is still very traditional in many ways, not least the set of subjects and the historiographies taught. Yet this sense of historical empathy, if not part of the assessment burden, is increasingly deployed as a pedagogical tool. This empathy drives educational development, with research suggesting that children 'become increasingly able to make suppositions, to understand other points of view and values different from their own'.[50]

Horrible Histories addresses the needs of the historical student – empathy, a sense of period rather than of fact, a narrative interest in detail. At times the fascination with the minutiae of the unpleasant and the relaxed tone can lead to a problematic equivocation. For instance, on Hitler's blaming the Jews for Germany's problems: 'Rubbish, of course, but sadly most people at that time believed his big lie and millions died'; the Holocaust is not mentioned directly or named.[51] The excerpt is bracing and on the edge of dismissive. Yet the books also attempt to engage the empathy of the audience:

> When Russian ruler Joseph Stalin sent his secret police to arrest and execute 20 million people, what did Mr and Ms Ordinary do? Nothing. They shut their doors, drew the curtains, shut out the horrors and let their neighbours die. When your Rotten Ruler tells you to kill and die for them, what will *you* say, you ordinary person?[52]

The brand is so popular that it has spawned spin-off products including merchandise, special series (on cities, or countries, or pirates), a television series, a magazine, a stage show and an exhibition at the Royal Armouries in Leeds. The Armouries exhibit emphasises interactive learning and empathic engagement with the past, for instance with a courtroom that encourages the visitor to stand in the dock. The books have had tie-ins with newspapers (*The Telegraph*) and breakfast cereals. Their style has been mimicked to educate children in science, geography and maths.[53] *Horrible Histories* illustrates a popular iconoclasm, a challenge to standard narratives, and a pedagogical desire to present information in complex and dynamic ways. Yet, despite some interest in social and 'everyday history', the books are still interested in the actuality of the past: 'history books designed for use in the home ... still focus almost exclusively on imparting the facts of historical knowledge'.[54]

The status of the popular history author

One way to measure the impact of the new generation of public historians – or historians in public – is to briefly consider their reception in the press. This provides some, albeit biased, insight into the ways in which working professional historians as public figures are conceptualised in relation to the most important aspect of their profile, their work. The military historian Richard Holmes is high-profile enough to have been a judge on *Great Britons* and introduce several BBC documentaries. His work has focussed generally on the experience of the common soldier. The critical response to his published output allows us to see a cross-section of contemporary attitudes to history. It illustrates various ways that the past is imagined, and the ways in which an audience's use of and engagement with the past are imagined to work. Most reviewers suggest that Holmes' approach is crucial, his opening up of the past by allowing the marginalised to speak being the main selling point for his work. One element of the reviews is the use of the landmarks of fiction to orientate the reader. The historical novelist Bernard Cornwell, creator of the 'Sharpe' series of novels about the Napoleonic era, was used by the *Daily Mail* to judge *Redcoat* (2001). The use of 'celebrity' rather than professional book reviewers with some relevance to the book under consideration is commonplace practice. In this instance Cornwell's review suggests that Holmes' particular skill is in many ways similar to his own:

> I have never met Richard Holmes, but I am deeply jealous of him for *Redcoat* opens with the re-enactment of a Napoleonic battle that I wish I had written myself ... The redcoat and his family were never appreciated, but Richard Holmes has written them a marvellous memorial. *Redcoat* is a wonderful book, full of anecdote and good sense. Anyone who has enjoyed a Sharpe story will love it, anyone who likes history will want to own it and anyone who cherishes good writing will read it with pleasure.[55]

The historian is the keeper and constructor of the memory of those marginalised by history; the narrative chronicler and reanimator of events such as combat which the reader has no access to; the repository of 'good sense' and the giver of pleasure and enjoyment. Cornwell collapses the distinction between narrative historian and the writer of historical narratives, enviously eyeing Holmes' ability to vivify a scene (Cornwell also wrote a novel entitled *Redcoat* in 1993). He highlights the style with which Holmes writes, again plainly terming it 'good'; this imprimatur of decency (somehow not complex but straightforward) assigns Holmes a solidity. In contrast, Andro Linklater, writing in *The Spectator*, indicted Holmes for his rigid approach and his empathic mythmaking: '[Holmes] inclines to ... the romance of cannon-fire, trumpet calls and tattered regimental colours'.[56] This vivacious quality is what Simon Heffer enjoyed about the book: 'vivid, comprehensive, well written, pacy, colourful, and above all, highly informative'.[57]

Responses to Holmes repeatedly return to his use of anecdote to drive the narrative and the notion of 'empathy'. Writing in the *Independent* about Holmes' *Tommy* (2004), Gary Sheffield suggested

> a historian with the flair of a novelist lovingly recreates the British Army of 1914–18, often letting the soldiers speak through their own words. This technique is not new, but what sets Richard Holmes apart is the sheer quality of his writing and his empathy with his subjects.[58]

Similar to Cornwell's review, then, uppermost is the written style and the ability to engage imaginatively with the past.[59] Holmes' use of direct quotation from marginalised figures is emphasised continually. The suggestion that the use of 'anecdote' drives this type of historical writing – along with rigorous military scholarship – is problematic. It supposes that Holmes is a sifter through stories, a compiler of others' narratives. More accurately, he allows the common soldier to speak and his arrangement of these voices creates fast, moving history.

Holmes' book *Dusty Warriors: Modern Soldiers at War* (2006), an account of an Iraq tour of duty of the Princess of Wales' Royal Regiment (PWRR) during the summer of 2004, demonstrates a peculiar relativity – coming after accounts of the British Army 1700–1900 (*Redcoat*), WWI footsoldiers (*Tommy*, 2004), and the soldier in India (*Sahib*, 2005), the decision to bring the story to the present represents one of the only serious interventions in the conflict to be made by a high-level historian. Holmes deploys similar techniques to his historical work, using the words of the combatants themselves to describe what is happening. His empathy is both an emotional connection and a desire to help non-professionals to understand the military (he himself was Director of Reserve Forces and Cadets, and 1999–2007 he was a colonel in the PWRR). The book is an attempt, then, to rationalise a wider conflict and to communicate it by concentrating on the particular stories of those ordinary soldiers taking part. It uses the techniques of history, and the cultural capital of the historian-soldier, and is a unique document in the developing status and social definition of the historian. Reviews of the book reminded the reader of Holmes' pedigree as a military writer, giving his thoughts on a contemporary conflict legitimacy and authority; the reception of the book similarly emphasised its immediacy, fluency, pace, narrative and brilliance of description. In some fashion the fact that Holmes was writing it, as a military historian, took the political sting out of the book and allowed reviewers to celebrate the army's bravery and professionalism: 'They give us the privileged chance to glance into the heart and soul of today's absurdly small but extra-ordinarily good British army, our army.'[60] The courage, determination and ability of the common soldier are emphasised, in terms which clearly echo the char-acteristics that reviewers found in soldiers described by Holmes in his earlier books. Continuity of some description, therefore, was emphasised.

The response to this one popular writer, then, points us to a selection of cultural tropes associated with the writings of popular historians. First, it demonstrates the complexity of the reception of historical work – criticised by novelists, historians, professional critics; compared to fiction, judged on readability and interest. The popular historian is judged on their literary qualities as much as their historical skills: clarity and written style are as important as factual precision and innova-tive historiography. The populism of this popular writer – giving the voice back to the forgotten of history – is emphasised, although the possible conservatism that this might signal (a revisionist account of the armies that conquered the Empire, according in some ways with Niall Ferguson's rethinking of that insti-tution) is played down. Furthermore, it is possible to pick out key words and ideas: accuracy, clarity, a robustness of approach and a direct style. Holmes is historian as story-teller, informative and enjoyable. He is also able, through his work on the PWRR, to make a clear and important intervention into contemporary political debate.

Popular circulation: magazines

History magazines show robust figures in terms of circulation. *History Today*, a semi-academic, educational monthly magazine circulates on average 26,000. This is roughly equal to a specialist film magazine such as *Sight and Sound* (22,000). The BBC's history magazine, *BBC History*, which is more populist in appeal, circulates 54,000. This is dwarfed by much of the BBC's suite of magazines (*Good*

Food circulates 342,677; *BBC Homes* circulates 129,778) but compares well to titles such as *BBC Wildlife* (46,094) or *BBC Music* (56,096). Ancillary publications for specialised interests (*Women's History*), local history (*Local History, History Scotland, Yorkshire History Quarterly*) and genealogy (*Ancestors, Practical Family History, Family History Monthly*) stand up relatively well. For instance, *Family Tree Magazine* circulates some 16,498 which is impressive given that the main genealogical information is more readily accessible online (and also that it is competing with three other titles). Magazines of this type are aimed at affluent professionals, ABC1s in general (89 per cent of *BBC History* readers fall into this category, 73 per cent for *History Today*), who buy history books and biographies. Readers of these magazines tend to be both genders (for *BBC History* there is around 55/45 per cent male/female split, although for *History Today* it is 75/25), over 40 and educated.

The prestigious monthly magazines like *History Today* and *BBC History* have achieved the status of educators, attracting eminent contributors, sponsoring prizes and publishing branded books. Magazines are print media (albeit with online manifestations) and their articles combine historical analysis with images, polls, adverts and editorials. Magazine readership implies intent (subscription) and repeated monthly interest in the subject. Rather than buying a single book, the magazine implies a recurrent interest; similarly, the diversity of articles suggests an audience able to investigate in a number of historiographical styles and complex historical contexts. Furthermore, much of *History Today* is given over to book reviews, suggesting an interest in the wider scope of the discipline, a desire for an overview of current scholarship, a critical engagement with the production and consumption of history, and an ease with diversity of methodology. Both *History Today* and *BBC History* incorporate directly educational elements, publishing online study guides, archives, reference works and teaching news. They present themselves as a resource for students, so their articles in their online manifestation become a research store. *History Today*'s website (www.historytoday.com) has discussion lists related to the articles in that month's edition (free to access even if the online user has not bought the magazine). There is a prize given to the best comment. There is also an interactive poll on the site, and a 'classroom' section with references, links and study guides. This kind of meta-content encourages an interrogative reading of the magazines and attempts to foster an enfranchised sense of involvement in the consideration and understanding of history.

These magazines and their supporting websites give the interested amateur information, exposing them to multiple historiographies and debates. The reader is interested and informed, participant in a wider intellectual conversation of which the articles are a synthesis. Importantly, the information communicated is print-based and, in the case of the history magazines, print is still given precedence over electronic information, and is conceptualised differently to tele/visual information. These magazines occupy a complex and important interface between academic history and popular history. Magazine articles in the higher quality publications tend to be relatively prestigious, written by acknowledged global experts in their fields. At the same time the magazine is a commercial operation, needing to sell copies and earn advertising revenue.

Reception and consumption: reading groups and reader-reviews

After the success of Oprah Winfrey's reading groups in 1996, the book club phenomenon has become a familiar part of contemporary life.[61] Radio 4 has a longrunning show *Bookclub*, and libraries, cafés, newspapers and museums now run them. Generally the format is designed so that members get together once a month to talk over a book they have all read. The 'reading group' has its roots in the 'Book of the Month' club and subscription publishing, insofar as it suggests an audience somehow literarily disenfranchised and desiring a safe, directed way of accruing cultural capital.[62] However, the method has become much more widely influential, and incorporates a much broader social demographic. The reading group is a grassroots phenomenon, bypassing traditional cultural gatekeepers and ignoring critics. Richard and Judy's book group is the single most powerful entity in publishing in the UK, able to create an instant audience for a book. It is not surprising that publishing houses have seen the reading group as a natural progression from other types of subscription publishing and set up support websites with introductory guides (Random House is the biggest player in this field).[63] The groups suggest an enfranchised way of dealing with cultural product – a desire to discuss the text and create book-based communities with others outside of the aegis of traditional institutions such as the university, school, arts show or newspaper and magazine review.

Quite apart from the fact that there are dedicated book clubs for historical fiction, increasingly reading groups are taking history and biography as their subjects.[64] This again demonstrates a popularising of the reading of history, and an emergent enfranchisement as non-professionalised discussions take place without organisation or direction. Reading groups online also contribute both a social networking and a globalising element to this phenomenon.[65] History reading groups emphasise discussion outside of the academy as a way of forming community and as a means of accruing cultural capital. In some ways this phenomenon is akin to the extra-mural education movement of the 1960s (the Worker's Educational Association, the Open University), although outside of the purview of the profession as they are user-directed and user-oriented. Similarly, their contexts are complex, being generally online or domestic, so models of grassroots historical discussion fracture and develop. Reading groups demonstrate that the popular audience for history is complex and dynamic, able to be interrogative and creative as well as simply to follow a more standard passive reading model. Reading groups – both virtual and physical – encourage an enfranchisement of sorts, allowing the user of the text to interrogate it publicly.

Similarly the advent of online review websites and blogs – and the incorporation of customer-led reviews in web-based bookstores – have further eroded the power of traditional cultural gatekeepers. The marketing model is of friendly recommendation by someone *just like you* – a purported democratisation which circumvents traditional routes.[66] Amazon's consumer profiling database innovation which recommends other books based on the purchasing habits of others who bought it ('Customers who bought/viewed this also bought') creates a set of virtual relationships with unknown buyers which again subverts mainstream cultural gatekeepers. They also link consumer-generated 'lists' related to the product being viewed. This relationship-based presentation emphasises (probably illusory) user-generated economic systems and marketing. Rather than navigate by traditional methods the 'new hybrid consumer' engages with information in a new set of ways, and one of the most important is a sense of user-led community.[67]

In November 2006, a controversy surrounding the novelist Susan Hill brought into focus issues surrounding web reviewing and word-of-mouth marketing. The critic and academic John Sutherland wrote a column in *The Telegraph* in which he bemoaned the increasing (unaudited) power of internet reviewers (blogs, Amazon reviews, websites, chat forums). In particular, he mentioned the controversy surrounding the Amazon UK reviews of Victoria Glendinning's biography of Leonard Woolf which were universally derogatory apart from one posted with fawning praise which turned out to be by Glendinning's husband.[68] Sutherland used this as a platform to attack web reviewers for 'shooting off their mouths'.[69] He continued:

> There are those who see web-reviewing, whether independent bloggery or commercially hosted, as a 'power to the reader' trend – the democratization of something traditionally monopolized by literary mandarins. And there are those who see it as a degradation of literary taste.[70]

Sutherland's appeal to 'literary taste' betrays a cultural gate-keeper increasingly unable to engage with a dynamic and complex marketplace. Susan Hill blogged an entry entitled 'Just who do they think they are' on her site, attacking Sutherland, and expressing her boredom with reviews:

> I have been growing more and more sure that the traditional book pages of most of the national newspapers are largely irrelevant. The TLS is not because it caters for a different and largely academic readership, but the rest spend yards of column inches reviewing books few people will buy/read and arrogantly ignoring what is going on in the world where the real dedicated and committed readers live.[71]

She continued:

> The fact is that the tide has turned and the people have power now. Not that we do it in order to have 'power', we do it because we love books and want to recommend a wealth of them to others, so that they may enjoy them and for no other reason. We do it for nothing and for fun and for the book/literature.[72]

As a consequence of her blog, Hill was informed by a still-anonymous literary editor that:

> After reading your blog about book review pages, I would like you to know that no book either published or written by you will be reviewed on our

literary pages. In the light of your expressed views, I am sure you will be neither surprised nor distressed.[73]

Hill published this email on her blog but has declined to name the author of it.

Hill's assertion of 'people power' and the cultural democratisation she describes demonstrate the new power dynamic of online reading communities. Her view is idealistic – much online reviewing is increasingly being controlled and directed by publishers – and her forthright anti-intellectualism betrays a cultural affectation. However, she illustrates the new recommendation marketing, the online creation of a community of 'real dedicated and committed readers' outside of traditional boundaries or discourses. One example of this for history books is a subsection of the massive site *Review Centre* which encourages the involvement of the ordinary user.[74] *Review Centre*'s pieces ask the amateur contributor to list value for money, whether they would recommend the book to a friend, and for an overall rating out of ten in addition to enumeration of Good and Bad points. The creation of web buying guides and review accumulator sites like this testify to the importance of a kind of 'word of mouth' marketing, as practised by Amazon and iTunes (the deployment of customer reviews and associative 'people who bought this also bought' structures).[75] There is a clear sense that the 'ordinary' experience of a book is more important than – or at least *as* important as – the opinion of a critic or professional historian. This kind of site also clearly inserts the marketing and recommending of books into a consuming continuum – the advice is given to ensure an 'informed choice' as to which book to buy. Reviews are therefore educative and utilitarian. The rest of *Review Centre* is given over to customer-generated comments about commodities from car insurance to laptops and wedding dresses, demonstrating that books are increasingly just one part of a general leisure experience and the quantitative element of the review is more interested in the experience of a consumer than a reader.

It is increasingly the case that 'quality' broadsheet papers have taken to incorporating readers' views, with comments, reader-led lists and discussion. The boundaries between official content-generator and user are increasingly blurred, underlining Hill's assertion that 'national newspapers are largely irrelevant'. Furthermore, it does not end at reviewing – although this kind of cultural judgement is the most obvious element of a newly 'enfranchised' online community. User-content-driven sites such as Helium and Wikipedia suggest an increasing encroachment into professional and institutional areas that were previously clearly demarcated: writing, publishing, commenting, reviewing. This babbling multiplicity of comment might promise a type of enfranchisement and voicing of the marginalised but it is occurring simultaneously with a shoring up of the popular historian's gatekeeper status. There is a dichotomy between the status accorded to the public historian and the seeming grassroots revolution in historical participation that many of the genres and media examined by this book encourage. Historians are more visible than ever and with this comes a concomitant cultural capital and authority, drawn, in contrast with Hill's blogging revolution, greatly from the power of the printed word – as most of this chapter has demonstrated.

3   The historian in popular culture

'That's you, that is': historian as child, adventurer, and hero

One of the reasons for the erosion of academic authority in public and the concomitant raising up of the individual, dynamic, undonnish celebrity presenter is the complex representation of the historian in popular culture. Outside of specific paradigms the humanities academic in the popular imagination tends to be relatively stuffy, fusty, male, and often homicidal (those who appear in *Inspector Morse*, for instance, are generally all four). Like Dylan Moran's foolish David in *Shaun of the Dead* (Edgar Wright, 2004) – 'A 30-year-old lecturer, in more ways than simply vocational' – humanities academics are prissy, mis-directed, not up to action and ultimately expendable.[1] University historians specifically are petty and childish, emphasised by the 'History Today' sketch on *The Mary Whitehouse Experience* (BBC 2, 1990–92) which consisted of two eminent professors of history beginning to debate but descending into a series of increasingly baroque playground-style insults.[2] Similarly Andrew Lincoln's English teacher in the Channel 4 drama series *Teachers* is more interested in his students liking him than in poetry. Alan Bennett's character Irwin in his play *The History Boys* (2004) is a secondary school History teacher who looks for the alternative, the almost counterfactual (or at least counterintuitive), and who recommends his students argue against the grain and think outside the box. Clearly inspired by Niall Ferguson, at the conclusion of the play Irwin has emerged in the 1990s as the presenter of historical documentary. His brand of slightly ruthless and definitely amoral historical investigation is seen to be actively bad for the boys he teaches, and, it is suggested, for the society which he advises. He is directly contrasted with Hector, the unique, passionate English master, out of time and sadly pathetic. Here is the historian as malign influence, creating problems and active destruction due to the baleful influence of maverick methods and historiography.

The more cerebral processes of teaching, understanding and learning in the humanities do not lend themselves to popular tropes. An exception might be the inspiring English teacher, like Robin Williams' character John Keating in *Dead Poet's Society* (Peter Weir, 1989) who helps his boys discover the truth within themselves through a dynamic love of literature.[3] The inspirational teacher motif suggests that eccentricity and uniqueness are the characteristics. Of course, this is to focus upon the minority representation – by far the most high profile academics in popular cultural product tend to be scientists, mathematicians, mechanics, medical doctors or computer experts whose knowledge is obscure, often world-threatening, and either sends them mad or leads them to a bad end.[4] The fictional scientist is repeatedly represented and – at least since *Frankenstein* – has become the repository of cultural worries and fears. The humanities scholar – historian or archaeologist or literary theorist or philosopher – tends to be someone who might help unravel a code, point towards the truth of some description, or give arcane contextual information. They generally work at Oxford or possibly Harvard, and are rarely the central characters.[5]

That said, archaeology and the investigation of ancient history – due to their links with adventure, exploration and field work (and therefore with getting out of the stuffy confines of the university) – have provided popular culture with several key tropes. In film, minor figures like John Hannah and Rachel Weisz in *The Mummy* (Stephen Sommers, 1996), Ralph Fiennes in *The English Patient* (Anthony Minghella, 1996) and James Spader in *Stargate* (Roland Emmerich, 1997) clearly present the scholarly, slightly unworldly expert historian-archaeologist. The two most important adventurer-archaeologists-historians are Lara Croft and Indiana Jones. The game *Tomb Raider* (1996–) allows the player as Lara Croft to follow a set of clues and perform a series of increasingly difficult physical tasks in order to claim the ancient treasure. Croft is unusual as the female heroine of a major action game (in contrast, for instance, to *Max Payne*, 2001, *GoldenEye*, 1997, or *Splinter Cell*, 2002). The games present the archaeologist as romantic heroine, as protagonist, as problem solver and explorer. She is an athlete with an intellect, skilled in investigation as well as gunfighting. Significantly enough for a global game she is English, and her patrician links to a tradition of gentlemanly pseudo-imperialist archaeology are emphasised by the training level which obliges the player to get to understand the game by exploring her stately home. The games cast the historian as adventurer, inserting Croft into an ergodic process whereby eventually she will discover the 'truth'; similarly she is part of a game, her investigations contextualised by the player's desire for entertainment, interactivity and eventual – wished for – conclusion. *Tomb Raider* also physically renders the central character as unreal (Croft's bust size is famously unfeasible), and desired. In casting Angelina Jolie the film versions of *Tomb Raider* (Simon West, 2001; Jan de Bont, 2003) continued this presentation of the female adventurer/ archaeologist as a sexual object and undermined her intellectual or cultural authority. The films lose all connection with the purported intellectual matter of investigation, placing Croft into a familiar genre of archaeology-fantasy-action similar to *The Mummy* and *Stargate*.

Indeed, popular archaeological films cannot seem to get away from secret societies, mumbo-jumbo, magic, ritual and the undead. Even Harrison Ford's resolutely materialist Indiana Jones is saved by the vengeance of God and meets priests who seek sacred stones. The Indiana Jones series (1981–2008) at least has scenes with Jones teaching at university, giving his finds to a museum and appearing to have some actual historical and linguistic knowledge.[6] In *Raiders of the Lost Ark*, Jones' lecturer is initially bashful but when liberated from the bounds of the academy he is decisive, heroic and virtuous. The films consciously channel the 'boy's own' style of episodic serials from the 1920s and 1930s, creating a kind of pastiche stylisation; they are historical adventure films and as such involve a double nostalgia, not least for a time of clear conflict between right and wrong. Jones, like Croft, is an adventurer with a conscience, a clean figure in comparison with René Belloq, his corrupted nemesis in *Raiders* who collaborates with the Nazis (there is a similar figure, Dr Elsa Schneider, in *Indiana Jones and the Last Crusade*). Archaeology is seen to have moral impetus, both in terms of not aiding evil but also because the artefacts discovered should be in museums, not private collections. The archaeologist has public conscience, moral clarity, idiosyncratic rumpled charm, and an ability with weapons as well as ancient texts. Again the films emphasise the notion of discovery and map-following, and indeed, the narrative form of the film demands the following of a trail to a final conclusion. The engagement with the past is at the level of artefact, the discovery of ancient objects and the solving of clues by deploying specialist knowledge being more cinematic than more humble historical work. Investigation of the past is framed as adventure and intrigue. The analogues for many of these characters are old. Indiana Jones harks back to a time of 1920s adventure films but his character also owes something to H. Rider Haggard's Allan Quartermain from *King Solomon's Mines* (1885) and *Allan Quartermain* (1887). Archaeology and ancient history have continually exerted a fascination particularly over English writers for at least a century – possibly as a consequence of Empire or of the British Museum, as for instance can be seen by the fact that Agatha Christie wrote some four novels centred on the topic.[7]

Novelists in general seem more interested in writing about complex scholars, possibly because external appearance and good hygiene are not so important. Campus novels have for years presented academia to the public in all its dynamic, strange, and self-absorbed oddness.[8] The madcap introspection of the British university campus is lampooned from *Lucky Jim* (English Literature, 1954) through David Lodge's *Changing Places* (English Literature, 1975) to *A Very Peculiar Practice* (campus medical doctors, BBC1, 1986), all of which emphasise the obsessive unworldliness of the academic.[9] Lodge's novel *Nice Work* (1988, filmed for BBC 1989) dramatises the conceptual conflict between a literary critic and an engineer factory owner, emphasising once again the humanities scholar's distance from the real world. Don DeLillo's *White Noise* (Hitler/Cultural Studies, 1985) and Jonathan Frantzen's *The Corrections* (Cultural Studies, 2001) both highlight the problematic moral vacuity of academia. This – mainly American – sense of the intellectual gatekeeper as unfortunately priapic or morally flawed can similarly be seen in John Updike's *Roger's Version* (Divinity, 1986), Malcolm Bradbury's *The History Man* (Sociologist, 1975), J.M. Coetzee's *Disgrace* (English Literature, 1999) and Donna Tartt's *The Secret History* (Classicist, 1992) in which the cult of personality surrounding Classics professor Julian Morrow leads eventually to murder.

In A.S. Byatt's *Possession*, the central character argues that 'Literary critics make natural detectives' and humanities scholars have become detective-heroes in Matthew Pearl's *Dante Club* (2004) and Umberto Eco's *Name of the Rose* (1980), for instance, deploying their disciplinary approach to the study of crime.[10] Elizabeth Kostova's *The Historian* (2005) makes this research focus a gothic tragedy, as the scholar's obsessive searching for quantifiable truth is what provokes and sustains the threat of the vampire. The entire novel is predicated upon academic historical research, from the initial discovery by the protagonist of a sheaf of strange letters in her father's library through the obsessive search by various individuals in the archives of Turkey and Eastern Europe for clues to the whereabouts of Dracula's tomb. Dracula chooses his particular victims because of their research abilities and their focus on discovering all they can about him; the one who comes closest to finding him, Professor Bartholomew Rossi, is kidnapped and forced to arrange Dracula's terrible library. Dracula tempts him with knowledge and partnership:

> With your unflinching honesty, you can see the lesson of history ... History has taught us that the nature of man is evil, sublimely so. Good is not perfectible, but evil is. Why should you not use your great mind in service of what is perfectible?[11]

He foresees a fundamental shift in historiography as a consequence: 'Together we will advance the historian's work beyond anything the world has ever seen. There is no purity like the purity of the sufferings of history.'[12] This cruel and cynical interpretation of the past is then made personal: 'You will have what every historian wants: history will be reality to you. We will wash our minds clean with blood.'[13] Dracula is both historical and current, archaic and Undead, the ultimate expression of a cruel and destructive human history; he is quite possibly the 'historian' of the novel's title, an amoral but actually honest scholar who sees the innate cruelty of the past. The various researchers of *The Historian* finally do track and kill the vampire; the historian might, then, ultimately be the hero.

In Robert Harris's novel 1998 *Archangel*, Fluke Kelso is a smoking, drinking, brilliant but tortured historian with a messy life (often considered to be based on Norman Stone). Generically, his character is more akin to the protagonists of pulp detective fiction. Yet Kelso is also recognisably an academic – part of the romanticised version of academia in which fusty research is derided and brilliant, controversial instinct is celebrated (although it makes him an outcast maverick, naturally). Kelso is the historian as inspired figure; as truth teller and tortured repository of the nation's conscience: 'He glanced around the reading room and closed his eyes, trying to keep hold of the past for a minute longer, a fattening and hungover middle-aged historian in a black corduroy suit.'[14] He finds 'an aesthetic pleasure in the sheer detective work of research'.[15] In contrast, as played by Daniel Craig in the 2005 BBC adaptation of the novel he is sharp, rakish and instinctive (see Figure 3.1). He is a young, dashing, blond, greatcoated version of the hero historian. Kelso's ability to track historical detail through

Figure 3.1 Daniel Craig in the BBC production of *Archangel*, 2005, directed by Jon Jones. Reproduced with permission, copyright © BBC.

archives and follow a warm trail through present-day Russia allows him to be inserted into a heroic narrative, albeit one with analogues to hard boiled detective fiction and which therefore suggest that the protagonist might be a flawed, troubled hero.[16]

The Da Vinci Code

Dan Brown's novels *The Da Vinci Code* and *Angels and Demons* similarly present academic life as a near heroic labour to detect the truth. His central character, Robert Langdon, is Harvard Professor of Religious Symbology.[17] In the 2006 film of *The Da Vinci Code* he was played by Tom Hanks, famous for his solid, decent charm. In *The Da Vinci Code*, Langdon is teamed with a trained police cryptologist who has no purchase on history and therefore is unable to apply any kind of technical expertise. In *Digital Fortress* his partner is a scientist who is unable to understand ambiguity. The historical expert in these novels has the key to understanding – and finding – the truth. Brown's Langdon is academic as matinee idol:

> Although not overly handsome in a classical sense, the forty-five-year-old Langdon had what his female colleagues referred to as an 'erudite' appeal –

wisps of gray in his thick brown hair, probing blue eyes, an arrestingly deep voice, and the strong, carefree smile of a collegiate athlete. A varsity diver in prep school and college, Langdon still had the body of a swimmer, a toned, six-foot physique that he vigilantly maintained.[18]

Like the televised *Archangel*, Brown's novels portray historian as hero, the serious worldly scholar able to bring both intellect and athleticism to bear on international conspiracies. A similar character is the gymnast Art Historian Anna Petrescu in Jeffrey Archer's *False Impression*.[19] Nicolas Cage plays a Langdon-esque combination of adventurer and obsessive historian in *National Treasure* (2004, Jon Turteltaub), a film which channels *The Da Vinci Code* and clearly contrasts the moral historian-adventurer (Cage and his archivist partner Diane Kruger) with villainous, anti-intellectual treasure hunters (led by Sean Bean).[20] In all three of these examples the expert desires knowledge (generally in the form of artefacts – letters, paintings or the Declaration of Independence) – and solves clues in order to share the information and the treasure with the world and contribute to the sum of human understanding rather than make an individual fortune or gain fame. This selfless pursuit is what marks the historian out.

What the *National Treasure* films and *The Da Vinci Code* and its brood demonstrate is the intersection of historical investigation in the popular imagination with conspiracy theory. Robert Langdon is an expert in the residual influence of what Brown terms the lost sacred feminine, essentially the worship of the female and its repression by the Roman Catholic Church. Langdon's value to *The Da Vinci Code* is his ability to ally historical knowledge of symbol with a logical mind for the solving of ciphers or codes. History in the novel becomes an elaborate patch-work of codes – geographical, sacred, ritualistic, artistic – that if solved or under-stood can be shown to refer to the central truths which the Church attempts to suppress in order to further its own agenda. 'History' as it is known is a set of smokescreens put in place to shore up the power of the Vatican. The book reads European history by drawing out an ancient battle between Rome and the Priory of Sion, the political and mystical wing of the Knights Templar. The Priory protects a great secret – documents relating to the Holy Grail, and the truth about the bloodline of Christ – and this is threatened in the action of the novel.[21] The novel knits together a huge amount of religious and historical information into a well-ordered and relatively persuasive alternative account of the last 2000 years, suggesting that Mary Magdalene and Christ were husband and wife, and that this has essentially been an open secret ever since. Discovering proof of this conspiracy – and therefore changing the interpretation of two millennia of history – is the central impetus both of the characters and the plot: "'Learning the truth has become my life's love," Teabing said. "And the Sangreal [Holy Grail] is my favourite mistress.'"[22] Yet the novel is also interested in the fact that codes can be hidden in plain sight, and that they are essentially languages to be used as tools: '*There is more there*, she told herself. *Ingeniously hidden … but present nonetheless.*'[23]

The *Da Vinci Code* opens with a page headed 'FACT:' that stresses the historical veracity of the Priory of Sion (citing Les Dossiers Secrets, documents found in the Bibliothèque Nationale in 1975), presents some relatively subjective information about Opus Dei ('the topic of recent controversy due to reports of brain-washing, coercion and a dangerous practice known as "corporal mortification"') and concludes by stating 'All descriptions of artwork, architecture, documents and secret rituals in this novel are accurate'.[24] *The Da Vinci Code* traces a line of conjecture and conspiracy while cleaving to a sense that the truth *is* out there and can be understood (although it is apt that the main theorist of the Grail is ultimately unmasked as the central villain, his motivation the forced uncovering of a truth he has been seeking all his life). Brown's novel is generically straight, but it presents a view of history in a state of flux – certainly the central motif of the novel is that history is a whitewash and that academic investigation can demonstrate the complexities and irregularities of the story as it is told. He himself argues for the subjective nature of history: 'Many historians now believe (as do I) that in gauging the historical accuracy of a given concept, we should first ask ourselves a far deeper question: How historically accurate is history itself?'[25] Yet *The Da Vinci Code* also suggests that history is a set of ciphered discourses that can be understood and read with the correct training and approach (or if armed with the correct knowledge). Historical documentation and evidence are presented as a set of codexes that can be deciphered, with generally one single meaning rather than ambivalent or ambiguous interpretation.

Furthermore, all the gatekeepers of this knowledge are male. The innocent of the novel – despite the Greek inflection of her name – is Sophie Neveu, the trained Police cryptographer. Large swathes of the central part of the novel consist of the credulous Neveu being initiated into knowledge, taught by a Harvard professor and an Oxford-educated British Knight. They decode history for her, thus informing her of the untold story. In many ways the passive reader is put into her position of confusion moving to a final revelation and understanding. Her lack of knowledge is projected onto the reader (and that initial 'FACT' note anticipates this). The reader is presented with an 'alternative' history, a conspiracy theory presented as academically-inflected (tested by an academic) fiction. Yet 'key' to the novel is the possibility that things we take for granted are not true, and it is importantly the reader who is given the details and left to make up their mind, as Brown points out: 'The "FACT" page makes *no* statement whatsoever about any of the ancient theories discussed by fictional characters. Interpreting those ideas is left to the reader.'[26]

The novel was controversial, and religious scholars are still writing learned articles disproving and rebutting the ideas Brown presented. A small publishing industry has emerged particularly driven by Christian publishers refuting, debating and illustrating what have been termed the book's 'heresies'; Lincoln Cathedral was accused of simony when it accepted a financial gift in return for allowing the film of the book to be shot in its cloisters (Westminster Abbey had refused). The historical and its intersection with the theological became live popular issues as a consequence, and it might be suggested that Brown's novel – sixty-one million copies sold, translated into forty-four languages – has done more to stimulate historical discussion, or a rethinking of familiar discourses, than most historical teaching. Certainly the novel's success made readers aware of the historical development of institutions – the Church, governments, nations, universities. The theological implications invoke another interesting historicised relationship, that between the individual worshipper and the physical manifestation of Christ (although this could equally apply to relationships with Mohammed, or the Buddha). The contemporaneity of the worshipper's relationship with Christ *now* and engagement with his death *then* suggests that religious experience enshrines within it a dynamic past–presentness, an ability to relate to events from millennia ago as the mainspring for one's faith.[27]

The discussion of the book's issues in many ways now inflects the actual reading of the novel itself (there is, for instance, a *Rough Guide* to the novel, giving it a kind of non-fictional cachet). The notion that history as told to us, and therefore our day-to-day lives, might be the consequence of a massive conspiracy suggests an active understanding of ideology, a paranoid willingness to distrust the stories told by cultural gatekeepers like schools or churches, and a pseudo-humanist or liberal desire to be able to define oneself outside of such frameworks once one has all the facts at one's command. The investigation of history, then, might lead to revelation which could shake the very foundations of Western civilisation and allow the investigator or the holder of knowledge access to a new model of self. The novel and related phenomena present history-as-conspiracy, the pseudo-situationist mantra that 'everything you know is wrong', but also suggest that informed investigation (and continental travel) will allow personal revelation and understanding of the truth. *The Da Vinci Code* addresses a global culture soaked in conspiracy and keen to see the documents which undermine the lies.[28] The book has spawned a multitude of imitators (although it also is itself part of the wider conspiracy thriller genre, as seen, for instance, by its similarity to Michael Cordy's massive-selling (1997) novel *The Miracle Strain*) relating the untold histories of the Church, the Masons and the Templars.[29] This popular subgenre which might be termed the historical conspiracy thriller posits history as fluid and presents the hero-adventurer as investigator and iconoclast, pursuing knowledge in order to further the plot and attain narrative satisfaction, as well as to demonstrate the fallaciousness of the institutions underpinning modern society and civilisation.

Historians as popularly represented are dusty, particular, crumpled, possibly Undead, and obsessive; but they are also potentially heroic. Films eschew complexity, preferring the sensational, but in novels the figure of the historian is often complex and potentially troubling. Dana Polan has argued, 'History, in the popular conception, is not about imagination, is not about re-construction, but at best about positivist restoration, about a non-interpretative mastery of bits of facts.'[30] A number of books have been written considering the manifestation of various academic disciplines in popular culture.[31] These works often point to a decentring of authority, suggesting that to succeed, the expert needs to distil their character and their message. The academic historian enters the public imagination as often speccy and donnish, rarely easily heroic, a searcher for truth among the dusty archive. They might be an adventurer, but will have to shed the tweeds of the university for a fedora and bullwhip in order to make this work properly. In contrast to the scientist, repository of hopeful fears and a figure of potential, the historian is more solid but less interesting, a channeller of knowledge rather than the creator of anything new or compelling. However, at the same time their search for truth, their insight, and their ability to discern patterns of information might give them the opportunity and the means to remake the world.

Part II

Enfranchisement, ownership and consumption

'Amateur' histories

Serious leisure and enfranchisement

Part II considers the purported enfranchisement of the historical consumer through material means – the opening up of access to the tools, artefacts and texts of the past. Previous chapters suggested that, in addition to the popularity of the celebrity–presenter–historian, audiences were beginning to take control of historical information from the academic gatekeeper and develop their own narratives, stories and experiences. The circumventing of reviewers recorded by Susan Hill, for instance, gestures towards the seeming agency of the historical consumer. Technological innovation – in particular, database technology and the internet – has increasingly enabled the bypassing of institutions and professional historians. The status of the 'amateur' historian – if such a distinction is possible – is increasingly complex, and such figures are well resourced and visible. The opening-up of access to historical information via the internet and the personalising of history imagined in genealogy suggest an enfranchisement of the individual into history, the evolution of an historical subject with investigative agency. As Vivien Sobchak argues, increased popular engagement with the tools and artefacts of the past suggests 'a more active and reflective historical subject'.[1]

The *Oxford English Dictionary* defines 'enfranchisement' in the following way:

> The action of enfranchising; the state or fact of being enfranchised
>
> 1 Liberation from imprisonment, servitude, or political subjection
> 2 (a) Admission to the 'freedom' of a city, borough, or corporation, or to the citizenship of a state; admission to political rights, now *esp.* to the electoral franchise.
>   (b) The conferring of privileges (now chiefly the right of parliamentary representation) upon a town
> 3 The action of making lands freehold. To enfranchise is to 'admit to personal freedom', and to 'admit to municipal or political privileges'.

There are a number of things to pick out here. Enfranchisement is a political issue, enlargement from subjection and servitude. In general, it involves the conferring of privilege (the vote, or a public democratic voice). Sense 2 reminds us that the word has citizenship issues associated with it; to be enfranchised is to be a political subject. The historically enfranchised are seemingly afforded more agency and cultural capital due to their engagement with the past. At a basic level, enfranchisement is a liberal mode of theorising access to the past which attempts to somehow allow the ordinary citizen democratic access to the institutions and discourses of their history.

Of course, there are several sub-disciplines of history which for years have given the tools of investigation to the 'ordinary' user: local history and genealogy. While the local history movement has a long ancestry, the 1990s saw an acceleration of access to records and thus of relatively direct engagement with the past.[2] Genealogy and local history are two of the most important phenomena in 'public' history of the past decade. Their popularity suggests an emancipation of the historical subject, as 'ordinary' unschooled participants can discover their own history using means and information previously denied to them. A consideration of the variety of tools available to the general public enables the tracing of the methodological and cultural distinctions between the professional and amateur historian. The different types of historical knowledge available, and the range of ways that this knowledge is accessed and valued, can be analysed. The enfranchised subject has many ways of engaging with their various pasts.

Furthermore, the following chapters demonstrate how history – both as artefact and a set of investigative practices – has become increasingly conceived as part of an economic nexus. In particular, Part II shows how the leisuring of history over the past decade in British society interfaces with the commodification of historical knowledge. On the one hand, the opening-up of knowledge through the increased accessibility provided by online databases suggests an enfranchisement for the user. Yet this is generally paid for, increasingly via gateway pages. On genealogical websites, national knowledge, such as censuses, wills, and social information of all kinds, is fed into a financial matrix. Cultural artefacts, in the form of historical knowledge and information, here become commodities in an economy in which the consumption of such goods is driven by a desire to understand the self and make that self complete. Genealogical websites operate within a (globalised) historiocentric cultural economy, their information commodified. However, because of the status of genealogical information – rather than, for instance, of cultural artefacts – this economy is closed and rational. History can actually be valued, rather than be part of a circulating set of meanings and values. Information is a product, something created by the labour of history, which can be desired and paid for.

The past has become electronic information that is product. History as an area of scholarly inquiry will have to respond to this 'virtual', hyperreal or performative turn as it did to the cultural or to the linguistic (which in many ways has foregrounded contemporary worries about the malleability of history-as-text). Virtual history has arrived with digitised archives, CGI effects in documentary and games blurring the line between fact and fiction, authenticity and experience. History is interwoven with culture and therefore is experiencing the same complications as any discourse in its interface with the complex technologies of postmodernity. New media and new technologies diffuse identities and notions of self both in terms of the mediation of culture and our definition of the past. The *Oxford English Dictionary* definition of 'virtual' sense 4g relates to computers:

> Not physically existing as such but made by software to appear to do so from the point of view of the program or the user; *spec.* applied to memory that appears to be internal although most of it is external, transfer between the two being made automatically as required.

This definition has suggestive implications for the 'virtual' turn insofar as it clearly renders cyberhistory something which is very much a construction of software with no materiality. This disjunction of coded signifier from signified clearly presents virtuality as unreal and ephemeral, a ghost in the machine.

The leisurising of genealogy and local history, or 'history as hobby', models such cultural participation as part of a particular set of pursuits which can be analysed more generally. Recently sociologists have begun to note the 'importance of leisure in shaping social identity'.[3] Hobbies and leisure pursuits feed into the formation of a public social self. Local history and genealogy fall into the category of 'serious' leisure, a 'disciplined, systematic acquisition of knowledge and skills' and the 'organisation of this activity in the life course as a "career" involving programmatic benchmarks of achievement'.[4] Local and genealogical research form part of a suite of leisure pursuits which involve 'durable benefits such as self-actualisation, self-enrichment, enhancement of self-image and intensification of solidarity'.[5] Furthermore, these types of popular historical enquiry demonstrate the value of collaborative research and networking, both virtually and physically, achieving high social density. Serious leisure pursuits consolidate social capital. Genealogy, family history and local history as amateur leisure illustrate that the pursuit of history has a particular social function and is part of a continuum of non-work-related pastimes.

4   The everyday historical
Local history, metal detecting, antiques

Local history

Local history traces its roots to early modern antiquarianism, and was formalised as a discipline with the formation of the English Local History Department at the University of Leicester in 1947 and the publication of W.G. Hoskins' *The Making of the English Landscape* (1955) and *Local History in England* (1959).[1] It is closely linked to the expansion of adult education and extra-mural university education during the post-war decades, and therefore is from the beginning tied to a sense of democratisation of learning and the expansion of academic boundaries. Hoskins argued that the upsurge in interest in the local was tied to a sense of the fragmentation of the world, a claim which is repeatedly made for the subject.[2] According to Hoskins, there were particular themes that the local historian should pursue, or would unconsciously reveal: 'the origin and growth of his particular local community or society'; 'records about the ownership and occupation of the land'; 'population changes over a long period of time'; and the way that the local community 'has disintegrated during the past hundred years or so'.[3] His colleague, H.P.R. Finberg, agreed, writing in 1952 that 'the business of the local historian, then, as I see it, is to re-enact in his own mind, and to portray for his readers, the Origin, Growth, Decline and Fall of a Local Community'.[4] This sense of decline is the overriding theme of all local history for Hoskins, the way that local areas have become 'hollow shells from which the heart and the spirit have been eaten away by the acids of modernity'.[5] This melancholic, conservative sense of the loss of local wholeness characterises the local as something precious and in some ways a set of practices and actions (a community) threatened by the wider sweep of history as a whole. Local history complements 'history from below' models of social history while at crucial moments providing a model in which the local is detached from the national and international.

It also emphasises site-specific fieldwork: 'no local historian ought to be afraid to get his feet wet'.[6] Hoskins' emphasis here is that the text of a map may lie, and that the physicality of location is key to the search for truth: 'some of the best documented local histories betray not the slightest sign that the author has looked over the hedges of his chosen place'.[7] Hoskins' approach was long on accuracy and warmly democratic:

primarily I regard the study of local history and topography as a hobby that gives a great deal of pleasure to a great number of people, and I think it wrong to make it intimidating, to warn them off because they may not have the training of the professional historian. It is a means of enjoyment and a way of enlarging one's consciousness of the external world, and even (I am sure) of the internal world.[8]

This sense of the humanistic potential of historical knowledge for educating the individual and leading them to an enlightenment of sorts still underwrites the subject. Finberg termed the discipline 'humane' and emphasised its interest in the individual: 'it enables us to see them as flesh and blood, and not just as pawns on the national chess board'.[9] Local history interrelates in the academy with regional studies, historical demography and microhistory, all offshoots of social history with an eye to the material and the importance of the individual event.[10] Similarly, though, the focus on local, small-scale family history itself impacted upon social historiography. Family history, historical demography and new social history all interrelate in their commitment to 'reconstructing the life patterns of ordinary people and to viewing them as actors as well as subjects in the process of change.'[11] It is this notion of the way that local and family history might feed back into a wider sense of historical dynamic that is interesting – do local historians and genealogists see themselves as part of a continuum of social history, their subjects affecting world events? There is often a lack of understanding of how the local relates to the wider national or international context (a standard statist historical paradigm), or how local events affect or are affected by wider occurrences. The narrowness of the approach can lead to a certain marginalising of particular types of information, as Carol Kammen argues: 'Local historians censor local history by limiting the topics investigated.'[12]

Amateur or non-academically located local history allows the non-specialist to participate in historical investigation. There are numerous books designed to introduce the casual user to the tools required for historical investigation at a local level. These books range from glossaries to more thorough guides to using archives, oral history techniques, finding documents and reading maps.[13] They are intended to support practical research, and therefore their historiography is target- or goal-driven, generally geographically specific, and particularised. In his 1972 *Sources for Local History*, W.B. Stephens claimed the historiographic importance of 'local significance', emphasising the importance of archives to a study of locality.[14] Key to local history is a sense of place, and a desire to understand the narrative of that place: 'Every house has a tale to tell.'[15] This sense of discovery, revelation and local particularity is key to local history. J.R. Ravensdale's (1982) BBC series *History on Your Doorstep* emphasised this sense of multiple interleaved historical architectures, considering the archaeology of local areas in order to explain their meaning.[16] It is an extremely material type of historical inquiry, and, as Hoskins' two books suggest, often overlaps with archaeology.[17]

Key to the phenomena of local history is a sense of the importance of personal interest and fulfilment. The action of historical investigation is liberating, rewarding, fosters a sharper definition of selfhood and community. There is a sense that formulating the correct question and then pursuing the right archives and sources will enable the participant to understand the past. Local history has great affinity with genealogy as an amateur pastime and hobby, as both are similarly enfranchising to the participant and relatively straightforward to undertake. Both approaches bring the local – that which is close and familiar – to life, and use similar tools: archives, libraries, oral history, institutions, maps, topography. They also both enable the participant to take ownership of the locale or of their family. For instance, local history groups are active in surveying, conserving and displaying land in their area. The Local Heritage Initiative, funded by the Heritage Lottery Fund, funds hundreds of projects. Certain counties have Community or Parish Archaeology Wardens who monitor and conserve countryside and local landscape. This legislative drive to local community access reflects contemporary political interest in widening participation but similarly demonstrates a grassroots engagement with the local past.

Social and local history in the popular imagination was given a visual aspect with the rediscovery of the Mitchell and Kenyon films of Edwardian life. This archive of films made for local exhibition were found in 1994 and restored by the British Film Institute. They have subsequently been shown on BBC2, released on DVD and have been toured in cinemas. The massive popularity of this documenting of everyday life demonstrates a huge popular interest in the social and the local. The local past also figures crucially in popular romance imaginings of the past, in particular the work of novelists such as Catherine Cookson (Gateshead and Newcastle), Freda Lightfoot (Manchester) or Katie Flynn (Liverpool). These writers situate their novels clearly in the urban locale and create a genre of working-class local historical romance.

There has been a boom in demand for local history books and guides in the past decade. The two key local history presses, Sutton Publishing and Tempus, have massive global brand reach and success; Tempus announced huge profits in 2003.[18] The quarterly journal *The Local Historian* lists around 25–30 newly published books in each edition, as well as numerous journals and local societies. Peter Christie, rounding up the best books of 2004, praised one by claiming it demonstrated 'all that is best in local history – it is accessible, interesting and helps to connect today's population with its roots'.[19] Christie's comment demonstrates the importance of 'roots' in contemporary local history. Rather than the account of dying communities propounded by Hoskins this suggests a sense of personal connection to the locale (something which also feeds from the intertwining of local with family history). The popularity of local history, as testified by the expansion of publishing, the increasing demands on local archives and the various Heritage Initiative projects, demonstrate a keen amateur desire to invest time and energy in investigating the past. It also illustrates a direct engagement with the tools of historical work, and emphasises the value of the individual's research and direct understanding of locale, geography and artefacts, rather than the imposition of historical meaning by cultural and institutional gatekeepers of one kind or another. The following analyses consider the various ways that local historical investigation – in these instances, accruing around objects and artefacts – can allow complex articulations of historical subjectivity.

Metal detecting, popular archaeology, treasure hunting

This local investigation of the past has conceptual and material manifestations and outcomes. A traditional way for under-educated – mainly male, mainly working class – members of the public to get involved in object acquisition and artefact engagement is metal detecting and the discovery of what are known as 'portable antiquities'.[20] Metal detecting as a hobby has often been seen derisively by archaeologists as short-termist treasure hunting, which it might be, but the impetus towards collecting, searching and finding in this fashion demands attention. It is relatively solitary, defiantly amateur, and undertaken outside of many of the academic or professional frameworks that other historical and archaeological investigation deploys. There are around fifty detecting clubs in the UK and hundreds in the USA; as a means of engaging with historical artefacts and considering remnants of the past in the present, it is an extremely popular and varied pursuit.

The Council for British Archaeology now runs workshops on metal detecting, and the antagonism between professional archaeology and amateur searchers has lessened over the past decade.[21] Since the creation of the National Council of Metal Detectors in 1981 there has been a code of practice for the investigation and discovery of portable antiquities using specialist equipment. The Treasure Act of 1996, which replaced the common law 'treasure trove' principle, legislated for the discovery of gold, silver and coins more than 300 years old; subsequent to the Act, the Portable Antiquities Scheme (PAS) was set up for the voluntary registering of archaeological finds.[22] The Treasure Act imposes a legislative framework upon the activity of metal detecting and portable antiquity hunting, obliging the individual to work within a particular code and to consider their finds within the broader concerns and demands of the national heritage.[23] The PAS further brings the metal detecting individual into the heritage fold, although voluntarily; furthermore, they are nearly 50 per cent from demographic groups that would rarely venture into a museum (49 per cent of finders are from groups C2, D and E, who make up 29 per cent of museum visitors).[24] Things that are unearthed are part of the national heritage fabric, and the discovery process therefore is legitimated; those who metal-detect are validated by the PAS and their finds become part of a wider discourse of national understanding and history.

There is no such legislation in the USA (although there are more land access issues), where metal detecting is much more of an object-driven competitive pastime (the national magazine, *Western and Eastern Treasures*, lists the top ten 'best finds' of the year) that also includes panning for gold as part of its remit.[25] In the UK, metal detecting is low key by comparison, forming part of a suite of marginal treasure-seeking leisure pursuits such as wreck-diving and bottle collecting. They are all 'serious' leisure pursuits with educational arcs and requiring a great deal of skill to master. Metal detecting suggests a desire to search, independently, for objects and to engage with them outside of any formal institutional setting. The searcher needs particular skills, from technical to historical, in order to be successful.

Popular archaeology in general suggests a wide public interest in front-line investigation of the past and literally getting-one's-hands-dirty in the cause of history. Popular archaeology works on a national level, with institutions and television programmes such as *Time Team*. The movement is also local, with around 150 societies in the UK and fifty county organisations. These societies are funded by volunteer subscription, Heritage Lottery or Local Heritage Initiative money. Like local history, local archaeology demonstrates a keen interest in the psychogeography of particular areas and suggests a desire to see the historical in the everyday. Similarly it is a way of engaging with history at a micro-level, validating the individual experience instead of simply eliding the local in thrall to the more narrative-driven national history.

Time Team has run continuously on Channel 4 since 1994 and, with *Antiques Roadshow*, is one of the longest running popular history programmes on television. The team respond to suggestions from the public about sites that might be of interest but which are not, at the moment, excavated (they have done around 130 digs). This sense of the archaeological potentiality of places echoes local history's assertions that everything has a tale to tell. It is a levelling impetus, seeing the historical in the mundane locale rather than institutionalised cultural and national centres. In common with antiques shows, occasionally the programme does not work as little is found, but this sense of unpredictability is crucial to the programme's appeal. The generic flexibility of contemporary documentary applies here, as the team only have three days in which to do their work; this artificial drama undermines the professional ethos. The programme uses recon-struction and CGI in order to reveal the past visually, too. This diversity of representation is concomitant with other historical documentary-making techniques, deploying educational and historical material in diverting style. This is developed in the spin-off series *Extreme Archaeology* which solves archaeological mysteries in remote and dangerous places using cutting-edge geographic and satellite technology. This importing of science into the investigation recalls the use of DNA testing in genealogy, a further hybridising of documentary style which deploys leading technological investigation as a prop for illustrating the past and solving mysteries.

Time Team ran a national 'Big Dig' in 2003 in which members of the public were encouraged to excavate test pits. The 'Big Dig' encapsulates the populist approach: 'a great opportunity for members of the public to get involved in some real archaeology, using appropriate methods, to learn something significant about their own area and to contribute to archaeological knowledge'.[26] This breadth of appeal – local history, 'real' investigation, methodology and educa-tion (both learning and participating in creating a knowledge base) – illustrates the complex appeal of populist archaeological programming. It presents archaeological investigation as a time-specific adventure, a voyage into the unknown and the harvesting of the hitherto unremarkable site's historical relevance.

In some ways the locale becomes the subject of genealogical investigation, a digging into the past in order to understand the journey from that past to the present. *Time Team* suggests that archaeology is all field work, and that historical investigation can lead to revelation and understanding; that artefacts can be a way of connecting to the past.

The secondary life of the programme on DVD is underpinned by its use in schools.[27] The programme allows for participation at the same time that it enshrines the expertise of the 'team' against that of the amateur. Like genealogical programming it suggests that the ordinary individual might find themselves validated in historical investigation, so long as it is done within particular epistemological frameworks. It is the inverse of BBC's ruined house popularity show *Restoration*, deconstructing a site in order to understand its meaning and value rather than advocating a reconstruction. Another popular archaeology programme, *Meet the Ancestors*, investigates human remains from digs, reconstructing lives and social contexts from bones and other evidence. They generally respond to work already being done by archaeologists, for instance, investigating what was known as the 'Forgotten Battlefield' in Ypres in March 2002, a site which had attracted much attention from local amateurs.[28] Both *Time Team* and *Meet the Ancestors* testify to a public interest in reconstructing the past using historical investigation and scientific techniques. They suggest a forgotten, unseen history that can be reclaimed – a past that is local, but also general and part of a wider national story, rather than the very personal genealogy shows.

History as hobby: collecting and antiquing

One way in which an individual might interact with the past is through artefacts and objects, most commonly to be found in flea markets, antique fairs and auctions. The past is literally commodity. Auction sites create a sense of 'floating value' and a lack of concrete – but publicly negotiated – worth.[29] Auction websites such as eBay make the past easily purchasable. The selling of artefacts provokes various questions about past collecting practice (such as the Elgin Marbles debate). There is also a thriving black market in looted goods.[30]

Antiques demonstrate a complex commodification of the past – the fetishisation of the object due in the main to its age and historical context as well as any innate value or craftsmanship.[31] At the high end, antiques are art and significant pieces of work, but the majority of antiques or old objects that people engage with are simply minor second hand goods, books, memorabilia and pieces of furniture (although vintage clothing items also come in here). They are measures of cultural capital, objects which enhance the owners' sense of worth and allow them entry to particular discourses of taste. Raphael Samuel's illustration of how authenticity intersects with what he terms 'retrochic' demonstrates the commercial fetishising of historical artefacts such as clothes.[32] 'Collecting' is key to people's sense of self-identification and a massive phenomenon; it has been calculated that around 25–30 per cent of adults in the West identify themselves as 'collectors', and around one-third of the population in Britain.[33] Importantly, the practice of collecting generally ignores class boundaries.[34] Much of what is being collected has some kind of age-value. We can use crude figures about collecting to suggest that contemporary culture is obsessed with order, completeness and the arrangement of commodities which have value only in relation to each other.

Collecting is often different to seeking, bidding for and buying antiques, and collections can be of items from the contemporary world. Antiques and memorabilia both interact with the wider culture of collecting and are separate from it; a key part of the collecting culture, they are not the dominant element. Certainly antiques fit the 'history as hobby' model and are 'serious' leisure pursuits requiring tenacity, education of sorts and commitment to self-improvement. Amateurs can understand antiques easily enough and they have mass popular appeal, demonstrated in their television manifestations. Antiques and memorabilia are a closed system in economic terms, their value relative rather than intrinsic. Objects have monetary worth due to scarcity, originality, arbitrary value (their original ownership) or workmanship. Age, in antique terms, becomes something which confers value; it is the particular labour the object undergoes to become commodity, and therefore 'history' itself, in the sense of the passing of time, is here turned into something that might be physically consumed. Rarity and age confer value upon an otherwise inert object, in somewhat of a contrast with artefacts preserved in museums which accrue value because of their historical, cultural or social significance.

Antiques on television: *Antiques Roadshow*, *Flog It!*, *Bargain Hunt*

A consideration of the status of antiques on television shows how they ascribe random and floating economic value to the historical artefact (and how this adds to the cultural capital of the owner). While thousands of people collect and buy antiques, a greater number still follow the hobby vicariously through television. This form of history-related television enables the viewer to manifest their wish for inclusion in the world of the collector while being able simultaneously to distance themselves and articulate a rational response to the phenomenon. The most popular, *Antiques Roadshow*, has been running on the BBC since 1979. Imitation shows are also shown in the USA (since 1997), Sweden (1989), Holland (1984) and Canada (2005). The show involves ordinary people visiting a particular location with their artefacts which are then examined by experts in the following categories: Porcelain, Furniture, Pictures, Jewellery, Silver, Clocks and Watches, Arms and Militaria, Books, or Miscellaneous.[35] Artefacts are considered, dated, authenticated, given a brief history and, most importantly, valued. The best or most interesting cases are presented on a weekly programme.

What *Antiques Roadshow* offers the viewer is complex. It dramatises economic desire (to discover how much something is worth) and the commodification of the past. However, this commodified past is prey to academic knowledge (the expert says the artefact is worthless), randomness (the artefact is not part of a collection often but just something found) and the market (it may be unique but it might not be worth anything). Historical value here interacts with taste and cultural value – an artefact may have significance (both historical and personal) but not have monetary worth. The show allows heirlooms and therefore family history to become valuable; yet this is serendipitous, and history's financial worth to the individual depends on chance. Often objects brought along are judged to be unimportant and not worth anything, rendering them economically neutral and historically inert. At the same time many of the collectibles that have worth only achieve this relatively, through rarity or some fluke of desirability.

The experience of attending the roadshows is slightly different to the televised event, more participatory and sometimes problematic.[36] The roadshow effects the dramatisation of authenticity, wherein owners' projections of value and historical validity onto objects are confirmed or denied by the expert. This relationship between expert and individual demonstrates an interesting dynamic. The owner of the object generally has some kind of relationship to it (family heirloom, the gift of a relative, part of a personal collection, something that has been in the home for years) which is informed by its historicity but which also creates for the object its own particularised significance. What is the motivation for having its value – historical or monetary – tested and authenticated? Often the test denies basic assumptions about the object – so it might be a source of anxiety – while at the same time there is the possibility of revelation and the transformation of the object into something new and enabling. The travelling roadshow element of the programme makes the investigation of personalised items (antiques owned by individuals) part of a nationalised valuation of the past.

Antiques Roadshow is successful but staid and academic in approach.[37] Over the past five years the BBC particularly has evolved a suite of shows interested in the ephemerality of commodity value and very much more predicated upon the public value of objects. These (generally daytime) shows have had massive success, and are easily the highest viewed history-related programmes on terrestrial television. *Flog It!* (BBC2), *Cash in the Attic* (BBC1), *Car Booty* (BBC1) and *Bargain Hunt* (BBC1) were, together with *Antiques Roadshow*, the top performing history-related programmes 2005–6.[38] These shows (apart from *Car Booty*) consistently 'contributed' more than 10 per cent of those viewing when they were screened, which for under-advertised low-budget television is significant.[39] They are daytime shows so in terms of raw numbers their audience figures are not massive, but they are important nonetheless. Daytime television is generally thought to be watched by the old, women and those in low social groupings. These shows allow us to posit a socially more interesting or complex resonance of history. They are cheap, sensationalist programmes which nonetheless are part of a daytime-history phenomenon. Such shows are also generically complex, demonstrating the evolution of the antiquing genre from the traditional educative format of *Antiques Roadshow*. *Flog It!* follows a traditional journey narrative inflected by the drama of the auction house; *Bargain Hunt* is a competitive game-show; and *Cash in the Attic* is a makeover show in which ordinary household objects become transformed into valuable commodities. Decorative antiques provide an instance of historical artefacts in the material culture of everyday life, part of the day-to-day fabric of the world. *Antiques Roadshow* and the other television shows on antiquing warp this relationship, particularly those which emphasise the value of objects hitherto overlooked within domestic spaces (*Cash in the Attic*) or the ability to find artefacts of value not spotted by others (*Bargain Hunt*). *Flog It!* simply renders the relationship between individual and object in overtly financial terms.

Flog It!, the most successful of the daytime shows in terms of audience share, is an imitation of *Antiques Roadshow* which extends it to its logical conclusion and thus demonstrates the financial imperative in the original. Individuals bring old objects to events where they are valued, then those which are most interesting are chosen to be taken to auction and their progress monitored. The programme relies on the desire of the individual to have their object ratified as valuable and thence to attempt to sell it. It also demonstrates that the programme is not interested in taste, intrinsic artistic value or the sentimental associations of objects but in the monetary value that they will have in relation to other things. The imperative of the title suggests a persuasive aspect to the experts' authenticating of an individual's objects. The slang term 'flog' – generally used about something sold illicitly or sold slyly – does not help this impression of second-hand car dealing (and the objects are generally worth less than *Antiques Roadshow*). The nation-building roadshow element is emphasised by sections in which the presenter Paul Allen samples the local culture.

Bargain Hunt is the splicing of *Antiques Roadshow* with profit-driven programming, an updating of BBC's *The Great Antiques Hunt* (1994–99). It involves two teams competing to raise the most money at auction. Their lots consist of objects bought from second-hand sales in consultation with experts. The teams first visit an antiques fair with an expert to advise them, choose three items for a particular sum (generally around £300), and then take them to be sold in more formal settings. There is also an educational sequence where the presenter of the show visits stately homes or museums. The show dramatises the search for a bargain, the unearthing of something valuable in the randomness of second-hand bric-a-brac available. The teams can keep any profit, making the show part of a relatively new genre of active fixed-time money-making task shows. The artefacts are given value only by context – at a sale they are worthless, while at auction they (often) gain value. This gain is not guaranteed, and regularly objects thought to be bankers fail to sell. The show illustrates the 'floating value' of the object at auction.[40] The ascending auction model presented here itself is a site of price negotiation which demonstrates how historical artefacts can develop from second-hand goods into valued commodities.[41]

In *Cash in the Attic*, individuals or families raid their lofts and houses for things to sell either at auction or car boot sales. They are advised by an expert about which heirlooms or unwanted items might raise the most money. The money they raise is for a purpose – holidays and house improvements are most popular – so unlike the other shows in which the highest monetary value is the sole point, they have a target to achieve. The show is an expression of waste and surplus – contestants have too much and they want to exchange their old artefacts for new services. The show dramatises the hoarding of items which is then transformed into contemporary consumption of goods and services. Often the contestants are understandably attached to various items but they are persuaded to sell them for the good of their immediate future. Both shows work on the excitement and unpredictability of auctions or sale areas as well as demonstrating the worth of seemingly everyday household items given value simply through rarity or age.

Bargain Hunt has the educational value of *Antiques Roadshow*, as the expert calmly describes the function, use and probable value of each piece. They can even offer the team an object to 'swap' with one that they deem to be unlikely to gain much profit. However, the expert's views are often seen to be out of step with the market, undermining their authority and, as the market is what drives the game-show format of the programme, the expert here is a figure merely in thrall to the economics of commodity rather than the enshriner of historical value. *Bargain Hunt* had impact beyond its daytime format, including celebrity and children's versions. From 2002–5, a higher budget prime time version was shown. The popularity of the format demonstrates how antiques pervade popular culture but similarly suggests an interest in the game-show element of the programme. The 'winners' of the show successfully cherry-pick items of value from the flotsam of the past; the losers are not as astute and make a loss from poor speculation. However, the show also attempts to suggest other arbiters of value, particularly personal taste; presenter Tim Wonnacott argues: 'It's always nice to find a bargain and have the thrill of a financial reward but if you didn't get a bargain, but got the thrill, what's the difference?'[42]

The BBC particularly likes to employ colourful characters to enliven these programmes. The eccentric expert draws on various tropes: gentleman/dandy/ amateur expert (Wonnacott in *Bargain Hunt* or the foppish Lawrence Llewelyn-Bowen in *Changing Rooms*), the enthusiastic young fogey or donnish type (Ptolemy Dean in *Restoration*), and the rough diamond (David Dickinson in *Bargain Hunt*, drawing on the example of the TV character *Lovejoy*). These presenters have, in the same style as TV chefs and designers, attained a level of celebrity themselves. The most famous, David Dickinson, has a high public profile including a catchphrase and appearances on *This Is Your Life*, *Who Do You Think You Are?* and *I'm a Celebrity, Get Me out of Here!* Similarly to those designers and chefs, they are celebrities who found significance initially because of their expertise but who become abstracted from this into a wider nexus of signification. They are contrasted with the more sober aspect of documentary-historians, emphasising the game-show element of this style of historical investigation. The celebrity-presenter enlivens the journey into the past, encouraging the viewer to enjoy it.

These shows demonstrate that the past can provide a subject for leisure-driven daytime television programming, but only if yoked to elements of competition and financial worth. They communicate to the viewer that the past might be valuable, that the expert can guide you, and that anyone can undertake it. Like TV chefs and make-over designers, such shows contribute to a democratisation of the historical, with knowledge and ability moving from the elite – as represented by antique experts, connoisseurship and collectors perhaps – and an emphasis on the intervention of 'ordinary' people into previously fenced off arenas: 'We've reached a stage where we live in a design democracy: stores instantly respond to what is on TV and in magazines. Taste is no longer prescribed by the few for the majority.'[43] Leaving aside the problematic elision of democracy with television – suggestive though this is – this comment suggests that programme-makers are alert to this levelling of the intellectual and taste-making playing field. Popular daytime history shows with an element of individual-driven content similarly suggest a democratisation – that historical understanding might be the preserve of the ordinary participant. Television shows such as these seem to perform a historicised makeover of the participant, transforming them into subjects with agency and ability. At the same time, those with more cultural capital – expert, presenter – are foregrounded still as the most important element and uppermost focus of the programme. In the case of antique shows, furthermore, the choices of the participants (and the advice of the experts) are completely prey to the vagaries and functions of the market, so their particular intervention might be proved valueless. The enfranchised historical subject, then, is only given agency through the workings of the television show, not through their actual knowledge or actions. Their perceived shift in status is purely temporary and result-driven.

5 Genealogy

Hobby, politics, science

Another key forum for the 'amateur' interaction with the past is genealogical investigation. Genealogy has facilitated academic research in a number of ways. The field of family reconstitution studies became important during the late 1980s, particularly with the publication of John Knodel's *Demographic Behaviour in the Past* in 1988. Family reconstitution and historical demography have roots in the same historiographical movements as local history.[1] In 1964, E.A. Wrigley and Peter Laslett founded the Cambridge Group for the History of Population and Social Structure to investigate local and micro-social structure, household organisation and demography; they also founded *Local Population Studies*. The local becomes the site for exploration of social change, focussed through family structures and demographic data. As a model for critical and philosophical inquiry genealogy has also been theorised in relationship to subjectivity as a means of writing the self.[2]

Popularly, genealogy has become one of the most common historical activities in the world. It is certainly in the top five contemporary leisure pursuits, if not the top two, with millions of people participating around the globe.[3] The numbers of users run into the tens of millions, and they are persistent. In the UK, partly as a consequence of funding shifts and the need for public institutions to gain wider audiences, archives have been opened up and made accessible over the past couple of decades. The boom in genealogy was demonstrated by the opening of the Family Records Centre in 1997, formerly the General Register Office.[4] The need for a dedicated, centralised public institution to service the genealogical demand illustrates the growth in this field over the past 30 years, a time when genealogy turned into 'family history' – a more inclusive term suggesting a sense of identity rather than the more traditional proving of (paternal) bloodline. The pursuit of personal history became an important leisure pursuit:

> Family history is one of the most popular global hobbies. You are in for hours, if not days, weeks, or years, of endless fun tracking down your ancestors. It really is endless, because every stage throws up new challenges and surprises, as you progress.[5]

This hobby is driven by the desire of detection: 'to find out who exactly our ancestors were, where they came from, and what they got up to'.[6] Aside from this inquisitive element, the increasing desire to delve into origins possibly betrays a contemporary anxiety about social atomisation and the fracturing of family structures; it similarly might demonstrate an upsurge in nationalist concern with identity in the face of an increasingly devolved and complicated country.

There is certainly a sense of national and individual identity folded into this, of a nationhood built from the histories of past individuals, despite the often transnational results of enquiry. David Lowenthal argues that 'massive migration and the loss of tangible relics' have contributed to the rise in genealogical inquiry, and this sense of a desire for an articulating and organising narrative is crucial to an understanding of genealogy.[7] The historiography of family history can suggest an unseen, or untold, story within the arching narrative of country: 'In Britain, we are blessed with a rich history but historians have tended to chronicle major events and the people who defined our nation's development. The everyday folk who lived through those momentous events have tended to get overlooked.'[8] Indeed, investigating personal heritage has a key political function: 'Family history allows you to bring your ancestors back to life; by telling their stories you are giving a voice to Britain's forgotten sections of society.'[9] Despite the ingenuous prose style, this demonstrates that family history has a political purpose which grows as much from the social interest of academicised local history as traditional genealogy.

Family history, as much as local history, starts geographically with witness testimony, in this case, that of relatives: 'gathering as many facts, memories and memorabilia as you can from members of your family'.[10] This sense of the importance to family history of the local, of artefacts, and of the particular witness testimony of those remaining family members, pervades the guidebooks and webguides to the subject.[11] The historiography of family history, such as it is, is invested in the local, the specific, and the material from the beginning. It makes the familiar more luminous or meaningful, as well as enfranchising the participants – both in terms of the actual investigator (who is able to pursue research with little or no training) and in terms of the family member (whose information becomes valued as evidence and source). The flexibility of the internet fuelled genealogical research from its inception. The news-group net.roots started in 1983, the ROOTS-L mailing list in 1987, and postings began on other sites as early as 1981.[12] Early users wrote their own software in order to locate and present the information they needed. The internet allows for collaborative genealogy, with listservs and discussion forums on sites' ways of transmitting information and expertise; indeed, they were crucial to the initial development of genealogy on the internet.[13] The newsgroup and the discussion forum were the first ways in which web genealogy occurred (actual information not being served until the late 1990s, the National Register of Archives, for instance, was not accessible until 1998). This model of consultative, educative process of information gathering, and the collaborative trajectory of the process demonstrate that at base online genealogy is about sharing information and engaging with a community of like-minded, generous investigators. It is estimated that there are more than

50,000 English-language genealogy mailing lists; the facilitator site RootsWeb alone hosts 30,000.[14] RootsWeb also hosts user-contributed databases and the WorldConnect project, which links user-created family trees (there are around 500m names on file, with contributions by around 300,000 users).

The expansion of the web in 1991 and 1995 along with commercial investment gave more impetus to the process.[15] In particular, the serving of census records, parish registers, wills, civil registration (birth, marriage, death) information, property records and newspapers online enabled genealogists to pursue their research. Much of this information is transcribed rather than digitally scanned, so the researcher is immediately distanced from the original text; similarly, reliability is often an issue. There are now hundreds of entry websites that collect the raw data for the user from innumerable sources. Websites sell family tree software, provide specialised search engines, link to databases and also allow access to their own archives. This has meant that the tools of investigation are no longer the preserve of the College of Arms, the Society of Genealogists or the Institute of Heraldic and Genealogical Studies. However, most of the websites that have evolved around the raw databases are designed to support investigation in a structured way: offering tips, routes for research and online classes. So, on the one hand, a certain authority and gatekeeper institution are eroded, yet websites become supporters, creating a virtual information economy in which the individual user is the driving force.

This is a model of the internet as tool, and genealogy on the web provides us with a useful example of what Chris Rojek calls the 'active consumption' model of the internet.[16] His conception is that the internet by default is interactive and therefore consumption becomes more complex than simple passive models suggest. Certainly theorists of the internet consider that its basic state presupposes a reconfiguring of relationship between user and provider.[17] Genealogy websites provide a usefully dynamic example – they are predicated upon national archives and resources, they provide a service which is both material and conceptual (information and tools), they foster collaboration while emphasising the importance of the individual. In pure economic terms they are also complex. Many gateway and academic websites are registration and subscription-based, although the key public sites such as the National Archives and the Familyrecords.gov consortium are generally free to access. Historical knowledge therefore becomes part of an economic nexus, something desired and consumed within a standard late capitalist framework. On genealogical websites, national knowledge, such as censuses, wills, and social information of all kinds, are fed into a financial matrix. Cultural artefacts, in the form of historical knowledge and information, here become commodities in an economy in which the consumption of such goods is driven by a desire to understand the self and make complete. Genealogical websites operate within a (globalised) historiocentric cultural economy, you might argue, their information commodified. However, because of the status of genealogical information – rather than, for instance, of cultural artefacts – this economy is closed and rational. History can actually be valued, rather than be part of a circulating set of meanings and values. Information is a product, something created by the labour of history, which can be desired and paid for.

However, the emphasis is on individual interactive use of information, a consumption which emphasises the educational. In some ways, this might be considered to be über-consumption, a pure form of economic desire for commodified knowledge which will make the user whole in some way but which tantalisingly never does (there is always something else to discover, or something we cannot know). Genealogy here is a form of knowledge acquisition, the drive to own the past quite literally. The lack of conceptual passivity (along with the complexity of the 'interpenetrative' cyborgesque relationship of the material body to technology and information) models the relationship with the past as something here actively engaged with.[18] Even more than television, film and fiction (as cultural modes of consuming history), internet research demands an interaction and a stated desire rather than a wrongly assumed passivity. The interactive, multimedia site rootstelevision, for instance, demonstrates the complexity of modern responses to genealogy. The site uses open-source technology in order to create a dedicated 'channel' for family history, complete with blogs, vlogs, short educational films and programmes from around the world. In addition to this complex information, the collaborative aspect of genealogical research makes its consumption process even more complex.

Often the web can create a false impression of completeness: 'Family history websites contain only a minute proportion of what is available to the dedicated searcher,' argues Amanda Bevan.[19] There is still an emphasis on what she calls 'traditional searches', using a variety of archives.[20] In order to pursue these types of searches participants will need to learn new skills, such as palaeography, or know about dating and money. Therefore the amateur historian quickly picks up a set of new, discipline-specific skills. They learn to search smartly, to think archivally. The emphasis is on searching and detection, however. The tracing of the family 'line' through the chaos of history is an elegant illustration of a kind of teleological thinking (a vertical line, albeit with some lateral digressions, from those stuck in history to us now in the dynamic contemporary) about the past as something which will and can explain the present.

Genealogy and history of the family present a road map, a set of disciplining boundaries to the understanding of history; the family as classificatory function enabling the chaos of the past to be taxonomised: 'You can dig deep into people's lives and preoccupations, in search of answers to the "whats" and "whys" of their actions. This adds an extra dimension as the searcher carves out his or her own personal slice of history.'[21] This personalisation of history is important, and the sense of ownership associated with genealogical investigation illustrates a key issue, that of self-revelation. Through understanding the actions of ancestors the searcher comes to truth and understanding; they own their family history. Genealogy provides a route to understanding, a principle of collection, a thread of taxonomy within the chaos of history. This limitation within the proliferation of information that the historical record represents is looked for, desired by the amateur historian. Genealogy emphasises an abundance of information whose controlling principle is the individual undergoing the research, as the modelling of the family tree presents a pyramid from the confusion and complexity of the past towards the present. Family trees are key to genealogy, easy diagrams demonstrating relationships and imposing an order on history. Similarly the importance of indexing and databases suggests a model of information which is taxonomised, ordered and searchable.

'I'm getting more and more Jewish as this goes on': self-identity and celebrity revelation

In order to understand contemporary genealogy more it is important to consider its manifestation in the public imagination. This means a turning away from the personalising of history to a much more conflicted, mediated version of the way that the individual might access the past. Genealogical programmes have been little considered in what writing there is on historical documentary, possibly because they are quite a new phenomenon or maybe because they do not seem like 'real' history, despite their insistence on sources, the revelation of the past, and rigorous research methods. The very formal complexity of historical doc-umentary challenges the blithe assertion that television history is overly simplis-tic. This multivalent format demands a sophistication of response. Consideration of genealogical documentaries made over the past couple of years brings out some of the issues already discussed; similarly, though, there is something of a conflict between this 'public' genealogical research and 'private' individual work. The dissonance between the two modes is intriguing and suggestive for locating the historical subject – if such a thing exists – within this nexus.

Who Do You Think You Are? (BBC, 2004, 2006, 2007) used celebrity avatars to great effect in order to explore historical issues relating to genealogy and social history. The show shadowed formats such as *Restoration* and *Great Britons* in its deployment of famous presenters opening up understanding of particular sub-jects. As a multiplatform event, it was also directed by the BBC to encourage use of the newly online National Archives. *Who Do You Think You Are?* reveals a great deal about the motives for and the methods of investigation of family in contemporary society. It tells us much about the ways in which genealogical investigation figures in the popular historical imagination, particularly in terms of the deployment of evidence, the personal narrative of history, and the key issue of revelation.

Shown initially on BBC2, the audience share for the second series was so great that subsequent programmes were screened on BBC1. The audience for the first episode was 5.8m with a 24 per cent share; these were the highest viewing figures on BBC2 for 2004. The first series averaged 4.7m viewers.[22] This demonstrates the huge – and relatively unconsidered – popular audience for this kind of documentary. *Who Do You Think You Are?* used the experience of each celebrity as they delved into their family history to explore issues of cultural and institutional change, social morality, and of immigration. The types of celebrity chosen were relatively wide-ranging, from newsreaders to comedians, and their backgrounds and social identities similarly ranged from the patrician Jeremy Paxman through expansively gay Julian Clary to black athlete Colin Jackson. While focused on the celebrity undergoing the investigative 'experience', the programme presented a social history, picking a route (the family) through a range of important events. The historiography of the programme was empiricism: the detective work of the archivist, the unearthing of unknown truths and hitherto silent stories.[23] It was also definitely populist, despite the initial celebritising: the programme is intended to encourage the viewer to act and use the very same kind of tools to discover their own past in their own time. While in many ways capitalising on the upsurge in genealogical interest *Who Do You Think You Are?* was also a genuine attempt on the part of the BBC to encourage interest in archival research. The programme was supported by genealogical software on the corporation's website, a magazine (from 2007), and links to the National Archives and local history organisations (the launch of the magazine demonstrates that commercial pressures also had a role in the development of the show's profile). In the first series, David Baddiel addresses the question of his identity. As he explores his familial roots, he exclaims 'I'm getting more and more Jewish as this goes on, I'm using more and more Yiddish.'[24] His sentiments demonstrate a clear sense among all those who use genealogy to understand themselves that there is some 'true' identity hidden in their family make-up. Exploration of the personal past involves learning and using – quite literally – a different language that reveals to the genealogical explorer more and more of themselves.

The programmes used a mixed set of evidence in their investigation. They regularly made use of experts – doctors, genealogists, social historians – to help the story along. These experts did not just give specific advice germane to the particular investigation but often appeared more as expert witnesses to make assertions and suggestions. In the same way formal elements such as archive footage and stills worked metonymically to suggest time period rather than specific experience. The expert authority here was deployed as guide, the image used as generalisation. At the end of each episode of the first series a consultant genealogist explained the research undertaken, conferring a concluding authority on the events. The programmes also made use of texts (death certificates, inquest information, BMD register, army records, photographs) as evidence. These two modes of historical enquiry clearly presented history as the piecing together of a set of clues in order to create an understandable image of the past. More useful, but also more problematic as information, was the testimony of immediate witnesses. This generally took the form of the stories of surviving family members which was used to make suggestions about people's choices in the past as well as simply to find out information. Family stories and oral history are an extremely useful tool but they also took on dramatic significance. Amanda Redman's mother refused to answer questions about her father's affairs on camera, and this lingering sense of disturbing personal invasion – and the possibility of real horror being discovered – permeate the documentaries.

Why investigate one's family at all? The celebrity avatars answered this in a number of ways, all of which are revealing for study of contemporary engagement with the past. Bill Oddie, subject of the first episode, set the tone with his confession that the motivation for his search had been treatment for recent clinical depression. He was motivated to seek information about his past in order to understand the pathology of his present. Oddie himself argued that 'This isn't curiosity, this journey, its self-help.'[25] Immediately, then, the series was grounded in a discourse of self-revelation and introspection, albeit within a public forum. This revelation was at once individuated – the further understanding of oneself – and communal – the greater understanding of one's family or community. Lesley Garrett suggested at the end of her programme that 'I've found a lot of qualities that I've puzzled about in myself in my various ancestors which has so helped me make sense of myself ... all these things I really identify with.'[26] Furthermore, she understands 'not just about who she is but why she is'.[27] Nearly all of the participants testified to this sense of exploring an unknown side of their origin: 'you're never entirely sure of how you ended up here', as David Baddiel argued.[28] Clear here is a sense of the revelation of history, but also of gaining an insight into selfhood that has not been disclosed hitherto. The concept that one might understand further 'why' one is has proven immensely attractive and keys directly into a contemporary concern with personal narratives. Genealogy provides points of reference, is an aid in the finding and defining of oneself. Memory is clearly tied to identity, and the series participated in creating an historical family memory for each participant. They moved towards self-definition and completion through an understanding of their ancestry.

Furthermore the series showed a clear interest in 'untold' stories, the reclaiming of narratives from the chaos of history. The archive is too big to appreciate but if one chooses an individual pathway one can thread one's way towards some kind of truth and understanding; the series tells individual stories within the horrors of history. For Jim Moir, the connection was clearly physical and emphatic: 'Its great to perhaps touch a piece of wood they might have touched, and see the same things that they saw, and that allows you to perhaps feel the things that they might have felt.'[29] However, *Who Do You Think You Are?* was intelligent enough as programming to appreciate that 'uncovering' the past does not necessarily lead to resolution. Again this is demonstrated in the Bill Oddie episode, uncovering the truth about his mother and a dead sister Oddie bitterly wishes that he had known earlier. This unexpectedly melancholic and downbeat conclusion is echoed elsewhere: David Baddiel is left at the Warsaw Ghetto imputing motive to his ancestors, fictionalising among the bare known facts; hoping his ancestors were part of the uprising there without evidence, he forces them into recognisable narrative strands (heroism, resistance) in order to somehow deal with the enormity of the Holocaust.[30] For each show that ended with revelation, there was one in which the poignancy and unknowability of history were emphasised.

The fascination for the audience was complex. First, there was a clear documentary narrative being deployed, a journey towards a greater understanding (the journey motif was accentuated throughout the series by numerous shots of protagonists on trains or driving to obscure parts of the country).[31] The programmes demonstrated modern Britain as a complex culture with roots as far apart as Jaito and Warsaw, and as such fostered a sense of inclusiveness and of a dynamic nationalism. The shows were controlled documentaries which promised sensation but did not necessarily deliver it – many of them ending in a lack of explanation or event ('I don't know that there is anyone left who has any answers,' concluded Jim Moir).[32] They worked, similarly to other reality history documentary, to produce a narrative of individual change through engagement with the past, providing an evidence-based epiphany and a personal becoming reflected in Baddiel's words about his Jewishness. *Who Do You Think You Are?* works to disclose new information to the protagonist and to the audience. They are biographical and autobiographical simultaneously, and formally therefore sit at an acute angle to other reality history documentary. They tell stories as well as teach understanding.

The interleaving of celebrity with history complicates this further. Jim Moir pinpointed a salacious motivation, for himself and presumably for the audience: 'your own personal soap opera … I suppose what everybody wants is a bit of scandal … and I suppose there rarely is'.[33] He points out that even normal people seek celebrity and cultural myth in their personal histories, although rarely find it. Moir did find scandal – including an unknown sister, bigamy and former marriages. The notion of the celebrity revealing something of themselves is key here, part of a culture of revelation in which the personalising of the well-known figure feeds a desire for a further understanding of the minutiae of their lives. The narratives of familial improvement presented by the show took many forms – immigration was key, as was class mobility – and lain over the top of this was an understanding that the celebrity was as ordinary as anyone else, their families prey to the same hardships and worries. The use of celebrity avatar therefore worked in complex ways – by encouraging a sense that you as an audience member could also do this, the distance between viewed and viewer was lessened; as an avatar, the celebrities literally stood in for all of us in some fashion. As the voiceover reminded us during Lesley Garrett's programme, 'we hope to show you how to use similar techniques in your own research'.[34] The sense of the celebrity tantalisingly being on a continuum with the audience rather than somehow made different is clear here. History seemingly democratises, allows for an identification and enfranchisement of the audience.

This purported inverting of the celebrity untouchable status is of a part with other cultural phenomena such as *Hello!* photoshoots welcoming cameras into domestic settings of all types (marriages, houses, hospitals) and also *Celebrity Big Brother* which, alone in the celebrity reality shows, encourages an almost aggressive normalisation of famous figures. *Celebrity Big Brother* demonstrates a kind of Jamesonian folding in on itself – people we want to be (celebrities) being made ordinary again through their enactment of roles in a reality game that celebrates the minutiae of the ordinary and everyday. They're just the same as us, but crucially othered, changed while we observe them within a familiar (to viewers of ordinary *Big Brother*) yet abnormal environment. As Andy Lavender argues, 'The fascination is in seeing how people with familiar onscreen personae reveal their "actual" personalities within the strictures of the house and the game.'[35] Banality, key to the *Big Brother* phenomena, pervades *Who Do You Think You Are?* and is part of the attraction – the famous self laid bare, the extraordinariness of the celebrity undermined.[36] For all that many arguments about celebrity suggest that the modern phenomenon demonstrates the 'inauthenticity of contemporary popular culture', these programmes clearly undermine that impetus by literally rooting the celebrity, giving them flesh and normality; these shows demonstrate celebrity appreciation as para-social interaction and the creation of new community relationships.[37] On this model, *Who Do You Think You Are?* fosters new interactions between individuals and the media-created personalities peopling the programmes by suggesting points of connection and identification. Like *Celebrity Big Brother* and other reality shows which feature celebrities, *Who Do You Think You Are?* demonstrates the overlay of celebrity onto everyday life in its combination of reality TV documentary elements with famous people (it is not strictly reality TV but it has key formal and generic similarities, including, most importantly, the notion of existential revelation into subjectivity).

Yet at the same time in *Who Do You Think You Are?* the celebrity was not simply avatar but fetishised icon, and their roots became somehow more luminous as we gained further insight into their lives. 'Mobility' was a key narrative theme, and most of the episodes include a sense of progression and escape from (in general) poverty and hardship. Therefore, the shows included a backwards narrative trajectory which then flowed forwards to the privileged now of the celebrity. Everyone has family history but only that of famous people is interesting – the scandal, horror, trauma and body count in their history demonstrated that, even before they were born, they were special. Equally, the diversity of the programmes was undermined by the celebrity involvement as their current status as classless celebrated individuals made the various chaotic transactions of history moot; *Who Do You Think You Are?* demonstrated the march of history not towards the formation of the current modern individual but to the creation of the *über*-person. The model of historical process was therefore teleological but only insofar as the new focal point for contemporary society is fame; this might be called celeb-humanism, where the notion of self-definition is tied directly to a confessional mode and to public profile. The programme suggested the movement from an ideological, immobile, class-riven society of the past to the (purported) meritocracy of contemporary social networks.[38]

However, the experience of the audience was not simply passive, but importantly interactive. The BBC planned *Who Do You Think You Are?* with an integrated pan-platform media strategy in mind. Key to this strategy was the premise that the programmes were just the beginning of people's experience. While this had an educative value there is also an element of branding associated with this – a desire on the behalf of a corporation to facilitate historical research at every point. The BBC is evolving and part of its response to the challenge of new media, interaction and complex participation is to tailor the post-programme experience in several ways. The first series of *Who Do You Think You Are?* was supported by 5-minute 'How To' sections at the end of each programme, further documentaries on practice on BBC4, 1.3m leaflets circulated in the *Radio Times*, a dedicated website, a phone line, radio information, interactive TV (both digital stories and 'How To' guide), and, most impressively, 48 Family History roadshows and in total 395 events in partnership with the Archives Awareness Campaign. The response to this suite of support options was massive: 29,375 calls to the phone line resulting in 18,850 leaflets sent out; 530,000 users of the programme website after the Jeremy Clarkson episode with 9m users across the series; the National Archives' website experienced a 77 per cent increase in traffic; 40,000 people attended the roadshows and the AAC events saw a 36 per cent increase in new visitors.

This unprecedented response demonstrates the popularity of genealogy and also that it possesses great 'stickability' – an audience will continue to be involved long after the TV series has concluded, and the conversion rate of 'viewers' to 'users' is significant. The numbers vindicate the BBC's integrated strategy and also suggest that this pan-platform approach appeals to audiences of historical documentary. The use of archives is not simply related to personal history; investigation of the history of houses, locale, and institutions are all encouraged and supported. History and the archive, therefore, are engaged with in a variety of ways here and for a number of reasons: understanding, revelation, personal storytelling. The past is something which can explain and something which can be easily appreciated with the right tools.

This style of programming is continually evolving, which demonstrates the instability and warped dynamism of forms of engagement with historical knowledge. In 2006, ITV commissioned an imitation entitled *You Don't Know You're Born*, a hybrid format in which celebrities investigated their ancestry and then spent some time following their forbears by doing their jobs under historic conditions. It takes genealogic elements from *Who Do You Think You Are?*, adds an interest in socio-economic historical roles from the Channel 4 show *The Worst Jobs in History* (2006–7) and frames it within the experiential-reality documentary models of the 'house' reality history formats (see Chapter 11). The model of truth-seeking here is muddy, and the shows dramatise an interest in historical caricaturing as people in the past are defined economically rather than, for instance, socially or culturally.

The specialist production company Wall to Wall made both *Who Do You Think You Are?* and *You Don't Know You're Born*, and several important lessons can be extrapolated from this fact. The dissimilarity between the shows is what is of most interest, demonstrating the flexibility of historical formatting: *You Don't Know You're Born* develops the format, showing the innovative possibility and flexibility of contemporary historical documentary. Where *Who Do You Think You Are?* is straightforward in some ways, an educative series with serious intent (and tied to a national education institution, the National Archives), *You Don't Know You're Born* is more firmly populist in focus and commercially supported (the series was sponsored by the website GenesReunited.co.uk). *You Don't Know You're Born* evidently, then, is aimed at a different market demographic and no longer desires to get people researching but more to communicate about the difference of the past. There was no concerted supporting information, no outreach and no dedicated website. *You Don't Know You're Born* is not interested in the vague empathy of the BBC show but forces the celebrity/avatar to engage physically with the past. *You Don't Know You're Born* complicates the celebrity genealogy documentary genre by adding social history, creating a strange public history format.

There is a further heritage and living history aspect of the show, as the celebrities have to use traditional methods. The job-following segment, which makes up the majority of the programme, is empathy-driven reality history, whereas the genealogy is archival searching for 'truth'. This truth here is displaced by the experience, as the 'historical' (that which is found through reference to archives) is replaced by the contemporary-experiential (the actions of the working celebrity). History becomes effaced by nowness, and the focus shifts into the potential pitfalls and serendipity: 'they explore the road they might have travelled themselves if their lives hadn't taken them into the world of show business'.[39] This is the vanishing point which *Who Do You Think You Are?* and *You Don't Know You're Born* both see, that there but for the grace of God go the famous; 'actual' historical subjectivities become something to experience briefly before they are rejected, a kind of biographical tourism. Actor Ken Stott, for instance, seeks 'to find out if he's inherited his ancestor's traditional tailoring skills'.[40] He also spends some time working with traditional bakers who, through a quirk of genealogy, are his distant relatives (again, there but for the grace of God). History is presented as a place of privation and poverty, harsh economics: 'It's hard work, all night long [pause] which [pause] isn't for me.'[41] He also becomes an Italian fish seller, which the voiceover prefaces ominously: 'Ken is about to discover for himself just how tough his great-grandfather's life was.'[42] Far from being too onerous, though, living history here is however more like 'celebrity work experience', a brief insight into the world of the plodding proletariat gained by the celebrity aristocrat. The method of presenting the celebrity as workshy dilettante in this instance does not have the malicious vengefulness of *I'm A Celebrity, Get Me out of Here* or *Celebrity Big Brother*; instead it affords the celebrity enshrined status.

Celebrity here becomes an accident of history, fame something which allows the subject to individuate themselves from the mass. Certainly what celebrities do not do, by definition, is work, and this sense of an historical identity which is defined by economics informs the sense of difference here; how quaint that our ancestors should be tailors or farmers. If celebrities are the ultimate expression of an empty, service-driven postmodern global economy, then this show allows them to demonstrate the insubstantiality of modern economics through the contrast between their luxurious life in the contemporary imagination and their playing the parts of their ancestors. The title refers to this, suggesting that the celebrity subjects have no sense of the value of 'real' work. The jobs they take on are seen to be roles, something to be put on in order to empathise with and understand the past, of little lasting value. The programme suggests that there are such things as inherited values, abilities and skills, but that they are not known to us in our cosy modern world. For this programme, the past is something we have to investigate but it has little real impact on our contemporary lives; it is a hobby, little else, something to be tried on and given back.

Roots, identity genealogy and America

Much popular genealogy, particularly in the USA, is influenced by the writings of Alex Haley. Haley's family narrative, *Roots: The Saga of an American Family*, was published in 1976 and won the Pulitzer Prize; it was later translated into 37 languages. *Roots* was made into a television mini-series, with astounding results – the audience reached 135m in the USA, 20m in the UK. It was event television, and sparked a politicised interest in discovering one's past. The impact of the pro- gramme on Afro-Caribbean communities was immense and the family-seeking that *Roots* prompted continues. The genealogical phenomenon associated with the book and series is redemptive and deeply felt by those who engage with it.

The book is a fictionalised account of Haley's family from the birth of his ancestor Kunta Kinte in mid-eighteenth-century Gambia.[43] Based on scholar- ship and archival research, the novel relates Haley's personal family history, up to and including the moment when he arrives: 'The baby boy, six weeks old, was *me*.'[44] He enters the account late; subsequent to his birth the book relates his search for meaning through archives and libraries. The arrival of the author in the book provokes a kind of metafictional moment; the story's movement has been to this point, just as genealogy generally tends to the moment of '*me*'. The author/researcher is the purpose of the research and the novel, the focal point of everything that has gone before.

Significantly, Haley was inspired to discover his family history by seeing the Rosetta Stone: 'The key that had unlocked a door into the past fascinated me.'[45] Haley sees a 'rough analogy' between the oral history that he has been exposed to in his family and the scholar's deciphering of the Rosetta languages. This model of the translation of the unknown past through research into an important part of the identity of the present figures a functionality to genealogy. With the right tools – the equivalent of the Rosetta Stone – the user can understand the language of history. Furthermore, Haley actually uses words that have been kept in family stories to trace his way back to Africa: words remembered from his boyhood were 'phonetic snatches of whatever was the specific tongue spoken by my African ancestor who was a family legend'.[46] The language motif in the book, therefore, suggests that the original language spoken by his ancestors is the thread through history which connects the entire family.

Roots demonstrates the political trajectory of some genealogical work. Haley's story of his family exposes the horrors of history. His family stands in for all: 'My own ancestors would automatically also be a symbolic saga of all African-descent people.'[47] Genealogy can be used to cleave to an identity and a community, to discover one's context in the world and to tell stories which were only kept just alive by family and ignored by the main narrative of history. Family history can be a route to fuller historical understanding of oneself and the membership of a community. *Roots* presents interest in the family as a path to enlightenment. In a key moment of self-revelation and completeness Haley weeps when, in the Gambian village of Juffure, he is called '*Meester Kinte*'.[48] The fact that his account of this may or may not be true is interesting here as he has created a narrative of birth into self-awareness, deploying extremely familiar tropes of revelation in a way which becomes extremely influential on how genealogy is approached. Similarly the moment of emotion allows Haley to make his broader political point: 'I just felt like I was weeping for all of history's incredible atrocities against fellowmen, which seems to be mankind's greatest flaw.'[49]

One the most important resources for research and model for shared, collaborative genealogy is the information gathered by the Church of the Latter Day Saints (Mormons). Mormons have a doctrinal interest in family history in that the dead can be redeemed and baptised into the Church so that families can be united eternally. The Church has 12.5m members and as a consequence their genealogical resources are huge. Family history for the Mormons is part of an investment in community, a reclamation and salvation of one's ancestors. This concept of retrospective reclamation of a family emphasises the importance of bloodline in defining community. It also presents the notion of the claiming narrative of genealogy (the family rescued from the obscurity of history to become part of a whole unit). This practice returns family history to a more straightforward model of linearity; Mormons are interested in their family rather than in more generalised research. Their website Familysearch.org is one of the most important global gateways to genealogical research, and their free software products (such as the file format GEDCOM, or GEnealogical Data Communication) are used by most websites. The use of religion-based information and technologies implicitly frames genealogical research in a narrative of salvation, here attained through family knowledge.

The models of genealogy presented by *Roots* and the approaches of the Mormons square awkwardly with most contemporary genealogical writings, which emphasise the value of research for personal and individual reasons rather than the accessing of community identity. A suggestive case relating to genealogy and identity is that of black American politician Barack Obama, who, when he was campaigning for Presidential office, was revealed by a genealogical website as the descendant of slave owners (black leader, the Reverend Al Sharpton also found out that his slave ancestors were owned by the family of racist politician Strom Thurmond).[50] This high-level entry of genealogy into political discourse, or at least the media storm surrounding the American presidency, demonstrates fascination with family trees and ancestry as an explanation of contemporary identity. It provoked a rash of celebrity genealogies being discussed in the public domain. Yet Obama effectively ignored the issue, claiming sensibly that by another route he was related to Confederate leader Jefferson Davis and Union soldier Christopher Columbus Clark; such relations simply made him 'representative of America'.[51] This point attempts to neutralise family history at a stroke; one's past is simply metonymic for nation. Obama's very public case inverts the *Roots* model insofar as family history is demonstrated not to be the following of one particular route to political and cultural identity but the uncovering of multiple possible backgrounds and through that the neutralising of any community relationship. Haley's model gave him security through a final, revelatory identification, whereas this present version (although obviously politically spun) suggests the cleaving to a melting-pot model of America rather than a polemic political interest.

Science: genetic genealogy and daytime detection

The notion that genealogy can explain or somehow lead to personal revelation about present-day character derives from popular understanding of genetics as well as a contemporary faith in the relationship between the past and the present.[52] Popular genealogy is intertwined with genetic science in cultural conceptions of the past, and this provides various interesting paradigms.[53] Conceptually the notion of genealogy and communal ancestry is nuanced by understanding of genetics. Typing, characteristics, ancestry, and family fingerprinting are all concepts which underlie popular genealogy. This flows both ways, as the Diversity Project noted that the upsurge in interest in the past in Europe meant that the ground was prepared for a gene bank; the ethical questions associated with this might be considered in a more positive light as a consequence.[54]

In terms of practicalities, increasingly DNA testing is being used to support usual textual evidence-based searches. This has the added advantage of being able to give physical information where there is no archive. The organisation Family Genetics claims that it holds the world's biggest genetically based genealogy database, creating a non-textual archive. Faceless science becomes of a part with narratives of the individual.[55] Genetic genealogy adds to a popularly imagined sense of the scientifically definable self. Personalised genetic histories (PGH) enable researchers to develop understanding of population demographics and medically inherited syndromes as well as contributing to the new fields of genetic anthropology and forensics.[56] They also allow for the opening up of commercial companies providing PGHs to individuals in order that they might pursue their family history.[57] This leisuring of scientific discourse has been termed 'personal interest genomics'.[58] Genetic data is extremely useful for inferring ancestry. In men the Y-chromosome, particularly polymorphisms or mutations of this cell, can tell us much and for women mitochondrial DNA is key. The types of testing available allow the user to either test paternal and maternal lineage or to use informative markers to judge biogeographical ancestry.[59] The first type relies on a single line model of investigation, the second on estimating the percentage membership of ancestral groups. The company Genetic Genealogy, for instance, invites the user to come on a journey to seek their 'deep' ancestral origins; Family Genetics has two options, Deep History Testing or Relationship Testing. Oxford Ancestors, a knowledge transfer company started by Oxford University, claims 'we are all human and we can prove it', imposing a model of scientific rigour and precision to the process.[60] Each of these companies has relationships with the major genealogical entry websites, creating a package which combines various technologies with standard family history research.

There are numerous issues associated with these tests, from scientific queries to worries concerning racial profiling.[61] They are quite difficult to read and mainly consist of statistics; similarly the technology is predicated upon sampling, likelihood and broad comparison. What it gives the user is a set of possibilities, percentage points that might point towards something concrete but which are still interpretable in different ways. PGHs are not easily accessible to the lay reader and therefore the companies that provide such testing have to account for this. Despite this difficulty, and the problems of interpretation, the sense is that the individual will gain self-knowledge and self-definition from knowing the results of a DNA test.[62] This presents a model of an infallible scientific proof which will lead to personal revelation, an authority given to the DNA test which supersedes other investigations. The effect this has on 'normal' genealogical investigation is twofold. On the one hand, it suggests it is more fuzzy than the scientific approach; on the other, it demonstrates to us the enormous faith users put in what genealogical information or knowledge of a family past can give them now. Matrilineal genetic genealogy also has the interesting side effect of allegedly giving a final authorship to the current world. Mitochondrial DNA changes slowly over time and as a consequence such testing demonstrates that everyone is pretty much related at base to one of 36 ancestral mothers: 'mtDNA traces an unbroken maternal line back through time for generation upon generation far further back than any written record'.[63] This idea of humanity pre-civilisation, and of the sudden ability to go back to a past that was lost, is crucial to the appeal of this approach. The 36 are themselves able to trace their maternal ancestry back to the 'Mitochondrial Eve' who lived 150,000 years ago. This sense of a final mother to which all humanity owes at least part of their existence inverts the normal trajectory of genealogy (from the proliferating past to the individual of the present) by neatly tying everything together several hundred thousand years ago.

For popular history the entry of DNA testing is suggestive for the relationship to evidence. DNA as a determining phenomenon is most familiar from forensics, particularly the hugely popular *Crime Scene Investigation* series (2000–, two spin-offs with *c.*20m viewers in the USA alone) which follows a team of criminologists and scientists as they investigate unusual deaths. This model of forensics as scientific detection – familiar also from contemporary novels and films – suggests the ability to reconstruct events and to come to truthful conclusions. There is also a troubling sense of the materiality of pathology, insofar as the inflexibility of DNA information presents the past as something inescapable. DNA testing is (despite several public court cases) considered infallible. The other popular cultural aspect of DNA testing comes from a series of high level paternity suits, similarly conferring a legal gravitas on the procedure.

While DNA testing has been used in *Who Do You Think You Are?*, for instance, in the episode with Colin Jackson, its real entry into the popular imagination came in two series, *Secrets Revealed – DNA Stories* on daytime ITV (2007) which followed the success of the BBC daytime series *Gene Detectives* (2007). In the latter series Melanie Sykes and genealogist Antony Adolph investigated the genetic backgrounds of members of the public; in the former Lorraine Kelly helped normal people to discover important things about their family make-up through DNA testing, from histories to paternity and relationships. Its very title demonstrates the thrust of *Gene Detectives*, a desire to discover the past. In the show DNA testing becomes the final arbiter of identity. The programme's trajectory was that of self-revelation and the discovery of new identities (a counsellor was on hand to aid the protagonists in their adjustment to new reality). *Secrets Revealed* has more of a revelatory quality, disclosing information in order to reconfigure the lives of the participants. *Secrets Revealed* presenter Lorraine Kelly claims that 'the results we will discover through the programme are potentially life-changing for those taking part, makes this series something quite special.'[64] Genealogy therefore becomes part of the revelatory reality genre here, with ordinary people being made extraordinary through the intervention of television (and science). Both series relied heavily on set-pieces, to the extent that *Secrets Revealed* had a repeated scene in which the individuals received their results. The fact that both of these shows are on daytime television and about 'ordinary' people suggests that they are part of a different genre to the more formal and prestige programming such as *Who Do You Think You Are?* The presenters are more associated with daytime programming, particularly Kelly as the face of Good Morning Television (GMTV). *Secrets Revealed* keys directly into a genre of confessional lifestyle programming similar to *Jerry Springer* and *Trisha*.

The relatively low-level and populist deployment of DNA and population genetics in British popular programming is in contrast to the practice in the United States. In the major series *African American Lives* (PBS, 2007), eminent academic Henry Louis Gates, Jr. combined standard genealogy with DNA testing to investigate the backgrounds of a group of eight accomplished African Americans. In contrast to *Who Do You Think You Are?* or *You Don't Know You're Born* this group was not totally made up of cultural celebrities and indeed this diversity was pointed: they included well-known figures such as Oprah Winfrey, actor Chris Tucker, musician Quincy Jones and actress Whoopi Goldberg but also among their number were astronaut Mae Jemison, surgeon Ben Carson, Bishop T.D. Jakes and educationalist Sara Lawrence-Lightfoot. Celebrity here was leavened with measurable achievement and this range of ability was part of the series' celebration of excellence in the African-American community. The use of the heavyweight figure Gates as a presenter signalled that this was prestigious television. The narrative of self-revelation is even more pronounced in this kind of genealogical investigation, and the ability to define oneself through family history had a profound effect way beyond straightforward transformation of self. Actress Whoopi Goldberg expressed it well: 'We're the only ones who came against our will, so whole stories are gone, whole lives are gone, whole histories are gone.'[65] *African American Lives*, then, uses science and historical investigation in order to write back, to give those marginalised by the past a presence, a voice, and a resonance in the contemporary.

DNA genealogy inverts the family tree of mainstream genealogy – rather than being at the top of the structure, the contemporary individual is part of a mass, a

node in a model that traces itself back to an originator. The author[s] [...]
tific information privileges such ways of identification, suggesting a sh[...]
paradigm of popular kinship.[66] The genealogist using DNA investigatio[...]
find themselves quickly abstracted into a general set of values rather [...]
emphasise their unique selfhood. This new direction in genealogical inqui[...]
suggests a conflict with traditional text-based forms, and, as such, a replacing of [...]
one family-epistemology with another.

istory

formation architecture,
as, community websites and
s

New sources, new tools, new archives

When *Time* magazine decided to elect 'You' its person of the year for 2006, the point was that the tools of media and cultural production had been taken over by the consumer: 2006 was a story 'about community and collaboration on a scale never seen before', and, portentously, 'about the many wresting power from the few and helping one another for nothing and how that will not only change the world, but also change the way the world changes'.[1] Web 2.0, the various innovative tools and techniques upgrading the internet's communications and compatibility framework, opened up wide interactive possibilities. These were seized upon by various key brands, all of which suggested that they devolved programming and content power to the end-user: Google (search engine), MySpace and Facebook (social networking), and YouTube (DIY broadcast space).[2] Part of the potentiality of this new generation of programmes was the hybridisation of software – essentially splicing and rewriting freely circulated (open-source) code; also known (no longer pejoratively) as 'hacking' or mashup.[3] This kind of revolutionary grasping of the means of production by the savvy independent information consumer has been part of the idealised version of the internet and associated information technologies ever since its inception.[4] However, 2006 seemed to be the tipping point, both in terms of participation (millions of users), cultural consequence ('Google' entered the *Oxford English Dictionary* as a verb) and community significance.

Does this make any difference to history? Ludmilla Jordanova queries the revolutionary impact of the internet: 'it already has altered modes of learning and teaching, access to original sources and to information', yet she argues that it 'remains unclear in 2005 precisely how the internet will radically transform, if at all, the nature of historical scholarship'.[5] Many professional historians are sceptical of the validity of the web both as repository of information and as research tool.[6] This chapter argues that the way that people engage with history currently is fundamentally interactive, and it follows that the internet and the suite of tools for it known generally as Web 2.0 can work to challenge structures and hierarchies of knowledge. Therefore the way that historical information is presented, engaged with, searched and protected online is crucial, something archivists have known for some time but historians are slowly noticing. The global knowledge economy includes 'history' and as such information relating to the past has become currency. It is within this context that any discussion of the information consumption must now take place, and it is a context which is constantly shifting away from older models of interpretation: 'The new global economy has to be seen as a complex, overlapping, disjunctive order that cannot any longer be understood in terms of existing center–periphery models.'[7] The information revolution fundamentally changes the paradigms for understanding, engaging with, and owning the past.[8]

Arjun Appadurai comments on the deterritorialisation of information which is a consequence of globalisation:

> As group pasts become increasingly parts of museums, exhibits, and collections, both in national and transnational spectacles, culture becomes less what Pierre Bourdieu would have called a habitus (a tacit realm of reproducible practices and dispositions) and more an arena for conscious choice, justification, and representation, the latter often to multiple and spatially dislocated audiences.[9]

Users need not have connections, either conceptual or physical, to the information they download; that information is used, retrieved, and deployed, in newly particular fashion. On this model, 'history', or rather the sets of information relating to the past – document, artefact, image, database – become another group of strands in cyberspace, accessible and usable to just about anyone who has access to the internet. This dislocation of authority models or hierarchies of meaning is crucial to the fragmentation of cultures in globalisation.

Theorists have suggested that the internet's creation of a fully accessible digital archive will 'not only change the form in which culture is produced and recorded, but the wider conditions under which it is enacted and lived as well'.[10] The internet is predicated upon the archiving and searching of information, and as a cultural phenomenon therefore is based upon the opening up and sharing of files (despite increased attempts at controlling access). Thus, as a phenomenon new web media necessitate a model of engagement – both creating and using – which encompasses sharing information. Mike Featherstone reminds us that Tim Berners-Lee, the creator of the World Wide Web, saw it 'as not merely a mechanism for information retrieval from a global archive. Rather it offered the potential of a new inventive relationship to knowledge that overcame the hierarchical relationship found in the traditional archive.'[11] The internet continually evolves but in its current raw state it provides sufficient dynamic challenges to standard models of knowledge and information retrieval to effect genuine change on the ways in which we understand and engage with the past. The use here of the term 'evolves' suggests a problematic teleological conceptualisation of the internet, echoing the ecological metaphors used by many technology theorists, and the question of 'progress' is a vexed one; certainly it is more the case of fragmentation and interference creating hybrids which denote new modes of engagement rather than better ones.[12] Raymond Williams considers the problems of thinking teleologically about culture:

> If we call the process, not human perfection, which implies a known ideal towards which we can move, but human evolution, to mean a process of general growth of man as a kind, we are able to recognise areas of fact which the other definitions might exclude.[13]

William Dutton puts it succinctly: 'Technological change can also alter the role of gatekeepers in the dissemination of information.'[14] This – possibly idealistic – notion of the undermining of authorities and the shifting of relations is clearly the case at a purely material level. Gatekeepers of knowledge increasingly have to either modify their practice or be simply ignored.[15] A useful example here is that of history teacher Lars Brownworth, whose podcasts on Byzantine rulers have a worldwide audience of around 140,000.[16] This is still a relatively straightforward communicative phenomenon, with global reach, and suggests a shift in audience rather than professional practice. Yet does this really demonstrate a fundamental shift in engagement or simply a new way of presenting the same information?

The electronic archive can enfranchise the user, and implement social history models in contradistinction to more personality-led hierarchies of knowledge. In 2007 Andrew Marr's personality-led documentary *History of Modern Britain* was supported by a website entitled 'Your history of Britain' which encouraged viewers to upload images, video and audio from the decades covered by the series (1950–2000).[17] The hybrid site (it includes links to youtube, Wikipedia and interactive polls) enfranchised the viewer – their memories were important evidence – while establishing the authority of the presenter. The BBC, particularly, has made use of its online presence to include the user in the compilation of history. For instance, the WW2 People's War project, which between 2003 and 2006 collected some 47,000 stories and 15,000 images, was predicated upon the desire to hear the stories of ordinary participants and to use web technology to archive their experiences.[18] This testimony-based project followed in the main from the 26-part *People's Century* (BBC/WGBH, 1995), a compilation of witness stories with contemporary footage. This series itself developed the historiography of local and social history, particularly within the paradigms set out by social historian Howard Zinn's million-selling (1980) *A People's History of the United States* (and its more analogous companion book, *Voices of a People's History of the United States*, 2004).[19] Unlike other such attempts at revoicing the marginalised which tend to ventriloquise through dramatisation, such as the 32-hour Canadian series *Canada: A People's History* (2000–2001), *People's Century* consisted of interviews with those who lived through events.[20]

The storage, interface with and conservation of electronic information affect historical research, and the issues associated with this are even more complex for 'born-digital' information: that which does not materially or physically exist in analogue form. This includes a huge range of materials: emails, online documents, electronic information, CCTV images, office suite documents, websites, audio files, blogs, databases. Born-digital historical documents profoundly affect the way that people use them and the types of knowledge that are accessed and created. There is a new and emerging sense of dynamic textuality and techno-logical literacy. Mainstream, older definitions of information fragment, transform and develop into something new and complex; the implications of born-digital materials for archives and for researchers are profound. Archival structures arrange digital information differently from analogue, and the multiple changes in the organising principles of these institutions and the way that documents are arranged, preserved and accessed will of necessity alter methods of research and scholarship. The impact of new technologies on education systems, research, knowledge conservation and information archiving is profound. It is also difficult to conceptualise, due to the pace with which it has happened. A massive amount of information is being used and generated at exponential speed. In 2000, zero documents were downloaded from the National Archives website; now the number is around 66m annually. Millions more were viewed and used online.

Study of the virtual archive is at an extremely early stage. The pioneering work of scholars such as Roy Rosenzweig, Mike Featherstone and Tara Brabazon has begun to analyse born-digital information, but there is still little historio-graphic work. Digitisation of collections and born-digital materials shifts our understanding of management, transmission, interaction, copyright; there are multiple associated issues including compatibility, migration, security, life-cycle, interoperability, authenticity and reliability, and obsolescence. How sustainable is the digital record and how is its authenticity assured? New methods of appraisal for electronic records are being developed, strategies for digital continuity are being implemented, and new presentation systems are being pioneered. Seamless flow models link together existing components and automate manual processes for information architecture and archiving. Key projects include Electronic Records Online or the Digital Continuity project at the UK National Archives, and the September 11 Digital Archive 'at' the Library of Congress.[21] This last demonstrates the vibrancy and range of materials collected in these new archives: mobile phone images, animation, emails, daily pdf action plans from the FDNY, audio files. The September 11 Digital Archive also demonstrates the new instantaneity that communications technology has imported; for instance, news programmes regularly request eye-witnesses and by-standers send in their own mobile phone footage and recordings of events. Some of the first images screened of the 7th July 2005 bombings in London, for instance, were taken with mobile phones.[22] These images are part of the historical record, but in thrall to numerous problematic issues associated with facilities for storage and models of collection, integration and organisation.

Networked interfaces with information: search engines, Wikipedia

The web and associated database technology, then, presents new types of investigation for the humanities scholar:

The digital era seems likely to confront historians—who were more likely in the past to worry about the scarcity of surviving evidence from the past— with a new 'problem' of abundance. A much deeper and denser historical record, especially one in digital form, seems like an incredible opportunity and gift. But its overwhelming size means that we will have to spend a lot of time looking at this particular gift horse in the mouth—and we will probably need sophisticated statistical and data mining tools to do some of the looking.[23]

The 'culture of abundance' described here has multiple implications for archiving, researching and sharing information.[24] Digital information is fragile, prone to corruption (either intentionally or otherwise), expensive to store and prey to multiple copyright issues. Information is not kept within national boundaries, for instance, and therefore the question of ownership and who pays for archiving electronic information becomes important. The internet has profound implications not simply for engaging with historical information as a scholar but also about how historians might understand contemporary life: 'The historical narratives that future historians write may not actually look much different from those that are crafted today, but the methodologies they use may need to change radically.'[25] Already research methods have shifted demonstrably in response to what is known as interoperability (relational databases) and new generation technology software such as *Zotero* have been produced to help scholars data-mine, collect and manage information from the 'infinite archive'.[26] Fundamentally the internet changes the way that historians might work – be it simply reading articles, searching archives, taking notes or composing. Those critics who have approached this software have emphasised how scholars might use new tools for dissidence and warned of idealising Web 2.0.[27] Technologies change the relationship to information, suggesting and creating new hierarchies, hegemonies and ways of imagining society.[28]

Certainly search engines have affected the way that people *ask* for information and therefore how they engage with and understand historical knowledge.[29] John Battelle argues that if we analyse the 'Database of Intentions' – what people search for – we can understand contemporary culture, and furthermore it is clear that the search engine's reduction of knowledge to a set of (even advanced) query answers institutes an electronic epistemology of sorts.[30] Analysis of the patterns of searching can inform scholars about the structures of understanding and engagement that the web fosters; it also demonstrates the conceptual approaches that users bring to historical research. This is not simply at the level of amateur-users; sophisticated software can also be used to data-mine archives and data-bases on behalf of professionals, too. The raw information created still needs to be interpreted, and the correct questions asked, but the speed of research has increased and the type of information generated is new: 'These computational methods, which allow us to find patterns, determine relationships, categorise documents, and extract information from massive corpuses, will form the basis for new tools for research in the humanities and other disciplines in the coming decade.'[31] At a practical level, using independent software to mine data implies a cyborg element to scholarship (in the same way that using a laptop to write an article does) which partially excludes the human element and shifts our relationship with the information. Abstracting information from electronic sources and utilising computer technologies to present it mean that fundamentally the computer–human relationship underpins all scholarly historical inquiry. This implies some distance and some deferral of meaning, a cinematic gap between viewer and image.[32] Similarly, using sophisticated search engines alters the relationship that scholars have with their raw material. Google's algorithms are on the edge of being AI and therefore deploying them involves a newly technologically defined interface. Utilising sophisticated feed generators and automated gathering systems (like Google) to 'information trap' allows information to be abstracted from the chaotic whole. These systems are based on the principles of 'spidering' – an automated indexing of the information and links on a page and the subsequent following of all these links through to other pages, an exponential creation of data (this is what search engines do) – and 'scraping', a less sophisticated, automated text-based searching. These tools let the scholar navigate the chaos of information – Rosenzweig's 'abundance' – yet they are rough technologies and provide only a skewed image of the available resources. They are in essence ways of reading and formulating and are updated versions of standard historical tools; at the same time, they change the way that users engage with historical information.

New technologies and media have affected the way that general or amateur users interface with information. Gaming technologies have, for instance, the potential to significantly alter the way that users learn and access information.[33] Search engine models such as Google Scholar have allowed users to, as the advertising hook goes, 'Stand on the Shoulders of Giants'. This specific incursion into academia demonstrates that Berners-Lee's conception of the internet as something which circumvents existing hierarchies of knowledge might be valid. The design, purpose and methodologies of the internet are still in a state of flux. As Louis Rosenfeld and Peter Morville have argued, 'There is a dynamic, organic nature to both the information systems and the broader environments in which they exist.'[34] Such natural, ecological motifs and metaphorical language abound in discussion of the web, and phrases such as 'information ecology' are commonplace; such conceptualisation demonstrates the potentiality and the fluidity of the web, as well as the lack of a particularised discourse with which to describe it. Information architecture, for instance, is the discipline of organising and presenting information (as opposed to the technicalities of doing this) and is a growth field. Information design is closely linked to the concept of user experience. The fact that internet theorists conceive of the web in these terms suggests an underlying dynamism and flexibility in writing about the phenomena. Theories of information architecture – particularly in terms of content organisation, access and the hierarchy of presentation – are concerned with how it affects the user's engagement with content and therefore how they understand what is given to them.

Crucial here is the complexity of information presented – a common web database page now has print, image, video, audio, virtual modelling, Google Earth tags, scholarly cross-reference, bibliography, blog, and podcast associated with it. The depth of information and the complexity of linkage create a dynamism (particularly visually) which print media cannot mimic. The Gutenberg-e project endows a prize run by Columbia University Press and given to the most innovative and creative use of new digital technology.[35] Publications include further documentation, hyperlinks to further databases, music, images, links and video. As a model for the presentation of scholarly information it demonstrates the potential for multi-layered presentation. The architecture of the page is much more complex than a normal book – and the links make it part of a constantly evolving and changing network of information.

The web page, then, exists in a state of simultaneity. Partly this is economically defined. The freedom model of the internet is mitigated against by the increasing incidence of websites charging for access to content.[36] Subscriptions to databases and journals are standard; free content is generally supported by in-page advertising. Information is currency and 'history' has simply become part of this global knowledge network. In this set of relationships the user of the information becomes, in John Fiske's terminology, a 'commodified audience to be sold to advertisers'.[37] Yet most web use involves a dynamic relationship rather than a passive one – a user generally cannot be simply fed information but must seek it. Chris Rojek argues that the net emphasises 'active consumption [which] abrogates part of the creative role to the consumer'.[38] Conceptually and materially, then, the web is an interactive resource; indeed, for Lee Manovich, computer use is by definition interactive.[39] The audience of the internet is mainly active at most points in contrast to the audience of, for instance, television, which has led to the argument that the web represents a new public sphere and a possible gateway to political or social engagement.[40] However, this interactive, participatory user also loses bodily physicality, identity and accountability: 'The ephemeralization of labor and the evanescence of the commodity, in cyberculture, are paralleled by the disembodiment of the human.'[41] The web user is simultaneously a commodity to be sold to advertisers, a potentiality for creating a newly hacked interactive identity and a disembodied presence alienated from society and production.

A key challenge to traditional systems of knowledge is that of participatory publishing. The website Wikipedia, launched in January 2001, attacks intellectual commonplaces about the ownership of knowledge as well as undermining legal (copyright) definitions of information possession.[42] It is the largest multilingual free-content encyclopaedia on the internet, with nearly 2 million pieces in English, and hundreds of thousands in German, Dutch, French, Italian, Polish, Spanish, Swedish and Mandarin. It has an inbuilt translation engine. Wikipedia has also become the model and the source for many other sites, as it is fed through and used by web authors (it is common to search for a term and find multiple results for the Wikipedia entry). Wikipedia presents information – including historical information – as an encyclopaedia, a fully searchable database. The model, then, is of focused investigation rather than browsing, of the directed interrogation of a body or repository of knowledge rather than a more complex engagement. The term 'wiki' refers to a multi-user, collaborative website, and is a form of page creation that is used commonly in programming and education. Like Google, MySpace, and eBay, Wikipedia has taken on a life outside of its original application and now has a brand recognition, marketability and prevalence (it is constantly in the top 15 of the Alexa global web traffic rankings). In itself this tells us much about the way that the web is used – Wikipedia holds its own against sites with more obvious economic, practical or entertainment elements and suggests that, while communication is key to the internet, cultural, social and historical information are also important. Rosenzweig argues that it represents 'the most important application of the principles of the free and open-source software movement to the world of cultural, rather than software, production'.[43] It is not-for-profit, funded by a foundation that accepts private donations, and as such is an example of a new virtual information institution. Users administer the site themselves, electing overseers to keep an eye on things.

Anyone can contribute or revise an entry, although there are certain rules.[44] This emphasis on user-created content suggests a participatory model wherein the production and circulation of information rely on the engagement of the common user. The editorial process, though, tends towards conservatism and consensus – the emphasis is on the site as a resource. One of the key contributor policies is to present a 'neutral point of view' ('Debates are described, represented, and characterized, but not engaged in'), an attempt to avoid accusations of bias.[45] Another is that original research is not allowed – an attempt to avoid personal theory which leads the site towards the middle ground. Key to the project is the sense of collecting information rather than writing something new: 'The threshold for inclusion in Wikipedia is *verifiability, not truth*. "Verifiable" in this context means that any reader should be able to check that material added to Wikipedia has already been published by a reliable source' (their emphasis).[46] The definition of a reliable source is divided into primary (eyewitnesses, archives, letters, autobiographies), secondary (books, magazines, newspapers) and tertiary (encyclopaedias). Anyone may engage in history as long as they observe the standard practicalities of history – research, scholarship, reading sources, writing articles. The tools of historical scholarship are given to the user, but it is still straightforward, if consultative and interrogative, historical practice.

Wikipedia presents knowledge, then, as something which is in a state of continual revision, with numerous points of view, reliant on other sources to establish factual based truth. It presents an 'objective' consensus. Critics have suggested that this model is poor history as it is simply interested in a truth or factuality which does not really exist. The phenomenon of Wikipedia in microcosm presents the infinitude of the internet – a multitude of information that lacks form and needs modelling by users. Wikipedia is not alone, as user-driven sites such as Helium encourage non-professionals to write and publish articles on a huge variety of subjects including historical ones. It also demonstrates the effect that database technologies – from storage to searching – are having on the modes of engagement with information. The web is encyclopaedic rather than holistic, audited by exponential spiders relentlessly searching for all the manifestations of a single term or set of code.

Hacking history: Google Earth

Google Earth (GE) is a database technology that uses satellite images to present a dynamic, streaming photographic 3D map of the world. Users can explore by inputting locations, global co-ordinates or areas; there is also the ability to simply scroll around using a compass and a zoom function. As a service technology it provides location finders, directions and images of key tourist destinations. The consequences of the information found on Google Earth are clear – a seemingly real-time image of the world both enfranchises (giving access to the globe) as well as imaginatively disciplining space in the way that all cartography does.[47] In terms of scholarship and communication, the potential for using the images is widespread – the program can, for instance, allow for geospatial tags in database or encyclopaedia entries, significantly shifting the way that information is presented.[48] It is an example of how a technology can be hacked in order to facilitate historical inquiry. Google Earth can also be use to break down information hierarchies. It publishes application programming interfaces (api) which allows the user to embed maps in their webpages, providing utilities for manipulating maps and producing mashups.[49] The software allows the user to add image overlays, literally to impose their own image on the map. This means that the map can be disrupted, fragmented, interleaved and rewritten. Jeremy Crampton and John Krygier have persuasively demonstrated how 'map-hacking' and open source technologies have allowed the by-passing of standard practice in map-making: 'open-source mapping means that cartography is no longer in the hands of cartographers or GIS scientists but the users'.[50] They also usefully point out that the technologies which make this possible are not interested in the content *per se* but in the *presentation* of information; 'history' becomes just one more set of data. The consequences of this, in a discipline in which spectacle, power relations and surveillance are crucial issues, are far-ranging and suggest a wider application: if users can escape the gatekeepers of cartographic knowledge and begin to construct and use their own maps (particularly of contested sites or places), what might they do with histories?[51] Technology here allows for the disruption of hierarchies, giving the user free rein to create and control their own sense of space.

Google Earth has set of historical functions, in that various maps of the past are programmed in to the basic software.[52] Choose, say, a map of London in 1843 or Asia in 1710 and the image of an historical map is overlain onto the contemporary satellite image (with all its tags to modern locations still showing). There is a psychogeographical element to this – an archaeological sense of the past literally mapping onto the present and melding in – and this is emphasised by the fact that there is a transparency slider function which can make the overlain image bolder or lighter. This sense of the dynamic relationship between past and present also establishes a very physical relationship between then and now. Yet the historical maps are presented as a viewing option alongside, for instance, transportation networks, tourist locations, places to eat or sites of ecological interest, suggesting that 'historical' is just one of a set of viewing tropes. The 'old' maps are also *wrong* – either in terms of topography or borders or the naming of places – which on the one hand establishes them as less authoritative than contemporary images while also subtly undermining the authoritative assumptions of 'maps' in general.

Google Earth software and the multiple add-ons it has generated demonstrate an interest in the physicality of history and a further understanding of the flexibility of that materiality. There are bespoke history hacks with users – institutions and professional organisations as well as individuals – adding their own overlay maps and photographic images (complete with topographical mapping) of historical sites.[53] These range from archaeological echo images to shots of ruins, from ancient maps to locations of shipwrecks in the Atlantic. This cartographical archiving shows users rearranging information, remaking their world with an historical perspective. Historical 'map-hacking' points to an inflexibility of the past – as a fixed topographical moment – while the dynamism of the software and the ease of use allow each individual to engage with the history of the 'world' in a unique way. This potential for disruption inscribed within GE allows historical 'fact' to become another set of data to be manipulated in whichever way the end-user wishes.

Open source code and community websites

The websites that present these hacks offer a multiplicity of historical perspectives on the fabric of the globe. They are dependent on use, trust and, to a large extent, on advertising revenue – a combination which is common in the knowledge economy. Hack and user-content-driven websites are a hybrid of enfranchisement and global capital. The design of most blogs, websites and search engines is complex and its dependence on advertising clear. This fundamental commercialism is in conflict with the 'liberating' model of the web. Information freedom is subsidised and made possible through advertising, sponsor links and popups. Yet open source coding allows at least partial ownership of the tools of production, and the evolution and development of new methods of information retrieval and presentation which circumvent the mainstream centres of economic power: 'while this [the internet] creates new opportunities for commercial exchange it also enlarges the scope for infraction and transgression'.[54]

In his work on the incipient public sphere Jürgen Habermas describes the process by which 'the emergent bourgeois gradually replaced a public sphere in which the ruler's power was merely represented *before* the people with a sphere in which state authority was publicly monitored through informed and critical discourse *by* the people'.[55] This shift in authority leads to the creation of the dynamic political subject. The impact of new media technologies enables a further nuancing of this effect, the creation of a proliferation of information, albeit with little direction. At the same time what is being presented through new technologies is simply a mediated selfhood, a subject defined through their relationship to the global media interface rather than through community or innate qualities. *Time's* nomination of 'You' as the key mover of the year does not differentiate between individuals but makes the user a mass part of a system of self-referential signs.

Open source software and open content websites (designed to be copied and reused), however, mean that knowledge and information become more flexible entities; that epistemologies might be interrogated; and that the user becomes the director of investigations. It points towards an open society, or a new means of governance in the way that Habermas suggests, creating new ways of communicating and understanding the modalities of the global economy; however, it is only a tool. Open source emphasises the sharing and circulation of information and ideas. It allows software to be, in effect, owned by the online community, with utilities ranging from local history databases to the tracking and data-mining of public financial information.

One of the ways that these new tools have been used in innovative, interrogative ways is in the creation of community archives. Community-based media are generally not-for-profit and enable members of a particular group to take part in the process of creating content.[56] This encourages participation and develops local access, enabling non-professionals. Community-based projects give agency to the participants and encourage cultural participation. Community archives on the web are an extension of this collectivism, being local, small, individual projects interested in creating a record of a particular group. The community creates the archive, administers it, edits and owns it. The archives consist of documents (scanned or photographed), images, audio and video. They are often personal, or extremely particular in their focus. Archives do not simply relate to particular social identities but accrue around areas, institutions, hobbies.

The majority of these collections tend to be online, creating a virtual, disembodied community (the geographical location of the user or participant is not important). For the main part, these projects have the potential to enable the community to engage with its own history directly, develop skills related to information management and reach a wider audience. Community archives can also preserve unofficial history, and provide communities with spaces for reflection, consideration, self-definition and identity formation. They give people the chance to claim their past back from official versions of events, to preserve fading ways of life, and to dissent from mainstream historical narratives. The range is diverse and complex, from social history to material culture. The Brighton Ourstory archive, for instance, was set up to collect and preserve lesbian and gay history (their statement 'Our approach is very much that of an oral history group interested in ordinary lives: our primary focus is not academic or theoretical' sums up the marginalised and consciously non-professional approach of these archives); The Ball Clay Heritage Society archive is dedicated to preserving the records of firms in Devon that produced ball clays for the ceramics industry; Apples and Pears Past is an archive dedicated to oral history of Cider and Perry; Ironbridge Gorge Community Archive collects information relating to that area.[57]

Community archives devolve power from the central institutions of national preservation, and, once set up, are independent with their own collection policies and preservation principles. They demonstrate the levelling function of the internet, the way that it can allow communities to create spaces in which to interrogate and develop identities.[58] This networking function of the web both strengthens existing communities as well as creating the possibility for new ones. However, participation and access issues are still uppermost, for instance, the creation of an archive still involves money (for software, hardware and storage), IT literacy, and the preservation of particular types of information (although generally more dynamic than standard archives).[59] They also mimic macro-developments in web development, for instance, through the use of merchandising and book sales to support their work.

In 2004, the National Archives set up the Community Access to Archives Project (CAAP) in order to facilitate the building of local collections. The project 'aimed to empower potential archive users and archive professionals to work together to identify the sources users require, whether for family, community and local history, for lifelong learning, for educational projects or for other purposes'.[60] The organisation recognised that by giving over the means of information, collection archives might become more relevant to communities that generally had little to do with them. It established a best practice model for consultation and a set of general guidelines. Archives are understood here to be materials that 'encapsulate a particular community's understanding of its history and identity'.[61] The archives challenge standard models of collections, focusing on the group's needs rather than a wider desire to tell a story or represent a history externally. The motivation for CAAP was also social inclusion, a desire to create networks of communication. The charitable organisation Commanet, which provides the software for most of the databases, makes grand claims for the purpose of the community archive:

> Community archives promote understanding, tolerance and respect between generations and between diverse social, ethnic and cultural communities. By enabling communities to record and share their heritage, they foster active citizenship within a multicultural democracy.[62]

The archives allow the creation of imagined communities irrespective of prac-tical or physical issues. For Commanet they have a humanist, enlightenment purpose of fostering communication between groups; they also provoke political engagement. The vocabulary of 'active citizenship' and the 'enabling' of the community suggests that freedom of information, of access and of software might promote humanist values, political transformation at a grass roots level, and the establishment of a better society. Certainly such archives suggest the wider intervention of a minority community into a public forum, the creation of and public presentation of a sense of cultural identity and heritage.

Part III

Performing and playing history

Seeing and believing: re-enactment culture

So far, this book has argued for a twofold engagement with history – through the offices of a personality–celebrity, and via material engagement with the artefacts and texts of the past. History is both taught and experienced. In analysing further the personalising of history and individual agency in engaging with the past, the following three chapters analyse a variety of 'bodily' historical experiences and delineate the complexity of engagement they demand. They consider the implications of re-enactment, historicised cultural performance and games on questions of historical experience and authenticity. The phenomena considered here – re-enactment, Living History and computer game first-person history – offer a range of *experience* within history and a complexity of consumption. They seemingly enfranchise the audience, while also subjecting them to a viewed history, history as a performance and story (and a story with particular narrative rules overseeing events).

Both re-enactment and Living History as practices raise questions of education, ownership and authenticity while also being in many ways undertheorised by historians. They are activities, like first-person and role-playing games, which suggest an historical freedom in the 'bodily' or embodied experience. These activities – mainly new or newly popular – provoke troubling questions about 'how' history is as well as 'what' history is.

Re-enactment, a 'winning combination of imaginative play, self-improvement, intellectual enrichment, and sociality' spans cultural genres (re-enacting film, or theatre, or television), is art (the work of Jeremy Deller and the ICA re-enactors), or can be political activism (in the case of the Lifeline project).[1] The action of reinscribing the past through a particularised set of bodily actions – a reperformance, or reanimation – is widespread through culture, from memorial walks through to the use of medieval instruments. Historicised performance is keynote to contemporary society's obsession with 'authenticity' and this is in some part because the key to such legitimacy is seen to be personal experience. Re-enactment blends the experience of the historical artefact such as is experienced in museums with individual revelation.

Re-enactment is one of the key tropes for contemporary historical engagement, and can be traced in nearly all the media and forms considered by this book – in the need for interactivity at museums, for instance, or the embodied experience of reality history. Raphael Samuel traces in reconstruction and living history 'the quest for immediacy, the search for a past which is palpably and visibly present'.[2] Samuel links the vogue for historical re-enactment or 'resurrectionism' of all types – walking, canal restoration, floodlighting old buildings, steam trains – with the rise of local history in the 1950s.[3] Clearly, there is an attempted enfranchisement of sorts, a grassroots movement and DIY element associated with such re-enactment, and the cultural phenomena of historical recreation and re-embodiment certainly challenge mainstream historical models and modes of disseminating knowledge.

These chapters consider re-enactment and re-embodiment in multiple guises – professional (generally that at museums), as a leisure genre (such as practised by the Sealed Knot), as a set of cultural approaches to history (as in the Globe), as games, and as art. The various types of re-enactment and re-embodiment analysed here demonstrate the complexities of historical empathy. The prevalence of re-enactment throughout popular culture, in multiple varieties, suggests the importance of (bodily) experience to an understanding of history. Re-enacting reinscribes the self in relation to both the 'past' and to a set of tropes associated with a previous event or artefact.

7   Historical re-enactment

Combat re-enactment: WARS and the Sealed Knot

Contemporary re-enactment is a large, multifaceted industry, encompassing at one end committed, decidedly individualistic groups and at the other occasional participants engaging in easy leisure activities.[1] Re-enactment is not simply war-related, although a large proportion of it relates to combat (and it is not necessarily 'genuine' war-related, with live-action role play of fantasy scenarios increasingly common). It is global, with re-enactment occurring across the world. The membership is generally white, mainly male, and relatively well off in terms of money and time.[2] Re-enactment as a collectivised experience is defiantly outside mainstream professional ways of thinking about the past, as Vanessa Agnew argues: 'Reenactment performs political and cultural work that is quite distinct from more conventional forms of historiography.'[3]

What is the motivation for the amateur re-enactor? Many societies do exist for the presentation of, for instance, the society of Jane Austen or early dance. Within the Sealed Knot (SK), Britain's largest re-enactment society (formed in 1968), there is a range of living history activities ranging from Basketry to Cookery via the Renaissance Art of War. Their journal, *Order of the Daye*, is a knowledge base with articles on a range of historical subjects related to SK activities. The pieces are often footnoted and provide bibliographies, and the purpose is to add historical texture and variety to the entire activity. Yet it is combat re-enactment that is the most popular re-enactment activity; there are some 6,000 members of the Sealed Knot, mostly involved in staging battles. War may be bloody and chaotic in reality, but re-enacted it enables the combatant safe progress through history to a wished-for and satisfactory conclusion.

Re-enactment reminds the participant and the (potential) viewer of the essential otherness of history. In its purer forms it is predicated upon hardship, complexity and privation, presenting the past as continually different from now: a 'body-based discourse in which the past is reanimated through physical and psychological experience'.[4] Similar to reality history, the agency of historical investigation is found in the individual and their experience of the everyday – of cold, hunger, discomfort, difference – rather than any grander, totalising conceptualisation of meaning, purpose or progress. History is consumed by the re-enactor – obsessive, leisure participant or mere observer – as something which may be put on, worn, a set of tools and behaviours which relate specifically in the first instance to the corporeal body and thence to 'culture' or modes of behaviour. As Della Pollock has argued, the historicist performer is both subject and object, and the audience's reflection on this fact can open 'the way for an as yet unseen history, a history less in thrall to the visible facts than to embodied, performing subjects'.[5] Re-enactors recognise that they are both actors and audience, for instance.[6]

Yet re-enactment also offers enfranchisement, a complexity of historical interaction which is missing in much academic or 'official' history. The complex set of discourses circulating within the re-enactment experience offers us interesting paradigms for thinking about other, newer forms of populist historical consumption. The interaction of re-enactors and their audiences with the past is a crucial paradigm for contemporary historical consumption. They present an 'authentic' inclusive or participatory history which lacks the messy 'edge' of events. Public reconstruction is interested in presenting a sanitized, closed version of warfare, of avoiding the unpresentability of war. Re-enactment of the past – discovery, presentation and categorisation of any text and narrative – is concerned with avoiding the fragmentary process of history and with demonstrating the ongoing value of rationality and completeness. Re-enactment history seems enfranchising but it also presents an inflexible positivism and an oppressive subjectification – wars are still won by the same people, and the good soldier is he who unquestioningly obeys the orders of history. Public combat is turned into narrative, a linear story of nationhood rather than a complex development.

Re-enactment, crucially, has a performative educational purpose. The Sealed Knot's primary purpose is 'the performance of public re-enactments of Battles, Sieges and other events of the period with a view to educating the public and encouraging an interest in our heritage'.[7] This rhetoric situates re-enactment within the portfolio of 'Living History' as an educative performance, an accurate and verifiable version of history. It is possible to place the phenomenon in performance theory terms, arguing that the postmodern play involved in dressing as a Cavalier soldier might seem to undermine any fixed conception of 'historical' or 'social' identity. Yet equally an appeal to historical realism is inscribed in the process. The Sealed Knot warn that 'mixing seventeenth and twentieth century clothing styles is unacceptable when performing re-enactment events in front of any audience'.[8] History is a role, but it is not particularly open to interrogation – the 'verifiability' issue makes history something with inflexible rules and specificities. Historical actuality orders and disciplines this activity. William C. Davies recommends that when re-enacting the participant 'become that person, talk like him, act like him and never stray from the 1860s as your time'.[9] The dynamic is between 'authenticity' of representation and the factuality of the history being presented. There is a drive toward the importance of performance and education (and the two being combined) which rests on this guarantee of authenticity. At the same time, though, the re-enactors are performing and portraying historical figures (and therefore divorced from the ideological or material implications of their actions). So this is, on the one hand, a set of leisure activities with particular rules and, on the other, a serious, authentic performance that educates and delights.

History here also interacts with discourses of 'leisure' as something on the one hand useful (the educative aspect) but also something undertaken in non-work time (weekends, evenings). The re-enactor is teacher and hobbyist. They are familiar – they talk to the audience and each other – but othered – they dress differently. The dynamic here between audience and participant is incredibly complex and fluid. Furthermore, the audience is generally on holiday or out of work bounds – and also outside of an institutional framework for their historical experience/ education. Culture here is something out of institutional bounds, in some ways ordered but also part of a leisure-time activity. Much like genealogy, re-enact-ment is a 'serious' leisure pursuit (see Chapter 5), insofar as it allows the parti-cipant to develop their profile, learn, and become better and more proficient in their activity. It is fundamentally educative, therefore.

While the American Civil War has the largest number of participants (some 12,000 celebrated the 125th anniversary of Gettysburg in 1988), increasingly re-enactors are turning to WWI, WWII and the Korean and Vietnam wars.[10] This raises ethical issues in terms of authenticity: 'is re-enacting a proper way to represent war?'[11] There are issues of trivialisation, of authenticity and violence. The re-enactors often see their work as commemoration of those who died in battle, and dedicate films to their memory. Yet there are many issues of anachronism, ranging from inability to find particular kit to modern body shapes. The hobby is a paradox, and relatively self-consciously so. It is about the performance of a history which happened but which, in modern hands, might take different courses (and not have the ultimate arbiter, death). It very much is interested in local, specific, rather than wider issues. The activity is authentic – and very much desired so by participants – due to outside forces (academic history), the skill of the combatants, and their will to reality. It is at once a postmodern pastiche of history while it is also just a leisured way of engaging with one's present self.

Re-enactment, then, offers a range of *experience* within history and a complexity of consumption. It enfranchises the audience, while also subjecting them to a viewed history, history as a performance and story (and a story with particular narrative rules overseeing events). The audience's gaze empowers them (and their ability to walk or look away extends this) and gives them a certain interpretative authority. However, the re-enactor also takes on a power role in this relationship, as they have the authority of 'verifiable' truthful history on their side. While one may walk away from a performance it still happens; furthermore, if you choose not to be educated, then you cannot engage with the discourse of humanist perfectibility and understanding that is implied in the entire process. If you are not interested in your heritage, then you disenfranchise yourself from your national story and identity. This humanist drive to understanding the nation through history is common in contemporary history teaching at all levels.

However, this re-enactor's national story is relatively monolithic. It seems to invest in a transcultural notion of shared history that ignores ethnic difference or cultural complication. Re-enactors generally tend to shy away from historical controversy and complication – although one might cite Clairséach Óir who re-enact the Irish War of Independence while other Irish groups re-enact World War I. Another Irish group, O'Neill's Company, are based in Carrickfergus Castle and re-enact the 1640s, again not an uncontroversial period. Ireland is perhaps a peculiar case; certainly Irish history is superficially more related to the political present.[12] There are, though, also companies that simulate the American war in Vietnam. In general, however, re-enactment societies present themselves as non-political groups. Given this, though, the concept of the 'enemy' in these activities is interesting. On the one hand, the enemy is foretold by history, on the other the enemy is part of your organisation – a truly recognisable other. Those joining the Sealed Knot choose to be either a 'Roundhead' or a 'Cavalier' and their subsequent re-enacting identity is diffracted through this definition. The problematic notion of civil war – fighting a recognisable enemy other – is in some ways a virtue for re-enactors of the 1640s as it allows each side to perform victories and 'win' particular local battles without considering the bigger historical picture; the enemy is folded into the entire holistic 'experience'.

A number of societies take it upon themselves to actively portray the 'enemy'. The World War Axis Re-enactment Society (WARS) is an umbrella group of British organisations that portray German troops. For instance, one society portrays the 2nd SS Aufklärungsabteilung ('reconnaissance') battalion of the 2nd SS Panzer division 'Das Reich'; another portrays the HG Flak Abt – Herman Göring Division. Society websites distance themselves from right-wing and racist politics; the first rule of WARS is 'never perform a Nazi salute, even as a joke'.[13] That said, the drive toward authenticity is still key: 'Members will not be accepted with long hair, pony tails and full beards. This is due to WARS trying to portray German soldiers of the period.'[14] Practitioners often speak German to each other, and their kit is as authentic as possible. The dynamic is between 'authenticity' of presentation and the factuality of the history being presented. Yet it is an authenticity compromised by ideology. By denying the practitioner the historical motivation of Nazism such re-enactment emphasises that this exercise is a game or role, and gets us no nearer to understanding the past; in fact, it enables an othering, a distancing of the past. What WARS acknowledges is that we can understand the fact of the past but not the motivation of the practitioners. This is scripted performance, the inhabiting of a 'role' rather than empathic recreation.

The re-enactor seeks the authentic while *always* understanding themselves as othered from History. They do not claim total understanding and so inscribed within each experience of the historical is the aporia of History (there is almost a teleological ideal of progress towards authenticity which knowingly will never be attained). Re-enactment, then, plays out the shortcomings of history and instead turns it into another aspect of the 'historical'. Fundamental to the experience is a lack, an absence, an othering, and in this othering the true 'historical' experience occurs: an awareness of historical contingency and multiplicity. There is almost an aesthetics of illusion, a knowing transubstantive loss of self in the moment and the experience. Re-enactors lose themselves in the game of playing at being 'historical' while striving for, but never attaining, 'History'. The game is always unfinished.

Indeed, this might lead us to consider that the postmodern play involved in re-enactment is more authentically human than that of 'normal' life in its rejection of a positivist 'whole' identity.

A great deal of re-enactment is private, and there is a keen difference between such events and the more crowd-pleasing public shows (not least that the open enactments have scripts – so are relentlessly 'authentic' in terms of a wider historical narrative – while the closed events are more 'real' insofar as they are more random and do not unfold within a set pattern). As Thompson observes, 'Ironically, it is only in the absence of a pre-determined historical script that they believe they can achieve any degree of authenticity'.[15] Most re-enactors prefer the private functions as rather than performing they are asserting their own ownership over history rather than being told how to think about it by professional or intellectual gatekeepers.[16] They 'lie outside the boundaries of established academic and public history'.[17] They are also more interested in being normal and average soldiers – it is unusual to wish to lead or be anyone specifically famous. This reflects the interest in normality and in experiencing the day-to-day of war personally. This desire to personate, perform the normality of historicity is key to the hyperauthenticity of re-enacting. The absorption of the enactor means that 'they are free to act autonomously, governed by their knowledge of what could have happened more than what actually did happen'.[18] Again, this is the projection of a personalised narrative onto an authentic background, self-creating a persona and story for oneself by using 'history' as a backdrop. We can posit a dual nature of re-enactment – a public, educational element which desires simply to teach, and a private aspect which is less interested in historiographical issues and more with a deeply personalised historicised experience.

At the same time increasingly YouTube and video-sharing websites are being used to circulate films of re-enactors. This also allows the addition of elements some hardcore re-enactors find problematic as romanticising the activity: soundtracks, voiceovers, overview, information screens. Sharing sites create communities, and allow the public audience to experience the more unpredictable 'performances'. They also re-insert the activity into the historical genre of the war movie (and further complicate the 'authentic' use of re-enactors in documentary). The *YouTube* movies emphasise the randomness of re-enactment, the unpredictability of the combat zone, and the impossibility of knowing what is going on more generally around the enactors. The use of YouTube demonstrates how the phenomenon has created a supporting industry in recent years, with multiple global companies, magazines (*Skirmish* and *Call to Arms*, in the UK, for instance, or *Civil War Historian* in the USA) and websites starting up to support the various activities, and with increasing numbers of public events and a wider public profile.[19]

Re-enactment and place as historical evidence: documentary

Michael Winterbottom's (2005) film of *Tristram Shandy, A Cock and Bull Story*, includes a sharp cameo from comedian Mark Williams as the historical re-enactment advisor, obsessing over irrelevant but authentic period details: 'I've got a list of the men that fell ... 92 died that morning ... I can fix up your lot with real, accurate names and then they could shout out their names to each other in the heat of the battle.'[20] He condemns other films (which the stars and the director of the film within a film admire for their dramatic effects) as 'shite ... woefully inaccurate from end to end. We wouldn't be interested in participating in a pantomime like that.' This is part of *A Cock and Bull Story*'s self-reflective quality – an attempt to show what happens behind the scenes and to demonstrate the falseness of the final output (and in this motif it follows the source text extremely closely). This metatextual element attempts to undermine the realism of the costume drama and demonstrate that cleaving to the 'authentic' is undesirable and misleading. Williams' character shows that drama is something which does not necessarily equate to authenticity, neatly undermining the unspoken realistic trajectory of the costume film and also forcing the viewer to reassess their generic engagement with the past. Is authenticity necessary, and, if so, how much authenticity is necessary? Re-enactment in film – a double performance – foregrounds various issues about re-enacting in general and which allow us to suggest that the pursuit is extremely good at creating historical dissonance. *A Cock and Bull Story* allows the audience to see the filming of the battle, in effect a bunch of actors dressed up running around a field. Yet when the finished sequence is watched the audience is expected – and submits – to see the past, authentic or not. Similarly re-enacted sequences are evidently not contemporary footage so an audience is aware that those in the scenes are modern actors. When a well-known 'star' is part of these scenes – or is cast in a leading role in an historical or costume drama – the dissonance between the recognisable star cloaked in the recognisably historical fractures the fragile mimesis of the film (or at least induces the need to hold multiple ideas in the imagination simultaneously) (Figure 7.1).

   The key thing that the *Cock and Bull* section reminds us is that re-enacting is used regularly within the historical cultural industries, from film and documentary through to museum theatre. Cultural historical product is evidently 're-enactment' in some fashion and generally works on various levels from macro (the authentic extras in fight scenes) to micro (well-known stars in battle dress). Films, drama, television and games reanimate the past, be it literary or 'historical' and as such create a live performance of history. Historical documentary's use of re-enactment is particularly interesting. 'Re-enactment' has been used increasingly since 1990 by a wide variety of TV history documentaries both to dramatise narratives and to emphasise audience involvement (before 1990, it was relatively unseen). As Robert Hewison fulminates, 'Heritage is gradually effacing History by substituting an image of the past for its reality.'[21] This is clearly shown in Simon Schama's *History of Britain*, for instance, when the same footage (say, of men on horseback) is deployed in different contexts (see Chapter 1 for a discussion of how this metonymic style became ripe for parody). David Starkey's series accelerate the combination of documentary and drama. Rather than the use of cut-away shots favoured in *A History of Britain*, *Elizabeth* has long sequences in which actors playing the Queen, Cecil, Dudley and Mary Queen of Scots

Figure 7.1 Steve Coogan and Rob Brydon in *A Cock and Bull Story*, 2006, directed by Michael Winterbottom.

wander around country houses conversing with each other or mimic key portraits. Several of the scenes of re-enactment involve the reading of letters or eyewitness accounts, adding an evidentiary authenticity to the performances. The series, as with *A History of Britain*, blends historical 'fact' with conjecture, music and performance to create atmospheric and 'authentic' television. The use of what might be termed 'dramatic re-enactment' rather than Schama's staged cut-aways turns this history into drama, placing the historical events that Starkey's academic narration others into a discourse of performance; in particular, into a recognisably televisual entity.

In both these instances re-enactment is replacement, the visual and corporeal 'experienced' history becoming the authentic – in the same way that for Williams' auditors *it did not matter* that the scenes he hated were wrong, what was key was that they engaged with them as if they were. The use of re-enactment in documentary demonstrates again that this is a key trope in popular historical representation, that it is unremarkable, and argues a need or desire for a visualisation of the past (Figure 7.2). Documentary about periods for which there is archive footage rarely uses re-enactors, for instance, since the film can give an audience the necessary visual experience. The innate falseness of the practice is apparently fine with audiences, although it annoys professionals:

> Firstly, they are inherently phoney. They neither reconstruct the past nor the appearance of the past, but are inaccurate, distorted and misleading. For example, seventeenth-century people were different from twenty-first-century actors: shorter, thinner and often disfigured by disease and bad teeth. Actors portraying actual historical persons usually have scant resemblance to them.[22]

Figure 7.2 Simon Schama and Andy Serkis as Vincent van Gogh in *The Power of Art*, 2006, BBC.

Stearn's righteous anger at the inauthenticity of reconstruction in documentary ignores the imaginative element which is being invoked – possibly problematically – by reconstruction. An audience is aware of the dichotomy being offered them, but the inaccuracies are forgotten, somehow. The point is not that these dramatisations are wrong *per se* but that they happen at all; that an audience is happy to watch reconstructions in the knowledge that they are 'inherently phoney'. It inflects the documentary with a performance and a fictional element, gives it life. It isn't a 'problem' but the mode of doing documentary history now, and as a way of presenting historical evidence or creating a narrative is as biased and subjective as any other tool the professional historian might deploy.

Despite the reservations of academics, re-enactment in historical documentary is now commonplace and rarely commented upon as an unusual technique. It can range from mere illustrative backdrop to more complex embodiment. In the Brunel episode of *Great Britons* a pre-title sequence has presenter Jeremy Clarkson walking through the tunnel under the Thames that Brunel had built (the first under water), and in voiceover: 'They knew that the river had been dredged and there were holes in the river bed, they just didn't know where.'[23] All of a sudden, the wall breaks and Clarkson is flooded, going underwater as he narrates the death of those working with Brunel. The sequence emphasises the danger of the moment and its importance to Brunel's biography, but also presents Clarkson *as* Brunel, understanding his subject – and communicating that to us – through a bodily empathy. The episode uses artefacts to demonstrate Brunel's brilliance: diary, texts, mechanical objects and possessions which enable a reconstruction of the man's mind. This concern with objects is a favoured technique for reanimating individuals within the narrative of an historical documentary.

This need for visual authenticity raises a set of issues relating to realism. The trope of realism in cinema generally relates to an attempt at producing authenticity.[24] Documentaries which use re-enactment are striving to create a realist discourse – the battles are hardly in the style of Monty Python's 're-enactment of the Battle of Pearl Harbor by Mrs. Rita Fairbanks and the Battley Townswomen's Guild' or the National Theatre of Brent's comic replaying of the French Revolution. Documentary re-enactment gains authority through its 'realism' and confers an authority upon the proceedings. Certainly the widespread use of the style suggests a documentary audience that is comfortable with an evidently anachronistic and illusory set of visuals, an embodied history articulating and amplifying the words of the presenter while simultaneously drawing attention to the falseness of the exercise.

The substitution of Clarkson for Brunel suggests the keen importance of the experience being overlain on the personality or presenter. This is most commonly achieved through the representation of the historical locale. Historical documentary's emphasis on site – the presenter being in the actual spot, the *real* place – demonstrates a cultural move to the importance of location. The psychogeographic presumption that being somewhere can address a connection between then and now, or that location emphasises empathy, argues that visitors to the location themselves become re-enactors of a sort, desiring a physical linkage between themselves and the past. While ostensibly literary and intellectual history, Peter Ackroyd's *The Romantics* (BBC2, 2006) spent much airtime discussing the political and social context of the period *c.*1789–1830. The series, in common with general contemporary documentary practice, relied on presenter narration onsite, interspersed with reconstruction and some CGI images. The location-specific element of the series is fundamental to its *mise-en-scène*, and the importance of place in these films suggests that the physical heritage site is still fundamental to our understanding of history (even of the history of ideas such as 'liberty' or 'the imagination'). Ackroyd's encounter with the historical site is somehow fundamental to the programme, both in terms of his physical presence at the place of history and his explanation of what and how it *means*. He wanders around Paris talking about revolution, for instance, or visits the sites of London's radical presses. This presents something of a problem for the visual experience of the viewer: the site of the Bastille now is, after all, a roundabout. It might be suggested that this kind of history views the site as a palimpsest, a series of maps and spatial encounters overlaid on one another. You have to imagine what happened here, or engage in some kind of psychogeographical decoding of the site. A more everyday version of this kind of tagging would be that of the Blue Plaques, signs of a resonant past in a bustling present (and of course of a history which is predicated upon the individual, and generally refers to that person's contribution to social progression).[25] History somehow has to 'live' while acknowledging its very 'pastness'.

On television, Schama and Starkey achieve this historio-spatial effect mainly by going to places which are relatively unspoilt (even if they are just ruins). Occasionally they will use CGI to re-enact site details. Other series use such CGI to recreate the site, a further instance of the increased sophistication of television history in re-imagining the past. This kind of effect is used in *Battlefield Britain*, a BBC series which turns what are now open lands and pastures into digitalised killing fields:

> [The CGI graphics] allow us to show in meticulous detail the various episodes of the battles and bring alive the composition of battle lines and their movements. Understanding the ground a battle is fought on is an essential key to following its course.[26]

The series is historiographically conservative in its presentation of battles being 'key' to British history but innovative in emphasising the physical experience of warfare. The use of digitalised effect presents us with a further melding of the virtual with history; it also plugs directly into contemporary popular culture tropes of the presentation of war influenced by the mass digital battles of *The Lord of the Rings* (Peter Jackson: 2001–3). Of course war is a key cinematic trope anyway, and it is difficult to engage with these programmes without any number of filmic signifiers intruding between viewer and subject. On the one hand this series is about absence – there are few markers of these battles, and some of the programme consists of presenters Peter and Dan Snow marching around empty spaces physically demonstrating what happened where. However, talking-head interviews with actors playing soldiers, captains or leaders are used to give the action a human face. *Battlefield Britain* uses digitisation and reconstruction to create a visual representation, filling the space in rather than leaving it to the imagination. This has the effect of imposing a visual version of history and perceptive 'truth', although it is only one discourse of truth among many, as discussed below.

Location is particularly important to military historians, who regularly visit the scenes of battles to gain empathy. Richard Holmes, for instance, the presenter of *War Walks* (BBC2, 1997–2003), emphasises the importance of empathy to the historian: 'travelling by road in India at the tail of the monsoon told me as much about the man as *The Maratha War Papers of Arthur Wellesley*'.[27] This kind of argument suggests that physical empathy and enactment are crucial to understanding the mechanics of combat and the motivations of the key players, or at least as important as 'actual' historical evidence.[28] *War Walks* follows Holmes as he tracks around key sites; each show has some element of combat re-enactment undertaken by various companies and organisations. In this programme the urge to re-enact meshes with the need to physically be on the site of history, as practitioners physically personate their historical antecedents. Similarly, Peter and Dan Snow undergo 'Battle Experiences', ranging from firing a replica cannon to charging a modern police riot squad's 'shield wall' and flying a stunt plane in a 'dogfight', as well as deploying the familiar re-enactors to demonstrate combat detail. The accounts of battles also emphasise the feelings and motives of the soldiers, who must have 'regretted their decision to follow their ambitious duke'.[29]

There are layers of 'experience' here – the digital re-enactment, the showing of actual historical artefacts such as weapons, the personal experience of the avatar-presenter, the updating of combat conditions to make it understandable to a modern audience, the CGI visuals – which make these shows both empty of event (the battles have left little mark) but stuffed full of semiotically dynamic materials and possible experiences – imaginative and physical – for the viewer. The book accompanying the show demonstrates this complexity, shown in the dynamism of the page formatting. These include fact boxes, narrative prose, maps, images of artefacts, CGI images of battle charges, contemporary woodcuts and photographs, pictures of re-enactors, photographs of locations in the peaceful present day, and strange conjunctions such as the van Dyck portrait of Charles I next to a CGI version of his face (this is true of all leaders in the book and series, who have a 'real' and a 'CGI-real' entity).

The influence of the virtual on the presentation of historical information reached a high water mark with the screening on the Discovery Channel of *Virtual History: The Secret Plot to Kill Hitler*.[30] This exercise in virtual history was trumpeted as a watershed, and it is true that the programme was innovative. However, this innovation is troubling on several levels.[31] The programme narrates the events of 20 July 1944, the day that rebellious factions of the German army attempted to assassinate Hitler. Colonel von Stauffenberg, a discontented senior officer, planted a bomb which narrowly failed to kill the German leader. The programme uses standard narrative techniques common to this kind of piece – historians telling the story and giving context, testimony by von Stauffenberg's son, contemporary news footage and photographs. Computer imaging is deployed to demonstrate the geography of the situation and to show the viewer three-dimensional plans of the various settings (Roosevelt's train, Churchill's bedroom, Stalin's dacha, Hitler's Eastern command bunker). The historiography of the programme is conservative, concentrating both on the key importance to events of the war of particular personalities and on 'what if' scenario tropes wondering about the consequences of a successful army coup.

Yet what set *Virtual History* apart was the attempt to 'recreate real historical events':

> By using look-a-like actors and the latest computer animation history's most famous characters are brought back to life in the style of authentic film archive. This gives the viewer the feeling of being present on a crucial day in history.[32]

The Discovery Channel made the ingenious claim that 'In effect, it recreates archive footage that was never shot at the time.'[33] The programme creates a visual narrative and fills in the gaps, relying heavily on personal eyewitness testimony. It is an attempt to 'to bring the viewer right in to absolutely leave him believing he was there'.[34] Re-enactment and dramatic rendition are no longer sufficient; this style of film-making mimics the actual footage of the archive, striving for a visual authenticity.

In contrast to such recreative industry, Ackroyd's series takes a new approach in order to emphasise the relationship between then and now. The central tenet of the series was that 'The Romantics are important because they helped to define, and indeed to create, the modern world. They helped to fashion the way in which we all now think and imagine.'[35] In pursuit of this, the programmes deploy what might be termed anachronistic reconstruction. Actors perform the roles of various key players – reading from the works of Byron, Wordsworth, Rousseau – while clearly in modern-day environs. Road signs and graffiti are used as signage and props. An impressionistic camera rarely settles, even on Ackroyd as the central performer, somehow making him more an addition to the scene than a focus (often the actors are in the background over his shoulder, again effacing the line between reconstruction and presenter). These effects suggest the contemporary resonance of the Romantics' thoughts, the continuously evolving presence and importance of their ideas. The actors quote at length, and these lines are footnoted at the bottom corners of the screen. These texts, the building blocks of contemporary society according to Ackroyd, come to be physical things. Their ideas are not simply cerebral but have effect, and this has the consequence of making the writings somehow analogous to the historic place or artefact. They are sites of resonance that layer our social existence, and Ackroyd's series is psychogeographic insofar as it physically and psychically lays bare the textual origins of the contemporary mind.

Living theatre: museums, live and Living History

Similar to re-enactment, Living History provides first-person interpretation of the past allied with a sense of the educational value of that performance of history.[36] The process is generally interactive, with an audience engaging with the performer to create a dynamic relationship. Goodacre and Baldwin, advocates for 'peopling historical space', argue that:

> the establishment of a relationship with the past is most realised when there is a representation of people in the past to be related to ... the fabric of a building or a collection of artefacts cannot be fully understood unless the people who inhabited the space in the past and created, used and disposed of the artefacts are considered.[37]

The material artefacts are only given meaning, in this view, when considered in relation to people rather than to a more amorphous historicalness. Performance animates the artefact or place. The involvement of the audience with the performance encourages a different style of learning and engagement with the past, particularly when improvisation is involved. Such interaction – as an active or a passive audience member – articulates a personal response to the past, and stimulates new ways of learning. At the same time it can confuse or embarrass a visitor – changing the traditional relationship with a collection.[38]

Reconstructed and living history is, for Raphael Samuel, a prefiguring of 'some of the favourite conceits – or genial tropes – of postmodernism. In place of facts it offers us images – hyperrealities – in which the old is faked up to be more palpable than the here-and-now'.[39] The presenting of knowledge is often as pre-scriptive and problematic as any taxonomising museum, yet is presented as 'experi-ence' rather than 'education'. It is no longer scholarship but 'learning', an ongoing lifestyle decision. However, as Jacqueline Tivers points out, 'Living' history is not necessarily interested in education or finance: 'to this extent, "living history" stands in some respects to one side of the general commodification of history which creates heritage, although it may well be used to commercial advantage by tourism managers'.[40] This sense that Living History might stand outside of the commercialisation of history – in the same way that private re-enactment similarly might dissent from this tendency – is key to the phenomenon's inde-pendence. Similar to re-enactment, Living History participants strive to lose themselves in historicity:

> It is interesting to consider *how conscious* are these re-enactors of taking a role. They seem to work very hard to make their role *un*conscious, and in that sense might perhaps not be described as 'performer' [… they] remain in character until they leave.[41]

Skansen in Stockholm was the first Living History museum, using musicians and crafts people to create a community. Opened in 1891, and still welcoming around 1 million visitors a year, the open-air site consists of historical buildings with live interpretation including Ironmongery, Baking and Furniture Making. The buildings come from all over the country and so the site is the national history in microcosm, a kind of simulated metonym of Swedish history. This is the case in most open-air museums, where an historical site is brought together, constructed from architecture formerly scattered around the country. There is no reason that this should be seen as particularly unusual – after all, most museums draw their collections from a range of geographical sources – but the immersiveness of the design and experience of the open-air museums effaces this range somewhat. The rendering of the past is hybrid, with a range of time per-iods represented.[42] The overall settings vary in time, too, with the Ironmonger's shop mainly in 1930s style and the Bakery functioning like it is the 1870s. This is what Raphael Samuel terms, with some affection, 'historical bricolage'.[43] Other important museums followed Skansen in the presentation of rural-industrial life and traditions, including Old World Wisconsin, Ironbridge, Beamish and Colonial Williamsburg. These museums are part of a renewed interest in folk and social history and the representation of ordinary people's lives: 'oriented toward the collection, preservation, and display of artefacts relating to the daily lives, customs, rituals, and traditions of non-elite social strata'.[44] Beamish, for instance, in the North-East of England, tells the story of the people by focusing on 1825 and 1913. The museum prides itself on its innovative and immersive approach:

You will find here no glass cases and few labels. Within our buildings you will find costumed people who are trained to talk to visitors and to answer their questions. The staff are proud of their heritage. We believe that the reality of human beings is better than technological virtual reality. It is this belief that distinguishes us from other museums.[45]

This faith in the educational virtue of historical embodiment – 'the reality of human beings' – demonstrates an underlying pedagogical investment in performed reconstruction of historical periods. Beamish's constitution strives to combine entertainment and education: 'Inform our visitors, entertain our visitors, educate and involve our visitors, without compromising our historical integrity.'[46] Similarly, Ironbridge Gorge's mission statement talks of enriching the visitor's experience through live demonstration and innovative presentation.[47] Like other open-air museums Beamish's buildings are imported from around the region. Gaby Porter has argued that the implicit authenticity inherent in the Beamish approach is problematic, insofar as the museum still provides a particularised model of social relations.[48] These museums are immensely popular. The Beamish site attracts around 350,000 visitors a year; Williamsburg attracted 767,000 visitors in 2005. American open-air museums like Williamsburg aim for complete immersion in the past.[49] The sites combine education with experience, emphasising first-person historical interpretation and first-person engagement.

It might be argued that waxworks and animatronics have been embodying history in museums for decades, and certainly the desire for a humanoid element in displays to animate the artefacts has been reflected in standard practice since the beginning of the nineteenth century. Both types of model involve a conscious dissonance, being obviously not human but embodying and representing a clear replica of the past. Museum theatre, or 'content-based educational performances', provides museums with a new way of introducing and interpreting their collections.[50] They are generally interactive and can be used in a site-specific fashion or for outreach work. Practitioners professionalised in the 1990s, with the formation of the International Museum Theatre Alliance in 1990 and IMTHAL-Europe in 1999. IMTHAL defines its members' work in the following way:

> Museum theatre involves engaging visitors in the willing suspension of disbelief – in pretend, or imagination – to enhance the educational experience that happens within a museum. It ranges from storytelling and living-history interpretation, to musical and dramatic presentations, to creative dramatics, puppetry, mime and much more.[51]

Museum theatre therefore is keen to foster educational engagement particular to the museum's ethos. Key is the notion that the particular type of theatrical technique used relates to the particular educational aims of the museum.[52] Much museum theatre differs from Living History insofar as rather than replicate an experience to be viewed – even in an interactive way – as part of the collection, as an artefact, theatre is an adjunct which amplifies. It is a way of introducing narrative and possibility in order to enliven and animate the collection, and has been demonstrated to be extremely effective particularly in engaging children with museums.[53]

Getting medievalish: anachronism, faires and banquets

The Society for Creative Anachronism, Inc. was founded in 1966 in California and incorporated as a non-profit corporation in 1968. It presently has around 30,000 members worldwide. Creative anachronism is defined as that which 'takes the best qualities of the Middle Ages and selectively re-creates them in the modern world'.[54] A members-organisation with a constitution and subscription fees, they have their own email programme (*Known World Mail*), a sophisticated system of governance including ministers and royalty, and a specific cartographic way of conceptualising the world.[55] There are currently 19 independent administrative kingdoms (although this number varies), all ruled by monarchs who have won their position through combat. Each member creates their own 'persona' (although they are not allowed to be famous fictional or actual people) and constructs a biography and context for themselves. The group does not create a specific time in history, being more interested in general impression. In Board discussion the following was suggested:

> Our target market is:
> Any person who is in the taste culture that includes all of those who, at any time, have been interested in fantasy and SF, gaming, combat games (laser tag and such) or any similar activity that lies in the area of Romantic pursuits. More specifically within that group our prime age ranges are the 14–18 and 19–24 year olds and the baby boomers ... I view the SCA 'product' as primarily being an experience, as opposed to a good or even a traditional service.[56]

The notion of a 'taste culture' – positing the Society as a subculture or lifestyle choice rather than a specific re-enactment – is key here. The historical element is not important in this self-definition, rather the demographic profile is fantasy, combat and SF. The Society has its roots in science fiction (the name was coined by an originary member, SF novelist Marion Zimmer Bradley), and blends fantasy with re-enactment. However, there is a key nostalgic element in the fantasy: '"Romantic" is a term that derives from the period of Victorian times (and earlier) where there was often a yearning for something else in reaction to the perceived alienation of modernity.'[57] The SCA's approach to the past as a desired experience which is key to the formation of a like-minded subculture (importantly with an associated economic element) demonstrates that the physical re-enactment community is not wholly interested in authenticity or necessarily combat. 'History' – heritage – here is something to be consumed as an experiential leisure form.

Audience physical engagement with the past – a kind of controlled re-enactment taking place at times more associated with passive leisure – takes multiple guises.

Medieval Fayres and Festivals are commonplace throughout the UK and the USA, with jousting, stalls, dancing, and musicians. History is literally consumed here as visitors purchase mead and historicised food. This commodification of the past is Hewison's effacing 'heritage' in action. The festivals emphasise fun and family activities. Medievalism is nothing new – the fetishising of the Middle Ages has antecedents easily discernible to the beginning of the nineteenth century.[58] Re-enactors have been visiting the period since at least the Eglinton Tournament of 1839. Yet the combination of a standard medievalist approach – celebrating minstrels, mead, romance and courtliness – with the personating of the past and the active bodily participation of non-professional and casual amateurs is new. Fairs are a particularly English form of countryside expression, so such events nationalise historicity by enlisting it to foster a particular sense of localised community. While there is an educative element to the events, fairs are attended traditionally on free holidays and so therefore the attitude of the visitors is different to, say, those visiting a museum or gallery. The biggest event in the UK is at Herstmonceux Castle and has been going since 1992 – 30,000 visitors attend the annual three-day festival.

In the USA, Renaissance Festivals and Faires are similarly popular (around 170 are listed by the Renaissance Festival website), and they have been running since the mid-1960s.[59] They are much larger in scale: the Maryland Renaissance Faire covers 25 acres and attracts 225,000 visitors over three weeks; the Pennsylvania Renaissance Faire attracts 250,000 over 12 weekends; the Bristol, Wisconsin Renaissance Faire – 'Where Fantasy Rules!' – had a highpoint of 400,000 over seven weekends in 1990.[60] The authenticity of the events is less important than in the UK, and they combine historical periods (Medieval and Renaissance) with fantasy elements, circuses, zoos, and particularly, with Pirates. The co-founder of the Bristol Faire, Bonnie Jo Shapiro, argues 'We can't be too authentic. We have to entertain ... clearly this is an entertainment vehicle.'[61] The American Faires demonstrate the ways in which authentic 'living' history and re-enactment are being overtaken by culturally-informed models of 'the past', particularly via film (the *Lord of the Rings* and *Pirates of the Caribbean* trilogies being the most important analogues here). The Faires emphasise an Amusement park ethos of entertainment and generic revelry rather than education. Certainly the key experience is sensual – visitors eat, drink, shop, and watch dramatised shows from belly dancing to singing plague victims. There are levels of visitor involvement – from the purely voyeuristic to those who become 'playtrons' by hiring costumes and taking part. 'Playtrons' engage in an amateur style with the experience, representing a staging post between professional entertainer and visitor; at the same time the element of choice is important, and the 'playtron' can at any point disengage with history, or choose another pathway. Hiring a costume is similar to creating an avatar in an Massive Multiplayer Online Role Playing Game (MMORPG) although importantly there is still a physical embodiment of the historicised figure (see Chapter 9).

At Bristol recently a 'Cleavage Contest' was rated PG-13, and the producer claimed: 'We have very definite rules of what part of the cleavage can be exposed and what cannot. It's not improper, but it is voluptuous.'[62] History is the originary point for these simulacra of the past but the Faires soon move away from that, turning the historical into a set of recognisably buxom tropes: competition, entertainment, food. Similarly to the SCA, these events emphasise community – there is a virtual-social networking site Renaissance Faire World, for instance, that combines the economic impetus of Faires with the creation of re-enactment personae by inserting the user into a virtual community where they can be targeted by Faire organisers and entertainers.[63] Physical Faires have also joined with MMORGs such as *World of Warcraft* to create hybrid virtual scenarios. Key is the desire for historicised entertainment and the deployment of the past as a commodity trope, as an experience entertainment leisure model that can be easily sold to consumers. Visitors are paying for the embodied experience, but are quite aware of their insertion into the theme park atmosphere. The Faires have been compared to Disneyland and in their anodyne 'theming' of history they create a similar experience, both authentic and unreal. The historical has a tenuous connection with the actual past but the spectacle is much more important than accuracy, and 'Medieval' or 'Renaissance' come to mean the events of the Faires rather than have any attachment to chronological periods. The events become self-constructing, and self-referential. This is history turned into commodity, 'heritage' in action.

MTV's intentionally dumb stunt show *Jackass* has attempted to undermine the whole Faire process by introducing a dwarf dressed as a dragon to a Medieval Faire, filming him being chased by a knight – they also have a strain of medieval combat japes, including BMX jousting and gladiatorial tennis. The gleeful mindless violence of the *Jackass* approach (and the updating of conflict) reject the coded, commodified version of the past to be found at medieval entertainment sites or in the formalised revisiting of the past found at a re-enactment performance. It is random and violent, and this is both compelling and – at the risk of overanalysing them – more real (or less disciplined, in a Foucauldian sense).

A development of the Medieval Faire is the Medieval Banquet, a staple of heritage sites around the UK. While the authentic heritage setting is generally important to the experience, there is a Medieval Banquet restaurant in a purpose-built building in central London with nightly feasting and special events. Medieval banquets encourage the participants to indulge in a bodily fantasy of pastness, transporting themselves physically through costume and eating. While such banqueting re-enactment does limp into the Tudor period, it is worth noting that these meals are generally particularly associated with the Middle Ages, and with a set of modes associated in popular culture with that period. Customers are after an 'authentic' experience which is historically othered from themselves but attends to particular tropes – mead, buxom wenches, minstrels, jesters, olde worlde-style speech and haunches of venison. The experience is empathic and all-encompassing, addressing all senses: 'At a banquet you will step straight into the pages of Elizabethan history and savour a unique atmosphere that has been centuries in the making.'[64] The experience is two-fold, then – empathic (actually stepping back into the past, albeit a past which is conceptualised as a text), and ephemerally immersive (the ancient atmosphere). There is almost a teleology going on here which suggests that history has been a continual process leading up to the moment of the individual customer's consumption of it.

Eating the past is a commonplace way of literally consuming it. Since the publication of the best-selling *Pleyn Delit* in 1979, historical cookery books have become commonplace and are particularly to be found in heritage site book-shops. They allow the user to perform domestic duties in the style of medieval, Renaissance and other historical periods. This kind of historical enactment invites the audience or readership of a book to engage with history physically – both through taking on skill sets and by eating. Books such as *Shakespeare's Kitchen: Renaissance Recipes for the Contemporary Cook* (2003) and English Heritage's *Cooking Through the Ages* series (encompassing Victorian, Tudor, Georgian, Roman, Stuart, Ration Book) which splices history with recipes, encourage the consumption of historical information while consuming historically. Historicity in these collections is the action of using particular techniques in order to make something which is familiar – insofar as it is edible and made of recognisable ingredients – but strange. These books have scholarly impetus – introducing key terms such as the prevalence of *potage* – and citing their sources.[65] They are interested in introducing historicised cuisine and authentic cooking techniques to a modern audience. Some provide useful tips like 'Rather than trying to hull and pound whole wheat grain, use pre-prepared kibbled or cracked wheat' to enable a modern replica of a historical diet, although *Pleyn Delit* and others tend to eschew this approach, instead underlining authenticity.[66] At the same time, the books emphasise a revisionary historiography, recovering mainly women from the margins and demonstrating an interest in the minutiae and detail of histor-ical life (as is demonstrated, for instance, in *Take a Thousand Eggs or More*, an edition of BL Harleian MSS 279 and 4016).[67] These books are of a piece with Living History initiatives at heritage sites emphasising the domestic and day-to-day life rather than the state apartments – although these sites, 'one of the few vehicles for arrangement and display of artefacts traditionally associated with women' are popular, they have been criticised for being 'often inaccurate and unrepresentative, idealised images of the way we think people ought to have lived'.[68]

The historical cookery phenomenon has begun to combine with documentary, creating a strange cultural-historical coherence. Television chef Hugh Fearnley-Whittingstall's DVD *Treats from the Edwardian Country House* (2003), for instance, is a companion to the reality history television series with period recipes, cleaning, gardening and beauty tips. The DVD allows the viewer to partake of the foods that the participants in the series did, so their status as historical avatar is com-promised – the viewer replaces them. Similar are the BBC series *Carluccio and the Renaissance Cookbook* (2007), *The Victorian Kitchen* (1989) and the *Victorian Kitchen Garden* (1987). In this latter, using only traditional tools, the presenter Harry Dodson grew and cooked period fruits and vegetables. The show combines three strands of lifestyle programming – cookery, gardening and history – into a re-enactment and recreation of historical behaviours. *The Victorian Kitchen Garden* is about empathy – understanding, through sensual and bodily engagement with the past.

A stranger domestic re-enactment is that undergone by the families of the Channel 4 reality TV show *Bringing Up Baby* (2007) in which six families apply modified historicised childcare theories to their children for the first three months of their life.[69] It is a hybrid of the popular life-changing 'achievement' shows – historical ones like *That'll Teach 'Em* (Channel 4, 2003–5, in which children are taught according to 1950s state education rules), or the contemporary *Brat Camp* (Channel 4, 2005–6) – and childcare intervention programmes such as *Supernanny* (Channel 4, 2003–). The show explains: 'Every decade since the war has had its own advice when it comes to childcare. Depending on when he was born this baby would have been brought up completely differently.'[70] They take elements from the practices of Frederic Truby King (1950s), Benjamin Spock (1960s) and Jean Liefloff (1970s). The experiment puts influential historical methods into competition with each other to find out which is best. Much like the other reality history shows, the modes of action are text-based, as each family is given a manual. The families are under constant CCTV scrutiny to see how things work out. There is a certain bodily re-enactment undergone by the parent – particularly in terms of breast-feeding – but which is actively inscribed upon the developing mind and body of the child. The show posits that socio-cultural and historical difference can be traced in fundamental medical theory, and that the experiencing – and broadcasting – of these differences can allow us to come to understand a fundamental truth. The families are the audience's avatars, re-enacting historical actions in order to educate.

8 Recycling culture and re-enactment/cultural re-enactment

Music, performance and remakes

This chapter is a development of the previous, analysing similar phenomena (re-enactment and re-embodiment of past practices and events) taking place in a different cultural context and therefore has a new set of legitimacies associated with it. While musical historicism has been around for centuries, the reuse of instruments and Historically Informed Performance is a relatively new phenomenon, at least insofar as it informs both academia and public fora.[1] Historically Informed Performance is linked to the levelling practice of the Early Music revival, which attempted to undermine the starchiness and formality of most modern classical music performance, drawing on oral and folk traditions. Historically Informed Performance similarly moves to deny the key importance of the academic-composer, is performance- and experience-driven, and sits at odds with mainstream musicology. Such practice suggests that a return to the original instruments and performance style can heighten contrast, and emphasis tonal smoothness and transparency. As John Butt argues, Historically Informed Performance in some ways claims a transcendental text which can be approached through authentic performance rather than an artefact which can and does change in time – sometimes termed *Werktreue*.[2] This style re-enacts, using props, the cultural product and experience through a combination of research and performance. Music is an ephemeral as well as material phenomenon, and the assumptions of Historically Informed Performance often suggest that the ear is itself ahistorical, which it manifestly is not; the paradox of re-enactment is threefold: the trio of performer/performance/audience are inauthentic while all at some level striving for or desiring historicity. There is a very literal consumption going on here, in terms of a sense responding to stimuli; this is bodily historicity. The experience here is a channelling of multiple things – material object, ephemeral sound, research into technique, and audience expectation. Listening to such a performance is simultaneously 'old' – as it is the 'authentic' experience – and self-evidently in the 'now'.

Historically Informed Performance has become a key part of a tourist experience as can be seen, for instance, in performances in locations such as churches. This reconstructionist drive towards a more authentic experience is also evident in the rebuilding of Shakespeare's Globe on Bankside in London. The Globe was built between 1993 and 1997 on the site (just 225m away) of the original theatre on the Thames, costing around £30 million. The site houses a theatre, education complex and exhibition. It is therefore tourist attraction, heritage centre, cultural venue and educational establishment simultaneously.[3] As well as being built in the same place – again demonstrating the skewed motive of location – the theatre was built in the same style, being thatched, open-roofed, and the internal auditorium being as close a replica as could be made.[4] Audiences 'experience' plays there, and the authenticity of the surroundings both helps scholars and actors to understand the dynamics of staging and also gives tourists and theatregoers a sense of getting the play unvarnished, and in a version closer to that of Shakespeare's own.[5] Of course this feeds off transcendental 'not of an Age but for all time' Bardolatry; as Graham Holderness points out, Shakespeare has become more a tourist attraction than anything else: '[Stratford] is the spiritual heart of the Shakespeare myth: and the institutions of bardolatry and quasi-religious worship are the structures holding that myth in place.'[6] The Shakespeare myth fed the building of the Globe as a worthy monument to a national treasure; as such it is a museum as much as anything for the pseudo-living work of the playwright.[7] It is an ersatz experience – particularly now the various theatrical experiments it was built for (all-female and all-male companies, authentic costume) have been forgotten about. The Globe has become a theatre in its own right, though, staging newly commissioned drama in addition to Shakespeare, which then becomes a strange hybrid – a modern piece written to be performed on an archaic stage.

Globe performances are re-enactments in the same way that Historically Informed Performance is, but the dynamics are complex and challenging. The Globe's position, next to the Tate Modern Art Museum, exemplifies contemporary recycling of monuments and a concomitant flexibility about cultural experience and historicity. The Globe is mock-Tudor, quite literally aping an old style; the Tate is a modern exhibition housed in a reused power station. The Tate's building is the more authentic but it is not being put to its correct usage; the Globe is unreal but built for a particular purpose. The fact that tourists and audiences can happily move between both modes demonstrates a sophistication of engagement with cultural artefacts and their housing.

There is a kind of fetishistic equivalent in popular music – with the selling of memorabilia and the reuse of iconic instruments – but this kind of recycling of practice to enhance and change music more finds its equivalent in pastiche and the actual reusing of key motifs, either through shadowing practice, reusing sounds, or sampling. Retro-musical style is common, with many bands accused of channelling their forbears. Most new rock movements, for instance, owe much to a specific musical moment, and this has also often led to the serving of law suits for plagiarism.

Sampling has been around since the early 1980s and is a way of creating a back-beat in order that an MC can rap over it; in this manifestation it is used to make something new. Sampling is defiantly modern, insofar as it deploys a key new technology – the synthesizer or computer – to use the old to create the new, albeit with a key element of recognition. Since its origins in early 1980s hip-hop artists such as DJ Shadow (*Entroducing*, 1996), Girl Talk (*Night Ripper*, 2008), M/A/R/R/S ('Pump Up the Volume', 1987), the Beastie Boys (*Paul's Boutique*, 1989) and the Go! Team (*Thunder! Lightning! Strike!*, 2004) have created albums or songs made nearly entirely of samples knitted together to make new music. This is a patchwork or collage of inauthenticity, the construction of something from the innumerable tissues of existing culture. Yet at the same time the historical text is bent out of shape in order to become part of something previously unseen, something new rather than an artefact which mimics the old. Sampling is electronic part re-enactment, performance which recycles to make 'new'; this marks it as clearly different from the remix, which reorganises. It is similar to the cover version, although without its status as recycling being foregrounded in the same way. Cover versions obviously draw on their original and simply fold the historical artefact back into itself. Mark Ronson, for instance, has a stalled career as a rap artist but his cover album *Version* (2007) is huge selling; winners of television talent shows such as *X-Factor* or *American Pop Idol* generally release cover versions first as they have a clear niche market due to their recognisability and instant nostalgia value. The 'new' versions gain legitimacy from recognition and renewal, but are often simply recycling the tropes of the past into nostalgic commodity with surface value and little else.

A more obvious re-working and mimicry are performed by the tribute band. Tribute bands are a large industry, having been growing in popularity for about 20 years – they now stage their own festivals and have a large live following.[8] Tribute bands again demonstrate a demand for knowingly 'false' enactment of events and cultural texts. The bands faithfully replicate the music and the look of their chosen forbears. As Allan Moore argues, the notion of 'authenticity' in music is at the very least contested.[9] The key distinction between tribute bands and cover bands is that somehow the tribute band is presenting a more concrete, more authentic re-creation of the key texts.[10] 'Tribute' bands have much in common with the Historically Informed Performance movement – re-enacting songs live as faithfully as possible to their original setting and performance in order to reanimate them. In this case the historically informed element is contextual – to do with costume and attitude rather than the use of antique instruments – and technical, insofar as the bands do not innovate in their rendering of songs (to do so would be to lose the point of the exercise). As the Complete Beatles claim, 'Performance is totally live – no dodgy backing tracks or gadgets, just a totally authentic sound capturing the atmosphere and excitement from those fab early years!'[11] The experience here is both in the performance and in the 'authentic sound', a combination of Historically Informed Performance and ephemeral 'live'-ness. Bands have become abstracted from their actual manifestation as 'tributes' and become entities in their own right – in 2004 Led Zepagain were extremely pleased to have Jimmy Page, Led Zeppelin's guitarist, visit one of their LA gigs; Blondie mimics Into the Bleach include a note of support from Debbie Harry on their website and quote drummer Clem Burke: 'Sam can play Debbie. Pitch Perfect'.[12] Several claim that they have been officially endorsed by their originals, and Oasis tribute band No Way Sis had a top 20 single and stood in for the 'actual' band in Paris when they cancelled a gig.[13] The tribute band here becomes a stand in for the 'actual'; the real musicians are relatively irrelevant, and it is the product – performed in an authentic style – that is important.

Tribute bands intersect as a recent cultural phenomenon with globally successful nostalgia jukebox musicals such as *Buddy* (based on the songs of Buddy Holly, 1995–), *We Will Rock You* (Queen, 2002–), *Mamma Mia!* (ABBA, 1999–), *Never Forget* (Take That, 2007) and *Our House* (Madness, 2002). *Mamma Mia!* has toured globally and been seen by 10 million people as well as grossing over $1bn and being made into a film; *We Will Rock You* has run for six years in the same theatre as well as opening across the world. The primary text which these musicals look to is *Grease!* (1972; film 1978), a pastiche created in order to channel nostalgia for the 1950s. The musicals are vehicles of nostalgia, an 'event' in which the desired musical texts are importantly delivered live and in a public forum (rather than listened to alone and in privacy).[14]

Over the past decade, too, the remake has become a clear film genre, with directors re-shooting and recycling films from the art house *Psycho* (Alfred Hitchcock, 1960/Gus van Sant, 1998) to horror films like *The Texas Chainsaw Massacre* (Tobe Hooper, 1974/Marcus Nispel, 2003). As this suggests, cultural re-enactment and the reworking of the past are key to how we understand contemporary society. One of the biggest web phenomena of recent years is YouTube, a video-sharing site which initially began with people sharing their own versions of themselves performing classic music videos and film.[15] Undermining cultural hegemony by first 'playing', then sharing, cultural product, users of YouTube demonstrated a desire for DIY content, and an interest in reanimating or reworking that pervades contemporary life. Frederic Jameson suggests that it is this pastiching – the continual reworking of the dead tropes of art – which contributes to the unbroken surfaceness of postmodernism, yet he is working on a model of reified cultural hegemony whereas these YouTube models challenge and are dissenting voices – they fracture culture, and are, as Michel de Certeau might argue, strategies for forcing the historical and the cultural into becoming part of everyday life ('habitable') and therefore resistable. If culture and history are things which are not at arm's length but which might be appropriated and their emptiness demonstrated, then the power is in some ways returned to the user. Certainly cultural re-enactment might provide a political space for challenging hegemonies, as is suggested in the next section.

The first time as atonement, the second time as art: Lifeline and Jeremy Deller

The Lifeline Expedition Project is a religious organisation which seeks to make amends for the slave trade through education and a series of public physical apologies, including symbolic re-enactment. Europeans and Americans march in replica chains and yokes to symbolise their apology for the slave trade. They travel the slave trails and present themselves as ambassadors of reconciliation and apology, a 'journey to forgiveness and freedom'.[16] The marchers make their apology in the form of a kneeling confession and then are forgiven and their chains lifted. There have been expeditions to many of the Caribbean ports (Barbados, Martinique and Guadeloupe, Curacao) and two visits to West Africa (Gambia and Benin). There have also been walks in America through famous slave areas and markets, and, in the UK, the Sankofa Reconciliation walk followed the route of Thomas Clarkson in 1787 between the three major British slave ports (London, Bristol, and Liverpool), although this was a commemoration and not undertaken in chains. Such projects intersect with other types of ritualised pilgrimage, commemorative actions which have agency for the participant as well as a wider significance. The marchers posit themselves as representative of an entire set of nations and through their symbolic actions they hope to atone for historical crimes. This is re-enactment in the most metonymic and general of ways, and is an extraordinary moment which demonstrates the cultural power of re-performance, its ability to represent and mean in dynamic fashion, but also its tendency towards triteness. In order to actively configure an 'apology' for violence and brutality, the slaving nations have to be personated and bodily punished. The entirety of the trade can be rendered in one set of actions, but a set of actions whose significance is extremely broad and sweeping. In this action of commemorative re-enactment there is a possibility of reconciliation and therefore a move to understand the past and to forgive. Re-enactment here is not inert but has agency of a kind, a dynamic which is no longer representative but active.

No less politically, installation and video artists are increasingly interested in the re-enacting of historical moments to scrutinise social interaction and reflect upon postmodern mediated society. The fact that visual artists are interested in the notion of re-enactment demonstrates how as a concept it pervades the contemporary imagination. The Institute of Contemporary Art in London has staged a series of artistic re-enactments including the work of Iain Forsyth and Jane Pollard and, in 2007, Jo Mitchell's restaging of the famous Einstürzende Neubauten 1984 gig (the band attempted to drill through the floor). Re-performing events like this is what Pollard and Forsyth have been doing for a decade or so, in work which reflects upon the fetishising of performance, mimesis, and turns the artist into mimic. Their works in this series, *The Smiths is Dead* (1997), *Rock 'n' Roll Suicide* (1998) and *File Under Sacred Music* (2006) re-enact important musical performances – the Smiths' final gig, David Bowie killing off his Ziggy Stardust persona, the Cramps live at Napa Mental Institute.[17] These pieces see historical events as cultural readymades, to be reconceptualised and reworked (they also re-examine the works of key artists such as Bruce Nauman in a similar way). These re-enacted sequences commemorate events which have already become fetishised in the popular imagination.

Other conceptual artists have approached re-enactment in multiple ways. Sharon Hayes' *Symbionese Liberation Army (SLA) Screeds #13, 16, 20 & 29* is a re-performance of Patty Hearst's audio transmissions in April 1974, and reflects a kind of personation of the icon and a sense of the artist as chameleon/subject in the same vein as Cindy Sherman.[18] Romauld Karmakar's film *Das Himmler Projekt* (2001) takes Himmler's 'Posen' Speech and reperforms it to remind the viewer of its innate horror and to defamiliarise the figure of Himmler, already too easily inserted into the system of signs. Manfred Zapatka, the actor 'playing' Himmler, is what Karmakar calls a 'sonar' device inserted into the text to make it speak again.[19] Rod Dickinson recreated the FBI's 'Psychotronic Warfare', a mix of repetitive sounds used on the Branch Davidians in Waco, in order to reconsider the initial violent event as well as reflect on the brutality of state control (something that Jeremy Deller, below, also explores – both considering how acts of violence can be smoothed into historical narrative). Dickinson has also re-enacted other traumatic scenes in order to explore motivation and crowd dynamics, including the Milgram Obedience Experiment, and the Jonestown massacre.[20] He argues that art should be deploying and interrogating such tropes, as 'popular culture invests in forms of re-enactment, such as crime reconstructions on TV, it's a cultural convention that's now familiar to us and which we understand'.[21] This key claim argues a sophistication on the part of the viewer and an ability to conceptualise re-enactment intelligently; it therefore has profound implications for notions of 'performance' in contemporary culture.

A similarly politicised form of artistic re-enactment was Jeremy Deller's (2001) Turner Prize-winning restaging of the Battle of Orgreave. The clash between police and striking miners in 1984 was a turning point of the Miner's Strike. Deller restaged the battle on the original site. The battle was planned by Howard Giles, who had been director of events at English Heritage, and the film of the event directed by Mike Figgis; it was screened on Channel 4. Some of those who took part were former miners and policemen who had been at the original event. The re-enactment makes an iconic moment in labour history into a piece of art film. It also suggests that in terms of key moments of history to re-enact this is as important as the Civil War or WWII in terms of socio/cultural/political development (indeed, that it was part of another civil war itself). This is history that is not taught, almost folk-history being revived and re-shown. At the same time the formal issues associated with the event highlight contradiction, chaos and containment.[22] The enactment was part therapy for the local community and a reinvoking of a particular time. Deller argued, 'It's going to take more than an art project to heal wounds ... [This is] about confronting something and not being afraid to look at it again and discuss it.'[23] Deller's attempt here is creative re-enactment – to use the replayed event to try to understand further and to connect to the past rather than a postmodern pastiche, intent on smoothing over troubled histories.

The 'extreme historian': reinhabiting the past

Re-enactment is not just about costume and performance, however; it also has a spatial element. Certain types of re-enactment or historicised performance emphasise their locational uniqueness in order to sell themselves as special. Since 1994, Heritage sites have been able to obtain marriage licenses, for instance, and weddings commonly take place in historic buildings and museums (see also Chapter 15 for a discussion of the economic reuse of the museum space). Couples may nowadays choose to get married in medievalised dress with strolling minstrels at a Renaissance Faire, or in an ancient castle with historical surroundings, or at Ironbridge Gorge museum having ridden to the venue in a horse and cart. The Historical Houses Association lists 261 of its properties, for instance, as being open for weddings. The 'authenticity' which old buildings confer upon a marriage ceremony (both in terms of the age of the site and the couple's ability to find a unique venue) is key here. The male members of the wedding party often wear morning dress, an historicised affectation which emphasises the uniqueness of the occasion and the seriousness which the historical trope invests it with. There is a brief reflection to be made here on the secularisation of society in which the church has been replaced as venue of sanctification. Heritage venues, shorn of their ideological semiology (as in the case of industrial sites or stately homes, for instance) become sites which offer a historio-cultural gravitas purely because of their age, heritage status, and architectural significance.

Similarly, conversions of old buildings into residential apartments tend to ignore their former employment, hiding them behind heritage euphemisms and 'original' features. The vogue for conversions signals a peculiar involvement in the historical environment. The historical genre here in its architectural manifestation adds a recognisable class to property; it is a sense of history present in the contemporary. Fetishising old factory buildings, churches or warehouses by turning them into flats draws the sting of their material significance; they are neutralised. Yet the conversion also reflects a certain nostalgia, a willingness to physically inhabit the past (or even to suggest the architectonics of the past being drawn into the present). This is in direct contrast with the trend towards false external pastness exhibited by, for instance, the vogue for mock-Tudor superficial house decoration of the 1980s. Conversion keeps the 'authentic' shell while replacing the inside, as opposed to creating a false exterior; the apartments inside bend to the will of the historical structure rather than use a 'false' signifier of heritage to confer taste and authority. Mock-Tudor architectural style is akin to Frederic Jameson's concept of pastiche, the neutral practice 'the wearing of a stylistic mask, speaking in a dead language: but it is a neutral practice of such mimicry'.[24] In contrast, building conversion signals a social investment in the historical built environment, a kind of architecture of dialectic rather than surface. This process of gentrification is of course thoroughly class-based, and suggests an imaginative architecture that develops organically rather than replaces. Alternatively, refabrications of sites such as the Haçienda in Manchester or the Gainsborough Studios in East London trade simply on the name, not the building (both of which were demolished). The site is the same, but these buildings consciously hark back to an idealised history. The Haçienda apartments were sold with the tagline 'Now the party's over, you can come home', demonstrating the disciplining of the building – moving from dynamic cultural space (as a nightclub) to controlled financial investment. The re-development of older buildings is a physical occupation of the past but their purposes are changed; it is not re-enactment or re-embodiment, but a valuing of the 'old' severed from its actual ideological foundations or original meanings. Most of the buildings are old industrial sites, reflecting once again the movement away from early industrial-capital models, and demonstrating that the past is materially now part of an economy of service. Those who live in conversions are not bothered about their true or primary meaning, just that they have cultural capital now apportioned to them purely because of their age.

Historic spaces are therefore key social sites of anodyne 'embodiment', heritage commodities that allow for a low-level retro-residential *frisson*. This anodyne, economic heritageness has been questioned by some communities. Artistic and theatrical usage of old factories, ruined buildings and wasteland spaces is common practice, for instance, attempting to animate these locations and to fuse modern and ancient into a unique and unsettling experience. It is a way of taking back the past before it is 'heritaged' into flats and council-designed regeneration communities. Such use of abandoned space can be traced back to the early 1980s New York art scene and it is now standard practice to intervene in historical arenas. This can be both official and unofficial. For instance, the *Cobweb* project used the Victoria Baths in Manchester for site-specific works while it was being restored having won *Restoration*. *Cobweb* was interested in the transitional period undergone by spaces. Curator Alison Kershaw's involvement in the Victoria Baths project allowed her to consider the space as liminal and potent:

> Although 'semi-derelict', the space is by no means empty or abandoned. It's just not been redeveloped in the sense we think of. It is an in-between sort of place, a space still available to an extent. It is rare to have a huge building that you can explore with minimum restriction. Once the Victoria Baths is redeveloped, it won't have that freedom, that expectancy.[25]

Art installations in abandoned buildings challenge ideas of the formal gallery, creating fragile and short-term pieces. They also attempt to use the historical resonances of the space in order to create something new while being simultaneously aware of the vulnerability of the pieces. They engage with the historical space in order to use the confusion of the location to undermine hierarchical organisation and to use the dissonance of old and new to develop something extremely particular.

Similarly alternative in terms of attitude to the built environment is urban exploration. Over the past 10 years there has been a huge upsurge in interest in exploring abandoned and empty spaces. There is a massive subculture of urban tourists wandering around derelict places taking photographs: 'To me, it's not really an "extreme sport", it's more like being an extreme historian ... We like to really get into the place, to really feel the atmosphere inside.'[26] Urban explorers are interested in reclaiming heritage and making it new:

> when the weekend comes and most folk are spending money or soothing their hangovers you'll be underground exploring miles of abandoned

tunnels or caves … or reading the scrawlings on a wall in a cell of a derelict mental asylum.[27]

Such explorers often reject contemporary life, enjoying the isolation of the empty space. This 'extreme history' is importantly self-defining and eschews any kind of authority and ordering system; it is an attempt at reclaiming the space of history and engaging with the environment of the past first-hand:

> I suppose my motive to do this is simply that I like to explore new places and to explore the past. Not just to look in it from behind the dull glass of a museum, but to experience these places first-hand and to try to understand their stories.[28]

These adventurers are the first wave of tourists exploring contemporary British industrial/post-industrial heritage. The explorers are not particularly concerned with the age or significance of the building (although asylums, former hospitals, factories and tunnels are popular). Their motivation is to find 'anything derelict and abandoned or disused. Urban Exploration is about visiting and experiencing these often forgotten places and photographing them before they disappear forever.'[29] The attraction of abandoned building exploration is the unknown and the never seen, the idea of being a pioneer, but also, as Nicholas Royle says, 'I'm less interested in what might have taken place in a disused building, than I am in what I can imagine taking place in it in my alternative version of reality. The one in my head.'[30] It is a violent enfranchisement, a taking back of 'official' history and a grasping of the past. Urban exploration is an opening up of a space of possibility in the very ruins of the past. It is a way of eschewing heritage – of avoiding history as something packaged and commodified, and re-asserting a communal ownership of sorts over it.

9 History games

The previous chapter's discussion of the activity of re-enactment suggests that a large number of diverse groups are keen to embody 'history' for a variety of purposes. Analysis of history-as-experience illustrates that it is a set of narratives divorced from an institutionalised framework, used in different and dissident ways by a variety of social bodies. This chapter develops the motif of re-enactment with a consideration of another model of historical 'experience' – that enacted in contemporary computer games.[1] Initially, such games seem to offer an empowerment similar to that of reality history but this seems ambivalent at best and illusory at worst. The chapter then moves to look at the 'experience' of history in a range of other games, and considers the ludic historiographic possibilities that the past creates. These games are sometimes occasional leisure pursuits – undertaken irregularly – although for others they are hobbies and immensely important. They are played by a demographic which is global, across all age groups, and relatively often male. They represent, then, a complex set of cultural-historio phenomena which often entail a certain embodiment – either first-person, or deploying an avatar – and encourage a sense of experiencing history. The manifestation of history in such a range of gaming models and genres suggest a complexity of interaction on the part of the user. Millions of gamers worldwide engage with the past through their immersion in these virtual and ludic worlds, attaining some kind of – albeit skewed – historical awareness through an active engagement with a representation of the past.

First person shoot 'em up history

First person shooters (FPS), or point-of-view (POV) games, present a particular type of visualised historical experience. Such games have graduated from the first commercial types of the genre, *Battlezone* (Atari, 1980) and *Tail Gunner* (Vectorbeam, 1979) through to early successful franchises such as *GoldenEye* (Rareware, 1997) and *Doom* (id Software, 1993), but the principles are largely the same. Point of view games are rarely peaceful, and generally come under the category of 'shoot 'em ups', in which the only piece of the player's virtual body visible is their weapon. Such games dispense with an explicitly othered avatar body and instead use the screen as the viewpoint. The player is put in the position of performing a character while simultaneously seduced by point of view to identify bodily and wholly with this character. This can be disorientating in its scope – modern versions of these games enable the player to have both a direction of movement control and a direction of vision. The implications of point of view games can tell us much about historical experientiality.

The games of particular interest here are World War II first person shooters, in particular, EA Games' *Medal of Honor*. This suite of game was relatively unique when it was launched in the late 1990s as it was a successful first person shooter (FPS) which eschewed the fantasy element associated with the games, and instead relied on building an extremely believable background to the game.[2] The organisation and construction of the game invited the player to experience it as narrative. There have been several generations of *Medal of Honor*, ranging from secret resistance missions in France to the war in the Pacific. Based on missions undertaken during the Second World War, *Medal of Honor* puts the player in the position of the combat marine, and invites them to be part of a greater military framework: 'You don't play, you volunteer' goes the advertising hook. *Medal of Honor: Frontline* (EA Games, 2002), a recreation of the D-day landings, emphasises that this is 'your finest hour'. Claims for experience range from 'Storm the beaches of Normandy' to 'Defeat the Nazi War Machine' (a second version invites the player to 'Defeat the Japanese Empire'). As Barry Atkins has commented of *Close Combat* (although a strategy game, not a FPS): 'The grand sweep of historical narrative becomes comprehensible in miniature, and the individual is presented as being able to "make a difference" in circumstances where the outcome was so uncertain and not already decided by sheer weight of numbers.'[3] *Medal of Honor* builds a sense of linearity and historical direction through its landscape and gameplay. Further, the game is interested in selling a heroic individuality within the broader sweep of history, an existential neoliberal view of the soldier as freer than perhaps we might say they are: 'Can one man truly make a difference?' was the tag line for the first instalment, *Medal of Honor: Allied Assault* (EA Games, 2002), with the assumption, of course, that they could.

The game's visuals rely heavily on the *verité* documentary style of *Saving Private Ryan* and *Band of Brothers* (Figure 9.1). Similarly, the game deploys tropes from a number of war films, interacting virtually in the perpetuation of certain historical simulacra along the way. For the beach landings the game particularly deploys the 'shock' aspect of the handset – which will rumble and vibrate as the player comes under bombardment – to create an experience of the landings which is disturbingly messy, loud and disorientating. Players are required to crouch, jump, run; ragged breathing is constantly heard, there is constant bombardment and shouted instructions, and players are under fire for most of the game. The game is heavily organised, however, and involves the player achieving targets either military or geographical (by moving through levels and killing enemies) in a strictly ordered fashion. The player is not allowed to skip levels or decide not to fight. This plays heavily on the 'target' version of games – as a series of increasingly difficult tests which are eventually overcome. There is some cumulative progression, and the levels become more difficult.

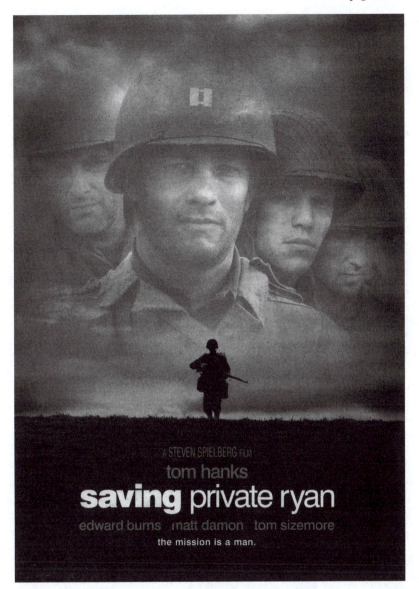

Figure 9.1 Promotional poster for *Saving Private Ryan*, 1998, directed by Steven Spielberg.

The player is required to enact and progress the story or it won't happen; this history won't move onwards without the player satisfying certain criteria, eliminating the correct enemies and staying alive. The player is therefore granted agency of some description within what is not narrative history but simulation – although simulation that mimics narrative history such as film and documentary. The game is not interactive or ergodic, being more a set of levels with increasingly complicated imaginative landscape.[4] The game is a simulation that invites an experience of interactivity and control, but which manages somehow to create a balanced dynamic between a passive experiential model and an illusion of control. It embodies the conflict within gaming studies between game as narrative and game as simulation – this is, in many ways, both. Key to the experience of the game is the balance between enfranchisement and narrative; the illusion of control is key to playing – the player is at once a powerful figure but at the same time an avatar that can easily be destroyed; at once a small cog in the military machine and at the same time crucially important to the war. The experience of history is at once othered and simultaneously enfranchising – the war takes place around and above the player, but their experience of history is fragmented, ontological and particularised.

Behind the jock rhetoric of *Medal of Honor* is something very sophisticated, the creation of a virtual landscape that becomes increasingly complicated in an updated incarnation of the game, *Rising Sun* (2003). This game's view of history is unreconstructed: players fight relatively faceless Japanese soldiers, and the bombing of Pearl Harbor is called the 'Day of Infamy'. This version emphasises the notion of the individual to the conflict 'you must claw and scratch to turn the tide of the War in the Pacific ... you begin an odyssey through the critical battles of the early parts of the Pacific Campaign'.[5] The game allows the player to unlock video clips, win medals, see news footage and receive letters from home. A dossier tells the player the background story of those they meet (one of whom is their brother), and of themselves. Online play allows the player to engage in increasingly complex situations. They can fight others online in 'deathmatches', too. However, the free levels are not part of the wider game – and again, if the player chooses to play with others they must work as a team to reach the various targets. Unlike, for instance, strategy games in which a player might plausibly play well enough to change the course of history, this kind of (much more popular) 'shoot 'em up' is relatively unsophisticated in its version of events. The player may pursue what seems to be their own mission, to mould or construct their own history – but crucially the element of interaction or recreation is lost. Their point of view is never their own, even if it looks that way. However, the games still encourage a notion of the importance of the individual to the conflict, and a recognition of the importance of the foot soldier.

Call of Duty (Activision, 2003), a FPS that built on the market for *Medal of Honor*, emphasises further this recognition of the common soldier. The game's rhetoric is more inclusive, and less individualistic than *Medal of Honor*. The tag line for the game is 'no one fights alone'. The emphasis is on teamwork and a developing sense of alliance: 'In the war that changed the world, no man won it alone. Through the chaos of battle, ordinary soldiers fought – and died – alongside one another'.[6] The game is more interested in filmic experience than *Medal of Honor*, but treads a fine balance between celebrating the ordinary soldier and making that soldier's version of the war a set of cinematic clichés. The war is consciously turned into film, at once othering history and simultaneously making it recognisable, part of a recognisable pattern or language of cinematic tropes:

Experience the cinematic intensity of WWII's epic battles including D-Day, the Russian Charge at Stalingrad and the Battle for Berlin – through the eyes of citizen soldiers and unsung heroes from an alliance of countries who together helped shape the course of modern history.[7]

The ordinary soldier can make a difference in this game, but their ability to do so is somehow compromised by that 'cinematic intensity' – the game becomes film, becomes a controllable genre. Indeed, the game went well beyond its forbears in linking with Hollywood – the screenwriting talents of Michael Schiffer, writer of *Crimson Tide* and *The Peacemaker*, were brought in 'to further immerse players into the game and capture the cinematic intensity of WWII … bringing a closer personal identification with the game's characters'.[8] Yet this emotional intensity is blended with claims to authenticity – the second instalment, *United Offensive*, brought in military advisors to help create 'authentic portrayal of squad tactics, formations and battle situations'.[9]

This combination of historical and military 'authenticity' allied to a Hollywood rhetoric of emotional attachment is immediately clear in *Battlefield 1942* (EA Games, 2002). The WWII version is reliant on film, but it is in the *Battlefield Vietnam* (EA Games, 2004) chapter that the game takes things beyond pastiche into downright quotation – the opening sequence of helicopters is played out to the *Ride of the Valkyries*, for instance, echoing the helicopter scene in the film *Apocalypse Now* (Francis Ford Coppola, 1979). This game, while strategic, returns to a sense of individual input: 'the outcome of the battle depends on the choices you make'.[10] The player is enfranchised but at the same time put into a recognisable chain of signifiers – performing a role (a similar cultural echo is found in the quoting of Jimi Hendrix in the title of *Vietcong: Purple Haze* (Illusion Softworks, 2004)). The 'freedom' allowed the player is compromised by the generic rules put into place before the game has even started.

Brothers in Arms (Ubisoft, 2005), promises 'unprecedented authenticity' and is based on a true story (not for the gaming community the delicacy of re-enactors in wondering whether replaying actual wartime experience is something to be ethically comfortable with). The attention to detail is lavish: the game includes 'historically accurate and detailed battlefields, events and equipment recreated from Army Signal Corps photos, Aerial Reconnaissance Imagery and eyewitness accounts'.[11] This combination of authenticity and film suggests that the games are actively investing in a notion of 'narrative' and historical actuality, but the blending of 'factual' history and cinematic trope creates an interestingly blurred space of identity. The game sees itself as an upgrade, an evolution – it is a 'tactical shooter' rather than a simple destructive FPS, a new kind of engagement in which strategy and teamwork are as important as marksmanship. The consumption of history is both academic and fictional. The experience of the game is narrative and simulation, part of a fixed set of signifiers and simultaneously part of the sweep of history. The player attains objectives and completes missions, but with a new emotional connection and intensity (*Brothers in Arms* portrays the squad leader as thinking of his men as his 'family', and the title consciously evokes *Band of Brothers*). The player is engaging in re-enactment, simulation, a game and history all at the same time. The games expect a complexity of understanding and response from their players, and the ability to inhabit multiple identities and experiences when engaging within the gaming platform is taken for granted.

The online community is incredibly important to these games. At any one time around 2,000 players are engaging with *Battlefield 1942* (compare that to *c.*6,000 Sealed Knot re-enactors in the whole of the UK and the size of this community is demonstrated). Gamers arrange themselves into regiments and communities with the same fervour and attention to detail of the re-enactment community. Regiments practise weekly, talk tactics; there is a sense of involvement and ownership. Names include 'New World Order', 'The Honor Squad', 'Doom Soldiers', 'RuffNecks', 'Screaming Eagles'. These organisations are taken extremely seriously, and deploy tropes learned from the games and from the rhetoric of war films, again folding back into postmodern historical experience. These communities also sustain the scholarly and mainstream academic element of the games – the *Brothers in Arms* website includes a 'historical forum' with links to museums, new books, maps, and information about weapons. Online skirmishing and fighting is itself evolving, with the user no longer tied to being in one place – PSP consoles and mobile phone game technology allied with wireless networks mean that players can carry on their missions and their involvement increasingly on the move. This mobility again changes the dynamic of engagement with the game. Networking through mobile historicised interfaces means that the user is no longer static and overlays a new level of embodiment to their engagement with the game. Another innovation is the HMD (Head Mounted Display) which makes the game a much more immersive bodily (or gives the illusion of bodily) experience.

History in these games has become a masculine backdrop to a leisure activity (there are no female characters and the demographic of players is resolutely male). The games are in and of themselves, relating to little else. The skills the player learns are not transferable; they cannot even use them in other games, often. There is nothing to be learned from this kind of history, no information to be gleaned; yet there is still an ontological kick to be got out of it, an involvement in historical discourse. The games are keen to stress the legitimacy of their view of the past, emphasising the 'authenticity' of their weaponry and uniform while suggesting that the player uses the games to 'experience the powerful realities of war'. These games are not that far away from re-enactment in their regimented enfranchisement of the individual within their historical nexus.

Games can also provide a space for contested historical narratives to flourish. American Vietnam games are in many ways enacting this historical amnesia, effacing the complexities of the situation in order to present a heroic sweeping narrative teleology. Other American games, for instance, mimic the actions of Special Forces in Iraq (*Conflict: Desert Storm* I (SCi Games, 2002) and II (SCi Games, 2003), although they are not FPS).[12] *Desert Storm II* casts the player 'Against the Might of a Tyrant' in combat to deal with some 'Unfinished business' from the 1991 war.[13] These games both shore up a sense of national identity (freedom fighting) and immediate resolution, while engaging in an Orientalist creation of the Middle East as an exotic, barbaric place. There are Hizbullah FPS games online, and Islamic Jihad games allowing the player to act as a Palestinian freedom fighter.[14]

In FPS games, the projected self is virtual, an unseen avatar allowing the player to engage with and in some ways understand history. Indeed, the experience is as 'realistic' as possible. The player is invited to be part of history, a wittingly small part of a teleological move towards the present. Taking their lead, in some way, from the edutainment first-person history experience as presented in re-enactment and living history, history in gaming presents at once a complexity of historical experience and a tightly organised, inflexible model of history. This type of experience suggests an investment in dynamic models of history, an economy of historical desire drawn inexorably toward the tension between 'experience' and 'authenticity'. 'Play' and variously controlled models of interaction frame contemporary consumption of history-as-experience as cultural product and economic experience.

Role playing and history as identity

This is further illustrated, but complicated, by online role-playing games, in which an othered virtual historical avatar becomes the embodied projection of the user. The blurring of the generic and factual boundaries, hastened by the integration of media systems and modes of representation, is demonstrably – and extremely suggestively – the case in historical online role-playing games. Massive multiplayer online games (MMOGs) and massive multiplayer online role-playing games (MMORPGs) combine game play with virtual and social software in unique and massively popular fashion.[15] Players design an avatar to enter the virtual 3D online world and to engage with the avatars of other players.[16] They can rent space, travel around, and undertake complex tasks as well as building and designing objects and products. The concept is a combination of gaming, role-playing and Virtual Reality simulation. Around 10,000 people are 'in' *Second Life* (Linden, 2003) at one time, and around 9 million users are registered. The scenarios are imagined and created in the main by the users, with certain framing principles (and increasingly 'real world' law is infringing); MMORPGs are more rule-based and akin to traditional 'games' insofar as they are quest- or task-based, less interested in mimicking the real world than in creating an imaginative forum for interactive play. Most MMOGs have their own internal economies which in turn have a manifestation in the 'real world'.[17] Their uses range from education through festivals to the US army designing a game to train soldiers in urban warfare. As Sherry Turkle argues, they also provide 'a new environment for the construction and reconstruction of self'.[18]

Popular MMOGs are generally based in the contemporary world (*Second Life*) where MMORPGs tend towards a quasi-historical romance fantasy combat scenarios (*World of Warcraft* (Blizzard, 2004) or *Age of Conan* (FunCom, 2008)).

Increasingly games are based on films (such as *Lord of the Rings* and *Pirates of the Caribbean*).[19] There are also hybrid MMOG-FPS crossovers, such as *Wolfenstein: Enemy Territory* (Activision, 2004). Pseudo-medieval games such as *Regnum Online* (NGD, 2007), *Rakion* (Softnyx, 2005) and *RuneScape* (Jagex 2001), in which players capture castles and are costumed in medieval style, are popular; *RuneScape* has 9 million registered users. There is furthermore a subgenre of games that incorporate Celtic, Norse, Greek, Korean or Chinese mythologies. This suggests that the vagueness of the audience's historical knowledge – and the attraction of various general historical archetypes rather than specific location and events – impact on and shape this game-playing community. Players have hacked games like *World of Warcraft* and used their graphics packages to recreate sequences from animated historical films; such splicings are then served on video sites such as YouTube, and these entities are pastiche texts implying a kind of tribute, imitation and willingness to replay cultural product in virtual contexts.

However, there is a strand of authentically historical MMORPGs and these are increasing in number as designers attempt to differentiate themselves from the host of games and experiment with possible outlines. Historical MMORPGs allow participants to act in history but the more sophisticated elements of MMORPGs – the interaction of human avatars with each other and their building and developing the world – mean that the games (and therefore their historical situation and development) will transform as their members change. These historical games are popular – *Roma Victor* (RedBedlam, 2006) has 5000 members, for instance. The developers 'invested years of painstaking research into bringing unprecedented levels of detail to the historical authenticity of this world', and again, like FPSs, the authenticity of the experience is key.[20] They develop economies in the case of *Silk Road* (Joymax, 2005), a trading game based in China, or pioneer in *Frontier 1859* (Cosmic, in development), or explore *Uncharted Waters Online* (KOEI 2004). *Voyage Century* encourages the player to take on a profession (such as a trader or merchant), as does *Roma Victor*, in which the avatar can craft nearly anything that is replicated in the real (historical) world as well as farm, fish, cook, smelt and brew. While most of these games are task- or quest-based, they encourage in the player a sense of economic identity and as a consequence a kind of skill-based autonomy (and potential development). MMORPGs are international (often made and served by Chinese, American or Korean companies yet played throughout the world), and illustrate a global gaming interface within an economic nexus.

Being part of history is necessary to accrue 'experience' or 'skills' which lead to points and rankings. The games – similarly to the FPSs that have online play – encourage community, solidarity and teamwork as well as a type of virtual interaction within their historical scenarios.[21] Replayability is not necessarily an issue as these games are continuous – players may die during combat, for instance, but all they lose is experience and possibly financial worth; the game itself continues (so the time-line is not affected). These games are also suggestive in terms of presenting history as a set of 'roles' that might be learnt and perfected. Identities can be effaced, put on and impersonated throughout the experience.[22]

The player both enacts their own role and – as part of the wider game – re-enacts an historical period. The chosen avatar projects the player into the game scenario while simultaneously effacing the actual self. The interaction with the game scenario is complex – the player is empathically and materially involved in the environment, playing and learning skills that have a value within the game individually and generally, while they are simultaneously performing historicity.

Research suggests that increasingly women are playing MMORPGs, and clearly the demographic of games is dynamic and evolving.[23] Taylor illustrates the 'multiple contexts' experienced in such games and argues that this complexity is key to the gaming experience and attraction; gamers in MMORPGs undertake a variety of tasks, engage with multiple scenarios and interact 'socially' with a wide selection of other players. These games allow ludic self-presentation, and as a way of physically engaging with and understanding the past they suggest a flexibility of approach and an acknowledgement of the gap between then and now – the avatar is the liminal figure who allows the player to connect with the world of the game, the consciousness which is not centrally self that leads the gamer through the other world of the past.

Civilization **and disc contents: strategy games**[24]

More cerebral and less embodied in their presentation of history-as-experience, but no less interesting in terms of their postmodern complexity and interrogative historiography, are strategy games. Sid Meier's successful *Civilization* (MicroProse, 1991–) suite of games is the most successful of what are known as reality strategy games. They use real historical, geographical or factual backgrounds to structure the game. The most venerable of these games is *Risk*, originally digitised in 1988 and a version of the 1957 board game. The aim of this game is straightforward conquest, whereas the turn-based *Civilization* and real-time games such as *Age of Empires* (Ensemble, 1997–) emphasise expansion through trade, scholarship and technological innovation.[25] There are also mafia games, arms-dealer games and railroad tycoon computer games, demonstrating the broad range of the long-term strategy model. Strategy games emphasise a teleology of development whereby the player wins or loses depending on the outcome of various decisions relating to technology, economy and military strength (this teleology is reflected in the structures of development, where new advances are dependent on already having invented or discovered something else in a strictly structured order).[26] These games 'visually and aurally immerse players in history' and as a consequence are more profound in their impact upon gamers' sense of the past than previous generations of historically based games; and, as Kevin Schut argues, the narrative of the gamescape tends to be patriarchal and systematic, presenting history 'as a matter of aggressive power'.[27]

Civilization enables the player to build 'wonders' of the world to supplement financial power and make society happier and more advanced. Culture is important, as is nationalism – and both can be augmented by diverting money and resources to them.[28] *Civilization* is a straightforward game that presents history as a series of progresses – there is nothing random other than the gameplay of your opponents (AI or human), and the average player can move towards success (i.e. 'civilisation') relatively easily. Realtime games are less predictable although similarly present a model of history which is predicated upon development, progress and the building of imperial dominion. Such games present (particularly pre-modern) history as the preserve of a set of contending empires. *Age of Empires* allows the player to progress their tribe through the Stone, Tool, Bronze and Iron Age. The past in these games is a framework, a system, that has various contingencies but very clear boundaries and edges: a 'crude caricature of the historical process', in Niall Ferguson's critical words.[29]

The gamer in these scenarios is ruler and has an overview of the historical process, navigating towards a successful outcome predicated upon economic and military decision-making in the main. Ted Friedman has argued that the player of such games does not associate themselves with an individual but sees the entire gaming field, and that the pleasure and purpose of the game is to think like a computer.[30] Certainly the simultaneity of engagement – a player sees the entire game and holds numerous roles some of which are specific (ruler/god), some metonymic (the player *is* whichever tribe or nation they decide to play) – argues a complexity of interaction and an interface with multiple roles. The combination of binary encoded ways of thinking (acting like a computer, or Friedman's 'Cyborg Consciousness') and historical framework suggests a virtual history that changes the way that users think about the past and engage with that past, encouraging them to see history as a set of tasks, problems, issues to resolve through the correct decision-making. Furthermore, the cyborgness associated with this game play illustrates that simulations are different from, for instance, re-enactment due to their overlaying of gameplay with an electronic framework. The experience of gaming is not embodied in the same way and so therefore is directed in other intellectual and cerebral directions.

In these games the process of history is driven by technological development and the skilful deployment of scarce resources. However, while this seems deterministic the scenarios boast such a wealth of randomness that history is replayable nearly endlessly with different outcomes. Replayability is one of the purposes and attractions of these games, and gamers would be expected to play repeatedly. Different decisions have different consequences, and the historical process is seen as a complex, multiple process. The games also emphasise co-operation, particularly in their online manifestations. The historiography of the games is therefore made complex by their very format, as they have an inbuilt reconfiguration with infinite outcomes. The games suggest the chaos of history while inviting the player to inscribe order onto a world envisaged in a 3D map (in itself ideologically problematic). They also ask the gamer to conceptualise historical development as something which is predicated upon the possible outcomes of various decisions – the player has to think of the consequences of what they are doing – and that there are various paths not taken; they have therefore been theorised as counterfactual, or at least presenting the possibility of different historical timelines (within the overarching move towards progress). Niall Ferguson argues that wargames are necessary for the historian precisely because of their counterfactual element.

He also praises them because they have the wider social effect of educating a 'strategically savvy generation'.[31] This point – that games are educationally and socially useful, particularly in terms of ordering and arranging unstructured information – is taken up by Steven Johnson:

> to non-players, games bear a superficial resemblance to music videos: flashy graphics; the layered mix of image, music, and text; the occasional burst of speed, particularly during the pre-rendered opening sequences. But what you actually *do* in playing a game – the way your mind has to work – is radically different. It's not about tolerating or aestheticizing chaos; it's about finding order and meaning in the world, and making decisions that help create that order.[32]

Games, for Johnson and Ferguson, allow a way of considering multiplicity while also imposing structure and order. They teach discipline and intellectual dexterity, and in the case of historical games a certain historiographical ambivalence.

Age of Empires was specifically developed as an historical one in order to differentiate it from other fantasy-based realtime games, as designer Bruce Shelley argues:

> Players already have some pre-conceived notions of what should be going on and thus have some ideas about how to play. They do not have to learn a pseudo-scientific rationale for what is going on. History gave us a framework upon which we could hang our game. We could pick and choose which interesting parts of history to include or discard.[33]

The idea that the player would have a rough idea of what 'should' happen in history argues a sense that these games allow one to replay and reorder reality. History is a 'framework', a model on which to project the game (and something which is easily plunderable). Authenticity is not an issue in these games particularly:

> Extensive, detailed research is not necessary or even a good idea for most entertainment products. The best reference materials are often found in the children's section because this is the level of historic interest for most of the gaming public. If you build in too much historic detail you run the risk of making the game obtuse. The players should have the fun, not the designers or researchers. We are trying to entertain people, not impress them with our scholarship.[34]

Shelley here effectively claims that most users' understanding of – or, maybe more specifically, 'interest' in – the past is at school level or below. Detail leads to an 'obtuse' experience. Shelley's honesty about the sketchiness of the history used in such games differs greatly from the way that FPSs such as *Medal of Honor* are presented. The player in those games is much less independent – their decisions may be wrong – than the strategy games, and they are – particularly due to the POV screen use – involved in the historical process the game enacts at a much more basic and visceral level.

The games have been used in secondary education, demonstrating their flexibility and attractiveness.[35] However, this in itself raises problematic questions about the historiography that is being demonstrated (and thence taught) through the game, particularly in the light of Shelley's comments (although other games pride themselves on authenticity). Similarly, the game engine for *Rome: Total War* (Creative Assembly, 2004), a hybrid turn-based strategy game with some real-time elements, was used in BBC's *Time Commanders* (2004–5) and the History Channel's *Decisive Battles* (2004), both of which used the technology to recreate famous ancient battles. *Decisive Battles* simply used the virtual model in tandem with location work to demonstrate what had happened – in itself interesting for the encroaching virtualness of television history and the viewer's need for visual representation (and their presumed familiarity with game *mise-en-scènes* for the presentation of historical scenarios). In *Time Commanders* two teams compete over a combat scenario and experts give their opinions and tell the audience what 'actually' happened and why particular decisions were costly, lucky, or strategically good. The virtual model allows the past to be presented as something malleable, highlighting the cost of particular decisions and demonstrating the contingency of (teleological, imperial, combat-based) history. This use of CGI and game technology in history programming illustrates the creeping virtualness of television documentary on the one hand and the ability to import history into the format of a television game-show on the other, and suggests that the relationship between video game, 'fact', and genre is fast being blurred.

Wargames and scale models

Of course, computerised strategy and role-playing games are merely more sophisticated updates of older modes of staging and personating combat. Static model and tabletop wargaming has a venerable history – stretching at least from H.G. Wells' *Little Wars* in 1913, a set of laws for playing with toy soldiers for boys and 'that more intelligent sort of girl' – and similarly demonstrates an interest in strategy, re-enactment, pattern and organisation, while also seeing an educational value in the pursuit: 'You have only to play at Little Wars three or four times to realise just what a blundering thing Great War must be.'[36] Recreational wargames were widespread in the 1960s and 1970s, driven by the company Avalon Hill, although have largely been superseded by online manifestations. Nonetheless they demonstrate a desire to approach the past – in general, what might be termed Whiggish turning points of history – in an informed and procedural fashion and to render that history subject to a set of clear rules and relatively predictable (although not necessarily resistable) outcomes.

Model-, card- and board-based wargames still flourish and with them multiple ways of envisaging, performing, and mentally conceptualising historical combat.[37]

We the People (Avalon Hill, 1993), a card-driven wargame (CDG), replays the American War of Independence and allows 'American' and 'British' players to 'simulate this first of the world's great revolutions in a fun and historically accurate game'; they can win, lose, or tie the war.[38] Board-based games such as *Diplomacy* or *Battle Cry* generally deploy dice to ensure that chance is a factor in the scenario, adding a random element.[39] Other wargames such as those played with miniature figurines are not tied to the tabletop but introduce multiple terrains and complicated rules (of course, many board-based games also use model figures).

Making scale model soldiers, tanks, airplanes, and boats as part of wargaming scenario building is an analogous hobby. Visual artists Jacob and Dinos Chapman used 5,000 Airfix model soldiers and associated hardware for their diorama works *Hell* (1999–2000) and *Disasters of War* (1993). The latter used fibreglass figures to imitate images from Goya's *Disasters of War* series (1810–20). *Hell* has atrocities committed by masses of figures that are recognisably German soldiers although they have been mutilated and melted into horrible figures. Using what are effectively gaming implements (or, for many, toys) to make such traumatic and unpleasant images – what has been termed 'abject art' – comments on the underlying prevalence of war in contemporary leisure culture.[40] The works suggest further that our understanding of war is at once distanced by such representation – soldiers are mere figurines in contemporary culture where in Goya's Spain they are rendered human and anatomically correct – and made manifest by recourse to historical caricature (the figures are generic, mass-produced and metonymic instead of individual) rather than actual understanding. The images use leisure models (toy soldiers) to present the simulacrum of contemporary violence – something unexperienced, a pastiche seemingly predicated upon an original (Goya) but cut loose from 'reality'. The Chapmans comment on the way that history can unthinkingly pervade society and render concepts like trauma, war and hell as part of a gaming continuum – a mere set of tokens to be won and lost as part of an allegedly ordered process. All of these types of ludic engagement with history – from the embodiment of the FPS to the cerebral teleologies of strategy games – demonstrate a complexity of modern understanding of the past and an imaginative intervention on the part of the player. This in turn might suggest that the historical imaginary is more diverse and complex than hitherto thought, and that audiences are extremely sophisticated in their engagements with historical products.

Part IV

History on television

Democratisation and deregulation

As has already started to become clear, television and visual versioning of the past are increasingly influential in a packaging of historical fact and a creation of history as leisure activity. What is produced is, for all it might attempt to be 'real' or 'educational', a subjective version of a constructed history. Chapters 10 and 11 look at the ways that 'history' is presented on television in order to consider how we think of the past as a cultural entity. The chapters consider the variety of genres of television history and the impact of new technologies and concepts upon those genres. They consider the key elements of the 'new' narrative documentary history as embodied in the work of Simon Schama and David Starkey, as well as comparing this personality-led programming with testimony-based and reality pieces. Forms of evidence are examined, particularly the 'inclusive' experiential use of popular culture, the importance of location, and the importance of the witness to documentary. The new techniques of television documentary, from CGI and reconstruction through to digital re-enactment, demonstrate a newly virtual history which emphasises a montage of 'real' and imaginary elements in the presentation of narrative.[1]

A key site for the rearrangement of the documentary in response to the pressures of deregulation after the UK 1990 Broadcasting Act, globalisation and competition, is the historical documentary. In particular, Reality TV has eroded the boundaries of the documentary form and heralded a raft of hybrid forms which encourage an investment in the personal, the experiential, and the active role (whatever active means) of the audience. Reality television programmes illustrate much about documentary and the ways that society accesses the past. In many ways, the intersection of history and reality has redressed the problems of the new documentary by reclaiming actuality and education as key aims. What is clear about contemporary historical documentary is that audiences are able to keep at least two kinds of ball in the air – Schama and Starkey and Ferguson essentially present in a tradition that goes back to A.J.P. Taylor and Kenneth Clarke, albeit with reconstruction, whereas reality history is more innovative and dynamic.

Chapter 10 presents a set of arguments relating to traditional popular history – documentaries from the 1960s onwards, and in particular those by David

Starkey and Simon Schama. The chapter explores how they present historical information, what their historiographical position is, and how they conceive of themselves as educational vehicles. The following chapter then considers the most innovative and interesting phenomena of recent television programming, reality history. The impact of reality TV on historical documentary making, in particular the form's 'emphasis on the experiential, the personal and the emotional', is highly suggestive not just of the way that contemporary society watches television but also of the ways that it conceives of the past.[2] The impact of Reality TV has massively influenced our televisual landscape, to the extent that 'Documentary and factual TV now exist in a space that is neither wholly fictional nor wholly factual, both yet neither.'[3] New programmes are hybrids and the televisual grammar is constantly evolving: as Annette Hill argues, this is 'how television cannibalises itself in order to survive'.[4]

A key question to be kept to the forefront when looking at all this documentary material is to what extent it contributes to the seeming democratisation of history and the enfranchisement – bodily or imaginatively – into agency of the historical subject hinted at in the previous parts. Simon Schama, for instance, has argued that television has contributed to the downfall of the 'usual hierarchies of authority' and has provoked 'a democracy of knowledge'.[5] Similarly, the digital revolution of which Reality TV is in many ways a part, offers to some critics the possibility of an 'implicitly politicized' form that through interactivity might 'revitalize citizen-based democracy'.[6] Mark Andrejevic, a key economic theorist of Reality Television, has on occasion argued for the revolutionary possibility of reality television, suggesting that 'the notion that collective participation in the creation of cultural commodities salvages their claim to authenticity invokes a critique of the top-down forms of control associated with the culture industry'.[7] This suggests that the inauthenticity of mass culture is due to the alienation of the audience from the production process itself, and Reality TV offers the possibility that 'including their participation might help cultural products reclaim an element of authenticity'.[8] In some ways, then, this model suggests a revolution whereby the consumers of the product become the producers, too. Andrejevic's analysis is more nuanced than this – indeed, he finally argues that being in Reality TV is more part of a culture of self-commodification – but his concepts are suggestive when applied to history programming. The involvement of the 'audience' in historical programming encourages a sense of common ownership of heritage and the history of nation rather than a history told to a passive audience.

10 Contemporary historical documentary

Documentary as form: self-consciousness and diversion

Mainstream documentary theory and practice for decades have been concerned with self-consciousness. Theorists of documentary are well aware of the innate inability of the medium to present 'truth': 'Documentaries are constructs, yet they seek to reveal the real without mediation. Watching a documentary involves holding these two contrary beliefs at once, a process of disavowal which is not terribly unusual inhuman behaviour, but is inherently unstable.'[1] Within the form itself, critics argue is, an acknowledgement that truth is insubstantial.[2] It is difficult to square these claims – that history on television is not complex enough and presents simple truths, or that it is innately self-reflexive and self-conscious and so obviously cannot claim the status of 'truth'.

Indeed, the very falseness of the relationship between camera and subject has been instituted since the first full-length cinema documentary, *Nanook of the North* (1922). Director Robert Flaherty changed material and staged events, distorting his subject. The very insubstantiality of documentary seems to lie, like theatre, in the audience's acceptance of the bias of the presenter and the 'arrangement' of information. As Richard Kilborn and John Izod recount, 'The production of a documentary is not simply an act of chronicling; it is just as much an act of transformation.'[3] They quote film-maker and theorist John Grierson's (1946) mandate that documentary is 'the creative treatment of actuality'.[4] Grierson argued that documentary had educational value and was key to the improvement of society; it enabled active citizenship by giving the individual information. Before the 1960s, documentary tended to approach serious subjects in order to educate the audience. Yet since the 1960s the problems of representation associated with the documentary form have been uppermost in its discussion, debate and practice. This crisis of legitimacy has clear echoes with the shaking of authority felt by History as a subject, a movement from unquestioning inflexibility towards a more complex, dynamic sense of the issues involved in articulating a position; documentary practice in general seems a good analogue for history insofar as it tends towards factuality despite an awareness of its own incompleteness.

The documentary theorist Nichols argues that history television introduces a necessary dissonance in our viewing consciousness which demonstrates the insubstantiality of all televisual media:

> Images, as we know, are always present tense. Their referent, what they re-represent, may be elsewhere, but this absent referent seems to be brought to life in the present moment of apprehension, over and over. Does this only further erase a fading sense of the historical in postmodernity, or does it leave open possibilities for historical representation beyond those of the written word? Something is clearly different. Historical consciousness requires the spectator's recognition of the double, or paradoxical, status of moving images that are present referring to events which are past.[5]

The fragmentary nature of the historical image in documentary leads to a certain absence and an unconscious but active appreciation as a viewer of the paradox of watching the past. The viewer is placed in a paradoxical situation which enables a more complex engagement with the past but similarly distances them from that past.

Writing of the Holocaust documentary *Shoah*, which consists mainly of eyewitness interviews, Thomas Elsaesser argues that:

> After six hours of testimony in *Shoah* – a testimony that, in different ways, records only absence, one is left with the overwhelming thought that no history can contain, let alone signify or represent, the palpable reality of so many individual, physical deaths.[6]

Here it is not the format of the documentary but the event itself which creates the dissonance; the sheer weight of the past is uncontainable. *Shoah* for Elsaesser demonstrates the inability of understanding the past, no matter what medium it is communicated in. Indeed, the conflicting and reverberating accounts voiced in *Shoah* demonstrate far more efficiently than historical monographs the complexity of the chaotic past. The complexity ascribed here to documentary suggests that the discomfort of professional historians is due to a misunderstanding of the complications fundamentally inherent in the form itself.

'Neither wholly fictional nor wholly factual': history on television

As long ago as 1976 historians were debating the problems of historical television documentary.[7] History on television is immensely powerful, and exerts subtle influence on the way that the past is considered. For instance, Adrian Wood has argued that popular conception of WWII is deeply flawed because it is mainly based on black and white footage; colour film of events from the 1940s, although relatively widely available, is little used and when it is creates an uncanny effect that unsettles the viewer.[8] This is not always simply an effect of historical documentary: revisionist historians of the First World War have argued that the BBC comedy series *Blackadder Goes Forth* perpetuates popular myths about the Western Front that have become deeply ingrained in contemporary consciousness of the war. Stephen Badsey points out, for instance, that in the BBC documentary *Timewatch: Haig – The Unknown Soldier* footage from *Blackadder* was intercut with interviews with historians in order to demonstrate the popular caricature of Haig.[9] The show was being used as evidence in an historiographical debate, demonstrating the increasing influence of popular culture on historiography.

As a consequence of this influence, and due furthermore to a flawed perception that the medium is simplistic, television has always had a vexed relationship with history. Historians are suspicious of the superficiality of television, its inability to present complexity. Tom Stearn argues that 'Mainstream history programmes divorce history from sources and research – as from historiographical controversy – and rely on the pronouncements of an apparently omniscient presenter and on "reconstructions" by actors.'[10] The medium is populist, problematic, impressionistic rather than clear, too interested in narrative. Ian Kershaw recognises that 'while it is unquestionably powerful, it is of necessity superficial'.[11] Jerry Kuehl, producer of *The World at War*, long ago noted the problem of immediacy:

> One characteristic of television as a communication medium is that it offers its audience virtually no time for reflections. It is a sequential medium, so to say, in which episode follows episode, without respite. This clearly means that the medium is ideally suited to telling stories and anecdotes, creating atmosphere and mood, giving diffuse impressions.[12]

Producer Jeremy Isaacs innocently reports the common practice of running still photographs together to create 'the illusion of living reality' from the late 1950s, and it is this imposing of (in this instance, false) linear visual narrative upon fundamentally chaotic events that for most historians is the key problem with television.[13] Dirk Eitzen more provocatively argues that 'popular audiences of historical documentaries are not particularly interested either in the complexity of the past or in explaining it. What they want more than anything … is a powerful emotional "experience"'.[14] Those interested in the authenticity of historical truth have derided the perceived simplifying of historical knowledge, concentrating on errors and problems of interpretation. Richard J. Evans, for instance, argues that: 'conveying history to a broad audience inevitably involves a degree of simplification or, in the case of Hollywood films, even downright distortion'.[15] 'Truth' is too complex to be communicated to a wide audience; the process of communicating to a 'broad' audience itself *inevitably* simplifies the message. Implicit in this view is a sense that real history should be left to the professionals. The issue such historians have with popular media is that they do not have the complexity to present an accurate view of the past, that they are necessarily circumscribed, simplified and straightforward. There is an underlying need to control the production and interpretation of the past (Evans claims a kind of trickle-down effect where popular history 'rests on the foundation of detailed research').[16] Crucially, for Evans, the problem is that 'truth' is distorted through simplification.

It is clear, too, in the writings of practitioners of television history, that historiography often takes second place to coherence and a drive toward storytelling. Simon Schama discusses his programme in personal terms: 'essentially it is all in the relationship between me the storyteller and you the viewer'.[17] The presenter Tristram Hunt argues that 'the creation of coherent narratives is one of the lead virtues of television history'.[18] Hunt praises the achievement of, among others, Simon Schama's *A History of Britain* and Kenneth Clark's *Civilisation*: 'Whether one agreed or not with the ideological agenda, the programmes nonetheless constituted engaging, authored narratives which engrossed millions of viewers with their historic take.'[19] The passivity foisted upon the viewer in this instance demonstrates the problems innate in using television as an educative medium. Clark's teleological positivistic series presented the march of civilisation as a movement from one cultural canonical achievement to another in a kind of join-the-dots history of western civilisation; Schama's series was more open to historical subjectivity but still presented a totalising, grand sweep version of history. These series present history as narrative, as progression, as progress. Crucial to Hunt's point is that television can enhance historical understanding – in a factual and possibly experiential sense – but he is still defending history as a definable discipline with rules and edges, a story to be told. All that television does is allow greater understanding of this story, and a certain empathy gained from that further understanding.

Television producer Taylor Downing asserts that 'a good history presenter takes the viewer through a slice of the past, by giving his own perspective on it' and claims that 'The Holmeses, Starkeys and Schamas are the storytellers of our age. They are the ones who bring the research out of the academy and offer it to the many.'[20] This trope of the historian as storyteller is key to the way that the popular TV historian is viewed. Yet inscribed within his celebration of the storytelling aspect of TV history is a sense of historiography and an elitist notion of audience: 'for there are millions of intelligent and thinking people who are genuinely interested in how the past has helped to make us what we are'.[21] A sense of nation and shared history is only appealing to the intelligent, seemingly. Again the notion of 'storytelling' is linked explicitly to the story of the present nation; the key point of these programmes is to explain to us who 'we are'. Problematic in terms of audience demographic, this statement is exclusive and excluding. Downing also claims that the academy should interact with popular history:

> Television historians should at their best be popular historians translating some of this [scholarly] work into narratives that will appeal to the many millions of intelligent viewers who don't want to spend their valuable leisure time in front of *Who Wants to be a Millionaire*, or *The Weakest Link*, or watching another episode of *EastEnders*.[22]

The audience Downing imagines for TV history is separate and elite, non-populist. He strives to differentiate TV history from the populism of television programming. It is somehow more important, more interesting, more intelligent than soaps or game shows. This despite the fact that TV history is part of the programming landscape in much the same way as these shows, and the fact that it attracts a massive audience which was not a first time audience turning on simply to watch the history. The audience for TV history is quite happy to watch soap, games, documentary. Indeed, in later manifestations of TV history gameshow, soap, and documentary happily mix. While special as a genre and part of an educational element of the channel profile, TV history is an important element of a rich programming culture, not apart from it. Key also to the present discussion is Downing's notion that history is something consumed during 'valuable leisure time'. Somehow an interest in 'how the past has helped to make us who we are' is a free time activity; it is simultaneously educational and leisured.

Postmodern theorists of history might suggest that documentary history-as-narrative is simply an explicit version of professional or institutional practice. Hayden White has argued persuasively for historians to recognise the narrative impulse and strategies within their own work.[23] Contemporary historiographical work emphasises the fact that engagement with the past is impressionistic, at best: 'Since "the past", by definition, does not exist, surely we can "know" it only by way of representations.'[24] As Keith Jenkins argues, 'All histories are inevitably troped, emplotted, figured-out and argued for from the historian's own position … [this is] history not as an epistemology but as an aesthetic.'[25] Historical documentary is acutely aware that it cannot reconstruct a true past and as a consequence presents a necessarily indeterminate and incomplete picture; similarly, it self-consciously presents the past as a series of narratives and stories. The very act of watching historical documentary is to engage with a set of tropes, formal concepts and technical elements that foreground the insubstantiality of historical knowledge. The epistemology of television history is *de facto* incomplete, biased, influenced by narrative and storytelling, biographical or mythmaking; it demonstrates the ability of an audience to deal with complexity.

Furthermore television documentary is a hybrid genre, importing audience expectation and technical practices from a variety of other forms and deploying a variety of systems of signification. The televisual grammar of historical documentary is complicated and can include among other things re-enactment and reconstruction, CGI, authorial presentation, archival documentation, archival footage and stills, eyewitness testimony, literary source, letters, diaries, recordings, diegetic and antidiegetic sound, audience participation in a variety of ways, location shots and interviews with professionals. Similarly, the practice of creating historical programmes demands a new set of skills encouraging different intellectual choices to be made by the presenter or producer: location; editing; music; sound mixing; script. The documentary is a work of collaboration between all parts of the production team, and it is also something developed within clear boundaries which are far from the standard limits of academia. Indeed, the very formal complexity of historical documentary challenges the blithe assertion that television history is overly simplistic. As Steven Johnson has argued, the non-linearity and complexity of popular culture have a cognitive effect and turn the viewer into a more sophisticated consumer of information than has been hitherto conceived of.[26] The multivalent format of contemporary historical documentary demands a sophistication of response.

'Contemporary, lively and egalitarian': Schama and Starkey

To consider this complex format it is necessary to turn to the premier exponents of television documentary history over the past decade, Simon Schama and David Starkey. Both produced epic personality-led, populist narrative histories aimed at wide audiences and global markets, and deploying the full palette of televisual tropes and techniques in order to divert and attract the viewer. The key domestic television documentary tradition that is being drawn upon in their practice is that of the epic series. Initially the BBC was the channel for big documentary series, and established the template with *The Great War* (1964), *The Lost Peace* (1966), *Grand Strategy of World War II* (1972).[27] These series were self-consciously grand in scale, distilling the complexity of the war event into digestible chunks. They used footage mainly from the Imperial War Museum's collections (despite the makers of *The Great War* falling out over historiographical issues with the then director Noble Frankland) but also used reconstructed scenes, stills, and interviews with witnesses, literary sources and commentary.[28]

The World at War (1973, Thames TV) was the first commercial series to employ this grand, wide-ranging style.[29] It was a series that intentionally changed the BBC's documentary practice, mainly through the emphasising of 'ordinary' stories, and the use of oral testimony and footage. Jerome Kuehl, the associate producer of the series, claims that they were trying to avoid official 'mandarin history', although they did deploy the gravitas of Laurence Olivier as voiceover for international sales. The series also moved away from a British-centric presentation of the war to encompass the experience of Germany, Russia and Japan – indeed, it was one of the first programmes to deal with the Holocaust in prime time, and the episode 'Genocide' received many press and public complaints due to its explicitness.

The second key tradition that contemporary documentary makers draw upon is the presented or authored documentary. The key analogues here are Kenneth Clark's art history series *Civilisation* (BBC, 1969) and Jacob Bronowski's anthropological series *The Ascent of Man* (BBC, 1973). These were unashamedly grand series, both in scale and chronology, and they presented teleological (although personalised) narratives. Robert Kee's *Ireland: A Television History* (BBC, 1980) introduced the more overtly interpretative style that Schama particularly deploys. These 'epic' documentaries have analogues in other disciplines, such as natural history or economics. They are sold on the personality of the presenter; as Schama warns: 'Note the careful use of the indefinite article in this series … it's *a* history because it's shamelessly my own version.'[30] These shows did not just have lives onscreen, though; they produced influential popular books to accompany the series. The most famous historian presenter before the 1990s was A.J.P. Taylor, whose programmes during the period 1957–67 and then from 1976 through to 1984 consisted of an unscripted lecture given in a studio to camera.[31] Taylor's history was narrative and populist, and his lectures were 'driven by stories and anecdotes', 'biased towards the biographical' and 'virtually all lent themselves to narrative and story'.[32] The shows were mainly on the fledgling commercial channel ATV rather than the mainstream BBC. Taylor's lecturing led to a profitable number of tie-in books on a variety of subjects.

Such personality-led programme-making fell out of favour during the 1980s. As suggested in Chapter 1, the revival of the form in the documentary *Simon Schama's A History of Britain* was the catalyst for the explosion in high-profile popular history in the early 2000s (and it is interesting that the pioneer for this movement was a series whose format had such ancestry yet was created anew within celebrity culture). Fifteen hour-long episodes were broadcast on BBC1 from 2000 to 2002. The series took an intentionally cinematic and epic approach to national history, progressing from earliest origins to the 1960s in an attempt to account for the emergence of a British identity. It always claimed to be a relatively subjective narrative, telling important stories in an attempt to have a contemporary audience. Schama's impetus was centralised on his four communicative tenets: immediacy, imaginative empathy, moral engagement, poetic connection. These ideas formulated his approach to making 'serious television history'.[33] Schama saw himself as the 'interlocutor between audience and protagonists', and, as Justin Champion points out, presented the historian as moral leader, guide, and continual presence in the narrative.[34] Schama says of Bede:

> [He] was not just the founding father of English history, arguably he was the most consummate storyteller in all of English literature ... it was this masterful grip on narrative that made Bede not just an authentic historian but also a brilliant propagandist for the early Church.[35]

Clearly Schama's own history is both keenly narrative and, in his 'unambiguous commitment to the moral function of history', subtly propagandist for a particular type of humanist History.[36]

Each programme took a period – around 130 years at times, as little as 40 at others – and used a particular set of primary motifs to read the particular stories: 'Dynasty'; 'Nation'; 'The Empire of Good Intentions'. Schama's script is interested in the repetition of image and idea in order to suggest a history rich in resonance. The use of the same cutaway shots to underline different points or the same clichés to describe events emphasises a history of Britain in which the same things keep on happening. It is also keen to emphasise that the past is present in the contemporary, shaping and influencing events. This is particularly striking in the episode 'Revolutions', in which Schama wears a yarmulke in a synagogue to emphasise his personal connection with Jewish history post-Cromwell; the episode ends with a description of the Battle of the Boyne overlaid with a contemporary mural commemorating the battle and soundtracked by both Unionist and

Republican speeches.[37] History is not something that is simply in the past, the programme suggests; it is full of repetition, resonance and echo. You cannot escape it, and those who do usually make a mistake. So the keynote is the educative power of history, the example that it holds up to us – a programme made in 2000 gave an opportunity to take stock and learn the value of the lessons of history. It was educative and exemplary, both in form and content.

Schama's appearance in the synagogue is an extraordinary moment of personalisation. Throughout the series, he speaks of 'our' history, emphasising a connection between audience, content and himself. However, the moment in the yarmulke creates an odd dissonance – this is Schama's personal history, a history he can specifically relate to. So it involves the audience, constructs an historiography of empathy. At the same time, however, the majority of the audience *aren't* Jewish, so the personalisation of history here is also an inscription of difference – the kind of polyvocal, hybrid difference that is key to Schama's view of multicultural Britain and Britishness. He is at once 'us' and other, the history he presents is complex but all part of us, tending toward this final moment almost teleologically.

Repetition is used to historiographical effect in the various visual images that the series deployed, suggesting, for instance, relationships between Charles, Cromwell and William III by the use of overlaying pictures and wiping between them – so Charles 'becomes' Cromwell as does William, emphasising visually connections (which are there anyway, iconographically, as those unfamiliar with portraiture the audience just has to be directed to them). Schama describes people using the same phrase ('his alpha and his omega' is a favourite; 'a public relations disaster' is another). This again emphasises connections and distills broad historical developments into understandable, cyclical entities. Schama's much derided use of demotic cliché, too, is part of this process – the placing of history into the familiar, creating a narrative of tropes that are recognisable and repetitive. These othered historical characters, all noble portraits and huge houses, are inserted into a familiar set of linguistic models – the threat of the Napoleonic armies meant 'it was sweaty hand time'; various Elizabethan nobles have 'sex appeal'. This slangy presentation of history annoyed purists, but, as with David Starkey's similar practice, it signals a familiarisation of history. Source, music, image, word, all work together to create a televisual experience that is finely wrought and well thought out as television first, then history second.

Of course, all this presentational material impacts on the historiography. One of the points of *A History of Britain* is that the development of the nation is a set of cycles and progressive events. Dynasties, empires, monarchs are all part of a process of accumulation toward 'Britain' and the present. Hence the proprietorial 'our' and 'we' that Schama peppers the narrative with – both involving the viewer in the narrative of nation but also emphasising the connection between then and now. Essentially, the programme presented history as a revolving cycle of religious violence, celtic rebellion, anti-European feeling and political expediency, all intersecting with the abilities and characters of a set of key personnel – Henry, Anne Boleyn, Elizabeth, Mary Queen of Scots, Charles II, Victoria. Key was a sense of the growth of liberal democracy in England, the union between the countries and the creation of 'Britain', religious conflict and the rise of capitalism. Schama traces his themes through the ages. Britain veers from battle to battle: from Marsden Moor to Culloden to Waterloo. The nation is reflected – even represented metonymically – by a series of major figures: Cromwell, Pitt, Wordsworth, Wollstonecraft, Walpole, Cobbett. There is very little about the common people, the day-to-day life of the nation, or the social, economic and cultural shifts undergone. Instead Schama knits together a history of personality, from Cromwell as half pious visionary, half ruthless politician through the romanticised image of Bonnie Prince Charlie, to port-drinking Walpole's gregariousness and Charles II's 'reason'. In between there are 'human' elements – the keepsakes left by mothers for their children at Thomas Coram's foundling hospital, for instance, are considered at length as a way of demonstrating the social ills of the early 1700s. These artefacts allow Schama to personalise history, in the same way that using one 'ordinary' figure such as Mary Wollstonecraft to commentate and experience key events gives those events individualised resonance and allows the viewer to connect and empathise. The important issue here is of recognition, of understanding the experiences of the past. Yet ultimately this history is one of important figures doing particular things – Clive in India, Wolfe in Canada, Pitt's 'Empire of Liberty', Victoria's 'Sisters'. It is narrative history, a story with human elements but a clear plotline nonetheless.

History is enshrined in the guidelines set out by Ofcom for public service broadcasting. It is part of a public service broadcaster's (PSB) educational remit, and history programming is presented by both Channel 4 and the BBC as evidence that they satisfy their duty to programme content of an educational nature and educational value. Therefore the channels conceive of history as part of an educative portfolio. Channel 4 uses the style of its history programming to further its institutional profile as an alternative view, quoting a number of respondents in its annual review:

> Viewers recognised Channel 4 had a different approach to history, more contemporary, lively and egalitarian. 'It makes it more accessible … it's not sort of stiff upper lip history programmes' (Female 50–69); 'The war on Channel 4 would be from a soldier's point of view. On 2, it would be the politician's' (Male 30–49).[38]

The channel's flagship documentaries are made by David Starkey, and they emphasise this liveliness. His series *Elizabeth* (2000), *Henry VIII* (1997) and *The Six Wives of Henry VIII* (2003) presented Tudor history and his *Monarchy* (2004–) approached that institution through the ages. The series are monarch-based, interested in personality politics, and their use of multiple problematic fictionalising devices make them more like essays than documentaries. The approach of this work, striving to be 'contemporary, lively and egalitarian' in many ways demonstrates Corner's point about 'diversion' in postdocumentary work (see Chapter 11). Starkey's series use multiple types of evidence and present their information in multiple styles – from docu-drama to lecture to music to textual evidence – all striving to keep the attention of – to 'divert' – the viewer.

Elizabeth opens with a summing up of the importance and appeal of his subject that is terse and pointed:

> In January 1559, Elizabeth I was crowned Queen of England. She was the last of the great Tudor dynasty, a bright star who dazzled both the nation and the world.
>
> The achievement of most stars fades quickly, but Elizabeth's has lasted for nearly four centuries – and it is easy to see why. She reigned for 45 tumultuous years, her ships defeated the Spanish Armada and sailed around the globe. In her time Shakespeare wrote plays and Spencer wrote poems. English noblemen and foreign princes wooed her but she, the virgin Queen, made love to that loyalest of audiences, the English people.[39]

In his trademark brisk and clipped style Starkey conflates the achievement of the monarch with that of her armies and population, and immediately presents us with at least three of the key cliché facts about Elizabeth: her virginity, the Spanish Armada, the time of Shakespeare (no matter that Shakespeare's career outlived her). It is a bravura passage in a direct, clear style, and as such it provides the framework for the series as a whole. *Elizabeth* is gripping docu-history, both personalised narrative and grand sweeping history. Starkey balances the personal and the wider political issues. He seeks to understand Elizabeth's 'achievement'. Further, he suggests here that he is simply filling in the gaps of a story already well known, four hundred years later – her reputation precedes him.

Starkey's presentational manner is in great contrast to that of Schama. He wears a suit and tie, and is generally pictured in distanced full body shot rather than the more intimate close-up shots that Schama favours. He is not the audience's friend, is not their guide (not for him the inclusive elements of *A History of Britain*, no 'us' or shared history). There are few jokes in Starkey's script, and the seriousness he brings to the subject is key to his projected gravitas. Starkey isn't part of the scenery in the way that Schama often is. Indeed, he strides around country houses lecturing the camera with great if distancing authority. He is a serious academic historian on television, rather than a presenter who happens to be an historian.

Yet his historiography is as much, if not more subjective as Schama's, and his work is more populist in trajectory. The series is on the experimental Channel 4 rather than the establishment BBC; Schama has the reputation of a British institution behind him, whereas Starkey has to ground his work lest it be accused of superficial flashiness. While he avoids Schama's insertion of himself into the historical narrative (and therefore attends to a different type of historiography with the historian as independent recounter of truth rather than subjective interpreter), Starkey's series does emphasise the importance of connecting the past and the present in the choice of talking heads. Again eschewing the academic documentary approach, *Elizabeth* comments on particular key personalities by having their descendants discuss their actions. Thus, Lady Victoria Leatham, descendant of William Cecil, gives us the benefit of her insight into his thoughts during the 1550s; the current Dean of St Paul's reads the sermon of Dean John Noel and conjectures on the effect it may have had; a Catholic priest considers the destruction of the monasteries and the character of Mary Tudor's Catholicism. The heirs of Bedingfield and Seymour wander around their country seats and discuss their (in the former case not so illustrious) ancestors. Disarmingly unacademic, refreshingly familiar with their forbears (using their forenames, confidently ascribing their motives), these talking heads give Starkey's series a sense of witnessing absent from Schama's, a collective account rather than his particularised reading. Their accounts personalise political and distanced events, dovetailing with the acted sequences to knit together a performance of history which is then focussed through Starkey's authoritative narration. In some ways the involvement of these figures demonstrates the massive historical shifts that have taken place – where once Cecil was Secretary of State, his descendant is irrelevant to the country; where the Dean of St. Paul's once affected political policy, his descendant has no national role. Yet the use of such 'experts' also suggests that personality is key – and in particular religious and aristocratic personality. Their subjective and conjectural opinion is as informed, the series suggests, as that of the academic expert. Indeed, these people may at least claim some kind of sympathy with the historical figure, an empathy the professional leaves at the door.

This notion of empathy is key to each series' historiographical impetus. Both want to use the medium to instigate a history of sympathy. Why alienate the audience from their historical past through jargon, footnotes and intensive detail, when the tools of television can be used to create a connection? This is the reason for the slangy script, the use of music and televisual trope. By presenting using the tools of familiarity, and by putting history into recognisable formats – drama, documentary, cliché – the series familiarise rather than alienate. While both invest in a Whiggish 'great men' methodology, they are interested in drawing the audience into a relationship with their history. Formally and generically, while both are recognisably 'narrative' personality-driven documentaries, they are complex entities. They use talking-head, witness (or relative of witness) testimony, text, metonymic footage, reconstruction, music and a range of camera techniques to inflect and package their central intellectual message. This complexity points towards the new typology of factual programming, the drive towards Corner's 'diversion'.

Schama and Starkey were massively successful, in terms of raw numbers. The first episode of *A History of Britain* was BBC2's top rated programme of that day, with some 4.3m viewers.[40] To put that into perspective, it would not have broken into BBC1's top 30; but it would have been third after *Brookside* (Friday/Wednesday) on Channel 4 and first by some distance on Channel Five. *Monarchy* was viewed by around 2m regularly, a really quite impressive reach and a substantial audience figure for Channel 4. As suggested in Chapter 1, they became part of British cultural life in an unprecedented way. Their programmes demonstrated that personality-led narrative history was marketable in the UK and the USA. The popularity of these narrative series meant that they were followed by Niall Ferguson's *Empire: How Britain Made the Modern World* (Channel 4, 2003) and Tristram Hunt's *The English Civil War* (BBC2, 2002), among a tranche of individual documentaries.

Dedicated history programming has gained a relatively good market share, for a minority lifestyle interest. There are a number of major channels: UKTV History (a branch of UKTV, part-owned by the BBC); the History Channel; Discovery Civilisations (a branch of Discovery); and this is notwithstanding specialist channels such as Simply Nostalgia (part of Simply TV) which is essentially an archival service. These channels represent a significant market portion, and there are few other 'lifestyle' programming strands that command three separate channels (other than shopping and travel). In late June 2005 these channels' share of weekly viewing time was as follows: History Channel (HC) 0.2 per cent; UKTV History 0.4 per cent (the equal best performance by a UKTV channel); Discovery Civilisations 0.1 per cent.[41] These share figures are about equal to those garnered by Sky Sports Extra (0.1 per cent) or CBBC (0.4 per cent). They translate into reach – and therefore number of viewers – as HC: 5.2 per cent (2,131,000); UKTVH: 9 per cent (3,472,000); DC: 2.7 per cent (1,030,000). In total, then, the reach/figures (despite their acknowledged vagueness as data) approximately equate all dedicated historical viewing (some 6,633,000) with that of all Sky movie channels taken together (18 per cent, 6,942,000). However, with the exponential growth in the numbers of homes with Freeview, and the developing of web- and mobile-based platforms for viewing television, the reach numbers will only go up, if the percentage of the viewing population probably will stay relatively static.

History on international television

Before moving on to consider Reality History it is instructive to compare the historical documentary on French, German, Canadian and American television.[42] In France, television history was initially used as a means of political debate in a rigorously controlled public television system.[43] Between 1953 and 1965, historical drama (there were 47) was used in this way: 'at a time when political discussion was avoided on French television, debates between Danton and Robespierre during the French Revolution were particularly appreciated by the audience'.[44] Historical documentary, when it was shown, was often used as the impetus for studio discussion, although continuing censorship meant that certain issues went unconsidered, such as the Dreyfus affair or the Vichy period. During the late 1970s and 1980s, entertainment became increasingly key, to the extent that now 'historical programming is no more a must for programme planners. These programmes are now considered as being at best a kind of cultural duty, a civic obligation that private channels will not endorse.'[45] The trajectory of French television history, then, mimics that of British in some ways – the doldrums of the 1980s, and the move towards entertainment – but they lack the authoritative element, and programmes were initially more concerned with wider issues and debate than the epic sweep and the academic style of British series. It is noticeable that French television has not imported the types of reality history common in the UK and the USA, possibly due to a residual commitment to propriety.[46]

German television has understandably found problems representing the immediate past. The screening in 1978 of the American NBC fictionalist mini-series *Holocaust* provoked a massive public debate breaking what Judith Doneson terms 'a thirty-five-year taboo on discussing Nazi atrocities' and led directly to political changes in the then West Germany.[47] While *Holocaust* was criticised in the USA for its sensationalist approach and its fictionalising, the effect of the series in Europe was to force the Swiss, French and Germans to 'confront the process of the destruction of European Jewry in all its enormity'; this process was painful and public.[48] Tobias Ebbrecht's survey of contemporary German drama and docudramas about the WWII argues that techniques such as dramatisation and the use of digital regeneration have been deployed by German producers in a particular fashion. In contrast to what he sees as the more conventionally objective British docudramas about the same period, German films 'use a combination of documentary and fictional modes of representation to create a special kind of tension and magical aura in order to offer the German audience a sensual and emotional space to empathize with the perpetrators'.[49] The programmes 'emotionalize history for a mass audience' in a style quite clearly at odds with British approaches.[50]

The most important – or influential – historical documentaries in the USA are those made by Ken Burns. He makes long 'event' television documentaries, as in the case of the 12-hour *The American Civil War* which was screened by PBS over five consecutive nights in 1990; the audience figures (14 million for the initial broadcast, many more projected millions for the rebroadcast and video release) ensure that it is probably 'the most popular history ever written or produced'.[51] Burns' approach is relatively hybrid. He uses a range of sources: footage of veterans from 1930, 1934, 1938, talking heads including Shelby Foote and various other historians, archive images, live cinematography footage of the battle sites, music, voiceover, newspaper accounts, lithographs. His aesthetic is kinetic and stately: the camera mimics movement – panning up, across, around; images are strung together to form a visual narrative. A key issue is that of the voiceovers – many contemporary sources are read out from Douglass to Lincoln, voiced by a range of famous names from Jason Robards to Studs Terkel – which lends credence but also celebrity and 'quality' to the whole event. The films begin with small, individual stories and widen their perspective; the epic sweep is the point. He claims a sort of historical empathy and gripping narrative innate in the materials:

> At a number of moments in this film, you suspend your belief that this is a photograph taken three weeks after the Battle of Gettysburg. You actually have the sensation of being there. When that happens, history is running on all cylinders. We have accomplished what we set out to do; to let the material tell its own story.[52]

The American Civil War, and his two other key series, *Baseball* and *Jazz*, were explorations of race in America driven by memory and witness testimony. Burns' films ensure that American historical documentaries achieve an epic range, speak to a sense of (albeit conflicted) nationhood, and are 'quality' events.[53]

Canadian documentary has spent a long time recovering from the controversy surrounding the 1992 CBC 3-film series *The Valour and the Horror* which considered the war in Europe and Southeast Asia. The series alleged incompetence at command level, suggested that unprosecuted war crimes had been perpetrated by Canadian soldiers in Normandy in 1944, and emphasised the Canadian Air Forces' involvement in the bloodthirsty and vengeful firebombings of Dresden and Munich. Canadian veterans societies sued the series producers, Brian and Terrance McKenna for libel.[54] The Canadian Senate sub-committee on veteran affairs consequently held hearings about the programmes (it was critical of two of the films), and the CBC Ombudsman produced a report claiming that the series was deeply flawed. In 1996, the Supreme Court ruled that the veterans' libel suit could not be pursued.[55] The series used re-enactment (scripted by diaries and letters) to highlight several events and these particular sequences were specifically attacked by the complaining veterans. The films sparked a lasting controversy which raged within contexts of memorialisation, public broadcasting responsibility, and investigative journalism. The incident suggested that revisionist film-making might be attacked extremely publicly, and, in particular, that techniques which seem familiar and unproblematic in a British context could be attacked for their lack of historical veracity and accuracy.

11 Reality History

Empathy, authenticity and identity

At odds with the formal austerity intertwined with a more or less explicit self-consciousness of the mainstream documentary are the various new forms and techniques being imported as a consequence of cultural and generic change. John Corner has argued that *Big Brother* in particular has had an aesthetic and a social impact on the genre of documentary, the shift towards what he calls 'diversion': 'a performative, playful element has developed strongly within new kinds of factual production'.[1] This influential analysis attempts to account for the 'imperative for playfulness and the erosion of the distinctions between the public and the private sphere, between the private citizen and the celebrity and between media and social space'.[2] Theorists of the classical documentary such as Bill Nichols suggest that Reality TV signals the death of the documentary and therefore the end of modes that encourage and mobilise the viewer to 'act in the world, with a greater sense of knowledge or even a more fully elaborated conception of social structure and historical process'.[3] Contemporary documentary has, in his view, eschewed this impetus toward education and citizenship. Linda Williams similarly argues that the weakening of historical specificity and the rise of populism mean that society has 'plunged into a permanent state of the self-reflexive crisis of representation'.[4]

Documentary, a form which in many ways (particularly in its British manifestation) relies on an underlying sense of sobriety, not to say educational seriousness, begins to fracture in the face of the new pressures. Corner suggests a state of 'postdocumentary' and argues that the form is undergoing a 'relocation as a set of practices, forms, and functions' as 'the aesthetic, political, and cultural coordinates that helped hold it together have both reduced in strength and shifted apart'.[5] He calls it the 'new ecology of the factual', and argues that 'when a piece of work in documentary format is entirely designed in relation to its capacity to deliver entertainment, quite radical changes occur both to the forms of representation and to viewing relations'.[6] In conjunction with these formal shifts, television channels began to eschew an academic approach to documentary and history in favour of an emotive, experiential-based approach. In 2002, the company Simply Television launched the Simply Nostalgia channel aimed at the 40–64 age group: 'The channel aims to provide an insight into 20th Century Britain from an emotional, rather than academic, aspect.'[7]

An example of this cheap, 'diverting', nostalgic programme making can be found in the archive list show. From 2000 onwards, television channels in the USA and the UK began screening a series of cheap 'recall' shows consisting of archive footage and talking head commentary. Shows like the BBC's *I ♥ 1970s* (2000), *I ♥ 1980s* (2001), *I ♥ 1990s* (2001) and VH1's *I Love the 80s* (2002), *I Love the 70s* (2003, 2006) and *I love the 90s* (2004, 2005) proved to be immensely popular and were shown on prime time. The shows were developed by the BBC and exported to the USA with few changes. They capitalised upon cultural nostalgia and a vogue for list-style documentary. Each episode covered a year in the decade. The format of the shows mimicked standard documentary practice but with a populist element and a pop-culture historiography. They deployed archive footage and the testimony of participants, along with an introductory voiceover and allied fringe elements such as websites. However, the focus was not on factual or newsworthy events. Instead, celebrity talking heads were asked to comment on and reminisce about diverse cultural phenomena such as films, television, fashion, toys, sport and famous figures. The shows established a cultural archive and a canon of experience. In the place of the academic, minor celebrities were invited to recollect and interpret their experiences, becoming at once the expert, the witness, and the avatar of the audience who were conceptually included in the reminiscences and recognitions. The experience of the viewer was intended to be that of inclusiveness and connection, of recollection and recognition. The shows project and construct imagined communities bound not by factual events but by shared cultural experience. As Bill Nicholls argues: 'These films naively endorse limited, selective recall. The tactic flattens witnesses into a series of imaginary puppets conforming to a line. Their recall becomes distinguishable more by differences in force of personality than by differences in perspective.'[8] They drew on a burgeoning mini-genre, the 'list' format of documentary. Similarly cheap, such documentary presents a countdown towards the 'top' event, selection or figure, with celebrity talking heads considering the significance or otherwise of each entry and evaluating them. Examples include *100 Greatest TV Moments*, *100 Best Sexy Moments*, *100 Greatest Sporting Moments*, *100 Greatest TV Ads*. The list as an evaluative historio-cultural tool is a key phenomenon and suggests a way of arranging or organising experience which tends towards the quantitative; it is a way of considering disparate cultural entities in parallel. The *100 Greatest* shows have an interactive element, insofar as they are generally voted by the audience of whichever channel they are on, and therefore there is a democratisation of cultural history. Viewers are enfranchised to a certain extent, and the fact it is artefacts from popular culture which are being celebrated and given importance similarly might argue for the fact that these shows are key levellers. The list shows allow the comparison of events which share few characteristics, and they create again an imagined community or audience bonded by the common experience of television. Whereas the top 10 list was often presided over by critics (for instance, in end-of-year summing up, or judgements of the 'greatest') the increasing popular involvement with these shows gives the power of cultural decision to the voters.

The shows are similar as they blend archive footage with minor celebrity expertise, yet of course the conceptualisation of these documentaries is slightly different. *I ♥ 1970s* trades in a collective cultural nostalgia whereas the 'list' documentary, whether serious or lightweight, presents an historiography of competition. Not for nothing was the final show in *Great Britons* entitled 'The Greatest of Them All'; the version of the archive that is presented to the audience in these shows is of a progression towards an historical winner, an exemplar. Yet similarly to *I ♥ 1970s* the list documentary presents a version of the past which is culturally constructed; social change is illustrated through cultural product such as film, gadget, music or television show. These shows demonstrate the multi-plying of the witness-documentary format, the drive towards populism and diversion.

Reality TV

In the debate on television history Reality style programming has played some-thing of a marginalised role.[9] Those most accused of 'popularising' historical presentation have often striven to disassociate themselves from such approaches; and those who have considered Reality TV have not looked at its historical manifestation in depth.[10] Given that, as a programming tool, it makes a clear contribution to the History profile of most TV channels, this distancing is inter-esting. Reality History is lowest common denominator television, re-enactment television inviting the viewer to identify with the ordinariness of the protagonist – and in many ways this clashes with the clean and coherent lines of narrative history; it certainly troubles the role of the academic or television historian as the gatekeeper of cultural product and historical fact. As John Dovey argues, 'Tidal waves of entertainment have flooded into discursive zones previously reserved for education, information and enlightenment.'[11] Reality History here refers to the suite of programmes which somehow involve and enfranchise the audience into historical experience, either by allowing them to participate in history through the game-style re-enactment of the 'House' format (in which a group of people are placed in a particular setting for a set amount of time and forced to act in the style of a historical period), or through interactivity of various forms such as voting, nominating, or commenting.

There has been much debate about the cultural implications of Reality TV, essentially, that which focuses on the experience of 'normal' people. One of the more idealistic views is well formulated by Jon Dovey in his book *Freakshow*:

> [Reality TV] has had a democratising effect upon the tired old formulae whereby the privileged commentators of the public service regime were allowed to speak on our behalf. Moreover this democratic impulse is not merely contained within strong narrative forms for our entertainment but is actually restorative of citizenship, actively soliciting our direct involvement

and interaction. It addresses new formulations of a social subjectivity in which what was formerly private becomes an essential component of public speech.[12]

This model relies upon Reality TV figuring a movement within television from it being a medium of transmission to one of consultation, a crucial interactivity empowering the viewer. Alternative models consider Reality TV as suspect due to it being the economic lowest common denominator and a product of market forces; further analysis considers Baudrillard's ideas of the simulacra in relation to the form.

Reality TV enacts a shift in the role of the audience. Where Reithian BBC models conceived of the educative power of television as a transmitter of information, contemporary television experience is more fragmented and far more interested in participation. Interactivity is the key word of the digital TV revolution, for instance. A greater sense of choice, interaction and control is fundamental to the way that television channels now present themselves. The audience is increasingly empowered. Reality TV is the ultimate expression of this, as the ordinary person is made extraordinary, either through makeover or public vote. Reality TV suggests that anyone could become a *Pop Idol* – and millions have tried – and suggests some kind of meritocratic system where the viewer is enfranchised, possibly part of the process and so therefore crucially invested in the conclusion. Reality TV, for many commentators, is important because of its key interactive quality. For Mark Andrejevic, this is both its attraction and its problem:

> On the one hand is the promise of interactivity – that access to the means of media production will be thrown open to the public at large … On the other hand is the Reality represented by Reality TV – that interactivity functions increasingly as a form of productive surveillance allowing for the commodification of the products generated by what I describe as the work of being watched.[13]

Interactivity can enable audience self-expression or self-definition, to allow for a consensus culture of personal investment and choice or participation. Andrejevic quotes Howard Rheingold: 'the political significance of computer mediated communication lies in its capacity to challenge the existing political hierarchy's monopoly on powerful communications media, and perhaps thus revitalize citizen-based democracy'.[14] Anita Biressi and Heather Nunn, for instance, argue:

> The visibility of ordinary people, the increasing audibility of their voices and the possibility of social mobility promised by their appearance on television raise important questions about the provision of space in broadcasting for the representation of ordinary people and their lives.[15]

Estella Tincknell and Parvati Raghuram suggest that the 'sense of participation engendered by this process … may thus have increased the feeling of ownership experienced by audiences and led to an intensified *engagement* with the text'.[16] On the other hand, however, are critiques such as Andrejevic's claim that Reality TV constitutes just part of a new self-commodifying capitalist system consisting of the 'work of being watched'. Gareth Palmer suggests that *Big Brother* represents 'an emotionalizing of the documentary project' as the new hybrids of the form shift their attention from public social issues to private concerns, to Reality documentary which is interested in the self-fashioning of the individual rather than a bettering of society.[17] Maybe the most nuanced consideration of this dichotomy comes from Justin Lewis who argues that Reality TV is 'nonetheless part of the continuum between Reality and fantasy that remains part of the ritual common sense of TV viewing … [it is] merely a reflection of television's own ambiguity: as an object, it is both external and internal to our world'.[18] What is clear is that rise of Reality TV and the new televisual grammar it has created demonstrates that 'significant changes are occurring in the way that audiences are consuming entertainment products'.[19] What does new form – or number of hybrid forms – mean for documentary and in particular for historical documentary?

In a recent essay, Simon Schama attempted to differentiate between what he terms 'historical Reality television' and 'television history':

> [Historical Reality programmes] sometimes seem as though they are in that same enterprise [television history], but actually they're not, since our involvement with the characters depends on us knowing that they are really 'like us', or that, in so far as they can be made unlike us, the agency of that transformation is social and material – washing with lye, tying a corset.[20]

On this model 'historical Reality television' is not History – and should be distanced from 'academised' television narrative history. The only difference between viewers and those they see is 'social and material'. The experience of the audience is significantly and importantly different due to the involvement of people 'like us' in Reality History. A notion of ontological interaction should be divorced from television history. In its place, Schama posits a mystical version of the 'poetics of television history' as a transformative experience that is grounded in a kind of alienation from history: 'Poetic reconstruction, if it is to work, needs to lose the characters, and by extension, us, who are watching them, entirely within their own world without any inkling of their return trip to the contemporary.'[21] This transcendent model involves a divorcing of visual experience from the lived world and somehow puts television history *outside* of history. It also ensures a model of history – or 'their own world' – as performance at a distance, something watched and apart from one's own experience. The protagonists are 'characters', and the whole thing plays into tropes of dramatic narrative. The model of the consumption of history here is passive, an audience observing rather than acting.

Quite apart from the various political and consequential issues involved in Schama's formulation of the difference between Reality and 'television' history, it seems that he misses the historiographical significance of Reality in contemporary consumption and transmission of history. While criticising those who would denigrate populist television history, he himself participates in the creation of a kind of hegemony that positions the historian as the gatekeeper to the past. Schama's attempt to distance his practice from the hybrids of Reality History suggests a certain anxiety about the role of the historian as master-of-narrative. The fundamental significance of Reality historical television is the fact that the people in it are 'like us' rather than idealised and crucially subjective reconstructions. While all historical presentation is contingent and subjective, Reality History at least acknowledges this and pursues its enfranchising agenda refreshingly free of the totalising claims of 'authenticity' that lie behind Schama's words. What follows is the sketching out of some ideas about how the involvement of 'ordinary' people in historical representation shifts received ideas of history.

There is significant crossover between the world of Reality production and historical programme making. For instance, BBC's *Restoration* (2003, 2004) and its spin-off programmes are produced by Endemol, the company responsible for *Big Brother*. In the programme viewers vote for which semi-derelict historical building they feel should be saved. Celebrities endorse buildings and the 'winner' is granted a huge amount of money and a high profile. This kind of historical restoration presents the reclamation of heritage as the responsibility of the somehow historically enfranchised individual rather than the community. When £3m extra was pledged to the series by the National Lottery, Nikki Cheetham, Managing Director of Endemol UK Productions, commented: 'We are extremely grateful to The Heritage Lottery Fund for this invaluable support. Restoring buildings like these can help breathe new life into communities and have a tangible effect on people's lives.'[22] This is history as regeneration, a discourse of the social utility of the past. Heritage becomes a literal national lottery and repositories of memory become part of a celebritised culture. Another example of this would be the *Great Britons* series. This demonstrates the cross-over between Reality formatting and historical discourses.

The key difference between *Restoration* or *Great Britons* and much Reality History is the lack of human involvement within the process, and the interactive voting element of the programme. More commonly, Reality History is about physical and emotional experience of the past. BBC1's *Destination D-Day: The Raw Recruits* (2004) trained a group of volunteers to simulate the Normandy landings. The diaries of the volunteers reflect the neoliberal rhetoric of personal achievement which is crucial to these reconstruction programmes:

> Jamie Baker: Practising the beach raid today, it was easy to imagine we were going to the Normandy beaches on D-Day. Bullets would have ricocheted off the boats, people would have died before they even got ashore. It would have taken a lot of bottle to do. Focusing on this puts any personal problems I have into perspective. People can do amazing things. The impossible can be achieved.[23]

BBC1 has also produced in recent years *The Trench* (2002) which recreated the experience of the 10th Battalion of the East Yorkshire Regiment on the Western Front in 1916. Volunteers from Hull and East Yorkshire spent two weeks in a trench system in France which had been authentically created for the series. *Why* they would voluntarily do this was unclear – in fact, the gap between Reality TV and history was demonstrated when members of the Trench squad refused to do various authentic things in the name of entertainment (volunteers on *Destination D-Day* also refused to do certain activities). Volunteers on *Surviving the Iron Age* (BBC1 2001) went even further, refusing to carry on with the experiment in social archaeology and walking out. The inability to withstand the privations of the past puts viewing figures through the roof. The space opened up between then and now is as interesting as the experiences of then – in fact, the notion of historical difference, or perhaps historical comparison, is crucial to the appeal. Dick Colthurst, the producer of *The Trench*, argued:

> We wanted to make a programme about the First World War accessible to a new generation. We've never thought of it as a Reality show, it's a new way of doing history. The problem of WW1 is a lack of archive film so if you want to tell a story of everyday life you have to find new ways.[24]

Is this a return to historical notions of 'empathy' – the creation of a narrative history connecting factual evidence constructed through the re-enactment of consciousness? Collingwood argued for a sense of re-enactment to understand historical events, to impugn plausibility to actions. What appears to be happening in some ways in Reality History is the attempt to 'put yourself in their place' and the creation of a empathy and experience. There is a gesture at empathic authenticity in the BBC programmes – the volunteers in *The Trench* are drawn from the same geographical area, as if that should have any relevance to the activity given contemporary population migration. The volunteers were trained and then expected to perform certain duties and tasks. There were no winners, and the entire point of the show was about recreating circumstances and gaining some kind of anomalous experience. There was an attempted emphasis on 'connection' to history, and through this a gesture towards a more profound understanding of the experiences of the past. This kind of re-enactment presents history as experience, a set of ontological skills that can be learned and mimicked. *The Ship* (BBC2, 2003) followed a '21st-century crew on an 18th-century adventure' as 'volunteers, historians and scientists recreated Captain Cook's epic voyage' around the east coast of Australia in the *Endeavour*.[25] A blend of expertise and ordinariness is foregrounded here. Volunteers become students of experience and the academic experts their guides. The erasure of the expert's status is enacted in *Tales from the Green Valley* (BBC2, 2005). The participants were a mixture of historians and archaeologists, running a Welsh farm for a year in the style of the 1620s. The experts were 'made' ordinary, their academic and theoretical knowledge undermined by the sheer physical difficulty of the past.

These types of show have a global appeal, and as such participate in the wider globalisation of cultural product. As Silvio Waisbord has argued, the global popularity of television formats (particularly Reality TV genres) demonstrates 'the globalization of the business model of television and the efforts of international and domestic companies to deal with the resilience of local cultures'.[26] Once the paradigm has been set – volunteers surviving the privations of the past – it can be mapped onto pretty much any country. There is even a competitive game version, *The 70s House*, which runs on MTV, and CBBC ran a children's version entitled *Evacuees* in 2006 which took 12 urban children to a 1940s-style farm (demonstrating the enormous demographic range of the format). The British production company Wall to Wall owns the 'House' Reality History format in the UK and the USA and makes docudrama, therefore being responsible for a great deal of the content discussed here. The success of Wall to Wall demonstrates the influence that private companies have on the BBC and UK terrestrial TV, and that formats are workable in several national media contexts. The development of programmes in the Wall to Wall portfolio shows furthermore the evolutionary sweep and potency of Reality History as a genre.

The global homogenisation of concept can work to flatten out national difference, yet it can also serve to emphasise a particular type of national mythos. American, Canadian, and Australian versions of the original *1900 House* (Channel 4, 1999) template have tended to concentrate on pioneers and foundational moments in programmes such as *Frontier House* (PBS USA 2002, set in 1883), *Colonial House* (PBS USA 2004, 1628), *Outback House* (ABC Australia 2005, 1861), *Texas Ranch House* (PBS USA 2006, 1867), *The Colony* (SBS Australia 2005, 1800s), *Pioneer Quest: A Year in the Real West* (Credo Canada 2000, 1870s), *Quest for the Bay* (Frantic Canada 2002, 1840s), and *Klondike: The Quest for Gold* (Frantic Canada 2003, 1897).[27] The publicity for *Outback House* illustrates the type of conservative (even survivalist) historiographies these shows are beginning to demonstrate: 'This is the story of the men and women who built Australia. The courageous entrepreneurs who, throughout the 19th century, ventured into the unexplored wilderness of the outback armed with dreams of making their fortune.'[28] This notion of extreme pioneering and 'untouched' history feeds into particular national myths. *Pioneer Quest* makes two couples 'survive just as the first settlers did', again placing them on 'untouched land'.[29] Participants in *Colonial House* take part in this rhetoric of nationbuilding:

> It has been said that the United States was built upon the great accomplishments of great men and women, but we discovered that it also stands upon the hard work and labor of countless people who performed these mind-numbing tasks, day after day after day.[30]

This has consequences for notions of active citizenship:

> As I expected, the project solidified my love for this country, as an American of African descent whose ancestors shed their blood in this soil for a better

life for me ... I better understand that democracy is not guaranteed, and that my participation is required to keep and enhance it.[31]

This sense of foundational events similarly informs the experiences of volunteers in *The Trench* or *The 1940s House* (Channel 4, 2001). These shows contribute to a teleology of national development (one gets to here from there), particularly emphasising the notion of the pioneers 'building' the modern civilisation and taming the wild frontier. The simplicity and tranquillity of past life are emphasised.

Reality History, then, often participates in the creation of a nostalgic shared past that demands memorialisation. However, it can also flag difference and contain historical dissidence. *Schwarzwaldhaus 1902* (*Black Forest House 1902*, SWR Germany 2001–2, 1902), for instance, explored the privations of farming in the early twentieth century with the central figure of the farmer being 'played' by Ismail Boro, a naturalised Turkish immigrant; the Black participants in *Colonial House* valued being part of an American history pre-slavery (it is noticeable that neither *Frontier House* or *Texas Ranch House* have Black or Asian participants), and *Outback House* includes Mal Burns, a member of the Aboriginal Wiradjuri tribe who wants to 'experience a little bit how hard my ancestors, as well as your ancestors, had it back then'.[32]

The interactive element of these shows is to the fore, with supporting websites presenting elements as traditional as photo galleries and as complex as podcasts, interactive quizzes, online forums and video diaries. The shows create an archive of their own, as the websites are still live on shows such as *Frontier House* which aired initially in April 2002. One of the most important elements of these series is their diversity and their generic flexibility as documentaries. They take place across several media – television (normal and digital), web (chats, forums, normal sites, links and further resources), follow-up books and magazine articles. They work in a number of ways, as Biressi and Nunn recognise: '[*The Trench*] was presented as commemoration and historical document in its attempt to construct and show the trauma of military service and it was also a group challenge.'[33] The shows deploy the standard tropes of historical documentary such as eyewitness accounts, archive footage, contemporary photographs and letters, while at the same time using innovative Reality techniques such as video diaries as well as their very form. *The Trench*, though, is more sophisticated in its approach to documentary than the various 'House' series, as it purports to tell more historical stories rather than simply focus on the experience of the participants.

Occasionally the programmes cheat in their presentation of the past, and in these slightly dissonant moments (such as the sepia-tinged footage of the Hymer family in the title sequence to *The 1940s House*), the programmes' dynamic is troubled. This photographic re/creation of a past also happens in the opening credits to *Outback House* as a shot of the entire 'cast' is rendered sepia after a mock-flash of a camera; similarly, the box for the game *Brothers in Arms* accentuates its authenticity with game screengrabs that morph into photographs. This visual trickery demonstrates the issues at stake with the aesthetics of presenting the past and the notion of authenticity and troping the past. Mock sepia-colouration adds a sheen of authenticity (even when the music accompanying is actually authentic) while simultaneously reminding the viewer that the history they are about to see is fake, a performance. Indeed, these brief moments invite the viewer to be constantly suspicious of what they are being told, as they demonstrate the ease with which the camera can lie. As opening sequences they immediately undermine any notion of camera authority.

Historical difference and ideology

One of the key elements of the Reality History show is difference. For all its empathic value ('how would I have lived through that?'), the shows also emphasise the problem of 'then'. One of the nexus points for this is animal rights (death, in wartime, is another). In a number of shows ranging in subject the treatment of animals demonstrates the dissonance of 'authenticity' both for participant and viewer. In *The 1940s House* the War Cabinet which was administering the 'game' of history provided rabbits to be eaten which had to be removed as the family could not bear to kill them. Mistreatment and mismanagement of farm animals in *The Outback House* led to public outcry.[34] Reality History demonstrates the flexibility of historical identities at the same time that it encourages a sense of historical otherness. History is at once crucially fragmented and simultaneously an othered discourse apart from our involvement, a game rather than an event. In contrast to other Reality TV in which the ordinary person becomes the subject, Reality History presents an elaborate drama of history with no particular objective. Reality History can challenge received ideas and imposed narratives of our past and heritage, but it replaces them with a muddle.

There is a crucial 'ordinary' involvement in history, and an audience investment in the story which is different from that of the audience for documentaries on *The History Channel* or Tristram Hunt's series on the Civil War. History is presented as lived experience, as a set of familiar privations, as something not mythic and different but familiar in many ways, undergone by recognisable people. As Juliet Gardiner has argued, 'The format allowed for an exploration of large issues not as debating points but as they might have impacted through the everyday.'[35] Reality History therefore presents a unique fissure in television history which has its roots in the re-enactment movement. It is history with the interesting bits left in.[36] History is lived experience, something messy and dirty and painful. Reality History still presents history as a 'fixed' thing, as something inflexible. The series present history as something which involves rules that cannot be broken. The subject undergoing history is not permitted to dissent or interrogate their chosen role.

The other major genre type of Reality TV of the last decade has been the makeover.[37] Key to this experience is the notion of the guide, the leader and companion in the journey to moral (albeit individually tailored) revelation and transformation through consumption. There are few historical makeover shows, and these in general relate to property – *Restoration* and *Period Property*. The key analogue between the makeover and historical television is the role of the expert/leader/historian in guiding us towards the finish line of personal achievement. In a far more subtle, classically humanist style than that of the makeover, television narrative history presents itself as entertaining education ('edutainment') that will lead to better understanding of oneself, one's nation, one's past – and so lead to perfection of some kind. There is an existential self-realisation inscribed into the Reithian version of television history, just as there is in the 'experience'-led Reality television shows. The audience better themselves, garnering and earning experience; like other 'serious leisure' pursuits, these things make them better (for instance, the BBC series *What You Wear Can Change Your Life*). Furthermore, the makeover transforms the individual through consumption; television history transforms the individual through experience. On the one hand, narrative history presents a perfectibility of nation; on the other, Reality History presents a perfectibility of self through empathy.

Central to these series is an interest in 'ordinary' people and the value of their historical experience. This is the point at which Reality programming intersects with historiography. *The Trench* focussed on volunteers living 'as ordinary foot-soldiers did in the Great War'.[38] The emphasis is that of 'experience', of using the 'democratising' format of the Reality show to create an historiography of empathy. As one of those involved in the series argues, 'The format allowed for an exploration of large issues not as debating points but as they might have impacted through the everyday.'[39] Through a combination of recognition and strangeness (which is the basic reaction to all Reality series – these are normal people, they are doing abnormal things), these shows force the audience to engage with history intellectually and emotionally. This is people's history, and the importance of personal testimony (witnesses, diaries, letters), the emphasis on the minutiae of experience, is the concern rather than larger issues of history. Mark Andrejevic's comment on the idealistic interpretation of the Reality format can be used to illustrate what is going on in terms of historical access:

> The promise deployed by Reality TV is that submission to comprehensive surveillance is not merely a character-building challenge and a 'growth' experience, but a way to participate in a medium that has long relegated audience members to the role of passive spectators.[40]

Reality History allows participation in a discourse which has 'long relegated audience members to the role of passive spectators', that of History itself. This has something of a moral issue involved, as is demonstrated in the disciplining of a particular soldier, thrown out for malingering and being AWOL. The Platoon Sergeant, when dismissing him, reminds the audience of the memorialisation that is occurring: 'You've not played the game the way that the rest of the guys are ... you've let the memory of the guys we're supposed to be representing down.'[41]

The Trench used an unsettling combination of information, particularly inter-leaving talking head testimony from surviving members of the 10th East Yorkshire

Battalion to describe their experiences of what was occurring. This technique encouraged a sense of connection between 'authentic' historical experience and the events of the series. The testimony of these historical witnesses was superimposed over that of the modern-day Trench.[42] At the same time, an extraneous and undiagetic voiceover explained events – both modern day and historical. The voiceover, as is the case in Reality History, becomes an authority in many ways above that of the witness testimony. The result of these two types of commentary is to emphasise the relationship between experience and explanation, the visceralness of the moment versus the understanding of hindsight. The audience is expected to engage on an emotional level (that of the experience) and the educational (that of the historical detail). The experiences of the volunteers were rarely related to historical or factual actualities (they never concentrated on their kit, or such specifics); instead their role was to demonstrate the effect of deprivation, hunger, confusion, sleeplessness, terror, bombardment on their personalities.

The use of the dramatic sequences here – being stuck in no-man's-land, going over the top (as, in *Edwardian Country House* (Channel 4, 2002) the creation of fetes and dinners, or in *The 1940s House* the privations and rationing) – creates a series of tasks. So while the shows are about experience of day-to-day life, they are also a task-orientated narrative. History is not random in these shows but has an outline. The show was criticised for not being able to really represent the horror of war (despite aggressive bombardment, and attacks by planes and snipers). The policy of 'disappearing' participants to follow the casualties recorded in the War Diary is one point, for instance, where the show rubs up against its generic boundaries. The regiment Corporal has to redirect post and collect the 'dead' man's greatcoat, which on one level is poignant but at another demonstrates that the show is a performance of history rather than anything authentic. This is then counterpointed with a survivor's witness account of the death of their friends and their desire for revenge by killing Germans, a visceral and emotive passage which highlights the emptiness of the contemporary experience.

One of the issues that have bedevilled most types of Reality shows in terms of 'authenticity' is the camera.[43] *Big Brother* dispenses with this problem by having hidden cameras, but for the majority of shows which do not consist of CCTV footage or hidden camera footage, there is a *frisson* of performance despite the standard convention of the camera being the POV of the viewer. The camera is allowed access to places that the participant cannot go – upstairs in the country house, into no-man's-land – and this creates a hierarchy of knowledge and access, with the viewer allowed an overview of events which is denied the 'ordinary' participant. These surveillance elements of the shows create for the viewer an illusion of understanding which is denied the participant. Similarly the programmes are organised in order to create narrative tension of a familiar generic type – in *The Trench* particularly that associated with 'going over the top'. The cliffhanger endings of the shows creates a false sense of narrative progression in a programme which is more about boredom and deprivation than explosion and event. It attempts to map a narrative clarity on events while simultaneously emphasising the everydayness of history.

Behaviour in these series is closely constrained and organised, and the programmes invite the viewer to wonder how this contrasts (or not) with their own lives. Such rules and codes of behaviour seem alien but are obviously only so because of historical hindsight. On the one hand, this has been argued to have the effect of demonstrating that ideology might also work (unseen) in contemporary life, allowing a reading of Reality History as dissident; at the same time the rules suggest that dominant ideologies are historically arbitrary and contingent, introducing a positivistic teleology of the individual which suggests a movement away from the constraints of the historical period towards the realisation and enshrinement of the self in the contemporary world. At the same time, the use of rule books, or war cabinets, or historical factual templates demonstrates that social life is a role. These paradigms demonstrate historical performativity; there is a set of rules to live your life through in order to be 'real'.

The Trench, for all its ability to create historical empathy and therefore effectively destroy hierarchies of historical knowledge, still utilises authority elements – narrators, experts, witnesses, the tyranny of authenticity – that attempt to create a framework. Participants in *Edwardian Country House* were governed by rule books (for the servants) and etiquette books (for the family). Their experience was disciplined, both by historical factuality and thence by behavioural specificity. In the instance of *The Trench*, as the volunteers were mimicking or echoing the experiences of a historically specific regiment, they had to obey the rules of the documents and texts of history (in this case, the War Diary or army manuals). Training manuals were used to recreate 'authentic' experiences, but of much more importance was the original 10th Battalion's War Diary. Not only did this allow for general information to be authentic, it was used to organise the experience of the Trench by setting the schedule for events, from the preparation for battle to scouting missions and casualties. This template, even more so in wartime experience than general everyday historical life, allows the series to demonstrate ideology at play.[44]

In *Edwardian Country House*, the rule books for the various roles were voiced by another, very clipped, female narrator (in contrast to the 'modern' voice of the VO). The authority of these sections in many ways superseded that of the VO, as they were the true 'voice' of the past. The rule book was voiced regularly in demonstrating how people should act, so in this there is a clear distinction between historical/contextual explanatory narrative and behavioural disciplining – so between history and experience. The behaviour of the participants in *The 1940s House* was organised by a wartime cabinet of historians who noted that 'this was probably the most controlled nation outside of the Soviet Union'.[45] Their aim is to create as authentic an experience as possible by 'controlling everything they do, from the kind of food they eat, to the amount of coal they can burn on their stove'.[46] In *The Trench*, the rules were imposed by the narrator (who talked the audience through them), the witnesses (who gave accounts of them), the military (who put participants on charges for malingering or not shaving) and the programme's producers, who instituted the action of the War Diary by withdrawing participants to replicate the disappearance of members of the regiment.

The Colonial House developed this diagetic hierarchy by putting the power of punishment in the hands of participants, particularly the Governor of the colony. The laws regarded the 'ordering of society', worship, royal proclamations regarding sports, trade and behaviour with Indians, masters and servants, drunkenness, profanity, and slander. The Governor and his colonists received a book of laws for the colony and a copy of Michael Dalton's (1619) *Country Justice*. Behaviour in the colony was therefore predicated upon printed, authentic information and a dramatised interpellation of ideologies:

> In reality, colonists would not have received such paperwork, but all colonists back then would have understood the laws of England, and would have known they were in effect. The law book served as a reminder to them of how they were expected to behave, and what the penalty could be for transgressors. The laws were not comprehensive, but provided a range of offences that gave the governor a framework for running the colony.[47]

This 'framework' for the correct running of society is ahistorically imposed in order that the inauthentic participants act correctly; their historical equivalents would have 'known' how to behave. The series foreground punishment and as such suggested a way of considering seventeenth-century life as being made subject to the rule of particular law. This imposition of ideology, and the demonstration of how the law is deployed as carrier of that ideology, are a key part of Reality History. These shows are interested in behaviour, and the historical constraints upon that behaviour – and in this ideology is as much an historical constraint as not having a washing machine.[48] Indeed, in most of these series the constraint upon behaviour is as much an issue as the privations of the past. The series suggest that historicity is simultaneously physical and social. Indeed, the very settings for these shows highlight the constraints of ideology upon behaviour, be they war (at the front or on the home front), colony or class-ridden manor house. History is a set of social and behavioural rules as much as it is different clothing or lack of technology.

Authenticity and the historical revelation of self

The 1940s House took on similar issues – wartime experience – but attempted to bring them even closer to home than *The Trench*. Similarly to *The Trench* there was a sense of memorialisation: 'it will be as nothing to those that lived through the war and we wouldn't want in any way to trivialise their hardships'.[49] Rather than build a trench in France, the producers found a property that itself had a wartime story – it had been bombed and requisitioned, and during the renovation a family bible was found with a note relating the death by heart attack of a man putting a fire out in the house – so the space of the programme itself was authentic, a piece of history. Similarly the introductory programme demonstrated the attention paid to period detail in the furniture, toys, cooking utensils and clothing. What was emphasised were the restrictions – fewer toys, lack of cigarettes or modern-day appliances.[50] There was a clear feeling among the participants of the educative power of the exercise: 'We have to show the post-war generation what it really was like … because our knowledge comes from books or films, this is where it is going to be different. We are going to be real people experiencing those hardships.'[51] Reality History attempts to address the problems identified with the new documentary, to somehow keep the Grierson ideal of the educative power of the form alive while innovating and changing the style of the genre and Corner's 'new ecology of the factual'.

The new televisual grammar of documentary is here an adaptive or evolutionary one which finds space for educative purpose in postdocumentary factual programme. Indeed, Juliet Gardiner, who was closely involved in creating the programme, claimed it was less 'Reality' than more traditional forms of 'living' history:

> It would be an experiment in trying to distil the essential features of the 'home front' into living history, to see how they would cope as a wartime family would have had to do with the privations and restrictions of war.[52]

In this view, the postdocumentary element of new documentary history is more down to the importing of elements of performative, educative history than to the deployment of Reality tropes. The 'living' history movement has involved 'ordinary' people in museums and historical locations for decades. However, the use of video diaries, voiceovers (diagetic and extradiagetic), expert visitors and the historical template of the wartime cabinet suggests that this series was as much Reality television as an experiment in living history. Key to this element of the series was an empathic response. The wartime cabinet of historians and experts saw their educative remit as being as much empathic as factual: 'I think we'll discover something of the psychology of people subjected to extreme circumstances'; 'it will be extraordinarily revealing to viewers because they will say to themselves "How would I have lived through that?"'[53]

One of the major dissonances that *The 1940s House* presented was due to the fact that unlike *The Trench* or *Edwardian Country House*, it was not a closed community. The neighbours help the Hymer family dig their Anderson shelter in Episode 2, for instance, or leave them firewood. In many ways this makes it into a performance, emphasised by the fact that the house was opened up to local people as a museum before the volunteers arrived. Unlike *The Trench*, in which 'witnesses' were given programme time and invested with authority due to their testimony, the witnesses in *The 1940s House* were presented in more complex ways. Lynn and Kirstie Hymer visited a retirement community (in costume as part of their WVS war effort, thus lending an extra performative element to the activity). They met and discussed their experience with the residents (asking about the the uniform of the WVS 'Does it look right?'; 'What did you do?'). This presents an interleaving of then and now, witness testimony and contemporary historical performance. The family also had visitors, such as Marguerite Patten, who worked in the Home Office during the war. She was another 'witness' (like their advisors on food and blackout) who tests the authenticity of their experience and congratulates them. She is seen speaking to camera about their experience: 'both Kirstie and Lynn typify how women coped during those war years'.[54] Reginald Long, a fireman whom Lynn makes friends with at the retirement home, becomes part of the programming as the audience hears his version of events and sees a newspaper article about the event (a bombing) that he is talking of. Some of these witnesses are authentic and official, judging the blackout or testing the food, but some are merely passers-by whose experience renders them more 'real' than the Hymers and continually reminds them of their duty to the past and particularly the ordinary people who survived such conditions.

Yet these shows still retain the importance of personal revelation. Biressi and Nunn conceptualise the 'revelation of self' and the creation of an 'authentic selfhood' through confessional or participative television.[55] Volunteers in these shows are seeking an imagined wholeness, a community which the anxieties of the 'real' world deprives them of: 'the subject's discontent is frequently coupled with a nostalgic yearning for a sense of authentic community'.[56] *Colonial House*'s Clare Samuels exemplifies this kind of connection: 'I relive much in my mind daily, I miss the closeness of newfound friends, miss the depth of sharing, miss the simplicity of life.'[57] In many instances this idealised community is allied to a personal revelation, a movement to a hoped-for self. In *The 1940s House*, Michael Hymer's 'boyhood dream' is to return to the 1940s (particularly to build an Anderson shelter).[58] Lynn Hymer admits at the conclusion that 'I never thought … that it would have such impact on our lives. It's made me look at things in a totally different light.'[59] Unlike most other series, both *The 1940s House* and *The 1900 House* have a final episode in which the volunteers are invited to reflect on how the experience has changed them.[60] For the Hymers, the experience educates them, teaches them the value of hard work, and improves their health (they lose weight (body fat), their fitness increases and blood pressure is better). The experience has been 'good' for the children and Kirstie, both in terms of material difference (no TV or Playstation) and conceptual (she is more experienced, they didn't argue as much with each other, they work harder at school, they appreciate what they have more). Lynn starts writing (letters and a diary) and finds that her memory for language comes back to her – all in all, she and her daughter live a less passive existence. Ben, the youngest, puts it plainly: 'since we've come back from the 1940s house, life is better'.[61] Reya, the daughter in *Schwarzwaldhaus 1902*, argued that her life was enriched and claimed that the experience has given her an 'auxiliary tank' ('einen Zusatztank').[62] There is an ahistorical sense of what historical deprivation might mean for the self, for instance, in Dan from *Outback House*'s particularised use of therapy vocabulary: he feels 'lonely and depressed' away from his family, and assumes that this would have been the experience of those at the time.[63]

Participants in *The Trench* – in this case, John Robinson – volunteered from a combination of historical interest and personal betterment: 'I volunteered for 2 reasons, first because it was about the history of Hull, second was personal – it was desire to put myself under pressure and see if I could hack the situation coming up.'[64] Subsequent to their experience, the volunteers expressed a new personalised understanding of the experiences of the past: 'I didn't have any idea of what the people went through, I now do without simulating the mortal fear they would have had to put up with'.[65] The experience appears to have focused on a sense of empathy, particularly emphasised through living near enough on a historical site: 'It was a sense of understanding where we were was of historical importance'.[66] Yet the Reality re-enactors kept a sense of perspective and historical distance in order, they claimed, to show respect:

> I was always aware of what I was doing and where I was because, for me, it would be disrespectful to claim I was back in 1916 for real but you did have insights at times, I was always aware I was not in mortal danger and was not a soldier for real.[67]

Through this historical 'Reality' enactment the participants claimed a personal transformation: 'It's given me a better appreciation of my life.'[68] Furthermore, though, they emphasised the educational importance of their experience and privation. There is a clear sense of awe at the experiences of those actually under fire, and a sober awareness of the very real difference between contemporary Reality show and historical event.

The butler Mr Edgar in *Edwardian Country House* sees a personal victory in the authenticity of his behaviour: 'I inhabited the world that my grandparents inhabited and they can be proud of their grandson, because I behaved like an Edwardian.'[69] This notion of 'inhabiting' the past is more alive in *Edwardian Country House*; indeed, while those undergoing hardship below stairs constantly conceive of their experience as performance ('you can't be yourself; you can hardly breathe', 'it's an absolute and utter prison'), the family who are privileged in the series drift further and further from 'now' into a fantasy of the past.[70] 'Lady' Oliff-Cooper has 'been transformed since she came here' says her maid, and she herself describes the experience as if she is suffering a kind of Stockholm syndrome: 'I am Milady and it is curious if people treat you as Milady how you grow in to the position. Sir John's taken to his title like a duck to water and in fact I think it really has brought out the best in his personality.'[71] The immersive quality of the three-month experience instigates a loss of the contemporary self, or a dissolving into historicity:

> I don't think I really like the 21st century ... we've worked out from experience how to act in every situation, so now we think like Edwardians ... we are the last living Edwardians ... I'm thinking Edwardian, I'm thinking nothing whatsoever to do with my modern life.[72]

Her sister Avril is disturbed by the situation to the extent that she becomes ill; according to the ladies maid, she is a 'victim of sticking to the rules, she's been a true Edwardian woman and she's paid the price for that'.[73] Mr Edgar describes her condition as 'a half-lived life. How very, very Edwardian' – so even failing in the show is somehow authentic.[74] For all its staginess, *Edwardian* is more akin to *Big Brother* than the other Reality History shows as it has a closed community cut off from the world for a *significant* time period. The moral universe of the participants begins to lose definition, as illustrated in this revealing remark from 'Sir' John: 'we do things within the house that conscience would not allow us to do in 2001'.[75] This differs, for instance, with the attitude of the more community-minded ranch owner of *Outback House*: 'we achieve more by cooperation'.[76]

Reality History documentary practice is immensely diverse and public engagement with the past through such programming suggests a sophistication and complexity hitherto unaudited by historians or cultural scholars. Reality style programming, on the one hand, turns history into something fetishised – the 'authentic' experience desired by the participant or viewer – and at the same time flattens it; history is just one other set of tropes, another type of privation akin to being on a desert island (like in *Survivor*) or cooped up in a house in Mile End (like in *Big Brother*). There is a clear sense of popular involvement in history – both as audience and participant – and of the various uses that history might have to the revelatory formation and definition of the contemporary self. Furthermore, there is an emphasis on individual achievement and the behavioural ideologies of history. Is it the 'democratisation' of knowledge? Reality History conceptualises the opening up of access to history and postulates a kind of 'public' history. Yet the active simultaneity of the project – from the presence of the camera to the use of documentary tropes such as archive footage – demonstrates the artificiality of the entire process.

Reality TV has eroded the boundaries of the documentary form and introduced a raft of hybrid forms which encourage an investment in the personal, the experiential, and the active role (whatever that means) of the audience.[77] Juliet Gardiner, historical consultant on *The 1940s House* and *Edwardian Country House* argues:

> men and women make their own history, but they do not do so in conditions of their own choosing. Setting people to live in the conditions of the past with the awareness and questions of their various presents can get satisfyingly close to interrogating this most profound of historiographical truths.[78]

This apparent dynamic between lived experience and broader arcs of meaning is a key element of the phenomenon. 'Reality' history can make a profound intervention into the ways in which people engage with and understand the past. Rather than proffer any thorough historiographical understanding of events – although it gestures to this, too – this style of programming presents the most profound example yet of 'history-as-experience' considered in various proceeding chapters. 'Reality' history suggests that the dominant mode of interaction with the past in contemporary culture is through embodiment, engagement and experience. By assessing their own experience and cross-referencing this with their physical understanding of the past, 'Reality' History promises the revelation of the contemporary self through the consideration of the historical subject.

Part V

The 'historical' as cultural genre

The genres of history

The following chapters consider the prevalence of the historical as a trope or representational context in popular culture and therefore its dynamism as a generic form. Once again Ludmilla Jordanova has pointed the way for this type of analysis, suggesting that: 'professional historians need to understand them [television and fiction] and appreciate their complex effects'.[1] The cultural representations of the past are crucial in contemporary society's historical imaginary. The breadth of this historical imaginary – stretching from best-selling romance stories through blockbuster films, from niche Graphic novels to classy costume drama – demonstrates the grip that the historical has on cultural production. The range of audiences addressed similarly illustrates that 'history' has a breadth, scope and range of influence that demand attention. These texts also demonstrate the fetishising of history and the commodification of the past through its being turned by the cultural industries into consumable product. Put simply, the ways in which society consumes these types of fiction, buys these kinds of text, visits these types of film, or rents these DVDs prove unanswerably that society is obsessed with various versions of the past.

History is prevalent to the point of saturation. While there have always been treatments of history, explorations of key events (particularly wars) and adaptations of classic novels, the 'historical' has become a commonplace in contemporary culture. These chapters consider the ways that this culture has interpreted, engaged with, and complicated 'history' to the point that the 'historical' becomes a genre in itself to be challenged and subverted. However, all the while, the pastness of the past is key, as most of these formats and media attempt to gain a certain legitimacy and orthodoxy through authenticity. Very few formal or stylistic experiments have been undertaken in mainstream historical drama and film, in terms of presenting rupture, fracture or alternative. Those that have, have still tended to cleave to certain rules (such as utilising realism) about representing the past. History on television strives to attain a kind of hyperauthenticity, a silently acknowledged un/reality.[2] Both drama based on novel sources and those based merely in period strive to present the 'reality' of the past in authentic fashion and therefore present their product as in some way true.[3] Truth and fiction are problematised, as the historical mode is deployed to present fictional accounts of the past. 'Authenticity' is an obviously empty category, yet these series strive for it and deploy a variety of tropes in order to attain a semblance of it. Only in comedy is the mask of authenticity shown to be just that, a caricatured illusion. The past in these shows is a set of tropes and gestures that are overlain onto a generic framework.

It is instructive to use the work of György Lukács, the theorist of the historical novel, to explain the kind of implicit, understood *Verfremdungseffekt* that the 'historical' text produces in the reader:

> [Walter] Scott's 'necessary anachronism' consists, therefore, simply in allowing his characters to express feelings and thoughts about real, historical relationships in a much clearer way than the actual men and women of the time could have done. But the content of these feelings and thoughts, their relation to their real object is always historically and socially correct.[4]

In other words, the character in such a work speaks in a way that is anachronistic, but necessarily so for the piece to work, and in a way that is tacitly understood by the reader. The historical text is constantly calling attention to itself as a construct but the reader happily forgets this. Brecht's *Verfremdungseffekt* – the dramatic text constantly bringing attention to itself as dramatic text – is here a fundamental element of the strange process that is creating the 'historical' mode. An historical novel is one step more complex than a contemporary novel because of its historical quality – it is continually illustrating to the reader that it is false while at the same time striving for truthfulness and authenticity. This seems to describe clearly the experience of engaging with an 'historical' text, insofar as the reader/audience/viewer is constantly aware of the 'difference' of the narrative whilst simultaneously understanding that this pastness is itself a falsification. The ability to hold all these things in the mind concurrently demonstrates that the consumer of historical product has a complexity of engagement that is a level higher or more complex than that of the 'contemporary' text. The process of 'reading' a text which is at once recognisable and at the same time consciously different from the present day necessitates this sophistication of response. The 'historical' text is self-consciously theatrical in its historicity, but simultaneously 'authentic' in its presentation of the past and performing that past as if it can ignore its status as something in the present. This kind of paradox argues a constant state of flux in such a text. It is the same as the *frisson* found in re-enactment or Reality History – the modern subject performing pastness and somehow able to inhabit their contemporariness as well as their performed historicity.

In this light it is notable that docudramas became increasingly popular during the 1990s.[5] The docudramatic simulation of documentary material through the deployment of actors allows a visualisation of the past much like the use of re-enactors. At a time when documentary practice was being renegotiated, John Ellis argues that this 'is clear proof of the idea that generic values are based upon assumptions shared between audience, filmmakers and institution'.[6] Derek Paget echoes this collaborative model, arguing that docudrama enfranchises 'the audience as active negotiators of meaning'.[7] Key films such as *Bloody Sunday* (ITV, 2002) or *Hillsborough* (ITV, 1996) demonstrate the uneasy marriage between television drama and history. They suggest an audience comfortable with dramatisation of key events, at ease with the reconstruction and fictional re-enactment of iconic historic moments. A docudrama is authentic and othered, simultaneously fictional and real, and this formal paradox is what underlies nearly all engagement with historical cultural product.

A great deal of work has been done on historical genres such as film and television, yet their very perpetuating, shifting, evolving form and the sheer number of cultural products designated as 'historical' make generalising problematic. History is fertile as source, backdrop, inspiration, setting or motif for a range of television and film genres encompassing comedy, serious drama and fantasy; it allows consideration of the modern world, the perpetuation of certain cultural hegemonies, or the exploration of dissident sexual identities.

12 Historical television
Classic serial, costume drama and comedy

Drama on television deploys the nostalgia mode in many forms, most notably the costume drama. Such 'heritage' product has been criticised for its appeal to a solely middle-class audience, its interest in superficial costume and the artifices of class. 'Heritage' product such as the classic adaptation is watched, on this model, by women, tends towards cultural conservatism and enshrines particular erroneous myths about historical identity. Historical television drama is generally associated with an educated middle-class audience.[1] Much of the fulminating about 'heritage', though, relates solely to film, and in particular was written during the 1980s and, as Claire Monk has argued, the 'monolithic critique' of them is 'a historically specific discourse, rooted in and responsive to particular cultural conditions and events'.[2] The classic serial on British television has been generally included in this criticism, part of a selling of heritage Britishness to the world. While this is in great part true – the series have established a cultural orthodoxy, a set of recognisable generic tropes and, in *Pride and Prejudice*, a cross-over hit – at the same time they can invoke complex models of historical subjectivity, confound expectations, and consider key political issues of the past in order to educate the viewer. As a consequence, they are not dry, conservative mythmakers and, in their later manifestations, are flexible and innovative. The dramatic representation of the past can emphasise a comfortable, easy set of recognisable 'heritage' tropes; at the same time it can also be problematic or challenging.[3] The ability of the postmodern nostalgic text to renegotiate form and include complexity and possible dissidence is theorised by Frederic Jameson as 'post-nostalgia', a mode in which the text's plurality and self-awareness in many ways allow it to critique through self-consciousness and ambiguity.[4]

In this chapter the classic form of the costume drama is considered before it is contextualised not simply with itself but with other types of television historical drama; this broader approach to history in dramatic form – or as cultural tele-visual product – allows continuum between, for instance, costume drama and historical comedy to be seen, and as a consequence fosters a more nuanced understanding of the models of the past which are being proffered and consumed. Key to historical drama is the question of authenticity, which is conferred either through cultural hegemony or – increasingly – within the *mise-en-scène* of the form. The chapter then considers two American series which seem to cleave so much to the authentic that they lapse into what might be called hyperauthentic, and then looks at the ways in which comedy and light populist drama have also queried and undermined historical legitimacy.

Adaptation and costume drama

The classic drama or novel adaptation series have an instant cultural value conferred by their source material. They convey a sense of the depth and richness of British literary history – it is rare to have an adaptation of something non-English, or of something not a novel. Canonical serial adaptation works to establish the cultural hegemony and standing of the channel (generally the BBC) in the first instance and is subsequently part of a worldwide strategy to sell a particular type of 'British', classic product. As Lez Cooke points out, the revival of expensive costume drama in the 1990s was driven by a need to create a saleable product, a national cultural brand that would be marketable outside of the UK.[5] John Caughie has argued that the drive to marketing programmes about the past in the USA and Australia meant that the product became tailored for a particular audience; he argues that classic adaptations simplify 'irony and wit' as 'English quaintness'.[6] The BBC, particularly, has funded and distributed classic adaptations with money from the USA, Australia, Holland, France and Finland. In the USA, PBS broadcasts the BBC productions with the umbrella title 'Masterpiece Theatre', highlighting the canonical and theatrical associations the adaptations have. They are now increasingly marketed as complete DVD sets, recasting the 'series' as an organic whole unrelated to their original televisual context and abstracted from their more complex origins.[7] The heritage television industry gave such notions of 'Englishness' commodity value, but the price was a dilution of the edge of the programmes and the development of a caricature; similarly the questions of nostalgia and the attitude of audiences to imagined history that the series raise are collapsed into a marketable national identity.[8] Yet, as is argued below, the classic serial has the potential to include dissident positions and to confound comfortable relationships between past and present, even while seeming to inscribe clichéd and unproblematic versions of history.

Costume dramas from 1990 include the following:

BBC

The Mayor of Casterbridge (1991)
Middlemarch (1993)
Martin Chuzzlewitt (1994)
Pride and Prejudice (1995)
Persuasion (1995)
Tom Jones (1996)
The Mill on the Floss (1996)
The Tenant of Wildfell Hall (1996)

Ivanhoe (1997)
The Woman in White (1997)
Our Mutual Friend (1998)
Vanity Fair (1998)
Tess of the D'Urbervilles (1998)
David Copperfield (1999)
Wives and Daughters (1999)
Great Expectations (1999)
Oliver Twist (1999)
Madame Bovary (2000)
The Way We Live Now (2001)
Lorna Doone (2001)
Daniel Deronda (2002)
North and South (2004)
He Knew He Was Right (2004)
Bleak House (2005)
Jane Eyre (2006)
The Diary of a Nobody (2007)
The Cranford Chronicles (2007)
Oliver Twist (2007)
Fanny Hill (2007)
Sense and Sensibility (2008)
Lark Rise to Candleford (2008)
Tess of the D'Urbervilles (2008)

ITV

Emma (1996)
Moll Flanders (1996)
Jane Eyre (1997)
Rebecca (1997)
Far From the Madding Crowd (1998)
Wuthering Heights (1999)
The Turn of the Screw (1999)
Doctor Zhivago (2002)
The Forsyte Saga (2002)
The Mayor of Casterbridge (2003)
Persuasion (2006)
Northanger Abbey (2006)
Mansfield Park (2006)
The Old Curiosity Shop (2007)
A Room with a View (2007)

Channel 4

Anna Karenina (2000)

Forty-odd prestigious, relatively expensive series in 18 years demonstrates the valency, tenacity and importance of this genre to the major channels. The standard authors tend to be nineteenth-century and English (the only foreign writers being Tolstoy, Flaubert and Pasternak), and indeed this period has near complete ascendancy: Dickens, Austen, Trollope, Scott, Hardy, Gaskell, and Eliot become the canon. The only writer who might challenge this canonicity is E.M. Forster, whose novels have been the basis for the most influential films in this genre. There is also a strand of BBC children's adaptations from classic – often fantasy – novels, including *The Machine Gunners* (1983), *The Box of Delights* (1984), *The Chronicles of Narnia* (1988–90), *Tom's Midnight Garden* (1989), *The Borrowers* (1992–93), *The Phoenix and the Carpet* (1997) and *Kidnapped* (2005).[9] These productions are similarly co-funded by American production companies, and marketed internationally. They are on a big scale and rely on similar models of 'quality' to their adult equivalents: literary source, high production values, good acting talent (particularly with the use of talented and well-known actors in adult roles). They present a model of quaint, quirky Englishness (generally dating from the early twentieth century). In *Kidnapped*, the children's series, the classic serial, and the swashbuckling genre all coincide as they do, to a slightly lesser extent, in the action-packed epic series *Robin Hood* (BBC, 2006–7).

The costume drama, then, has become part of the key televisual furniture for the BBC, a cornerstone of its drive to 'quality' and central to its scheduling. ITV do not do the 'classic novel' serial as regularly, but deploy them strategically in order to garner praise again for the 'quality' material they show.[10] This notion of 'quality' generally refers to the standard of acting, the costume and general production values, and the script. Other 'indicators of quality' include potential as 'heritage export', source material, and the obvious funds invested in the series.[11] The sheer number of these adaptations and their afterlives on DVD, world-syndicated repeats and in culture generally suggest that as a means of engaging with a (fetishised) past and with history as focussed through culture and literature they have a breadth and significance which outweigh their status as mere Sunday night entertainment.

The 'classic serial' in general obliges the audience to keep two separate concepts in tension – the idea of authenticity and that of fiction. A viewer is expected to be quite happy that this is a story or narrative occurring within the framework of authentic historical representation. Unlike, for instance, *ShakespeaRe-Told* (BBC, 2005) or Chaucer's *Canterbury Tales* (BBC, 2003), it is not the case that classic novels are updated or reset in any way.[12] They take place in their own cultural moment, and therefore represent history visually to an audience while their narratives give a flavour of the time despite being self-evidently fictional. Sarah Cardwell points out that adaptations of classic novels attain 'quality' status through their 'careful reconstructions of the past'; in many ways the engagement with the costume-drama is driven by a demand for authenticity.[13] Cardwell argues, 'Although the audience recognises the stories as fictitious, it accepts the validity of the programme's representations of the past.'[14] The visual aesthetic of these series and films, then, bleeds into popular conceptualisation of the past.

The audience, to develop Cardwell, can quite understand the narrative to be fiction while the setting is 'authentic'. This ability to conceptualise the past in such a complex way, as both fiction, live-action, a familiar aesthetic trope, and actual history of a sort again demonstrates the dynamism of television audiences and their capability of engaging with texts from multiple standpoints. This able and accepting response to an aestheticised and fictional past, though, might be troubling when texts veer from 'reality' – if they are based on historical novels, for instance, or if the medium is not a costume drama but, for instance, a series which deploys the same authentic *mise-en-scène* to gain credibility (as, for instance, *Dad's Army* did).[15]

In some ways, the television costume drama confounds the heritage theorists of the 1980s and demonstrates that they were very much part of their time; at the same time the series at their worst peddle lazy clichés about Englishness and present history in straightforward, unimaginative, elitist style. *Middlemarch* (1994) was one of the first of the wave of 1990s adaptations and in microcosm demonstrates the key elements of the genre: an impressive, canonical text by a leading English author; 'screenplay' by Andrew Davies, soon to become the man most associated with classy and elegant adaptations; high production values, expensive set-piece shots; the sheen of aestheticised history; stately music; fine English acting; epic sweep and length (6 episodes in 375 minutes).[16] The opening sequence seems to validate the criticism of such drama, a Constablesque pastoral landscape with sheep. However, this is disturbed by a coach driving through, metaphorically driving progress through the old country ways which echoes the attempts in the text of Lydgate and his friends to introduce reform and change to the resistant provinces. There is a wry joke in the first line, as, passing a half-finished railway cutting with a steam train Lydgate (Douglas Hodge) points and says 'Look – the future'.[17] This conflation of the obsessively modern Victorian outlook with a contemporary audience's interpretation of a steam train as very much old-fashioned categorically situates the serial in a past which is both part of a teleological progress towards now and an alien, unknown state of being. That said, the series' content examines the derailment of progress and reform in the face of the petty small-mindedness of an English village – including an attack by superstitious farmers on the railway builders. For Ian MacKillop and Alison Platt, the central issue of costume drama is knowing anachronism – while 'historical' the series must be recognisable, and this is 'valuably problematic'.[18] The very choice of adaptation, for them, demonstrates that the BBC was seriously interrogating the genre – *Middlemarch* is not a novel to be chosen lightly and itself is in dialogue with notions of history and presentation. It is not smooth and easy, and its complexity resists criticism. For all that *Middlemarch* is relatively straightforward as a classic series, it contains within it – as do all such adaptations – problems for a too generalised critique. While much of Eliot's irony is swept away, the overwhelming themes of the story are not glorious – pettiness as a bar to progress, poverty, bullying, illness, meanness and the horrors of an inflexible class system. The original 1871 novel is itself a piece of historical fiction, set in the reforming 1830s, and as such slyly invites the reader to judge the participants. Passive viewers of the series might fall into the same unselfconscious trap, thinking themselves more civilised and developed.

Similarly, the adaptation focuses more on Dorothea than the novel, emphasising (as does Davies' 1995 *Pride and Prejudice* treatment of Elizabeth Bennett) female desire for independence and education. Rosie's unthinking words in the first episode – '*I'm* not going to be a governess' – demonstrate the limited possibilities for women during the period.[19] The series concludes by suggesting that the model of reform and modernity that Lydgate desires – the great actions of great men – demonstrates an extravagant arrogance and ends in bitterness and failure. As the final lines of the novel are read (imposing a first-person omniscient authorial gravity lacking from the rest of the adaptation) the audience is clearly advised to remember the minor acts of kindness that are forgotten: 'for the growing good of the world is partly dependent on unhistoric acts'.[20] The historiographical impetus here is towards the local and the generous, rather than the march of progress. The status of women – oppressed, controlled, fallen – is a key concern of the classic adaptation and one way in which history in them is made other (this alien set of behaviours) and historical identities are demonstrated to be about ideological constraint and order. Similar to the country house reality shows, the classic adaptation and indeed all such historical dramas enact at once a distancing – these strange people in their odd costumes acting in their old-fashioned, ordered way – and a reconceptualisation, as the viewer uses the space of the drama to reflect on their own life. An idealised, conservative vision of England is in *Middlemarch* undermined as the pastoral landscape is filled with the dying and fractious poor who Dorothea attempts to aid. Her line 'we should all be beaten from our houses' as she is offered a useless pet as a love token from Sir James Chettham undermines the splendid glory of the *mise-en-scène*, and her refusal to wear her mother's jewels similarly demonstrates the shallowness of the obsession with costume.[21] Dorothea herself rejects the country house, choosing to forego money for love and 'live in a street'.[22] From the beginning of their more modern manifestation, then, the classic adaptation took on serious, morally complex texts and presented them in interrogative, challenging ways.

The classic adaptation attained a particular cultural prevalence after Davies' next series, *Pride and Prejudice* (1995).[23] This series was massively popular, repeated within a year of the original showing and featuring on the cover of *The Radio Times*. Demonstrating unlooked for afterlife – and thereafter changing the paradigm for adaptations and ensuring that they were strongly marketed on DVD and video after initial broadcast – the first 12,000 video copies sold within two hours and 70,000 were sold in the first week of release. The series, along with the Oscar-winning *Sense and Sensibility* (Ang Lee, 1995), confirmed the massive popularity of Austen adaptation.[24] *Emma* (1996) followed on ITV and *Persuasion* (1995) on BBC as well as films of *Emma* (Douglas McGrath, 1996), *Mansfield Park* (Patricia Rozema, 1999), *Pride and Prejudice* (Joe Wright, 2005), the Bollywood adaptation *Bride and Prejudice* (Gurinder Chadha, 2004) and the biopic *Becoming Jane* (Julian Jarrold, 2007). As a consequence Austen has become a tourist industry in Bath and Winchester, and her works still sell extremely well.[25]

In the main the film and television adaptations have been straightforward and have traded on a popular image of Austen, although Rozema's *Mansfield Park* attempted to highlight the issue of slavery in a postcolonial interpretation of the text influenced by the work of Edward Said.[26] Austen exemplifies a particular Englishness in these texts – demure, intelligent, reserved, self-sacrificing, witty, romantic.[27] The settings are lush landscapes and rich houses, the actors talented, the costumes gorgeous, the dialogue sharp; there is nothing nasty or unexpected, no real poverty or grinding historical reality (again, *Mansfield Park* does attempt to show the economic horror of 'real' life during the period).[28] Austen's novels have been characterised as offering 'an inoffensive experience to middle-class whites who like to think of themselves as discerning and endowed with the good taste of cultural capital'.[29] The massive success of *Pride and Prejudice* led to the ascendancy of a particular type of costume drama and the assumption of a cultural hegemony associated with 'quality' literary adaptation. Davies' *Pride and Prejudice* responded to the costume drama genre with great skill and conformed to this clear set of tropes. The series traded upon a particular type of idealised nostalgia associated with the genre and with Austen in general, a clear definition of 'quality'. It delivered a version of Englishness, and its massive popularity, alongside the rest of the Austen-industry, confirmed that this conceptualisation of an airbrushed Austen-lite past and national identity was desired by a wider public. Yet it is more complex than this account allows for. *Pride and Prejudice* introduced elements of soap opera, considered the dynamics of sexuality during the early nineteenth century and introduced a highly erotically charged scene with Colin Firth emerging soaked from a lake.[30] This updating of the elegance of Austen was of a piece with contemporary academic rethinking of her work which emphasised the irony, the edgy challenge of her writing, and her self-dramatisation.

Within the classic series, then, distinctions might be made and differences may be flagged, albeit often unsuccessfully. The eighteenth century, for instance, is generally imagined as Hogarthian, rather than Gainsborughesque. This sense of the 1700s as a time of rascals and criminals is perpetuated, for instance, by the ongoing Channel 4 docu/drama series 'Georgian Underworld' which has included documentary films such as 'An Invitation to a Hanging' (2002), 'Queer as 18th Century Folk' (2002) and the proto-detective series *City of Vice* (2008). The documentaries focussed on radicalism, black bareknuckle boxers, highwaymen and the Peterloo massacre; *City of Vice* was predicated on the fact that in the 1750s London was a melting pot of crime, prostitution and everyday violence. 'Georgian Underworld' emphasises the teeming dynamism of the time in contradistinction to the refinement associated with the later Victorian period.[31] The *mise-en-scène* and style of Simon Burke's *Tom Jones* (BBC, 1996), for instance, reflect the nature of the novel, and in its playful digressiveness, fluid narrative, caricatured characters and unabashed status as a 'romp' it differs clearly from other classic series adapted from more august sources. Similar to the mainstream series, such as *Middlemarch*, it opens with a vista of English landscape, before panning to the narrator Henry Fielding (John Sessions) who promptly gets knocked over by a carriage. The series develops this slapstick including mud-wrestling women outside church, farting squires and brawling rascals. It deploys choppy editing and a playful script. *Tom Jones* shares an irreverence and sexual flamboyance with *Moll Flanders* (1996) and *Fanny Hill* (2007). This perception of the eighteenth century as jolly and rambunctious in contrast with the serious, internalised, thoughtful world of the nineteenth-century novel first of all perpetuates old literary critical positions regarding the moral seriousness and therefore quality of the novel (suggesting that the more complex a novel, the better it is) and secondly creates a visual aesthetic of the eighteenth century in clear comparison to the nineteenth. It works to elevate a writer such as Austen in comparison – her work is dealt with in a serious, quality fashion. At the same time, the adaptations of eighteenth-century novels work to undermine the perceived stateliness of the Austen/Eliot/Dickens adaptations, suggesting that the 'classic' serial might be drawn from other sources, other time periods, and be approached in different styles. For instance, the two series' treatment of gender roles demonstrate a marked difference – the women in *Tom Jones* are sexually rapacious and generally free to move about (unless locked up by their fathers). In comparison to many of the women in later Austen adaptations, doomed to either wait by the window, be taxed for walking alone, or be kept indoors due to their infirmity, Sophia is allowed outside to participate in a hunt, during which Tom, not she, loses his seat.[32] *Tom Jones* presents sexual relations as being as hide-bound as in the later periods, but invites the viewer to critique this rather than to be complicit in it. More generally, the classic serial has been seen to undermine perceived normative gendered models; certainly the more gothic of the adaptations such as *The Woman in White* and *Rebecca* interrogate received notions of femininity and domesticity.[33]

The deployment of a narrator character in *Tom Jones* differs from many serials, interposing something of a distance between audience and story which is complicated by the fact that Fielding is both outside the text (narrating) and a diegetic part of the visuals. Much as he does in the source novel, he hovers inbetween, and, by replicating this voice, the series stays true to the original material. This attempt at fidelity to narrative style is relatively unusual. The metatextual foregrounding of the relationship between viewer and text, something which *Cock and Bull*, Michael Winterbottom's 2005 film of *Tristram Shandy* similarly uses, is generally lost in more mainstream, straightforward productions (although some do use voiceover). Subsequent series have tended to be less irreverent and more concerned with establishing a stateliness and an authority through their costume, script, music and presentation. Yet the examples considered so far demonstrate that there is great variety within the mainstream costume drama, and that to generalise about their purpose, their execution and their effect tends to ignore this multiplicity. It is the Austen adaptations above all which have given rise to a sense of the costume drama being comfortable, bourgeois and politically modest; at best novel adaptations engage with social issues (Gaskell and Dickens), ironise relationships (Trollope and Eliot) and force the viewer to deal with a vision of the past in which people do not behave according to cliché.

Adaptations also have a self-consciousness – formally and in terms of their content. *Bleak House* (2006), for instance, had the trappings of a standard BBC adaptation – an 'authentically' dirty *mise-en-scène*, a canonical author, famous stage actors – but challenged the normal stately presentation of the quality drama by showing fifteen 30-minute episodes twice a week, mimicking the regularity and timeslot of a soap opera rather than a classic serial.[34] *The Other Boleyn Girl* (BBC 2003) used modern camera angles and techniques as well as a partially improvised script. Often these decisions have been made on aesthetic grounds – *Bleak House* was designed to reflect the sprawling soapiness and episodic publication of the original novel, and *Moll Flanders* (ITV 1996) deployed direct-to-camera address to recreate the buttonholing style of the narrator in Daniel Defoe's text. The 2006 BBC production of *Jane Eyre* was supported with an adaptation of *Wide Sargasso Sea*, Jean Rhys' 1966 imagined prequel to the story. Rhys' book undermines the colonial impulse of the original novel, telling the story of Rochester's Creole first wife whom he unfairly casts aside, renames, and imprisons; the novel is a celebrated feminist rebuttal to the 'madwoman in the attic' model deployed by nineteenth-century writers.[35] The novel *Wide Sargasso Sea* is a critique of a certain type of novel-making, and the adaptation therefore is a criticism of the *Jane Eyre* television drama. The dovetailing of both versions establishes a dynamic relationship in which the idealised, imagined past presented in the classic serial is actively challenged and seen to be in error; indeed, the narrative itself (i.e. *Jane Eyre*, both as source text and programme) is seen as an anxious fiction attempting to ignore the realities of the time. At the same time, *Wide Sargasso Sea* was shown on BBC4 rather than at prime time, suggesting that the cultural hegemony represented by the novel and the classic adaptation was still solid, indeed, further implying that voices of dissidence could be easily contained and marginalised.

Queering the genre: *Tipping the Velvet* and *The Line of Beauty*

Sarah Waters' (1998) novel *Tipping the Velvet* tells the story of Nan King as she discovers her lesbian identity during the 1890s. The novel is a writing-back, an inserting of marginalised voices into mainstream history. BBC's *Tipping the Velvet* (2002) represents the classic novel serial attaining a self-consciousness about pastiche and aesthetic atmosphere. It is an adaptation of an historical novel rather than an historic novel (much as with the later *Other Boleyn Girl*) which is written in the first person and attempts itself to mimic the sensationalist style of late Victorian fiction. Thus some of the key elements associated with the classic serial – the gravitas and cultural worth accorded to the canonical and 'authentic' text – are undermined. Yet this is recognisably set in the same milieu as, for instance, *Pride and Prejudice*, and was shot, staged and marketed as a 'costume drama'. The decision to take such a pastiching, ventriloquial form and treat it as seriously as any canonical novel opened up a new space in historical drama.[36] The resulting serial is 'classic' in its production values and was presented as such, but at the same time its innate inauthenticity and the subject matter of the novel meant that this was a series which undermined its purported genre.[37] Similarly the narrative's purpose of reinscribing lost lesbian voices marginalised by history and culture is mimicked in the series' queering of its genre – by destabilising a hegemonic genre *Tipping the Velvet* gave the classic serial the opportunity to present dissident and non-mainstream voices.

The opening sequence of the series is a point of view shot with voiceover (again, mimicking the first-person address of the novel) in which the viewer enters the Oyster house where the protagonist, Nan, was born. The VO is inclusive, asking the viewer 'Did you ever go to Whitstable, and see the oyster-parlours there? … Did you, perhaps, push at the door and step into the dim, low-ceilinged, fragrant room beyond it?'[38] The use of voiceover allows for the representation of the authorial first-person voice, but this inclusivity further allowed the programme to invite the viewer to participate somehow in the unmarginalising of non-mainstream identities, to be complicit in this reconfiguring of the classic serial and thence of the historical as cultural genre. The programme was relatively explicit in its representation of sex and lesbian relationships, provoking some outrage in the press and public.[39] The desired effect of these complaints was twofold – first an urge to remarginalise the lesbian identities articulated in the text, and at the same time a suggestion that this kind of liminal, fragmented way of presenting history is not 'quality'. Those who considered the series offensive were mourning a particular type of conservative, culturally one-dimensional 'classic' series which the very fact of *Tipping the Velvet* demonstrated was a fiction; the history that was desired by conservative critics was that without the lesbians, in itself demonstrably a construction rather than an authentic entity. The BBC was relatively provocative in its presentation of the graphicness of the drama, in some ways courting controversy both to get publicity but also to create such a dissonance. *Tipping the Velvet*, then, might represent a point at which television costume drama became self-aware and politicised, evolving as a space of possibility rather than cultural hegemony.

Other productions such as *The Rotter's Club* (BBC, 2005), *White Teeth* (Channel 4, 2002) and even the counterfactual thriller *Archangel* (BBC, 2005) deployed the historical serial format in a more self-conscious style. *The Rotter's Club*, based on a novel by Jonathan Coe, was scripted by Dick Clement and Ian La Frenais, more commonly known for their work on comedy drama like *Porridge* (1974–77) or *Auf Wiedersehen, Pet* (1983–86); their presence gave the drama a populist feel rather than the more elegant approach of Andrew Davies. The key point is that these series mimic the style and production values of costume drama – the music, the attention to historical detail, the sweeping narratives, the personalising of the historical moment in the individual experience, and they are all of course adapted from novels.

The Line of Beauty (BBC, 2007), an adaptation of Alan Holinghurst's (2004) novel, is more conventional in many ways, but similarly demonstrates an interest in using historical fiction as source material for classical costume drama.[40] The series marks the entry of the costume drama into the recollected past, as it is set during the period 1983–87.[41] *The Line of Beauty* is in many ways an anti-heritage series, in the same way that *Tipping the Velvet* is a series which undermines its own genre. *The Line of Beauty* takes place at the high point of the heritage movie; several of its characters discuss going to see *A Room with a View*. The political characters it presents are those who are instituting the mid-1980s conservative Englishness that the heritage theorist Patrick Wright so decries.[42] Gerald Fedden, the MP whose family protagonist Nick Guest lodges with, opens a fete in his constituency with the words 'This is a classic English day and a classic English scene', keying into a sense of timeless heritage while playing the patrician. The dynamic of this moment – invoking a sense of Englishness articulated around a sense of history and a sense of political order – is the enshrinement of what Wright argued that the debates surrounding the national past during the early 1980s were doing – that our 'common heritage seems indeed to be identifiable as the historicized image of an instinctively conservative establishment'.[43] Gerald even takes to the ancient sport of 'Welly whanging' and beats the locals at it in order to demonstrate his ascendancy over the old ways.

Yet Gerald and his cronies are arrivistes, none of them have money or taste. The first episode consists of the visit to the ancestral family home Hawkeswood in which Nick is invited to look at the trappings of wealth. Therefore the fetish-isation of the country house and the spoils of ancient wealth are undermined; this is exactly what happens in the seminal heritage series *Brideshead Revisited*, when the visitor Charles Ryder is the only person to appreciate the splendour of Brideshead or to respond to it artistically. None of the people who actually own these things care, and in *The Line of Beauty* they are more interested in setting up a disco in the hall and getting drunk. The scene of the party has shots of ancient portraits with banging party tunes and flashing lights illuminating them, highlighting a kind of clash of the old with a modernity of flash and surface.

The series directly shadows *Brideshead*, with its ingénue narrator falling in love with a monied but flawed family and attaching himself to them first through the son (at Oxford) and then through the daughter; the paterfamilias becomes a monster that drags the whole family down. The novel itself makes reference to costume dramas: 'Martine slightly surprised him by saying, "I think it's so boring now, everything takes place in the past".'[44] The television series eschews this section but keeps the metatextual motif in which the protagonist Nick and his lover Wani set up a company to fund the production of a film of Henry James' *The Spoils of Poynton* (needless to say their American backers want more sex and to change the heroine's name from Fleda Vetch). The message of *Poynton* – it is about 'someone who loved things more than people' – will be lost to the American's cultural illiteracy, and so there is an innate little England con-servatism at play here, albeit one which celebrates nuanced, bleak writing (by an American).

The conclusion of the series has Gerald spitting in homophobic rage as he asks Nick to leave, the institutor of the conservative sense of nation actively ejecting homosexual difference. The family's eventual break with Nick – and implicitly therefore his rejection by the establishment, Conservatism, old England

and the notion of heritage incarnated by Hawkeswood – articulate a wider social dismissal; Nick's moment of understanding, of seeing the horror of the people he has easily fallen in with, allows the novel to critique the antique identities of the monied upper classes. The series shows the real, true face of Britishness here; similarly to *Brideshead* the family are fetishised in order to demonstrate just quite how unpleasant they are. Again the book demonstrates this well:

'What would Henry James have made of us, I wonder?' she went on. 'Well … ' Nick chewed it over. He thought she was rather like a high-minded aunt, proposing questions with virginal firmness and ignorance. He wondered condescendingly what her sexual prospects where. A certain kind of man might like to raise the colour in that plump white neck. He said, 'He'd have been very kind to us, he'd have said how wonderful we were and how beautiful we were, he'd have given us incredibly subtle things to say, and we wouldn't have realized until just before the end that he'd seen right through us.'[45]

This ironising effect is clearly at play during the series; as viewers we are invited, with Nick, to fall in love with the family before we discern their horror. As Nick wanders around the beautiful houses and places he is us, the audience, who fetishise the country house (something which is central to 1980s models of conservative heritage) and by extension the lifestyle that goes with it.[46] Similarly the audience is invited to fall in love with the period setting, enjoying its nostalgic value and its authenticity, before being reminded that the 1980s represent not success and wonder but AIDS, insider-dealing, homophobia and death. Yet this could be argued about all such adaptations; with the possible exception of Dickens (who was, all the same, a trenchant social and political critic), the writers chosen most regularly have tended to be those obsessed with irony, from Austen's proto-feminism through Trollope's gentle satire to Eliot's clear-sighted dismantling of pomposity.

What *The Line of Beauty* shares with *Tipping the Velvet* is sexual explicitness and an exploration of non-mainstream, marginalised sexual identities. Both series play with the audience's response and identification with the central figure. *Tipping the Velvet* uses a friendly voiceover to create a relationship between viewer and protagonist. *The Line of Beauty* presents Nick's fetishisation of the country house – which the audience shares – as included also in his sexual flaneurism, particularly in the party sequence in which he wanders looking at both boys and portraits. His awakening from innocence to experience, which the audience undergoes with him, is in many ways associated with his increasing under-standing of his sexuality. The series explore sexualities not included in standard historical models. They reinsert the marginalised, asserting first, that sexual relationships happened during the past and that they might have been welcomed and homosexual. Thus material explicitness – which, other than in *Tom Jones*, is generally lacking in the classic adaptation – becomes allied to homosexuality. At the same time these two series write a particular history of sexuality as at odds with and not part of heteronormative teleology. Lesbians and gay men are seen as both part of the historical fabric and at the same time self-consciously apart from it, at an acute angle with mainstream sexuality and historicity.

Boy's own authentic drama: Sharpe and Hornblower

Such innovation and complexity are part of the mainstream, but there are plenty of costume dramas presenting a less nuanced, more straightforward set of identities. *Sharpe*, adapted from the novels by Bernard Cornwell, has run for 15 feature-length episodes since 1993, screened on ITV. Similarly to *Tipping the Velvet*, the *Sharpe* adaptations demonstrate an acceptance of pastiche, given that they are adaptations of novels that are written in the present about or imitating the past. *Hornblower*, from C.S. Forester's novels (published 1937–57), was made into eight feature-length TV movies between 1998 and 2003, and screened on ITV. These adaptations satisfy the 'classic' novel remit insofar as they take Forester's beloved, canonical books and put them on screen, but they similarly complicate matters given that the original stories are historical novels. *Hornblower* and *Sharpe* gain large audiences and are event-television; *Sharpe* is shown at prime time on key dates such as Easter Bank Holiday or Boxing Day. They are not serials, as they are shown as one-off, feature-length episodes, but they complicate our understanding of the way that television drama deals with historical and historic fiction. These dramas do not attempt to attain the stamp of 'quality' that BBC historical drama does, but they still strive for authenticity and garner a different audience nonetheless still interested in seeing fictional narratives played out in historical frameworks. Both dramas are also marketed overseas, particularly in the USA and Australia, and sit at an angle to the more conservative presentation of Britishness represented by the BBC's classic serials. The programmes have the same high production values, attention to detail, to location and to class hierarchy as the Austen adaptations. The model of tough, decent, martial Britishness demonstrated in the two series is at odds with the witty, withdrawn manner of the BBC's costume adaptations. They present two differing types of man – an officer and an ordinary soldier – who can in some ways be metonymic for the nation in their devotion to duty, their steadfastness, and their wit. The Napoleonic wars do not present troubling political issues, unlike most any war since, and therefore the series are nostalgic for a time of certainty. Similarly, they deploy a vocabulary of masculinity and steadfastness, which, while akin to that of the country house costume dramas, is at considerable odds with them in terms of the projected audience and the models of authenticity and quality associated with the more prestigious series.

The first of the *Sharpe* series, *Sharpe's Rifles* (ITV, 1993), opens with a sequence of the kit of a soldier – weapons, uniform – over which martial music plays. From the outset, then, the series fetishises costume and accessory in the same way as country house costume dramas. The tropes are recognisable to those who might have viewed *Middlemarch* in the same year, but directed in different ways. The first establishing shot is still the landscape but rather than celebrate the pastoral beauty of England here the viewer is presented with marching ranks (in the later case of *Hornblower*, fleets). The elements of authenticity and tropes of quality are military wear, horses, strategy, weaponry and action sequences.[47] In contrast to the quality actors cast in the BBC series, lead Sean Bean is associated with action, is not obviously formally trained (although he did attend RADA), and speaks with a Sheffield accent. He is bluff and much rawer than those in the country-house series; the first the viewer sees of him is when he wipes his face clean, dressed simply in an open shirt.

The unconstrained sexuality and masculinity of Bean's Sharpe can be directly contrasted with that of the country house protagonists. In the opening of *Sharpe's Rifles* Sharpe fights in a river, emerging dripping wet much as Colin Firth in *Pride and Prejudice* but also covered in blood; the sexualisation of Firth in that instance is down to the presence of Elizabeth Bennett, whereas Sharpe's uncostumed moment is here constructed by homosociality, duty and violence. However, where Firth's appearance is the one moment of unguarded openness – a social nakedness which the series suggests is the moment they properly 'see' one another – Bean is constantly bloody, fighting, snarling, dirty. His earthy fleshiness, in comparison to the perfumed, beautifully clad Firth, effectively contrasts the controlled, stately 'quality' adaptation with the popular, more direct programme. Firth is the patrician conservative, Bean the yeoman who built and protects the empire Darcy is enjoying: 'All I know is how to fight.'[48] The notion of the upstart commoner being where he shouldn't is one of the key themes of the *Sharpe* series, particular *Sharpe's Rifles* in which Sharpe has to 'prove' himself an officer to his suspicious men. In the same manner that Austen's social hierarchies are incomprehensible to a modern audience, the *Sharpe* series introduces protocols, class differences and military discipline which is unfamiliar. The model of historical subjectivity here is similar in both adaptations – the protagonists are worked upon, rather than self-creating independent creatures.

Both *Sharpe* and *Hornblower* assist in the presentation of a particular type of nationhood and Englishness, a conservative, masculine, aggressive model of patriotic identity predicated upon duty, respect and honour. They both, for instance, deploy Irish characters to question the morality of the war.[49] In *Sharpe's Rifles*, Sharpe assists the Spanish in rising up on the English side by defeating a Count who desires Bonaparte's victory because he – like Sharpe, whom he questions on this matter – wants to be ruled by reason rather than superstition. *Sharpe's Rifles* and the series as a whole have a cynicism about idealising nationhood – 'Do you really think people will fight for a rag on a pole?', Sharpe asks; the answer is 'You do, Richard, you do' but it is clear that the national ideology of the King's war is relatively irrelevant to Sharpe, where in *Hornblower*, national duty is the utmost exemplar of good behaviour.[50]

These programmes, along with the similarly anti-Gallic *The Scarlet Pimpernel* (BBC, 1999–2000), fit into the 'swashbuckler' genre more popular in the 1950s and 1960s, attending to historic heroism and unnuanced motivation. They celebrate spectacle and often gorily suggest that manliness is forged in homosocial combat spaces, that respect is as important as social standing. They present a useful pause to the model of literary adaptation, undermining the stiffness of the

BBC costume dramas. Sharpe's own anti-authoritarian stance, for instance, his irreverence and tendency to ignore his social betters, figure him as a brilliant maverick (whom we should sympathise with) attacking the hide-bound hierarchical society he finds himself in; by implication the society he is troubling is that of Austen's novels. *Sharpe* is a series which demonstrates the cultural bankruptcy of 'quality' costume drama, both by illustrating the contemporary price of the stability of Austen's country houses but also complicating the audience's engagement with the dramatic representation of the past. That said, *Sharpe* also emphasises duty, order, and stability – and, unlike the costume dramas, rarely (despite Sharpe's maverick status) contains dissidence or complexity. A key example here would be the gender politics of both *Sharpe* and *Hornblower*: women are at worst problems and at best irrelevant, rarely considered or represented. *Sharpe* suggests that the army is a meritocracy, but one that you rise in through discipline; similarly *Hornblower*'s naval society is riven with hierarchy and order. So while the programmes directly undermine the cultural conservatism of the classic adaptations, they do not allow for the nuance or the postnostalgic querying of genre and representation that more seemingly mainstream series might.

Historical costume drama lends itself to all manner of genres, and in this hybridisation ITV have generally been more flexible than the BBC. Their shows range from romance (18 extremely popular Catherine Cookson adaptations from 1989 onwards) to detective genres (*Agatha Christie's Poirot* (ITV, 1989–), *Cadfael* (ITV, 1994–98)) and social comedy (*Jeeves and Wooster* (ITV, 1990–93)). Again the key issue here is that these shows are based upon novels, drawing on characters already long established and models of Englishness that are extremely familiar and have much cultural currency. They are also sumptuous 'quality' productions presenting a certain Englishness.

Police series *Heartbeat*, set in the late 1960s, was at its peak in the mid-1990s the biggest non-soap drama on television, consistently attracting an audience of between 10 and 15 million people.[51] It has wider cultural impact as the Yorkshire area it is filmed in is now marketed to tourists as '*Heartbeat* country'.[52] It has also spawned a spin-off hospital drama, *The Royal*, demonstrating that the blending of undemanding historical period setting with populist dramatic genres (medical, police) is immensely fertile. *Heartbeat* was designed to fit the market rather than conceived organically, put together in response to deregulation by ITV.[53] It reflects a strand of programming interested in presenting a nostalgic sense of the past by suggesting that past was more peaceful, straightforward and cosy than the present; it is of a part with Higson's definition of the nostalgia film: 'a narrative of loss, charting an imaginary historical trajectory from stability to instability'.[54] *Heartbeat*'s design-by-committee demonstrates in part the desire of the audience for historical programming which is generically familiar and historically undemanding. Nostalgia therefore works in this instance to comfort (things were better once) and to divert. Programmes like *Heartbeat* and *Sharpe* suggest that the link between nostalgia and bourgeoisness is not complete; they complicate an understanding of the ways that the past impacts on the popular imagination.

Heartbeat and *Sharpe* represent an audience share little considered within discussions of historical drama, a demographically different set of viewers than that of the mainstream adaptations. Costume drama during the 1990s was not simply a matter of country houses and conservative values. The standard critique of the costume drama rests on its innate conservatism, and this is in general associated with the BBC 'prestige' productions; what is clear is that the notion of an historical drama, an adaptation, and a 'classic' serial do not necessarily have to be party to this notion of stately quality television; indeed, the cultural heterodoxy that the BBC productions seemingly enjoy tells a skewed story about drama's interface with history. BBC heritage series are part of a wider dramatic popular interface with 'history'. Studies which insist only on considering prestigious or canonical adaptation miss the prevalence of the historical in the dramatic imagination and the way that it might be used to inflect genre, attract audience, establish prestige and open up markets.

Innovation and obscenity: *Rome* and *Deadwood*

Two series from the independent American network HBO demonstrate a newly iconoclastic and revisionist approach to key historical genres. They show that making quality historical drama is not simply a matter of authenticity – although both emphasise a particular gritty reality in order to break with past representations – but also of overcoming generic expectation. On the back of its showpiece drama *The Sopranos* (1999–2007), HBO gained a reputation and an audience by making labyrinthine, complex, epic and morally ambiguous series. *Rome* and *Deadwood* took this template and applied it to historical drama.

Rome (2005–7, in conjunction with the BBC) is an immensely expensive ($100 million budget), prestige account of the years 49–31 BC. It was syndicated worldwide. Jonathan Stamp, consultant and co-producer of the series, argued that the most important thing to do was to 'evade the clichés of HollyRome, all white pillars and white togas'.[55] How, he asked, 'do you take a world that is so mythic, so smothered in so many layers of invention and re-invention, and make it live?'.[56] The series had to contend with the cultural legacy of Shakespeare as well as more contemporary accounts ranging from the literary (*I, Claudius*, 1976), the comic (*Up Pompeii!*, 1971) and the action-packed (the film *Gladiator*, Ridley Scott, 2000), what the producers decried as a 'pastiche' approach. In order to surmount these cultural analogues the series emphasises the dirt, squalor and violence of the city, particularly shown in the explicit language, sex and violence. The setting was painstakingly detailed, and the grittiness is therefore a display of authenticity. This is intended to complicate the viewer's engagement with the series, to move them, first, to appreciate its authenticity and, second, to situate the historical period in a set of familiar contemporary tropes (these people are much like you). The show rescues figures from the margins – slaves, women, ordinary men. Roman history in the popular imagination, possibly more than any other given its historiography and cultural reach, is predicated upon key figures – Julius Caesar, Mark Antony – and where *Rome* does follow their fortunes, it also portrays the city as a whole.

The series' combination of authenticity and deliberate shock is seen in the opening sequence, in which phallic graffiti, fetishes, ritual sacrifice and images of rape, plunder and brutality are shown. These animated images are screened onto the fabric of the city – the walls and streets – as the citizens walk about out of focus, and the sequence is an elegant emblem of the series as a whole: it projects the imaginary on the concrete, inscribes something artificial but authentic upon a basis of 'reality'. Similarly the sequence shows the graceful use of CGI effects to create a kind of authenticity.[57] The series presented Rome's ambiguous morality, complicated pagan religion, problematic gender politics, and brutal actions (from gladiatorial contests to slavery) as context to clearly differentiate the characters from our contemporary understanding in order to emphasise authenticity – on this model, if a viewer did not recognise what was happening then it was accurate (and more satisfying as a viewing experience). The series dictates a new way of thinking about familiar settings and figures, and this new way is, allied to the strong narrative, the appeal of the show.

Set in goldrush Montana in 1876, *Deadwood* dramatises the pioneering West. The titular town has 'no law' and as a consequence presents the West as lawless, criminal, obscene and morally corrupt. Characters swear, use drugs, are casually racist and vicious – and this acts to emphasise historical difference and give the series authentic heft. Much of the action takes place in the town's inn-whorehouse and the characters are murky, complex and compromised. The *mise-en-scène* is grubby and dirty, emphasising authenticity and non-contemporariness. The mud and muck, as with Rome, is intended to flag difference from the clean, sanitised – and somehow less authentic – modern world. The show underlines its sense of teleology – as the show's website puts it, 'The outlaw camp of Deadwood marches slowly towards civilisation' – while suggesting that the things which make this historical setting stand out – violence, swearing, death, sexual explicitness – both reflect the contemporaneity of the show (these things happen now) and its historical difference (the audience would like to think that these things don't happen with such dirty rawness now).[58] The violence – both physical and conceptual (in the murky morality presented) – of the show chimes with that in *Rome* and suggests a way of presenting a raw history, a revisionist take on the follies of our ancestors.

The series' creator David Milch is associated with realistic, controversial and innovative genre shows such as *NYPD Blue* (1993–2005) and *Hill Street Blues* (1981–87). His desire to make the actors understand context and the subtleties of the period springs as much from his televisual experience as his first job as a college professor.[59] Similarly he claimed that he was driven to make a show which went against his understanding of the Western as a genre which presented 'to America a sanitized heroic idea of what America was … an America disinfected and pure'.[60] He continued: 'It seemed so obvious to me that the West I was encountering in my research … had nothing to do with the westerns'. Milch's account of his work on *Deadwood* demonstrates how a cultural trope can become an historical given, and clearly signals him positioning his series as more 'authentic' because it was not pastiche and caricature but something which got close to the real West.

The show is iconoclastic insofar as it attacks, like *Rome*, the sanitised and cleaned up *cultural* versions of the past, aggressively undermining and challenging accepted historical genres. That said, *Deadwood* clearly built on a seam of revisionism and iconoclasm in Western movies. The amorality of the West and the undermining of heroic exemplars is a common theme of the Western, from John Ford's *The Searchers* (1956) through to Clint Eastwood's *Unforgiven* (1992). The moral relativism and ambiguity of the text mine a rich seam of dissident films, then. Putting this into a television series argues for commissioning producers who see their audiences as ready for morally complex and problematic programmes, something which was initiated by the success of *The Sopranos*.[61]

The effect of these two shows on production has been immediate, and programmes deploying the same approach to history are increasingly common. Channel 4's *City of Vice* follows the fortunes of novelist Henry Fielding and his Bow Street Runners, London's first regularised police force. The programmes intertwine actual events and objects such as John Cleland's *Fanny Hill* or Jack Harris' published list of prostitutes. The episodes are generically hybrid, procedural police-dramas with period elements; they include sex, swearing and dirt. *City of Vice* offers insight into a London which is dirty, offensive, noisy and lawless. The series is not an adaptation, but a fictionalised account of real events, with many of the cases being adapted from the Old Bailey Sessions Papers and the Newgate Calendar. It was quite explicitly ranged against the 'mainstream' of costume drama: 'We wanted to create a historical piece that had nothing to do with the decorum and seemliness of most other TV period dramas, which are usually gentle re-adaptations of familiar and much-loved novels.'[62] Like *Deadwood* and novels such as Andrew Pepper's *The Last Days of Newgate*, the use of generic tropes such as those drawn from the Western or police show suggest the 'taming' of the past, the bringing of a certain type of rational order to a period which is rapacious and bestial.[63] 'Then' in these shows, is not idealised, but a place of horror; somewhere to escape from rather than nostalgically evoke. The attempts of Fielding to bring rationality and order to society show him modernising and establishing a more recognisable civilisation; at the same time, the invocation of the detective genre suggests that Fielding is attempting to establish order and truth in a chaotic society that will resist his actions. He vainly strives against the onrushing vice around him. The series producer Rob Pursey articulated a desire to challenge audiences' perceived views: 'I'm sure viewers will be shocked at the behaviour of our Georgian ancestors, but vice on the streets of London is by no means a new phenomenon.'[64] This type of programme dissents from the view of the past as a time of beauty and challenges the nostalgia of standard adaptations; it presents a historical period as dark, dangerous and unpleasant (and in need of controlling).

'Good moaning': comedy and time travel

History as a backdrop and setting for comedy and lightweight drama is a minor, although influential, strand of television programming. In the main, this kind of programme trades in stereotypes, but in the self-consciousness of the series is found the undermining of nostalgia. While not necessarily suggesting that light comedy or populist drama should be taken as serious engagements with and representations of historical events these programmes demonstrate that history can be played for laughs, can be used quite seriously to reflect on the definition of self, and can be part of the fabric of television genre. These shows have an ability to create and sustain received ideas, caricatures and visual imagination of historical period. All of the series discussed in this section have an afterlife on DVD and cable television worldwide – and in 2007 the makers of *'Allo 'Allo* were approached by a German company interested in screening it. Historical comedy and light drama are more influential than costume drama or serious docudrama; they have wider reach, a very much broader demographic audience and less specific afterlife. The shows attain a popular cachet, amassing far greater cultural capital than the briefly lived costume dramas (other than, perhaps, *Pride and Prejudice*), and they have much bigger audience figures. They are perpetuated in other media – live theatre shows, tie-in books, even music releases (tie-in singles and soundtracks).

'Allo 'Allo! (BBC, 1982–92 and 2007, also theatrical manifestation internationally) was set in wartime France and the members of each side represented (French, Italian, German and British) spoke in ludicrously amplified accents to signify their various nationalities. They also wore caricatured dress (although much of this was uniform-related). The show had roots in serious or straight representation of the past as well as forming part of an ancestry of historical comedy. It followed *Dad's Army* (1968–77) and *It Ain't Half Hot, Mum* (1974–81) as BBC historical sitcoms which traded on particular stereotypes to explore class and Englishness. Furthermore the show directly parodied the resistance drama *Secret Army* (BBC 1977–79). Obviously the 'history' of the series is a minor part of its purpose, yet it is influential in formulating a visual representation of the war for its audience, and for imposing presumed historical and national models of behaviour upon its protagonists.

'Allo 'Allo!'s Frenchified English, referencing of war movies and ludicrous plotlines arguably demonstrate Frederic Jameson's postnostalgia; history and heritage as authorities and facts are here undermined, shown to be mere disguises. In particular, this applies to the character Herr Flick of the Gestapo, whose Aryan secretary and penchant for leather are played for laughs – he is the Nazi ideologue turned into effete, sexually repressed fool. This undermining of the monstrous is part and parcel of the resistance motif of the series – a debunking of the horror of war possibly – but turning it into broad comedy undermines the valency of the signs here, and the trauma of wartime Nazism becomes occluded by slapstick:

HERR FLICK: I have a box of sharp needles somewhere. [*opens a drawer*] Ah, here they are.
HELGA: What have you in mind, Herr Flick?
HERR FLICK: I have an excellent gramophone and many old records of Hitler's speeches. They are quite amusing.

HELGA: Hitler's speeches quite amusing?

HERR FLICK: Played at double speed, he sounds like Donald Duck.[65]

While this works to undermine Hitler and suggests a dissident quality in the officer (Donald Duck was used throughout the war in Allied propaganda films like 1942's *Der Fuehrer's Face*), the following demonstrates the postnostalgic emptiness of this character:

HERR FLICK: [*to the tune of the Hokey Cokey*] You put your right boot in, you take your right boot out, you do a lot of shouting and you shake your fists about. You light a little smokie and you burn down ze town, zat's vot it's all about. Ah, Himmler, Himmler, Himmler ... [66]

Invoking Himmler and joking about burning villages – all accompanied by a raucous laugh track – turns the violence of WWII into a set of clichés and tropes, actions untainted by 'reality' or consequence. History becomes parody and pastiche – as demonstrated by the fact that the show drew clearly on and mocked *Secret Army* – a joke about itself with no central true referent point.

The terrible costumes and accents are, first, a joke and then quickly attain ascendancy, to the point that when the British undercover agent who impersonates a French policeman enters his terrible – and diegetically 'wrong' – accent gives him away (and provokes laughter in the audience). 'Good moaning' is the catchphrase here; the characters continually try to hide his obvious non-Frenchness (on top of his comically amplified Englishness) and the situation's ludicrousness undermines the historicity of the programme. The characters obviously 'perform' Frenchness while clearly not being French (they don't speak the language, just a clichéd approximation of it), in a comic rendition of Judith Butler's theorising of drag:

> If the anatomy of the performer is already distinct from the gender of the performer, and both of those are distinct from the gender of the performance, then the performance suggests a dissonance not only between sex and performance, but sex and gender, and gender and performance.[67]

'Allo 'Allo demonstrates for comic effect that nation is performance and that identity within the mode of 'history' is similarly predicated upon costume, gesture and action within a strictly ideologically defined space. The past is as inauthentic as the French accents of the protagonists, and their constant repetition of key phrases and plots demonstrates the viewer's desire for easily locatable and understandable historical figures at the same time that it undermines them by demonstrating their innate falseness. Engagement with the past via the programme is as garbled as the English character's attempts to speak French.

This trend is given much more force in *Blackadder* (BBC, 1983–89), which quite happily attacks historicity while still striving for a certain 'authenticity'. Blackadder as a character is found in four distinct periods of history (Middle

Ages, Elizabethan, Georgian, First World War), and each series follows his under-hand and sly attempts to make a better life for himself. The satire on 'history' in these programmes is the fact that the viewer is expected to at once recognise the history which is being travestied while respecting a kind of 'authenticity' expressed in the deployment of recognisable tropes (costume, music, set design). The series ventriloquises the past, putting on bad costumes in order to perform history as a backdrop to broad comedy.[68] However, many of the jokes in *Blackadder* depend on some historical knowledge – either of fact or more impressionistically of period – prompting the thought that there is a level at which 'historical jokes' might be more than just witticisms which take place in a fictitiously rendered historical space. *Blackadder*'s take on history is more sophisticated than *'Allo 'Allo* insofar as the past is intertwined with character and narrative rather than simply a backdrop for crossdressing and slapstick. Indeed *Blackadder* has begun to become folded into historicity, and the series has been criticised for its ability to spread broad caricatures and therefore affect public historical understanding.[69] It is used in schools as a teaching aid, for instance, and its effect on the way that the past is conceived of is great.[70]

In contrast to this postnostalgic way of presenting the past, another strand of mainstream programming dramatises movement between past and present in a way that emphasises historical difference. *Goodnight Sweetheart* (BBC, 1993–99), *Life on Mars* (BBC, 2006–7) and its sequel *Ashes to Ashes* (BBC, 2008) are popular programmes which centre upon characters that are surprised by finding themselves out of time. In terms of dramatising how one engages with history both these shows suggest a fluidity – the barrier between us and the past is more permeable than we would think, either imaginatively or physically. Yet they also suggest that the past can infect one. A good comparison is *Quantum Leap* (NBC, 1989–93), in which the hero is parachuted back into the past to 'put things right that once went wrong' or change timelines for the better. Similarly the children's series *Time Warp Trio* (NBC, 2005) sends a team of kids back to learn about a period and ensure that history happens correctly. The key film analogue, the *Back to the Future* trilogy (Robert Zemeckis, 1985–90), concerns travelling forward and backward in time in order to ensure that key events still occur and that there is a happy ending for all. Obviously the programmes have a huge debt to *Doctor Who* (BBC, 1963–), which imposes a set of moral absolutes upon time travel but does not generally consider movement *between* times so much as movement *to* particular periods; similarly the series is interested in the specificity of the particular moment rather than its relationship to anything else – the past in *Doctor Who* is simply a backdrop to have the particular episodes' narrative projected onto rather than inextricably intertwined with the events unfolding. The moral complexities of *Goodnight, Sweetheart* and *Life on Mars* ensure that these relatively simplistic ways of conceptualising time travel are too straightforward. Their interest in the dynamic between then and now is in dramatising historical difference and rendering it as generic entertainment. There is also an element of these series which is interested in disturbing the 'present' – both central characters are relatively ambivalent about their lives in the 'now' (despite the privations of the past).

In *Goodnight Sweetheart* (which is essentially a sitcom), the protagonist Gary Sparrow discovers that he can move between his modern life and 1940s wartime London. He evolves two lives (which somehow run concurrently in realtime) and gets props from the modern world's historical resources and archives (ration books, papers) to help him live in the past. Sparrow sells artefacts from the past as antiques in the modern world; when he first unknowingly enters the 1940s he decides that the first place he visits is a heritage theme pub. The series therefore gently satirises contemporary fascination with history while also demonstrating the pervasiveness of that past in the present, both materially and in terms of cultural tropes (the 'themed' leisure heritage space). The ethics of the programme are dubious and this works to give the show nuance – Gary has relationships in both times and marries both his partners; he attempts to make money through prediction and passes off songs by the Beatles as his own work.[71] These ethical issues are created solely by the tension between then and now, as a direct consequence of the central character inhabiting both dimensions. In *Goodnight Sweetheart* having actual, physical empathy with an historical period – actually living there at times – leads to murky behaviour.

Life on Mars is a kind of inverted *Heartbeat* insofar as the period DCI Sam Tyler finds himself in – as a result of being knocked down by a car, so his impression that he is immersed in 1973 is probably an illusion – is horribly contrasted with the present day rather than nostalgically remembered. Tyler's introduction to the past is visual first – he checks his wallet, clothes, the cars around him – and thence behavioural. He doesn't understand attitudes, phrases, lifestyle props and this lack of comprehension figures historicity as a set of performative indicators. The indexes of modernity and contemporaneity are either gadgets – a mobile phone, a Jeep – or a set of rules for behaving (not being sexist, racist, homophobic).

He works in the same police force as his modern-day self but dislikes intently the atmosphere and the procedures, from the casual racism, homophobia and sexism through to the violence used on suspects by his monstrous boss, DCI Gene Hunt (the show draws heavily on the example of the 1970s show *The Sweeney*). This dissonance is important to the series' effect, as is made evident by the title – *Life on Mars* indicating the ambivalence that Tyler feels about living in the early 1970s but also being a 1971 song by David Bowie. It is a state of mind and a piece of history. The 1970s are seen as being immensely different from now, almost unrecognisable. However, there is a nostalgic frisson associated with the chain smoking and the flares. Yet this nostalgia is not that of *Heartbeat* – a warmth associated with an idealised past. The nostalgic impulse is about recognition in some fashion, but it is in no sense a comfortable 'retro' show about a harmless, disconnected past. The programme also uses dramatic irony to reflect upon what has been lost as well as gained – particularly the absence of community in the modern world (in Episode 3, the team investigate the union at a failing factory and Tyler recognises the building as the flats that he lives in; in Episode 5, the fracturing of football crowds by hooligan violence is foreseen).[72]

Life on Mars also suggests that in general Tyler's methods are more effective – certainly he gets better results by not hitting as many people. He has a kind of historical smugness which Gary Sparrow also shares, a combination of hindsight and positivist thinking (we are better now than then) which is undermined by personal relationships which force both of them to consider staying in the past permanently. The assumption that the present is the best place to be – with no conception of how this present will itself be superseded – figures a hypocritical historical moral high ground.

Pressure groups complained that the programme's 'authentic' 1970s idiolect, which includes sexist, homophobic and racist insults, as unsuitable for BBC drama and could lead to copycat bullying.[73] This suggests that there are some things – verbalised bigotry, for instance – that are seemingly unsuitable for prime-time television. *Life on Mars* shares a visceral quality with *Rome* and *Deadwood* insofar as it suggests that life in the past was more violent, gritty, and unreconstructed. The nostalgic impetus in these shows is not towards the simpler existence of yesteryear but a desire to reimagine the past and examine it in more complex fashion. *Life on Mars* is a genre programme, though, and therefore the dynamic is slightly different – it dramatises the search for meaning (both Tyler's and the police force's) and the eventual attainment of truth and understanding of sorts. Even in the past the impetus is towards order from chaos. *Life on Mars* renders the 1970s morally inert – a site for the investigation of motive and the discovery of straightforward truth (in comparison with the present in which 'science' has taken over – as demonstrated in the opening sequence when Tyler is berated for being obsessed with forensics and not thinking with his gut any more). At the same time the 'past' is probably not real – it is a coma-induced dream – and so the representation of the past in the mind of a man who was born in 1969 is predicated upon television police shows (like *The Sweeney*) and musical sound-track; in short, it is a fictionalised account, a caricature of life in the 1970s complete with flock wallpaper and flares.[74]

Ashes to Ashes (BBC, 2008), the sequel to *Life on Mars*, extends and complicates that show's take on the past. DCI Alex Drake is shot and the effect of the bullet is to somehow send her back to London in 1981, where coincidentally Gene Hunt has moved to clean up the East End. The past is still rampantly homophobic and sexist, but again Hunt's real-man quality and his rude directness are fetishised. Philip Glenister's performance as Hunt renders him as a guilty pleasure for the audience, his aggressive non-PCness contrasted with Drake's priggish uptight-ness. There is a clear nostalgia for a simpler time when men were men and could talk as roughly as they wished. In contrast to Tyler's effectiveness, Drake is neurotic and talks in psychobabble, and her instinct is generally wrong. However, the fish-out-of-water motif is not developed overmuch – the tropes of the 1980s (red braces, New Romantics, the docklands) are so much more famil-iar and recognisable to Drake that she finds it quite straightforward to settle in.

The series is immensely self-conscious and self-referential. Drake is an expert on Sam Tyler's case, and the opening episode starts with her daughter reading aloud from his notes – reading the very words that he began each episode of *Life on Mars* with. Her daughter's reaction – 'Whatever' – threatens to undermine the carefully crafted believability of the first two series, but soon the audience is being asked to undergo another time travelling moment as Drake wakes up on a boat in the Thames in 1981.[75] Unlike Tyler, Drake immediately presumes that what she is experiencing is a delusion, a psychological reaction to the trauma of being shot. Having seen Tyler's reports she reads the situation immediately, thinking that it is her own fantasy of the past. At points she apologises for events that she thinks she is making up: 'I have no idea where this stuff is coming from.'[76] Similarly she presumes that, as it is her fantasy, she might be in control: 'I'm going to have to reimagine you,' she says to Hunt.[77] This self-consciousness renders the series quite conceptually fragile, but also alive with historiographic possibility. Drake's experience in the past is – she presumes – a fictive reaction to the circumstances of her present. The series expresses David Lowenthal's argument that heritage is all about a way of coming to knowledge about the present rather than understanding the past. *Ashes to Ashes* offers the past as a fantasy world that might allow the resolution of problems in the present. Drake bodily experiences a scene that she presumes is her imaginative version of the past (she expresses surprise at the tactile depth of the fantasy, but also worries that calories in her imagination might have a physical manifestation: 'a moment on the lips, an afterlife on the hips').[78] The *experience* allows her to understand her contemporary life. For Drake, it is all surface, a pastiche of the past, a knowing experience, rather than an immersive psychological understanding of historical otherness.[79]

Sam Tyler inhabits an odd netherworld, a coma-induced dream of history. In *Life on Mars* possessing an overactive historical imagination renders one effectively mad – and at the end of the series Tyler appears to commit suicide as a consequence of his visions. The show illustrates the way in which contemporary audiences (using Tyler as an everyman) engage with and conceptualise the past – through a series of fictional tropes, visual signifiers, odd behavioural models and in the main a mystification at what went on then. The historical imagination is authentic but contorted. Alex Drake recognises her fantasy of history, articulating a surprise and astonishment at the detail she creates and clearly conceptualising the past as a means of meditating upon the present. For her, the 1980s is something to escape, a nightmare that she would wake from, a set of problems that she has to solve to return to normality. The self-consciousness of her historical imaginary presents the past as a set of tropes and performances, depthless and purposeless. The binary enacted by these linked series demonstrates what this chapter has been arguing throughout – the potential and variety of the popular history drama in engaging with the past.

13 Historical film

National cinema, international audiences and historical film

Other than on television, the key form for visualised engagement with an imagined, constructed past is film. While it is important to consider the British historical film as an entity, it is also crucial to recall that the audience watching it will compare it to other historical film product, anything from *Goodfellas* (Martin Scorsese, 1990) to *The Pianist* (Roman Polanski, 2002); film is increasingly transnational and global.[1] Indeed, these two examples demonstrate the reach and complexity of the historical film. *Goodfellas* is a highly sophisticated, self-conscious, twisting piece of work examining life as a gangster. Drawing in some ways on the *Godfather* trilogy (Francis Ford Coppola, 1972, 1974, 1990), it was followed through the 1990s with a number of gangster and drug films set in the 1970s including *Donnie Brasco* (Mike Newell, 1997), *Blow* (Ted Demme, 2001), *Boogie Nights* (Paul Thomas Anderson, 1997) and *American Gangster* (Ridley Scott, 2007). *The Pianist* is an account of a Jewish Pole's harrowing escape from the Nazis, and is part of the ongoing filmic response to the Holocaust, including *Schindler's List* (Stephen Spielberg, 1993) and *Life is Beautiful/ La vita é bella* (Roberto Benigni, 1997). Spielberg's *Munich* (2005) complicated this set of tropes by making an historical thriller out of the vengeful Mossad counter-terrorist mission following the Black September assassination of Israeli Olympic athletes in 1972, clearly questioning the decisions of the Israeli state and reflecting on Jewishness as well as the American War on Terror post-9/11. As a consequence of this variety and scope there is not space here to consider historical film in real depth. The genre is vast and global.[2]

Historical film and allegory have been used by film-makers to work through issues about the recent past, particularly in relation to violence and national identity. In these films 'history' becomes both a set of reference points – the 'facts' that are or sometimes are not known – and an arena simultaneously connected to the present but also conceptually othered, a place where things happened in the abstract but which might be changed through understanding or reconsideration. Emir Kusturica's *Underground* (1995) is a surreal account of various stages of Yugoslavian history which debates how a nation is produced and sustained through violence. German film has begun to engage with modern history, for instance in the form of working through the figure of Hitler (*Der Undergang/ Downfall*, Oliver Hirschbiegel, 2004). *Downfall*, based on the memoirs of Hitler's secretary Traudl Junge, contributes to the strand of biographical film as well as demonstrating its own subjectivity by being bookended by an interview with Junge in the present day. It is both more truthful and less truthful as a consequence, and this uncertainty and desire for both understanding as well as a shying away from difficult wider issues characterise much historical biopics about key 'evil' figures. Recently, directors from Germany have begun to examine life before the wall came down, either presenting comic nostalgia for the Communist world (*Goodbye Lenin!*, Wolfgang Becker, 2002) or meditating on the humanness at the centre of the most mindless Stasi operation (*Das Leben der Anderen/ The Lives of Others*, Florian Henckel von Donnersmarck, 2006).[3] In particular, this last film reflects on the rewriting of history as a concluding scene has Dreymann, the subject of the operation, go through his Stasi file after 1989 in a newly opened archive. The scene emphasises its thematic matter by having the archivist spend some time walking through the collection, focussing the attention of the audience on the evidence filed there. The documents he reads, however, are those falsified by the leader of the operation to protect Dreymann and his lover. Having the Stasi officer as a kind of hero is a problematic move, and the film simplifies life under the Communist regime.[4] The 'Ostalgie' (nostalgia for Communism) of the film and its simplistic presentation of the Stasi methods and GDR repression rob it of anything other than narrative value and a certain material authenticity; the actions of the story and the characters are not historically truthful. The director argued in a statement released with the film: 'I didn't want to tell a true story as much as explore how someone might have behaved. The film is more of a basic expression of belief in humanity than an account of what actually happened.'[5] The film is fundamentally not real, but a representation of an ideal; a story which allows for forgiveness of a regime only by humanising it impossibly.

Chinese history was a potent way for the so-called 'Fifth Generation' of film makers in the 1980s and 1990s to examine national identity and culture. Chen Kaige's *Ju Dou* (1991) and the complex epic *Ba wang bie ji/ Farewell My Concubine* (1993) were both responses to the 1989 Tiananmen Square crisis which used the historical framework to explore the relationship between tyranny, compromise, politics and art. These films won awards and audiences worldwide, and made stars of their lead actors. Chinese historical epic during the early 1990s was a serious and political mode; it now means something very different. Some of the 'Fifth Generation' have exchanged politics for lavishness and gained massive audiences in their fetishisation of Chinese history and culture (although the breakthrough film that opened this market was made in America, Ang Lee's 2001 *Wu hu cang long/ Crouching Tiger, Hidden Dragon*). Zhang Yimou, for instance, has moved from thoughtful earlier historical work analysing gender and power relationships such as *Da hong deng long gao gao gua/ Raise the Red Lantern* (1991) to mystical martial arts epics *Ying xiong/ Hero* (2002), *Shi mian mai fu/ House of Flying Daggers* (2004) and *Man cheng jin dai huang jin jia/ Curse of the Golden Flower* (2006).[6] Where Kaige used history to reflect on nation, these films are escapist semi-mythological fantasies, although the movement towards this kind of conceptualisation of the nation's glorified past is certainly affected by state censorship to some degree after the absorption of Hong Kong (where most of the film industry is based) into mainland China.[7]

The films made by native film industries often have a polemic, political or purifying purpose. Contemporary Spanish films with an historic element demonstrate an attempt to engage with and understand recent events (in particular the civil war and Franco's reign), although this has been a motif of the industry for a while.[8] Relatively bleak or uncompromising films about Spain, such as Pedro Almodóvar's *La mala educación/Bad Education* (2004) and (despite his being Mexican) Guillermo del Toro's *El Laberinto del Fauno/Pan's Labyrinth* (2006), have found international markets for such national catharsis. This is the case with the majority of the films mentioned in this discussion – most of them won awards, too – and gives rise to a key question about the audiences for historical films: is the historical engagement that is going on in these films important to a non-national viewer, or does the past really become a foreign country?

Films exploring moments of national trauma often sit at odds – or in parallel with – popular crowd-pleasing work. The fact that a politicised film such as the account of the Red Brigade's murder of Aldo Moro in the Italian *Good Morning, Night* (Marco Bellocchio, 2003) can have some elements in common with more comfortable fare such as *Cinema Paradiso* (Guiseppe Tornatore, 1988) demonstrates that the 'historical' film or genre can be both politically interrogative or simply present a warmly nostalgic view of imagined historical events. Both posit a past which is somehow idealised, but the former analyses an obscure horror as key to national political development while the latter is clearly an exercise in indulgent nostalgia (the film is set up as the reminiscences of an older man, so ingrained in the form of the piece is a sense of melancholic and idealising remembrance of a happier time). The key difference, furthermore, is that one film is based on 'actual' events where the other presents a mood, an impression of the past rather than a reconstruction.

French film has often engaged with the recent past – generally in relation to colonial history – in more contemporary settings (in films such as Michael Hanneke's 2005 *Caché/Hidden* – although Hanneke is German). However, *Mon Colonel* (Laurent Herbier, 2006), *Days of Glory/Indigènes* (Rachid Bouchareb, 2006) and *Intimate Enemies/L'Ennemi Intime* (Florent Emilio Siri, 2007) all suggest a desire to explore the conduct and aftermath of the Algerian War. The French film industry's presentation of the past is more akin to the British – an emphasis on lavish costume drama such as *La Reine Margot* (Patrice Chereau, 1994), *Molière* (Laurent Tirard, 2007), out-of-time comedy such as *Les Visiteurs* (Jean-Marie Poiré, 1996) and literary adaptation such as *Germinal* (Claude Berri, 1994) or *Cyrano de Bergerac* (Jean-Paul Rappeneau, 1990).[9] French historical movies find their nostalgic touchstone – an equivalent of Merchant-Ivory – in the hugely successful (domestically and internationally) diptych *Jean de Florette* (Claude Berri, 1986) and *Manon des Sources* (Claude Berri, 1986).[10] Both films demonstrated a conservative mournfulness for simpler, rural community, and were – with *Cinema*

Paradiso – widely popular and successful outside of their domestic market (although abroad were distributed as art-house films rather than the mainstream epics they were at home).

The problematic prevalence of the tropes of historical film is demonstrated by M. Night Shyamalan's (2004) *The Village*. The film presents an isolated community from the early nineteenth century. The twist, which is only revealed at the end of the narrative, is that the community is actually made up of contemporary people who have fled to refuge from the horror of modern life in cities. The film undermines the audience's assumption that this is an historical movie and their consequent comfort with this mode. The twist is dependent on the assumptions associated with the generic form of the historical film. In contrast to this cunning deployment of historical tropes, comedies like *Bill and Ted's Excellent Adventure* (Stephen Herek, 2001) demonstrate an irreverence towards the representation of the past which can lead to sloppy caricature (*Black Knight*, Gil Junger, 2001) useful horror manifestations (Sam Raimi's *Army of Darkness*, 1992), and serious attempts to undermine the entire genre in wilfully anachronistic films such as *A Knight's Tale* (Brian Helgeland, 2001) or *Moulin Rouge* (Baz Luhrmann, 2001).[11]

The heritage debate and British film

Within this complex global nexus, then, British historical film is at once a distinctly national representational mode and also something that might be strong enough to evolve strategies for dissent and the interrogation of conservatism. Heritage products on television and film in the 1980s were in many ways considered one entity, and several critics have argued that the British 'heritage film' as a genre became defined during that decade.[12] The key productions in this particular narrative of the cultural phenomena of the historical film or television series were *Brideshead Revisited* (Granada, 1981), the film *Chariots of Fire* (Hugh Hudson, 1981) and the set of pictures that the production company Merchant-Ivory made between 1985's *A Room with a View* and 1993's *The Remains of the Day* (encompassing further *Maurice*, 1987, and 1992's *Howard's End*). Other films in this genre include *Where Angels Fear to Tread* (Charles Sturridge, 1991), *The Wings of the Dove* (Iain Softley, 1997), *The Madness of King George* (Nicholas Hytner, 1995), as well as David Lean's *A Passage to India* (1984). 'Costume drama' heritage productions were accused of pandering to a vision of 'a lost or vanishing country-house England', looking back with yearning to a time when life somehow was better and less complicated.[13] Key to this critique was the idea that the films presented a nostalgic Englishness addressing a culturally conservative elite. Andrew Higson, Patrick Wright and Robert Hewison all argued that heritage cultural products illustrated a desire for a particular form of Britishness.[14] Higson considered them 'middle-class quality products, somewhere between the art-house and the mainstream ... the artful and spectacular projection of an elite, conservative vision of the national past'.[15] They supported a right-wing vision of the country through their peddling of 'canonical cultural properties' such as novels, stately homes, and costumes; furthermore, they underwrote the privileged status of various texts and artefacts in the definition of nationhood and heritage.[16] Patrick Wright blamed the 'aristocratic-reactionary' ascendancy over society on the 'Brideshead complex', arguing that heritage was simply reactionary chic.[17] Hewison argued that the heritage film represented a return to a kind of feudal simpering over stately houses.[18]

Raphael Samuel pointed out in response that heritage had been happening a long time before the 1980s, but the associations of film costume drama with a conservative, right-wing, middle-class agenda have been hard to shake. They have been seen as instrumental in presenting a version of the past as homogenous, class-ridden, visually rich and viewed through the twin lenses of quality and authenticity. Many of the innovative costume films of the 1990s and early 2000s explicitly took issue with the staid image of the heritage series, and reacted by introducing realism, sex, fragmented narratives and moral complexity. Yet those texts which have followed this path, such as those that deal with anachronism, dissidence or additional story-telling (Jane Campion's *Portrait of a Lady* (1996), Sally Potter's *Orlando* (1992), Derek Jarman's *Edward II* (1991), Patricia Rozema's *Mansfield Park* (1999), Alex Cox's *Revenger's Tragedy* (2002)), have not proved particularly successful in the market despite critical acclaim.[19] However, they demonstrate that there is a strand of dissident heritage film-making.

When looking again at the heritage films and drama from the 1980s through the 1990s, it is clear that while a particular middle-class vision of Englishness is being articulated, these texts are more complex than they have been given credit for.[20] *Brideshead Revisited* expressed a sense of an England lost by the coming of war and attempted to engender empathy for a slowly decaying aristocratic family. It instituted the standard conventions of the heritage drama, with prestigious acting names, music, sumptuous historical recreations, excessive costumes and a characteristic note of nostalgia.[21] However, it is also melancholic and vicious. The decline of an England yearned for somehow is, even in the original novel, something at once nostalgic, bitter, and unattainable. This bittersweet element pervades the series which itself enacts the inability to return to the past and the insubstantiality of memory – dramatising and critiquing a concern with the nostalgic pull of history which was exactly what critics of the series said it was undertaking. At the conclusion of the series Charles Ryder leaves Brideshead and goes off to war, everything that it represented for him corrupted and decayed. He, as the voiceover so therefore the audience's avatar and something of an authorial figure, begins the text fresh-faced and innocent and by the end is bitter and lonely; the audience journeys with him and sees what is on the surface glittering and beautiful (Sebastian Flyte, Lord Marchmain, Julia Flyte) decay and die. The nostalgia in the series is for youth and innocence, rather than for a way of life. The audience enacts the same fall into knowledge and hard-bitten irony as Charles does. To complicate this further, the salvation that Charles finds at the end of the series is in the constancy of the Catholic Church, something which is certainly nostalgic and conservative but similarly challenging to a secular, generally Protestant British nation.

Of the Merchant-Ivory films one is unambivalently about sexual transgression (*Maurice*, based on a novel about homosexuality not published in Forster's lifetime) while the others articulate within their content debates about class and national identity (*Howard's End* dramatises class conflict particularly brutally).[22] The use of E.M. Forster to posit a sense of particular Englishness in itself raises complexities about that national definition, as *A Passage to India*'s ambivalences demonstrates. The film and the novel rest on the interpretation of a particular moment as a lens through which to dissect English attitudes to India. Coming two years after *Gandhi* (Richard Attenborough, 1982), the film is a meditation on the effects of imperialism.[23] The novels are not easily straightforward in their presentation of identity. The films do often present a conservative *mise-en-scène* but their content is complex. It ranges from naked homosociality in *A Room with a View* to the narrative of fragmentation in *Howard's End*, concluding as it does with the inheritance of the house by the defiantly middle-class but not quite English Schlegel family and ultimately the illegitimate son of Leonard Bast. Julianne Pidduck has argued that the Merchant-Ivory films can 'also be read as evocative dramatisations of female desire and transgressive sexuality'.[24] The final film in the sequence, *The Remains of the Day*, differs from the rest by being based on a historical novel rather than a 'canonical' source; furthermore the novel by Kazuo Ishiguro conceptualises collusion with received ideas, stereotypes, rules and cultural behaviours.[25] The novel and its film version are interested in complicity and a particular type of Englishness which is critiqued. As an endnote to their series of heritage films it seems a particularly bittersweet and dissident way to think about country houses, national identity and selfhood. Indeed the material status of the production company itself, a gay American-Indian partnership using a Euro-Indian scriptwriter (Ruth Prawer Jhabvala wrote *A Room with a View*, *The Remains of the Day* and *Howard's End*), suggests a cultural complexity – the films may have been read by their audience as a celebration of a particular type of Englishness but their roots are in a much more dynamic and less straightforward set of relationships.[26]

British historical film over the past two decades has seemed in the main concerned with analysing class, national identity itself, and the margins. Films that conceptualise recent national history are generally light, escapist fantasies such as *Billy Eliot* (Stephen Frears, 2000) which used the miners' strike as a backdrop, *East is East* (Damian O'Donnell, 1999) which gently satirised the racism of Britain in the 1950s and 1960s, or comedies like *The Full Monty* (Peter Cattaneo, 2001) which dealt with the problems of being unemployed in Thatcher's Britain. An exception is the social history film *Vera Drake* (Mike Leigh, 2004). British historical film has obsessed on biography (for instance *The Krays*, Peter Medak, 1990), and, in particular, royal biography.[27] This strand of film making unfurls from stage-based costume drama (*The Madness of King George III*, Nicholas Hytner 1994), through the more innovative *realpolitik* analyses of Shekhar Kapur's *Elizabeth* (1998) and *Elizabeth: The Golden Age* (2007) to sentimental pieces such as *Mrs Brown* (John Madden, 1997).[28] These films are companion pieces of sorts with British television drama biog-history, such as Ray Winstone's bruiser *Henry VIII* (ITV, 2003), Helen Mirren's *Elizabeth I* (ITV, 2005), *Charles II* (BBC, 2003), *The Tudors* (BBC, 2007), and *The Virgin Queen* starring Anne-Marie Duff (BBC,

2005). Stephen Frears' analysis of the monarchy's reaction to the death of Diana, *The Queen* (2006), was similarly concerned with reading political, cultural and historical events through the lens of the royal personage. The British film industry, then, produces a version of the country focussed through its past which uses that past to consider nostalgia and monarchy; sometimes to question, but often with little inflection.

History, complexity and horror: *Atonement* and *The Wind that Shakes the Barley*

In contrast with these straightforward examples, though, this chapter concludes with two self-conscious costume dramas that present a more complex historiography. It is clear how far the classic/costume/historical dramatic film might be developed as a sophisticated drama in considering *Atonement* (Joe Wright, 2007), one of a suite of films interested in complicating the tropes of the heritage film (others in this vein include Robert Altman's *Gosford Park*, 2001). *Atonement* is about the subjectivities both of seeing and of looking back to the past. In dramatising such concerns, the film – and the source novel – critique the costume drama and the historical film, suggesting that such works make those of the past (particularly the war) into icons, lie, and romanticise the way that things were. The film tells the story of one evening from the point of view of an imaginative child (Briony) who later admits she lied. The action is often shown twice, to demonstrate how the meaning of events depend on point of view, a metatextual element which comments upon looking back to the past (is it possible to understand things better the second time? It is unclear – the characters (Robbie and Cecilia) who are taking part definitely do not, and say as much to each other later).

The film signals its self-awareness in the opening shot, which has Briony putting the finishing touches to her latest play. The close-up shot of a doll's house further suggests the film's awareness of its genre, suggesting that the action will both be part of the country house model and also be a mere bagatelle.[29] This self-conscious opening – country house, novel – gives way to what appears to be a standard across the tracks passion between the daughter of the family and the housekeeper's son. Yet it is much darker – the real secret being kept here is paedophilia. The gentle country house genre is fractured.

After Robbie is arrested, the scene cuts to the days preceding Dunkirk in 1940. In one key scene, he arrives on Dunkirk beach and there is a five-minute steadicam tracking shot which follows Robbie and his men around the scene, taking in the beach, ships, pubs and the promenade generally. There are hundreds of extras, horses are shot, and a choir sings in the bandstand (1,600 people were involved). It is a grimly horrible place, bleak and full of hopelessness. The camera weaves around, losing the key characters at times to focus on other members of the evacuating army. Each of these men has a story and the audience's interest in Robbie is peripheral to what is going on around him. The individual is set within history, but not more important than it. The film is interested in one man's narrative, but there are hundreds of stories here. Furthermore, the audience is aware of the falsity of this particular shot – while it is immensely technically impressive, the alienness of an unedited shot, and the obvious dexterity with which it is being realised, actually draw attention to itself as a set-piece *tour de force* and move us as an audience out of engagement. The shot is over-authentic in its scope and brilliance and attempt to take in everything, and in doing so it demonstrates its bravado and breaks the connection between viewer and text. In being over-realistic, the shot undermines the authenticity of the film.

The film concludes, though, dissonantly, with the now extremely old Briony being interviewed as a famous novelist whose book the film stages. She admits that, while autobiographical, some of the events in the novel-film never happened. She has interviewed witnesses who were in similar situations and made some things up to atone her conscience. The narrative – the narrator – admits to lying to the audience, both in the same way that she lied about the original incident but also so as to undermine the value of everything that has gone past. Those characters the audience connected with are little more than figments of her imagination; that past simply what the author – novelist, film-maker – thinks might have happened. The unreliable narrator is a common device in fiction writing but less deployed in film, and the effect is to call into question the veracity of the historical film in its entirety. The audience, who attended a recognisable event – costume drama of a novel by a famous writer (Ian McEwan) featuring the cream of posh British acting talent (James McEvoy and Kiera Knightley) – are shown the trick. Again this undermines realism – the film is shot in such a way as to draw the viewer in to its 'real' setting (deployment of familiar tropes, props, locations and costume, as well as the standard authentic elements).

The tropes of literary adaptation and truly 'historical' film shade into one another so that the 'historical' becomes nearly seamlessly intertwined in the 'fictional'; it is difficult to know the difference between the genres. Historic authenticity becomes backdrop for a narrative, or the vehicle for a particular set of ideological concerns. Ken Loach's controversial *The Wind that Shakes the Barley* (2006), set in Ireland from 1920 to 1923, led to national debates in the UK and Ireland about interpretations and representations of the Irish War of Independence. The film begins with a generic 'local colour' shot of boys playing hurly in caps and old-style clothing, with characteristically 'Irish' folk music playing; there are stately long shots and the camera lingers on the landscape. This pastoral establishing sequence is brutally undermined in the next shots, and this undercutting of the tropes of the costume drama is keynote of the film's political purpose. First, the boys are arrested by soldiers for carrying offensive weapons, and then one is beaten to death for refusing to say his name in English. The 'Irish' music demonstrates resistance, then, and the 'costume' authenticity becomes the reason for brutality. The film continually challenges the easy assumptions of the heritage film, asking difficult questions about loyalty, empire and complicity. The date of the film's action suggests that while English heritage movies dramatise a worry about self and the end of empire what was actually going on in the name of that empire was vicious. The values of the 'country house' are attacked by the central characters, and literally invaded when the Republican gang arrests the local gentleman farmer in his library.

The film obeys generic rules (landscape, music, a scene of dancing, authentic use of accents, costumes and Gaelic) but shows the characters who would have worked the farms or built the roads for the characters in English heritage films.

The film is uncompromising in presenting the varieties of political faction in Ireland at the time (even the title comes from a song associated with the 1798 rebellion and used by the Irish Republican Army) and suggests that the British were capable of great horrors. While there is an attempt at justification – a British captain mentions the Somme and suggests that the traumas of the war affected his troops – the sheer level of brutality meted out by the British led some to attack Loach for his pro-IRA sentiments. The *Daily Mail* asked, 'Why does Ken Loach loathe his country so much?' and responded to the film by reminding readers that 'The truth is that, as empires go, the British version was the most responsible and humane of all.'[30] The director was compared to Nazi propagandist Leni Riefenstahl in *The Times*, and *The Sun* called the movie 'a brutally anti-British film ... designed to drag the reputation of our nation through the mud'.[31] These reactions suggest that an historical film merely *attempting* to comprehend and articulate complex political events is not welcome in the UK (such reactions were absent in the British press when *Land and Freedom*, Loach's equally bleak film about the Spanish Civil War, was released in 1995). In contrast, Jimmy McGovern's *Bloody Sunday* (1992), a docudrama about the events in Belfast of 1972, was extremely careful in the way it presented its information (but nonetheless expressed horror at the actions of the British police and army). Loach's film also generated great debate in Ireland about the accuracy of its representation (as had Neil Jordan's (1996) *Michael Collins*), and demonstrated that the country was still conceptualising and revisiting the key events in its formation. Both Loach's and Jordan's films were accused of simplifying complex events; the reactions to each film showing that discussion of history was able to provoke important national debate. In contrast, the hysterical reaction to Loach's film in the UK demonstrated an unwillingness to enter into that debate, a desire to avoid difficult questions.

However, the backdrop of brutality in *The Wind that Shakes the Barley* is put into relief, first, by an eloquent speech at gunpoint that Damien (Cillian Murphy) delivers asking the English to 'get out of my country', and, second, by the fact that the film's real subject is the intercine fighting between factions after the treaty with the British. Loach explores the way that nations derive from acts of violence, and the opening hurly game becomes a metaphor for the fighting between brothers. This becomes literal as Damien is executed on the order of his brother Teddy (Pádraic Delaney). Early in the film Damien articulates the horror of his situation as he prepares to execute a traitor he has known since childhood: 'I studied anatomy for five years ... Now I'm going to shoot this man in the head ... I hope this Ireland we're fighting for is worth it.'[32] Similar to *Land and Freedom*, the film demystifies romanticised moments (the glorious rebels, the birth of the nation in defiance of the English) and shows them to be messy, contingent struggles pitting horror against horror. It is a bleak, grim film which suggests that heritage epics can engage passionately with their subject at the same time that they present the indeterminacy of historical understanding.

14 Imagined histories

Novels, plays and comics

'A bodice-ripper with a bibliography': historical novels

History is other, and the present familiar. The historian's job is often to explain the transition from other to familiar. The historical novelist similarly explores the dissonance between then and now, making the past both recognisable but simultaneously unfamiliar. Historical novelists concentrate on the gaps between known factual history and that which is lived to a variety of purposes. The spaces scholars have no idea about – the gaps between verifiable fact – are the territory for the writer of fictional history. As Lukács pointed out, the historical novel is a form that deploys 'necessary anachronism' – it is innately false, and continuously draws attention to its otherness. While generally using the realist style – despite key examples which interrogate such authority, like John Fowles' (1969) *The French Lieutenant's Woman* – the historical novel is a self-conscious and self-reflexive form that implicitly communicates to the reader its illegitimacy and inauthenticity. A key site for this articulation is the material historical framework – the author's note, introduction or explanatory section appended to all historical fiction since Walter Scott's *Waverley* (1814). This self-consciousness can be demonstrated in a consideration of Mark Lawson's 'Afterword' to his *Enough is Enough*:

> While this novel was based on a large number of factual sources (detailed below), the warning of the Author's Note preceding it should be repeated here: it is a work of fiction and the characters, even when recognizable from an external context, are behaving fictionally … My general aim has been to avoid giving to any character dialogue or actions which the historical record indicates would have been impossible or unlikely. However, the dialogue, though trying to capture the cadence of their conversation as it is recorded in reality, is frequently invented … As a general principle, when a detail seems weird or ridiculously convenient … it can be guaranteed to be true or, at least, documented … The multi-viewpoint structure of the book is intended to reflect the conflicts that arise between different witnesses to history.[1]

Lawson's anxieties demonstrate the innate strangeness associated with historical novel writing. First up is the fact that this note appears at all – most fiction does without such information, and the apparatuses (bibliography, footnote, appendix) of the historical novel signifies it as something different to the novel in general. Lawson's historical novel is predicated upon sources, but at the same time it is fiction. It sits uneasily between authenticity and imaginative writing. Lawson's striving to avoid the 'impossible or unlikely' demonstrates an attachment to realism despite the self-awareness of the novelist that this is all 'invented'. The motif of attempting to 'capture the cadence of their conversation' suggests the artful mimicry of the historical novelist. They cleave to actuality and real events while at the same time acknowledging that the novel *must* disavow such reality. The multiplicity of viewpoint serves to undermine the notion of a singular history; this is clearly the mainspring for most historical fiction, which introduces another fictional voice to the babbling variety of the past. At the same time, that past is itself 'ridiculously convenient' in its apparent narrative and able to articulate something which is 'true or, at least, documented'. In this one note, then, we see the varieties of meaning and signification that the historical novel might generate, the ambiguities and problematic discourses that it deploys. The historical novel, then, articulates within it a complex of ambiguous imperatives towards the past – an attempt at authenticity, at real(ist) representation, at memorialisation, at demonstrating the otherness of history, working within the confines of the web of fact.

Over the past two decades literary novelists have interrogated history in a variety of interesting ways, from Jeanette Winterson's *Sexing the Cherry* (1989) and *The Passion* (1987) through Margaret Atwood's *Alias Grace* (1996) to Hari Kunzru's *The Impressionist* (2002). Rose Tremain's (1989) novel *Restoration* demonstrated the popularity and possibility of the literary historical novel, winning various prizes with huge sales. Tremain managed to combine critical acclaim with populist appeal. It is now commonplace for serious fiction writers to produce historical work, where it was not 20 years ago. On the other hand, the less interrogative historical novel as a popular form has become an even bigger seller than it had previously been, from Mills & Boon's 'historical romance' series to the global bestsellers by Philippa Gregory, Tracy Chevalier (*Girl with a Pearl Earring*, 2000) and Deborah Moggach (*Tulip Fever*, 2000).[2] The historical novel has scope for an interrogation both of fictional practice and the understanding and experience of history. The following discussion considers varieties of the historical novel and what they suggest about contemporary consumption of history. In particular, it considers brief examples from four female historical novelists, from the immensely successful to the critically lauded, in order to consider the varieties of historicalness manifest in contemporary fiction.

Philippa Gregory is immensely successful as an historical novelist. *The Other Boleyn Girl*, the first in her Tudor sequence of novels, is discussed in the introduction as a multiplatform entity; *The Queen's Fool* sold 50,000 copies in hardback in the UK; *The Virgin's Lover*, had advance orders of 180,000 in the USA alone. She is a trained historian and self-conscious about her practice in the way that all historical novelists tend to be:

Is not the imposition of the order of a story on historical facts the making of a lie? Am I not picking out from the enormous range of facts of that year the very few that I can thread together to tell, even to prove, the story that I want to write? … it is a prejudiced, biased view – just like any history book.[3]

This troubling of the record and awareness of creating something fictio-factual is what Lukács referred to as 'necessary anachronism'. He saw it as something utilitarian – it was 'necessary' – but it might be more useful to consider it as something which is inescapable when writing historical fiction. The otherness of the past is constantly foregrounded and the falsity of the exercise, the clear bias and subjectivity of the approach of the novelist, create a state of flux for the history being presented.

In the opening novel of Gregory's trilogy the 'other' Boleyn girl is Mary Boleyn, Anne's sister. In Gregory's version of events she comes to court and is the first Boleyn to catch Henry VIII's eye. The novel sets up a binary between Anne, the flighty, French-trained wit, toast of the court and ambitious over-reacher, and her sister Mary, English schooled, plain, slow-witted, unambitious. Mary only wants to be loved and to have children, and through the book she is explicitly contrasted with Anne. She is maternal, loving, generous and constant where Anne is wilful, hot-tempered and demanding. Mary is the heroine of this story because she strives for the ordinary, for 'happiness'. There are some proto-feminist gestures, and Mary desires independence from the demands of her family. Women are pawns in the games of men. Yet the book sides with Mary and her constancy against the ambition and agency of Anne. The secret heroine of the novel is Katherine of Aragon, the wife Henry abandons, and her poignancy is used to demonstrate the vulgar folly of Anne's desires. Women are empowered only to seek true happiness in marriage and family: 'A father and mother who married for love, who chose each other despite wealth and position.'[4] The novel celebrates love despite social division, an idealised, ennobling, pure 'love'. This love is the apogee of the story, and is presented to us as everything that one should strive for. It is directly contrasted with the 'false coin of vanity and lust'.[5] This love is morally pure and creative rather than destructive. The virtues celebrated by the text are those of constancy, prudence, obedience and domesticity. Katherine of Aragon: 'A woman needs to know her duty so that she may perform it and live in the estate to which God had been pleased to call her' and Mary adds a gloss: 'I knew that she was thinking of my sister, who was not in the estate to which God had been pleased to call her, but was instead in some glorious new condition, earned by her beauty and her wit.'[6] Katherine's constancy and stoicism are admired, whereas Anne's new mobility and dynamism are punished, not just by Henry but by the novel itself. She overreaches herself, and is punished for it.

The novel fleshes out the historical Anne but repeats the bitter judgements of the past upon her. For all that Henry's moves against Katherine of Aragon are arrogant and unfair, the cliché of Anne Boleyn as a calculating harridan is not much troubled by this novel; in fact, it is actively sustained. Mary exclaims toward the close of the novel: 'I loved her still … even though I knew she had brought herself to this point and taken George here too.'[7] Henry is a grumpy, lustful fool, but the one with historical agency and therefore liable for punishment is Anne; Henry is stupid and totally besotted, whereas Anne is calculating and intelligent. Women should not try to change the world but get on with it; they should be unsexual, dowdy, uneducated, loving and constant. The lesson of history here is that men will always be men and that instead of taking up the fight in the centre, one should retire to the margins and start a family. Mary shrugs and accepts her fate – 'women are the very toys of fortune' – and the novel applauds her withdrawal.[8]

Gregory's second Tudor novel, *The Queen's Fool*, foregrounds the dynamic relationship between history and fiction by incorporating a first-person protagonist, Hannah Green, who has the gift of Second Sight, a Holy Fool who is believed without question by all those in the novel. She is able to predict the future, and does so regularly with unerring accuracy. Creating this kind of 'foresight' character inflects the dramatic irony of the historical novel by giving the audience someone to identify with in their own hindsight. Hannah dresses as a boy for most of the novel, angrily asserting her independence. She is unique, untouchable, self-sufficient and confident. However, when she by accident takes over caring for her husband's illegitimate son she discovers maternal instincts that show her the way to happiness. Her desire for independence is broken and she wants to be made whole through family: 'I prayed in silence that perhaps even now, the queen might have a son and might know joy like this, such a strange, unexpected joy – the happiness of caring for a child whose whole life was in my hands.'[9] Gregory presents a very particular version of history in order to suit her moral purpose. Her Queen Mary is revisionist – she is not the clichéd tyrant but a generous, loving, pious woman – directly contrasted with the ruthless inconstancy of her half-sister. Elizabeth comes in for much criticism here, in the main based on historical conjecture and gossip. Mary is retrieved from her position as heretic burner whereas Elizabeth's flirtation with married men is emphasised. Elizabeth 'liked to choose her lovers from the husbands of other women, she liked to arouse desire from a man whose hands were tied, she liked to triumph over a woman who could not keep her husband'.[10] Elizabeth is as bad as her mother, and – for all her personal impressiveness – found morally wanting by the novel. This antipathy continues into the third Tudor novel, *The Virgin's Lover*, which directly compares the flashy, flighty Elizabeth with Amy, Robert Dudley's constant, if dull, first wife.

Taken together, Gregory's Tudor trilogy has a moral historiography – coquettish, adulterous, impious, inconstant, ambitious behaviour may get you the throne, but not happiness. The ambition of Anne Boleyn and her daughter drives the plot of history just as much as the constancy and emotional piety of Mary Tudor or the desire of Henry VIII. Public office and ambition are corrupting things in Gregory's fiction. Better to be married and safe, as both Hannah and Mary Boleyn discover: 'I don't want to be Mary [Tudor] or

Elizabeth, I want to be me.'[11] The novels idealise a love – both maternal and romantic – that transcends the dirty world of the court and of history. Instead the protagonists choose to step outside of history. Gregory presents a conservative version of history in which women should not interrogate their place. Instead they should seek true love and maternal happiness within the confines of family.

A more experimental but less successful (in sales terms) consideration of the Boleyn story is Susannah Dunn's *The Queen of Subtleties*. Dunn's characters swear at each other, speak in slang that is recognisable to the contemporary reader, and refer to each other as 'Charlie', 'Tom' or 'Billy'.[12] The dissonance created through the relationship between this informal style and 'history' is important to the book's development and purpose. The historical gap between how people spoke then and how audiences think of them speaking now suggests intriguing things about the fetishisation of the past. Dunn's version of things in many ways might seem to enfranchise her reader – these historical figures are familiar and recognisable, they talk in a way that does not alienate. However, what is evident from the reaction to the novel is that what one reviewer called 'half-timbered authenticity' is expected and demanded by readers.[13] Reviewers on Amazon, for instance, claimed the language was 'totally distracting, and unnecessary', continuing 'the story, had it been told in a more straightforward manner without all the silly names and more traditional language, would have been more true to the time'.[14] Another claimed that the 'modern slang ... ruined any hope of getting a real sense of the era'.[15] In both these instances the authentic fallacy is foregrounded – readers are after 'traditional' versions of history, they like their queens caricatured and formal: the vernacular is 'stupid, out of place and never allows you to feel part of the time'.[16] Among these responses is a keen outrage that someone might treat history in such a frivolous fashion, and a sense of protecting the memory of Boleyn: 'Anne Boleyn's life ended with a sword. Now she is getting a hatchet job.'[17] These reviewers desire the otherness and distance of history, a traditional approach that presents historical stories as events out of contemporary compass. The reaction demonstrates the problematic tendency of the genre to obfuscate through an appeal to a subjective and constructed 'authenticity'. In contrast, *The Other Boleyn Girl* was lauded by the website Newsday for its intertwining of quality and authenticity:

> It's the annual struggle: You need a book ... that will entertain and enlighten ... You want a real page-turner, but you don't want to tarnish your reputation for literary taste. *The Other Boleyn Girl* is your kind of beach book, then – a bodice-ripper with a bibliography.[18]

Dunn is not bothered by the politicking of the court, by overly foregrounded historical detail. She prefers a direct telling of what is in some ways assumed to be a familiar story. Dunn's presentation of Anne is intentionally more complex than previous fictional treatments. She tells her story from two perspectives: Anne's supposed confessional narrative for the benefit of her daughter, Elizabeth, and a story involving Henry's confectioner Lucy Cornwallis and her relationship with Mark Smeaton, supposedly Anne's lover. In some ways this is an interesting fragmentation of narration, implying a variety of perspectives. However, it also creates a historical hierarchy of agency. Boleyn's narrative is direct, brisk, a no nonsense counterpoint to that of Cornwallis – and the difference in many ways is about knowledge (or at least understanding). Boleyn is telling a story in the past, a story that she was central to and aware of; Cornwallis tells her story as it happens to her, emphasising that she is simply living through and in many ways outside the history that is happening around her. The lower orders have history played onto them, whereas Anne Boleyn has historical agency as an actor in the key shifts of the time. In contrast to Gregory's account, and versions of her story in general, Anne is aggressive, clever, bright and engaging; she is a flawed heroine who goes self-consciously to her death (although the reading of her fall makes her a victim rather than Gregory's ambivalent moral tone). She is aware of her status as historical recorder, telling a tale for her daughter at times cautionary but never admitting compliance or error. She repeatedly ridicules her plain and conforming sister, in a kind of macro-criticism of the gender dynamics of Gregory's novel. This is Anne Boleyn as the first self-conscious and self-fashioning modern woman – which you might argue historically is the case – acted upon by a patriarchal system, in contrast to the Boleyn of Gregory's novel who is blatantly (one-dimensionally) ambitious but destroyed by that patriarchal system in many ways because of her defiance of it. Gregory's modern woman chooses her own husband and enjoys her family; Dunn's rages against the actions of a male history. The novel also looks forward to Elizabeth and the liberating possibility of matriarchy.

Jane Stevenson's novel *Astraea* (*The Winter Queen* in the USA) is a more formally complex entity altogether. Similar to Gregory and Dunn, Stevenson situates a narrative of possibilities within the unseen margins of history, suggesting a relationship between the exiled Queen Elizabeth of Bohemia and her secretary, an invented freed slave named Pelagius. From the opening of the book the novel wears its learning lightly, if subtly. Stevenson's academic credentials – she is a Reader in English at the University of Aberdeen – are added to the brief biography that is on the first page. Her status as a novelist is also alluded to (she has written other works, also listed here) and this marries with her academic legitimacy to present the author as authority. This has already been confirmed in the back cover's assertion that the novel is 'An utterly convincing picture of seventeenth-century life and political intrigue' and the supporting quotation from *Image Magazine* praising the 'fascinating' period detail that renders 'faithfully the energetic Europe of the 1640s'. This quotation continues 'Their love affair itself, however … achieves timelessness', pinpointing the combination of 'timeless' love and historical authenticity that is key to the popularity of the genre.

The cover of the novel, too, bears closer inspection when considering the way that the text presents history. The image is a fabrication, a conjunction of three different pictures – a male figure from Hieronymus Bosch's *The Adoration of the Magi*, a female from Michael Jansz. Van Miereveldt's *Portrait of Elizabeth, Queen of*

Bohemia, a red drape from Sir Joshua Reynolds' *Alexander Loughborough, Earl Rosslyn and Lord Chancellor*. It is a compilation, in itself ahistorical (the pictures are painted across a 170-year period). The cover blends elements of the factual – the Reynolds and the Van Miereveldt pictures are of an actual person – and the fictional – Bosch paints an imagined King – and knits them into an authoritative hybrid image. This historical collage emblematises Stevenson's blending of historical reality and fictionalised elements. Stevenson shares with Gregory and Dunn a fundamental 'what-if' fictional postulation, but she supports it with more subtle and complex historical information. Furthermore, the image plays into the text, as both the Van Miereveldt and the Bosch paintings figure in the narrative. So this complex image folds back into the 'authenticity' of the text, lending credence to the thesis of the novel.

Stevenson's complex and self-conscious stylistic approach represents a continuation of this relatively explicit construction. The text opens with a date – 10 February 1639 – and a formal, distanced third-person description of a Dutch interior scene depicting a conversation between a barely seen woman and a man who fades into the shadows. He is unseeable in the dark, her skin is contrasted with her mourning dress. The font is smaller than normal in a novel – the same size as that used for an epigraph. After a page of this the novel begins proper, in standard font, also with a date (27 June 1634). The first account is a preview of a scene that occurs much later in the text and is described much more intimately in point-of-view third person descriptions from the perspective of both Pelagius and Elizabeth; a scene furthermore which revolves around the fulcrum comment 'Tell me a story'. The novel is self-reflexive, undermining the exactitude of the dating with complexity of viewpoint. The 'actual' opening of the novel is a brisk description of the Amsterdam docks on a particular day in 1634, beginning 'A great day for Amsterdam, daughter of the sea'.[19] These descriptions are given evidential credence: 'This is a matter of public record: clearly, established, abundantly corroborated fact – recorded, for example, in the Amsterdam *Courante uyt Italien en Duytschland* for 27–28 June 1634.'[20] This account has a sly punchline: 'which, since it spoke only to the readers of its day, can have had no interest in deceiving us'.[21] There is an implication of historical veracity, a conception of trope, genre and historical afterlife, and furthermore a refutation of the unreliability of source material. Stevenson cites authoritative source to frame her novel and give it credence. Yet she is also able to playfully manipulate her position as author, historian and factioner. The following paragraph discusses the movements of Pelagius van Overmeer, his movements 'attested only by a personal chronicle which he wrote almost thirty years later'.[22]

The fictional characters are juxtaposed with the verifiable 'fact' of history and slowly emerge as 'real' people. This rather elegant opening to the novel is at once playfully postmodern in technique while simultaneously anchoring the book in seeming factuality, albeit underpinned by facts that are interpretable. It presents historical experience from a detached, objective standpoint even when working in the same conjectural vein as *The Other Boleyn Girl*. The novel inhabits the gap between fiction and history and knits the two together well. Indeed, the point and the attraction of the historical novel as a form are this dynamic between the 'authentic' or factual and the rediscovery of untraceable experience which is the keynote of fiction. The reader of the historical novel inhabits both a discourse of history and a discourse of fiction, and the interplay between the two is the crucial dynamic to the genre.

After the massive success of her first three Victorian novels, particularly *Tipping the Velvet*, Sarah Waters' fourth novel *The Night Watch* was set in the 1940s, specifically 1942–47. Waters herself is a theorist of the historical novel – particularly of lesbian historical fiction.[23] For Waters, the historical novel might offer a space within which to articulate an alternative lesbian history. Her books revoice marginalised characters:

> I think that to focus on what you might think of as the lost or marginalised voices of history inevitably gives your books a political resonance; your novels are effectively making the statement: 'These people are worth writing and reading about; these people are worth paying attention to'.[24]

The Night Watch is less interested in uncovering lesbian history and instead is interested in how people experienced the war. Waters eschews her normal first-person voice for multiple voices, gay and straight. The novel concerns two groups of characters linked by a chance incident. One, Viv, is treated and helped after an abortion goes wrong by another, Kay, who is working as an ambulance driver, and it is this brief meeting and the selflessness of Kay's gesture toward Viv that provides the central moment of the novel from which all other events flow. Direction, in the novel, however, is complex, as it is told backwards ('1947', '1944', '1942'). This is a technique that Waters experimented with in *Affinity* (2005) but here it is particularly pointed and purposeful. Doan and Waters suggested that it would be problematic for lesbian fiction to mimic heteronormative models of historiography and this reverse linearity is a way of dissenting and disrupting the hierarchies of normal historical knowledge. The structure pulls the reader continually backwards rather than forwards, and this tug away from the diegetic now complicates the experience of the book. The reader's search for meaning is subtly undermined – they are led to uncover the beginnings of things already seen ending horribly, continually reading with foreknowledge. As such the book mimics the experience of history – something always understood in hindsight. *The Night Watch* is interested in ruins, too, the destruction of what was once incredibly familiar – it pores over the recreated map of London, the effects of bombs on houses (both Kay in her position as ambulance driver and another character, Julia, who is helping her architect father survey half-ruined houses, allow Waters to explore the shock of the ruining of the familiar). Again this is a kind of historiography, as understanding the ruining of the evidence of the past is key to understanding the brevity of our engagement with it. The ruined houses stand for a regularity which has been lost.

These four brief examples demonstrate the range of possibilities in the historical novel, ranging from straightforward genre fiction through more dynamic models of historicity, from formal innovation through to fiction written to articulate marginalised identities. They illustrate a variety of associated and interrelated issues, from material innovation to marketing and the problems of reader expectation. The historical novel is *de facto* challenging and self-reflexive, and offers the reader a complexity of interrelationships and histories.

Graphic novels and hybrid genres

Historical graphic novels present us with a manifestation of the 'historical genre' somewhat outside of the orbit of mainstream interpretation; influential, but ignored by scholarship. The format has in general been perceived as under-ground, trashy and simplistic and therefore any discussion has been strictly limited. Yet the hybrid nature of the graphic novel allows its considerations of history to challenge and interrogate received opinions, and, in the case of Art Spiegelmann's *Maus*, introduce an entirely new way of dealing with an historical horror.

Fictional 'sequential art' – graphic novels or comics – have traditionally eschewed history, being more concerned with fantasy (Neil Gaiman's *Sandman*, 1989–96), parallel worlds (Warren Ellis' *Transmetropolitan*, 1997–2002), or the present (James Delano's *Hellblazer*, 1988-).[25] Alan Moore has been a key figure in the reinvention of graphic novels as a format, in particular with his complex work *Watchmen* (1987) which posited a world in which the post-war McCarthyite witch-hunts had been directed at both Communists and masked vigilantes. Moore articulated a new way of thinking about the limits of the comic book genre and a more sophisticated take on 'heroism'.[26] His subsequent work, *The League of Extraordinary Gentlemen* (1999–) takes a cast of characters from Victorian fiction (Allan Quartermain, Hawley Griffin, Mina Murray, Captain Nemo, Edward Hyde) and pitches them together in 1898.[27] The collection is a fictional what-if pastiche, complete with accompanying breathless boy's own adventure tales, which again meditates on heroism and the iconic. Moore inserts his char-acters into a recognisable Victorian London and treats the fictional as real. The second collection places the group in H.G. Wells' *War of the Worlds* and they repel Martian invaders. In making literary heroes comic book characters Moore questions cultural hegemonies. His pastiche of historical genres – rather than the historical as genre – is subtly new insofar as the signs and tropes he is using are themselves already fictional. Moore extended this blurring of 'fact' with various ways of dramatising the world in his work *From Hell* (1999), an account of the Jack the Ripper murders. This psychogeographic work is truly hybrid, with academic footnotes supporting the main story as told in sequential panel art. Moore sees in one set of events the birth of the modern nation: Sir William Withey Gull, the suggested murderer, tells his coach driver 'It is beginning, Netley. Only just beginning. For better or worse, the twentieth century. I have delivered it.'[28] The book is at once an account of Victorian society, a detective fiction, an academic debate, an explanation of the material ordering of London, and a piece of Whistler-esque pastiche. The blending of the visual and the authentically historical suggests a readership comfortable with different levels of information and meaning. *From Hell* acknowledges the impossibility of finding the Ripper and is careful to present its solution as one of many possible or probable outcomes.

Graphic novels, much like film, rely on historical visuality. Writers have used the format to reflect on genre and the visual representation of the past. Max Allan Collins' self-conscious *On the Road to Perdition* series (1998–2004) marries hard-boiled noir with standard comic and detective tropes in a story of redemption and sacrifice in Depression-era Chicago (it was filmed in 2002 by Sam Mendes). The series is as close as sequential art gets to historical genre fiction, although it is channelling popular cultural tropes of gangsters and crime thrillers as much as historical themes. *300* (1998) is influential comic writer Frank Miller's retelling of the Battle of Thermopylae, a bloody and heroically determined version which sees the manly Spartans defending the civilisation and freedom of Greece against the effete and pierced Persian empire. Miller suggests that the Spartan's attritional stand kept back the non-European horde. The book emphasises heroic virtue and homosocial bonding, and is full of bombastic rhetoric and over-bearing speeches. In 2006, *300* was filmed mainly in a 'graphic' style of digitally enhanced live action which directly replicated the look of the original. This technique animates the frames of the film, with live actors migrated through what is called character capture into becoming themselves CGI effects. The cast act against bluescreen with the background added digitally and in a way which mimicked the muted grey tones of the original images. It was also a shot-for-shot version of the panels of the comic book, signalling the importance of sequential style for the film's narrative and underlining its formal origins. A similar technique had been used to adapt Miller's neo-noir *Sin City* (2005). *300* was massively popular, breaking box-office and DVD sales records around the world and, with *Gladiator* (Ridley Scott, 2000) and *Alexander* (Oliver Stone, 2004), signals a return to the mainstream historical imagination of epic narratives of classical heroism. Similar live action animated techniques were used for the similarly high-grossing *Beowulf* (Robert Zemeckis, 2007), suggesting that the retelling of ancient stories is associated with the fantastical and mistily pseudo-real.

Non-fictional sequential art is generally interested in reportage, autobiography or contemporary politics (for instance, Harvey Pekar's ongoing autobiographical series *American Splendor*, Joe Sacco's 2001 *Palestine*, or Marjane Satrapi's 2003 memoir of Iran, *Persepolis*). There are notable exceptions. Ho Che Anderson's *King* is an account of Martin Luther King which is both a piece of illustrative art which attempts to wrest the format into the mainstream and an educative biography.[29] Similarly Tayo Fataluna's *Our Roots* is an activist educational project, illustrating the achievements and struggles of black people around the world.[30]

Jack Jackson used the freedom of writing underground comix (as alternate to comics) to explore issues clearly outside of authorised historiography – in particular those of the violence and trauma undergone by Native Americans – in his *Comanche Moon* (1979), *Los Tejanos* (1981).[31] The fact that his medium was guerrilla and not considered mainstream gave Jackson freedom in his early work to present horrific images – the non-traditional genre allowed an interrogation of official history. His later work – multiple books up until 2005, some published in partnership with the Texas State Historical Association or Texas A&M University Press – demonstrated an interest in graphic rendition of local history and experience, and a desire to present controversial revisionist biographies of key figures such as Sam Houston and John Wesley Hardin based on archival accounts and images. Jackson argued that his work allowed his 'general readership to feel the mood and the tempo of the time, and understand what it was like … what I'm trying to do is take people back in a time machine to that day and time and let them see events as they occurred *through these people's eyes*'.[32] This notion of the importance of the visual in historical empathy is key to other documentary-style practice but unusual in this context.

Other graphic artists have used the medium's complex generic potential to reflect upon 'familiar' historical events. In *Maus* Art Spiegelman recounted his father Vladek's experiences as a Polish Jew from the 1930s through the war and his eventual incarceration in Auschwitz.[33] This story is alternated with moments showing the contemporary lives of Spiegelman and his father in New York and Florida. The key choices that Spiegelman makes are, first, to tell the story in graphic novel format and second, to present each different race in the novel as an animal (Jews are mice, Germans cats, Swedes are deer, Americans are dogs).[34] This latter motif allows the novel to be innocent and childlike while articulating great horror. The caricatures associated with the animals are also undermined by the book which suggests that such classificatory approach prevents you from seeing common humanity. The use of his father's biography allows Spiegelman to explore a 'normal' Jew's experience rather than generalise (his father is endearingly and annoyingly human, and he himself finds it difficult to accept racial difference; the first book finishes with Spiegelman walking away from his father thinking the word 'murderer' after discovering that he burnt his mother's notebooks).[35]

The novel draws on such forbears as Keiji Nakazawa's 1970s *Barefoot Gen* (about Hiroshima) and Jay Cantor's 1987 *Krazy Kat* (about nuclear weapons) as well as more obvious comic-strip tropes such as Tom and Jerry. The narrative and thematic complexity of *Maus* demonstrated that the graphic novel form was capable of emotional and conceptual depth; in 1992 it was awarded a Pulitzer Prize special award, underlining the entry of the format into the Western mainstream.[36] *Maus*' use of history is ambiguous – while eager to articulate the horror of war the artist finds it problematic. It is witness testimony – so aware of its subjectivity – and rendered in a style which defamiliarises generic tropes not generally associated with this type of narrative. Yet it is also keenly authentic, using maps and images with exactitude (the maps of Birkenau, for instance, or of the march to Auschwitz).[37] The testimony demands respect. His father articulates this: 'YOU **HEARD** ABOUT THE GAS, BUT I'M TELLING NOT RUMORS, BUT ONLY WHAT REALLY I **SAW**. FOR I WAS AN **EYEWITNESS**.'[38] Similarly, it is the account of one man and does not attempt to illustrate the whole.

Maus has been theorised by Marianne Hirsch as an example of 'postmemory', that experienced by later generations who did not directly experience the

Holocaust.[39] *Maus* demonstrates 'the son's inability to imagine his own father's past other than by way of repeatedly circulated and already iconic cultural images'; however, Hirsch also allows that the multiplication of images in the novel – both imagined and drawing on hitherto underused sources – 'is a necessary corrective which counteracts the canonization of a small number of images'.[40] At once personal and culturally metonymic, the hybrid form of the graphic novel allows Spiegelman to inscribe a familiar story with new resonance. Critics have argued that, despite its seemingly non-mainstream and hybrid format, the seriousness of *Maus* allows Spiegelman to position 'the subject psychologically and morally in history' in contrast to postmodern irony.[41] Spiegelman finds a way around the problems of representation in his form and his style. In *Maus*, the author is aware of his distance from history but is forced to review and engage with something he had (as a child) never wanted to hear. The graphic novel is not pastiche, it is metafictional without ironising, and concerned with representation and guilt. *Maus* challenges the seeming (or received) triviality of format and suggests that visual or sequential art, or comics – or whatever term one might use – are able to treat the most complex and horrible of stories with compassion, verve and accuracy. In this unlikely place, then, history is not effaced but relived and presented anew in its uncomfortable horror. The reader is made to review their own relationship with the past, eschew their own diffidence and see anew what actually happened.

Historical stage drama

Is there a difference between a play about an historical event – Michael Frayn's *Copenhagen* (NT, 2000), or Peter Morgan's *Frost/Nixon* (Donmar Warehouse, 2006) – and the consciously archaic staging of a Shakespeare play at the Globe theatre in original costume, or the revival of a contentious play to make contemporary points (such as the Oxford Stage Company's 2003 production of John Arden's 1959 *Redcoat*, or even the National Theatre's 2003 *Henry V*)?[42] The Globe's old-style performance in a particular space re-embodies the presumed original production and adds the imprimaturs of originality and authenticity to the staging. In some ways this is drama as heritage experience, an extension of living history. Yet there is also cultural value attached to it above and beyond its tourist appeal. Revivals can draw parallels or demonstrate how social life has changed – as was seen in the restaging of the previously controversial *Romans in Britain* at the Crucible Theatre, Sheffield, in 2006.[43] The importance of a restaging is the sense that this is in some ways a reimagining and a re-enactment of an originary event, and that the 'new' version will somehow have something to say about the difference between then and now; a revival might often simply present an historic text as part of a time preserved in aspic, rather than attempting to make points about the relationship between past and present – the case with any staging of 1930s drama by Noel Coward or Terence Rattigan, for instance. How about a text that has become historic through longevity, such as Agatha Christie's *Mousetrap* (St. Martin's Theatre, 1952–)? Is Schönberg and

Boublil's *Les Misérables* (worldwide, 1980–) an historical musical or simply an adaptation (of Victor Hugo's original novel)? *Les Misérables* represents the past, is a costume drama of sorts, but is also a recognisably modern sung-through musical. It is not a period piece, as it is a modern version of Hugo's novel, yet as it has been being staged now for over 20 years it attains a cultural gravitas. What these rather unhelpful questions suggest is that – much like film and fiction – the manifestation of 'history' onstage is complicated, and an audience's engagement with the multifarious discourses of pastness is similarly sophisticated.

Stage drama has always had a complex relationship with the past. The representation and embodiment of the past within a narrative and performance structure which drama allows for permit interrogation and reconceptualisation of history. Contemporary British drama has spent much time coming to terms with history. Rather than using it as a means to comment on recent politics (as, for instance, in Arthur Miller's *The Crucible*, 1953, which used the setting of the Salem witch trials as a means to comment on McCarthyite America) or simply presenting narratives within an historical setting, plays by Michael Frayn or Tom Stoppard have conceptualised history in more abstract terms, seeing it as just another system of knowledge that might be undermined and picked apart. They demonstrate that in dramatising history the author can investigate, undermine and challenge structures of thought in effective ways; and, this interrogation can be an integral part of the form of the piece, and more subversive as a consequence in what it is saying. Drama's ability to be momentary, dismissive, brief, enigmatic and intangible means that plays relating to history can be more ephemeral and therefore more challenging than, for instance, film or even novel versions.

Mainstream 'highbrow' British drama throughout the 1990s was interested in challenging the idea of history as something solid and in contributing to an interrogation of history as something tangible. Richard Palmer has pointed out that the ways in which playwrights have addressed the past have moved from 'historical'-based drama to plays which dramatise history as a concept.[44] On the one hand, playwrights have looked in much more forensic detail at the grand narratives of history – as demonstrated by writers from Caryl Churchill's feminist *Top Girls* (Royal Court, 1982) to the more cerebral postmodernism and undecidability of Frayn and Stoppard.[45] Alan Bennett's *The History Boys* (NT, 2004) involves multiple discussions about historical technique, value and methodology. In comparison, for instance, modern Irish drama – of immense influence in the UK, with writers like Brian Friel, Frank McGuinness and Sebastian Barry (all of whom have explored Irishness in historical plays) being regularly staged – has used representation of the past in order to explore contemporary political and cultural identity.[46]

British dramatists have explored previously marginalised histories and their relationship to contemporary identities, as seen in Mark Ravenhill's *Mother Clap's Molly House* (NT, 2001). Ravenhill's play cuts between a transvestite bawdy house in 1726 and a sex party in a loft in 2002, exploring transgressions and boundaries. This use of split-chronology is common – Churchill's influential play has a dinner party attended by five women from different times in history, and uses them to reflect upon the rise of the career woman under Thatcher – and deployed in order to meditate on our perceived ideas of the past as well as the ways in which the present is progress (albeit ambiguously so):

> *Tom*: All them years stuck at home listening to me dad: Fucking poofs this, fucking queers that. And I thought: You're history, you. Cos I'm a poof, but I in't telling you. Oh no. One day I'm just gonna up and go. Stick a note on the fridge. 'Fuck the family.' Little husband with his little wife and their little kids. That's history. And I'm the future. This is the future. People doing what they want to do. People being who they want to be. So why … ? Why do you have to make it wrong?[47]

Tom wants sexuality as newness, sweeping away the old prejudices, although the play suggests that sexuality is pretty much a constant, it is simply the ways in which it is consumed, packaged and experienced that shift and change: 'Morality is history/Now profit reigns supreme'.[48]

There is much radicalism in contemporary British drama – the work of David Hare and Harold Pinter comments incisively on contemporary politics; writing by Sarah Kane and Mark Ravenhill introduced a new violence to theatre; and there have been numerous reactions to global events post-9/11 from *Talking to Terrorists* (Out of Joint, 2005) to *Black Watch* (National Theatre of Scotland, 2006).[49] The use of history in modern drama, though, is often interested in understanding through personality – as seen in David Hare's *Albert Speer* (NT, 2000) and the revival of George Bernard Shaw's *St Joan* in 2006 (NT) – or in philosophy. The challenge of the latter type of plays lies in their dramatised interrogation of systems of knowledge. Tom Stoppard's cerebral plays *Arcadia* (NT, 1993), *The Invention of Love* (NT, 1997), *The Coast of Utopia* trilogy (NT, 2002) and *Rock and Roll* (Royal Court, 2006) investigate history as an entity rather than as simple context or narrative content. Stoppard's use of props in *Arcadia* – which shifts between 1809–12 and 1989 – demonstrates the drama's ability to literally present histories overlapping. The action of the play is in the same room, just in different times, and therefore props which are used in one time period are left for another. This ease of transformation/interaction between past/present demonstrates performance's fluidity and elegantly illustrates the ability of drama to subvert chronology.

The play which has most focused debates relating to history, objectivity, and undecidability, is Michael Frayn's *Copenhagen* (NT, 1998).[50] The play dramatises the controversial meeting in 1941 between physicists Werner Heisenberg and Niels Bohr at Bohr's house in Copenhagen.[51] The play attracted a great deal of discussion due to the sensitive material and Frayn's characterisation of Heisenberg.[52] Steven Barfield argues that Frayn's own concern relating to the historical validity of his play in the various postscripts and post-postscripts that he has written demonstrates an anxiety about the subject of the drama.[53] In fact, Barfield continues, it is these postscripts themselves which provoked the controversy, due in part to Frayn seeing the play 'as some form of history that needs to be accurate' ('Dark matter'). Had Frayn simply presented his piece of theatre, the argument goes, then there would be no debate. The point at which he assumes that he is making some kind of 'historical' intervention, his work is open to interrogation and challenge. Certainly Frayn's worry about the veracity of his presentation – the postscripts run to 54 pages in the most recent edition of the play – suggests a central discomfort about ascribing motivation, making assertions about individuals, and possibly distorting the historical record. At the same time, however, Frayn's meta-textual discussion of the complexities of the case simply adds to the play's central ambiguities and concerns with the indeterminacy of history. Despite swathes of evidence – letters, interviews, taped conversations, memoirs, autobiography – the meaning of the meeting and the motivations of those who took part (particularly Heisenberg) are still debatable.

The play is about science and responsibility, morality, and – ultimately – the unknowability of history itself. The play itself presents multiple possibilities regarding the events of the meeting and the meaning of the meeting. The characters rake over their own desires and motivations, referring to events in their futures and later interpretations of their actions. This chronological self-consciousness and forensic attempt at *understanding* figure the historical drama as a space which foregrounds a certain type of debate. Heisenberg's notion of uncertainty – the idea that a phenomenon (in his example, an electron) can only be understood by the effects it has on other entities, and that in attempting to observe it we influence and change it – is an elegant motif within the play for history itself. Bohr characterises it:

> Then, here in Copenhagen in those three years in the mid-twenties we dis- cover that there is no precisely determinable objective universe. That the universe exists only as a series of approximations. Only within the limits determined by our relationship with it. Only through the understanding lodged inside the human head.[54]

The meeting in Copenhagen had manifold outcomes and influenced so much, but no one can agree on what happened (in the play, Bohr cannot even remember which month it was in), what the significance of it was, why it took place, and who was there. The facts of the meeting can be reconstructed, but, like Heisenberg's hurtling electron, motivation can only be assumed and posited – never actually seen or understood in itself.

Ultimately, the play sacrifices unknowability to drama, and suggests that Heisenberg 'bluffed himself', helped by Bohr – that the meeting was a non-meeting, insofar as Bohr ended it before he asked the question that he knew would send Heisenberg down the correct path to creating a nuclear bomb. Had he asked – and in the play he does – whether Heisenberg had made a simple calculation regarding the amount of uranium needed to create a weapon: 'sud- denly a very different and very terrible new world begins to take shape' as introducing the idea in such a way would force Heisenberg to make the calculation, and see that he had assumed wrongly that tonnes would be needed.[55] This dramatic aporia – after constant conversations circling around the various events and motivations of the meeting, the actual point of it is an absence of a question, something unsaid – makes a genius of Bohr and a flawed hero of Heisenberg. The uncertainty staged in this play is an elegant metaphor for the problematic of all historical performance and cultural production – the knowledge that at base, the experience of the past is somehow mediated and influenced through the actions of the observing present.

Part VI

Artefact and interpretation

New theories of the museum

The numbers are impressive. During 1999–2000, there were 12 million visits to English Heritage sites; the National Trust currently has 2.7 million members. The British Museum recorded 4.7 million visits in 2004–5; the Imperial War Museum over 2 million during the same period; and the Victoria and Albert 2.4 million. These are just the big hitters: in 2005, there were over 100 million visits to museums and heritage sites in the UK. After charges were scrapped in 2001, nearly 5 million extra visits were made to museums in the UK by 2006.[1] Engagement with the national past at the level of the site and the artefact is important to the consumption of history in Britain, whether by domestic or international visitor.[2] The terms and conditions of this engagement have changed subtly in the past 15 years, in response to financial burdens, methodological and theoretical shifts, and consumer expectation.[3] Funding cutbacks meant that institutions had to radically change their fundraising practice; new museological and postcolonial theories meant that the politics and mechanics of display were hotly debated; the increased definition of the visitor as customer changed the power relationship, emphasising the visitor experience over the educative impetus. Add to these new paradigms, government rhetoric over access and citizenship, the concerns of an increasingly globalised tourist market, and the possibilities as well as the problems of new technologies, and it might be argued that museums are the places in which the experience of history has changed the most.

During the late 1980s and throughout the 1990s, debate on the nature and role of museums was a fertile and dynamic area, both academically and at a practical level. The movement which became labelled 'New Museology' emphasised the ideological function of the museum and argued that such institutions were 'a battleground between competing ideologies, but largely controlled by the dominant elite'.[4] This critique of museum practice attempted to democratise the museum and to challenge the tropes of representation, collection and display. As Peter Vergo has argued, it was a move to re-examine museums as social and cultural entities, an attempt to define museology as 'a theoretical or humanistic discipline' considering the purpose rather than methods of the museum space.[5] The various debates associated with this new movement galvanised academic debate on the subject, and in particular addressed the following key questions: *What* did the museum stand for?, *Who* was it for?, *Why* did it do particular things?, *What* is the *value* of a museum?, Is the museum *necessary?* Such questions generated immense discussion of the notion of the past and our ways of accessing it.

In particular, the New Museology is interested in emphasising the political aspects of museums. In recognising and understanding the underlying ideologies of the museum, we can come to see how they attempt to construct and delineate the viewing subject. A museum is defined by the *Statutes* of the International Council of Museums (ICOM) as 'a non-profitmaking, permanent institution in the service of society and of its development, and open to the public, which acquires, conserves, communicates, and exhibits, for the purposes of study, education and enjoyment, material evidence of man and his environment'.[6] The New Museology is interested in that 'society and its development', considering the ideological impact of the museum on culture. Museums make us, rather than the other way around; they are part of a disciplining state which seeks to organise knowledge in order to control its populace. Academic theoretical analysis of museums, then, sought to deconstruct this organisation and to reveal its repressive function; in order, thence, to point towards a newly self-conscious museum practice. Furthermore these theoretical debates often concentrated on the relationship between the museum and the visitor. Museums were seen as institutions of government, interested in 'educating' the population in a humanist fashion in order to discipline and manage it. The interaction with the museum would profoundly change or direct the subject; it was a space of participation. Museums, then, are not places of passivity but an arena in which the (bourgeois) visitor is worked upon, educated, constructed. They are an arena for class education, for the reification of society, and for the classification of knowledge. This 'active' model of the museum space demonstrates that there is a lot more going on in the visiting experience than might first be assumed, and certainly suggests that the various discourses at work in a public heritage institution should be analysed. As Charles Saumarez Smith argues,

> Museums are assumed to operate outside the zone in which artefacts change in ownership and epistemological meaning [yet] … the assumption that, in a museum, artefacts are somehow static, safe, and out of the territory in which their meaning and use can be transformed, is demonstrably false.[7]

At the same time, and in response to such debates, museums moved to change their practice in any number of ways, shrugging off their image as stuffy repositories of arcane information and moving to answer particular political criticisms (in the UK, mainly relating to the presentation of Britain's colonial past, but also to the representation of women and of minority groups). Often these changes were in response to the newly aggressive 'heritage industry', but at the same time it was both an attempt to garner new visitors and to revise their practice.[8] 'Museums have become self-conscious (at last!) about their power to interpret and represent "reality" in all its rich variations' argues Eilean Hooper-Greenhill, and this new awareness has led to multiple new practices, from consultation to interactive exhibits to outreach projects.[9] Simultaneously the running of museums became increasingly professionalised.[10] The ICOM's code of Professional Ethics were adopted at a meeting in 1986, formalising principles for the profession including museum governance, acquisition, and disposal of collections. The specialised training of specialist museum curatorial professionals had been common practice from the late 1960s but it is not until the late 1980s and 1990s that an explosion in more general professional qualifications was seen. This chapter also marks the entry of government into historical representation, as it covers materials, places and artefacts that begin to be valuable both to the economy and to definitions of nationhood.

In the past 10–15 years, then, museums have changed their strategies and their practice. Peter Welsh argues that they have moved as institutions from being 'Repositories', 'Educational' and 'Celebratory' towards becoming 'Stewards', 'Learning Centers', and 'Collaborative'. His analysis demonstrates that museum practice has shifted in response to social change and theoretical debate – away from concepts of the Museum as a collection towards an image of the museum as something transitive, self-reflexive, and self-aware. This concluding part, then, concentrates on the ways in which the museum experience has changed over the past decade or so.

15 Museums and physical encounters with the past

Museums and government policy

On 26 October 2005, David Lammy, UK Minister for Culture, gave a keynote address to the Museums Association Conference which demonstrated the wider agenda that museums now have and are expected to address:

> Everyone here understands the capacity museums have to contribute to enjoyment, to inspiration, to learning, to research and scholarship, to understanding, to regeneration, to reflection, to communication and to building dialogue and tolerance between individuals, communities and nations.[1]

Museums and heritage projects have become increasingly important to a political agenda of lifelong learning, diversity, access and education. Lammy presented the space of the museum as a kind of transcendent humanist sanctuary from the cares of the modern world: 'In a fragmented, less deferential, more mobile, more diverse society where globalisation affects us all, the role of museums as places for reflection and understanding is more important than ever.'[2] Museums, for Lammy, are places of reflection where the population can come to a better understanding of themselves and the world. The post-9/11 agenda is also to the fore, as 'Extremism of any form is more likely to prosper in the absence of informed debate. When the quality of the public debate is enhanced ... we as a society all benefit.'[3] Museums, too, play a role in 'cultural diplomacy and promoting understanding on the international stage'. Importantly, in 2001 this particular UK government made public museums free to the public in recognition of their moral and educational value.[4]

Lammy's humanist rhetoric is digested in the DCMS Secretary of State Tessa Jowell's 'Foreword' to the January 2005 consultation document *Understanding the Future: Museums and 21st Century Life*:

> Museums and galleries tell the story of this nation, its people and the whole of humanity ... most importantly, it [this story] is interpreted through scholarship and research. Teaching, education and scholarship, available to all: the values of the Enlightenment kept alive for each generation.[5]

She continues: 'The fixed points of history and heritage have an even greater meaning as our world becomes smaller, and our values develop.'[6] Lammy's points about the educative and social value of the museum, and particularly his notion of museums giving a fixed point of reference in a shifting world, echo Jowell's embracing rhetoric here. Both politicians emphasise a citizenship grounded in an understanding of Britain's heritage. Citizens have a duty to understand our past better. They are stakeholders – shareholders or part-owners of this idealised mythos that is British heritage. Nationality is held in tension with history here, as an understanding of the past can educate the subject into citizenship. This notion that one can 'learn' national identity is enshrined in the citizenship examinations given to new immigrants, or the post-2002 National Curriculum provision of Citizenship Studies. The rhetoric suggests that citizens 'own' the past, have a right of access to it, and should become historically and politically literate. Of course this rhetoric of ownership is problematic, particularly within the context of the commodification of heritage. The presumed democratisation of historical knowledge that attends interactivity and access is part of a liberal discourse of inclusion. Those who live in a land are stakeholders in its history, owners, clients, customers; they have rights and the ability to demand.

Tracey McGeagh, senior policy advisor at the Museums, Libraries and Archives Council (MLA, which replaced the Museums and Galleries Commission in April 2000) set out the agenda for 2006–8 by claiming that 'All the work we will do is now clearly focussed on the benefits for museum visitors.'[7] The MLA presents itself as a knowledge network, a repository of information that can be accessed in order to better oneself ('Investing in Knowledge' is the title of their five-year plan). Echoing Jowell's enlightenment vocabulary, the MLA suggests that this plan 'highlights the importance of the wealth of knowledge contained in museums, libraries and archives in underpinning community cohesion, learning and skills, economic development and creativity'.[8] The museum is useful and important because it enfranchises the population. Rather than inform and discipline, this idealised vision of the museum is one of inclusivity and liberation: 'MLA believes passionately that access to knowledge is what empowers people to learn, to be inspired. It enables us to understand ourselves and the world around us and to develop better communities for the future.'[9] It is hard to argue at times with this rhetoric of inclusivity and community development, particularly in the light of the fact that a 2004 MORI poll for MLA showed that the non-visiting reason 'Nothing particular I want to see' dropped as a response by 22 per cent in the five-year period 1999–2004 (down to 19 per cent from 41 per cent).[10] Clearly, the public was returning to museums and galleries and this surge (37 per cent of those asked had visited in the last month) has something to do with the visitor-centric models of access and museum design. This is also in line with popular museological theory about display: 'the subject matter of museums should arguably be material culture and its significance in people's lives in its fullest diversity, not just those fragments which curators deem to be authentic'.[11]

In 1988, Tony Bennett argued that 'new museum initiatives' dedicated to the 'collection, preservation, and display of artefacts relating to the daily lives, customs, rituals and traditions of non-elite social strata' was as significant as the legislative reforms of the mid-nineteenth century which transformed museums into organs of the state, 'dedicated to the instruction and edification of the general public'.[12] Bennett cautiously welcomed these museum initiatives as being possibly '*of* the people' while counselling about the risks inherent in sentimentalising those 'people'.[13] Bennett's critique of the myths of museum enfranchisement seem increasingly apposite when considering the inclusive, humanist rhetoric deployed by Jowell and Lammy. Their aspirational vocabulary suggests that museums are key social entities, yet there is a refusal to admit that the representational strategies of the museum are not ideologically uninflected. Museums are part of the fight against terror; they are important in national self-definition; they are Enlightenment treasure houses; they are repositories of knowledge. Lammy almost seems to conceive of museums as anti-postmodern spaces, an escape from the hectic pace of modern life into the comfort of the rigid, unchanging past. The liberal language used by these two politicians suggests that Bennett's criticisms of museums as places which simply demonstrate 'the bourgeois myths of history' hold true still.[14] Yet, with Bennett, it is possible to cautiously welcome the new museum practices. The influence of consumer culture and market models may be problematic, but the enfranchising of the visitor possibly presents a further example of the effacement of institutional power. The MLA conceives of museums as repositories of information which can empower rather than enslave the population.

Another seminal critique of museum and heritage culture, by John Corner and Sylvia Harvey, demonstrates how the direction of government thinking has changed, even if some of the conclusions and purposes have not: 'an intensified rhetoricization of heritage is one response to the perceived threat of weakened group identity in the changing contexts of Europe and of global finance'.[15] For Corner and Harvey, the heritage debates of the late 1980s were about creating a tribal identity, a nationalism focused through the use of the past. As is clear, the aims of New Labour seem more inclusive and dynamic than this, they embrace the global economy and seek to delineate Britain's position in it using heritage. Innovation and education are the key words, rather than a fixed sense of the past and an inflexible idea of 'Englishness'. Yet these liberal concepts of access and inclusion feed back into Bennett's 'bourgeois myths', creating the museum as a perfect space for the transmission of a particular ideology: regeneration, education and tolerance are the key tenets, but behind this lie commercial partnership, national identity and economic diversity.

One of the key reasons that the museum has been reclaimed during the past ten years is because of tourism. 'Internationally, the imprint of history on our environment is a powerful aspect of our image as a nation. And the value of this rich legacy as a magnet for tourists is massive in economic terms', claimed Tessa Jowell and Stephen Byers in 2001.[16] History is lost in a flurry of economic terms: we must 'manage' heritage properly, ensuring that 'public interest in the historical environment is matched by firm leadership, effective partnerships and the development of a sound knowledge base from which to develop policies'.[17] It is paramount that the 'full potential of the historic environment as a learning resource is realised'.[18] The manipulation of historical sites and artefacts for economic development gives us yet another manifestation of the central motif of this book, the 'consumption' of history.

British inbound tourism is managed by three separate entities: VisitBritain, VisitScotland and the Wales Tourist Board. This demonstrates the devolution of British institutional life, and such fragmentation has been attacked for leaving the UK at a disadvantage in relation to global competitors. Each tourist board celebrates the diverse history of its subject, emphasising the resonance of history in the everyday of each country. This seems at odds with the rhetoric of modernisation. The Welsh Tourist board, for instance, states that 'the sense of past can still be felt all around Wales: from a windy hilltop with a half-ruined castle, to the quiet darkness of a mine miles underground'.[19] Similarly, VisitScotland traces a clear connection between past and present: 'Such a history has left its mark on the nation's psyche – as well as the landscape – and has contributed in no small way to the fierce pride with which the Scots view themselves and their country today.'[20] Both organisations, however, find in the particularisation of national history the materials for robust tribal independence, and therefore their presentations of the past feed into discourses of proud difference. In Wales, the language is celebrated, as are the 'forward-looking people with their own National Assembly'; the 'fierce pride' created by Scottish history is in no small part due to the country's 'occupying a pivotal position, not only in a British context but in a European and worldwide one also'. VisitScotland's website has a section of 'Uniquely Scottish' things from Whiskey to Gaelic, while the Wales Tourist Board emphasises its diversity: 'You name it and the chances are you can do it in Wales.' So within the umbrella of the Union (both Boards are microsites of VisitBritain, although there is no Board dedicated solely to England) might be discerned dissident voices, or at least a variety of narratives. Similarly these inbound tourist boards emphasise the dynamism and diversity of contemporary British life, describing the vivacity of key cities as well as pointing to more traditional pulls such as landscape or religious heritage. The presentation of the various parts of the UK, then, and their unique history, seems to emphasise diversity. The tourist boards use heritage as a marker but by no means as the only way to sell Britain; indeed, there is a marked mixing of heritage with newness, a key sense that the past is alive and vital rather than ossifying baggage.

Government, again, is concerned with the influence of the material past on the contemporary imagination: 'the fabric of the past constitutes a vast reservoir of knowledge and learning activities'.[21] The historical environment is something

> from which we can learn, something from which our economy benefits and something which can bring communities together in a shared sense of belonging. With sensitivity and imagination, it can be a stimulus to creative new architecture and a powerful contributor to people's quality of life.[22]

This inclusive rhetoric masks a strong sense of the economic possibility of historical artefacts. The notion of a kind of nationalism rooted in the past and looking to the future is similarly key. Modern Britain becomes an architectural collage, using the fabric of the past to build for the future. More than this,

> [the] historic environment is more than just a matter of material remains. It is central to how we see ourselves and to our identity as individuals, communities and as a nation. It is a physical memorial of what our country is, how it came to be, its successes and failures. It is a collective memory.[23]

This clear sense of the symbolic importance of the historical, particularly in national self-definition, is indicative of government desire for the past to bind together the present. The historical can interact with the contemporary in order to blend a country; the historical – environment, concept, artefact – is able to create a 'collective memory', or, in Benedict Anderson's concept, an Imagined Community.[24] This conception of the importance of history in the public imagination is key to government thinking on the subject, as is the good economic sense that investing in such tourist sites makes. The past interacts daily in the lives of those in the present; it provides a framework both materially and conceptually for the definition of self and nation. This dynamic of interaction, of the environment as a narrative collage, is teleological (despite the 'failures') and positivistic in the way it accounts for nationhood.

Digitisation and economics

The two major material changes in the way that museums operate and that heritage is consumed within them over the past 10 years have been technological and financial. The digitisation of archives and artefacts to create an online museum has profoundly changed the way that their collections are experienced; museum shops (mainly developed due to cuts in funding) have inserted these institutions into a marketing discourse of competition and branding. In many ways, of course, these two things have combined with the advent of specialist online shops becoming part of the museum web profile. Online income generation is recommended to museums as a way of funding digitisation (and one of the benefits of a sustained web presence).

The need to support the institution financially was originally due to funding cuts but the more successful museums took the opportunity to compete aggressively for market share and brand recognition and to make increasingly confident inroads into the commercial sector.[25] Museums found themselves in a competitive leisure market and had to define themselves accordingly through aggressive branding and marketing. This has fed a shift in the organisation of the museum collections themselves, as demand-driven models have empowered the customer and emphasised choice, value and experience. Museums have been forced to commercialise. The entire industry – and it is now considered such a service 'industry' – has been forced to adopt a market-sensitive approach to education and attendance, and the concept of 'visit quality' is now an imperative issue rather than a by-product.[26]

The relationship between museum site and the business world is incredibly important to income generation, be it corporate event, conference, hospitality, gift or sponsorship. Museums have become sites of commercial interaction and celebration, franchises hired by companies to add gravitas to their events. They have become venues for hire, lending a complex cultural imprimatur to corporate proceedings. Similarly commercial organisations can purchase cultural capital by sponsoring buildings or generally contributing to the museum's running costs; philanthropy which helps the museum financially yet leaches some of its independence away. Corporations can literally buy cultural cover; it is also often suggested that they can thereby influence the organisation and presentation of exhibits.[27]

Furthermore, as Fiona MacLean has argued, business models such as marketing have become immensely more important to the restructuring of museum culture. She cites, for instance, the increase in full-time marketing posts in museums – from five in 1988 to 40 in 1992.[28] The professionalisation of the museum institution has demanded a corporate identity and structure. This experience is consonant with that of other public professions and institutions (such as universities or hospitals) during the 1990s and early twenty-first century under the New Labour drive to market-led modernisation, but this is given a more economic spin in the case of the museum. Museums now have brand recognition, market research, user surveys, accountability, corporate identity design, auditing and management structures at ease with selling the institution in a leisure marketplace. All of these new paradigms are instituted to the end of the user; they are deployed to enhance and sell the experience of the museum to the visitor. Therefore consumption of the artefact or historic site is increasingly structured. Visitors are profiled, institutions seek brand recognition and loyalty, the visit itself becomes increasingly well wrought and determined.[29]

Nothing demonstrates what Harvey and Corner call the 'commodified heritage culture' more than the massive growth of non-collection specific activities: picture libraries, publishing projects, and, most importantly of all, the gift shop.[30] Heritage has become something that can be owned. The past becomes something that literally – in the case of chocolates, cakes and biscuits – is consumed. Commercial wings generate income for museums using the name, brand, collection and exhibit programme. Generally the commercial arm of museums runs the shop as well as any picture library, publishing activity, and event management. There are also increasingly important 'friend' organisations which have a symbiotic relationship with the museum, providing financial support in return for increased access and discounts. Becoming a 'friend' or a 'member' of the museum creates a sense of community and identification. The protective rhetoric of these organisations can be traced back to the cuts in funding in the mid-1980s (although some 'Friends', such as those of the British Museum, are much older organisations). Becoming a 'friend' involves the process of protecting heritage for future generations, galvanising the museum visitor to become in some ways part of the museum process.[31] All these aspects of the commercial museum demonstrate the incredibly complex ways that one might engage with the collections at a level other than simply visiting and experiencing physically.

In terms of raw numbers, the commercial wings of museums have been growing massively over the past decade. For instance, the turnover for V&A Enterprises for 2004–5 was £8,450,420; in 1996, it was £3,723,754.[32] The company employs 123 people as opposed to 69 in 1996. Most profit for such companies is clawed back or paid in tax, but the sheer size of the operations demonstrates the scale that is now being worked upon, and how this has changed in a decade. Museum shops sell a huge range of products: DVDs, books, educational resources, toys, posters, prints, postcards, games, replicas and gifts 'inspired' by the collections and any number of other branded goods. The artefact of heritage becomes a brand. The original ICOM code of ethics clearly states:

> Museum shops and any other commercial activities of the museum … should be relevant to the collections and must not compromise the quality of those collections. In the case of the manufacture and sale of replicas, reproductions or other commercial items adapted from an object in a museum's collection, all aspects of the commercial venture must be carried out in a manner that will not discredit either the integrity of the museum or the intrinsic value of the original object.[33]

This tenet is being interrogated by museums in the drive toward greater competition and market share. The 'intrinsic value of the original object' is possibly sacrificed in order to brand and market the museum. Museum shops themselves have become flagship ventures, as, for instance, is the case with Tate Modern's new shop – designed by the same architects (Herzog & de Meuron) who oversaw the conversion of the gallery itself. The mechanics of this also has an influence on the galleries themselves, as Carol Duncan argues, 'These institutions look more like a part *of* the business world than a realm apart from it.'[34] Of course this is in many ways a simple updating of patronage networks and bemoaning it engages in a positivistic liberal discourse of state-led humanist heritage education. Yet it also signifies a shift in mass engagement with heritage and national culture, a move towards the commodification of history which makes the visitor a client.

The commercial impact and cultural implications of this shift toward competitive, market-driven institutions are manifold. Buying, joining and browsing have become intertwined with the museum experience.[35] It seems clear that the experience of a museum is not simply that of interaction with the artefact or site, if it ever was. There is an economic memorialisation to be enacted in the purchase of memorabilia. In some ways this breaks down the barrier between static museum and viewer, allowing an experience-based interaction with heritage in the same way that living history might. In this myth of heritage ownership, the customer is seemingly enfranchised, becoming part of the process of history rather than simply watching it happen.

The shop presents heritage as something to be replicated, made iconic and consumed. Visitors can 'own' history, purchase that of another country, or have it wrapped as a gift for their family. Obviously the artefacts purchased are not actually historical, but in purchasing them the consumer enacts a fantasy of ownership. Many museum shops sell products that are not based on their own collections, further muddying the cultural and 'authentic' waters. The rhetoric of the museum is that of individuality and uniqueness, but the reality of the commercialisation of the museum space is the increasing homogenisation of the heritage/historical experience. In making museums free, the New Labour government forced museums to efface their own uniqueness by expanding their commercial interests (although paying for a museum introduces a whole new paradigm into the relationship between heritage and those experiencing it).

Is the shop a space in its own right or an extension of the museum? As well as the shops within the institution, it is increasingly common for organisations to have outreach or satellite shops. The British Museum, for instance, sells replicas, postcards, books, jewellery and textiles based on the collections in the museum shop as well as a site at 22, Bloomsbury Street and a store in Heathrow Airport.[36] Most museum shops also have a mail order catalogue, and online retail is increasingly key. There are various websites which sell items from a variety of museums, as well as sites which sell reproduction ancient artefacts as if they themselves were a museum.[37] Outreach shops further blur the relationship between the original site or artefact and the replica. There is a conflicting dynamic between the iconicity of the object and the multiple versions of it which circulate as items for sale. Using the museum shop – online, in shopping malls or by mail order – without visiting the museum seems to further virtualise the experience: customers are buying the brand, not the particular experience.

Quite apart from this blurring of the value of the artefact and heritage experience, museums have become involved in what Shapiro and Varian call the 'economics of attention'.[38] They are often in direct competition with each other. Museums have become brand conscious, market-driven, concerned with reach and audience. Their function as repositories of heritage artefact, entertainment and learning is increasingly complex. Furthermore, the role of the museum as part of the public space has changed. As van Aalst and Boogaarts argue,

> The physical concentration of museums was and is generally tied to the redevelopment of public space and is usually combined with other facilities. In this sense, the intertwining of diverse functions – such as cafes and restaurants, events, museum stores – within a single space is an explicit goal.[39]

Museums have become part of wider branding issues – for instance, those relating to local, city-level (European capitals of culture, for instance), regional or national tourism.

The commercial wings of museums can have beneficial qualities. The museum café in the new American Indian Museum (called Mitsitam, or 'let's eat') serves authentic Native American food themed around the five geographic areas covered by the museum's exhibition. This introduces an element of education while blending economic demands with those of authenticity and experience. The importing of market models to museum structures has undoubtedly revived the sector, injecting funds as well as putting useful emphasis on issues such as marketing or audience experience. This has effected a transformation of the museum experience in the past decade. Furthermore, the democratisation of the artefact – the mass marketing of heritage and culture – might be read as a move towards inclusion. 'Ownership' of the commodity of history enfranchises the citizen, suggesting that history is community. Yet the mechanisation and com-modification of the artefact also devalue it, making it just one of any number of cultural signs rather than something particular within national or historical cul-ture. This notion of ownership is consonant with political models of access and ownership. The remainder of this section will consider how these ideas work in contemporary museum settings by looking in particular at the digitisation of museum collections.

The concept of 'access' has become key to museum rhetoric over the past decade, growing early from methodological and theoretical drives to encourage visitor engagement in the late 1980s into the government policy on citizenship and engagement articulated by Lammy and Jowell. Museum engagement with consumer and audit culture means that access is crucial. The visitor – or 'user' – is now at the centre of the museum, rather than education or conservation. Changes in the notion of access have a direct influence on the arrangement of collections, the presentation of materials, and the politics of display. As Kevin Hetherington has argued, 'Access within the arts and heritage industries has been associated most of all with consumerism.'[40] The social space of the museum has changed hugely over the past decade or so, as the example of the museum shop demonstrates. These changes have fundamentally shifted the purpose and meaning of the museum. The need for disabled access, for instance, changes the way that artefacts are considered and displayed.[41] The physical conceptualisation of the museum changes. Access is also now bound up with citizenship, national identity, and economic issues; widening participation in the heritage and cultural fabric of the country has become what museums do as much as their conservation programmes. This similarly shifts the conceptualisation of the artefact and its meaning, its relationship to its context, and its purposeful situation within the museum space.

What, then, does the idea of 'access' mean for both the experience of museums and the representational strategies deployed in presenting the past? In general, 'Access'-based initiatives in museums seemingly enfranchise the visitor, enshrining a movement away from elite cultural institutions concerned with scholarship and particularised storytelling. The emphasis shifts towards the experience of the everyday and the refracting of grand narratives into fragments. This would seem to chime with the general democratisation of historical engagement that this book has traced throughout various genres and media.

In 2005, museums in the North East began to put exhibits in shopping centres in order to expand their appeal. Curators would take over a space and put exhibits in from scratch, staying for a month or so at a time before moving the entire project elsewhere. The mobile museum, entitled the 'Curiosity Shop', was set up in empty units in Redcar, Stockton, Darlington, Hartlepool and Middlesbrough; more than 100,000 shoppers saw the various objects on display.[42] Mark

Simmons, Audience Development Manager for Hartlepool Museums, claimed that 'The Curiosity Shop is like a bizarre blend of Changing Rooms and Antiques Roadshow', demonstrating the combination of makeover and curiosity television formats driving the initiative.[43] The project claimed lineage with early cabinets of curiosity, updating this inquisitive model for a twenty-first-century audience. Turning shops into museums inverts the trend discussed above, and the 'curiosity' element of this project emphasises the uniqueness of the artefact. Heritage on this model is part of the fabric of consumption – the mall – but at the same time unusual and strange.

This kind of outreach project tackles key issues of access and availability with verve; it is an attempt at invigorating local heritage cultures as well as challenging the idea of museum experience as being something ordered and set. It is part of the government-funded Renaissance project, aimed at reviving regional museums. The project reflects government rhetoric of access and citizenship. Yet these dynamic projects also demonstrate a need to deal with a much more complex visitor experience and expectation. Innovation is necessary to keep audience share, and to develop ways of educating. What projects like the Curiosity Shop show us is that contemporary society demands new ways of thinking about old things; that mimicking the consumption process in order to engage people with history is a necessary part of the way the past is presented.

The drive to uniqueness in such projects contrasts strongly with the effacement of the individual in the selling of historical objects as commodity. This tension between the singularity of the museum experience (emphasised through branding and artefact) and the homogeneity of historical engagement is key to understanding what is going on in museums at the moment. On the one hand there is a drive to individuation, on the other a need to engage with the market and not be just another service provider clamouring for audience share. The uniqueness of the collection is what makes the particular museum stand out, but the levels of engagement with this unique collection are multiple and in the main tend to efface difference in order to gain visitor identification.

In 2006, for instance, the BBC's daytime show *The People's Museum* encouraged the public to vote for hidden 'treasures' in little known collections around the nation. This model of consultative, interactive, local/national self-definition certainly suggests an empowerment and shifts the power dynamics normally associated with the formation of a museum collection. It is the reclaiming of hitherto unseen treasures, emphasising a sense both of the potentiality of the past which is just there to be tapped and suggesting a sense of the density of historical white noise in the country – living day-to-day with history leads a population to ignore it, and there is such a depth of material, so many artefacts around that individuals can nearly afford not to take any notice of them. This is the kind of sense of historicity that Patrick Wright remarks upon in his book *On Living in an Old Country*, a phenomenon he theorises as 'everyday historical consciousness'.[44] Even within this initial innovative framework there were strange lacunae and improbable fractals. The show was shown in the early afternoon, on BBC2, meaning that it belongs to a whole genre of daytime 'amateur' history shows which combine brightness with generic dynamism and an irreverence. The audience for such shows is very different to mainstream, prime time documentary. The presenter of the show, Paul Martin, also presents the daytime antiques show *Flog It!*; the production company Reef Television specialises in lifestyle and factual pro- gramming. The opening credits are a point of view shot moving through a city towards a recognisably Victorian domed institutional building whose doors swing open to allow entry. Thus the show establishes itself as being still in thrall to the notion of a solid, physical museum as a place of display.

A further issue bound up with access is that of interactivity. Theories of interactivity often draw on the 'participatory' social model of museums which emphasises their status as repositories of information that manages the subject.[45] Yet they also discern a liberal strand in the history of interactivity, a drive towards empowerment. The first truly interactive museum was Frank Oppenheimer's 1969 Exploratorium in San Francisco, an institution which attempted *'democratic empowerment'*.[46] Such interactive models attempt an education of the visitor allied to a different understanding of the experience of the museum. This goes beyond the simple model of information communication towards a more pro- found conception of the visitor as an active participant in the museum. Interactivity implies an involvement and an enfranchisement for the visitor. It chimes with museological theory and government rhetoric on access to suggest a multiplicity of experience, an emphasis on the individual's engagement with history rather than an imposed narrative, and a certain ownership of the histor- ical experience. Rather than be shown the artefact and told its meaning, inter- active exhibits and museums involve the audience in the narratives of history. Museums have embraced new technology with a rash of innovations directed at empowering the visitor and enhancing their interactive, educative experience. Increasingly the museum experience is technologically-driven, a virtual experi- ence of one kind or another utilising hand-held mobile units, touch-screens, phones and laptops.

The idea of inclusion as a way of creating a community of museum goers is clearly connected to the increase in museum-based technology.[47] This can be seen in the 24hourmuseum project, an umbrella interface introducing all the museums in the UK in one site. Virtual resources allow offsite learning and distance engagement. Yet just who are they catering for? If the museum is in some ways an institutional machine of nation-building, the imagined community of the country is now created in a virtual space. The virtual museum is at once allied to a country while simultaneously made neutral. The citizenship and sta- keholder rhetoric of the UK government enables its subjects to engage with the past, but the digitisation practice of museums is opening up new, global markets instead.

Digitisation of archives and online museum presence can greatly expand the reach and audience of the museum. For instance, in 2004–5 some 4 million people visited the Tate online.[48] Over the same period around 6 million visited the Tate suite of museums physically. The demographic of the audience is entirely changed, and their purposes for visiting differ. As Ross Parry and Nadia

Arbach have argued, this brings with it an entirely new set of issues. Importantly, the visitor is not within the museum space, and their location (and therefore how they engage with the artefact) are entirely unique to their visit. Rather than the museum as a *place* being of importance, the way that the collection is presented is key.[49] Virtual architecture impacts upon the visitor experience and this has benefits ranging from easier language conversion to faster access for the disabled. This approach obviously also favours museums with international brand recognition and canonical collections. However, the development of virtual museum interfaces is constantly evolving. Key to their development is the idea of the dynamic, context and purpose of the 'visit':

> On-line experiences, after all, do not take place in some removed metaphysical *virtual* world. Rather, they are embedded in the actuality and physicality of the user's immediate sense of place, in the same way as the telephone (land line or mobile), newspapers, the radio or TV.[50]

In a very real sense the museum has to actively compete with other attractions for the attention of the visitor, and must bend to their will in terms of access, route, duration of visit. They are no longer able to physically impart meaning to an object, in the same way that the object is no longer experienced physically in any sense at all. The 'museum' as physical repository is replaced by the cyber-museum, a more negotiable space in all senses of the word. The engagement with the particular artefact is no longer the most important element of the 'visit'.

Since the late eighteenth century, museums have allowed visitors to experience the world and the past as foreign but tameable entities manifested in the comfort of their own city. The recent virtual revolution is the biggest conceptual change to the museum since, allowing such a visit to occur at any point in the world, whenever, wherever. It destroys the Eurocentricity of the museum structure and the authority of the institution, giving power and ownership back to some extent to the citizens of the world. Museums have embraced much faster than many other historical media the virtual turn, understanding history as increasingly a technologically mediated experience.[51] Of course, museum collections have always been mediated for public consumption, and this is in many ways simply a shift in direction. There are also curatorial issues related to digitisation of archives and collections. The creation of electronic resources is important and useful, but there are obsolescence issues as well as issues relating to the actual experience of the archive. As has been demonstrated throughout this book in relation to amateur, TV, film and computer history, the impact of virtuality on the experience of the past is unprecedented. History is always a mediated experience, but the movement away from text toward virtual or material or physical history presents us with a new and developing historiography. The physical consumption of the historical – economic or otherwise – has been revolutionised.

Conclusions

Nostalgia isn't what it used to be

This book has argued several key points which accrue around the following terms: experience; scepticism; enfranchisement; access; embodiment; variety; virtuality. These words are metonymic for the historical in contemporary society, whilst they also demonstrate how the past is various, multifaceted, and possible contradictory. The manifestation of history in popular culture is multiple, various, and worthy (even demanding) of further study. Generalised critiques of such 'heritage' or popular uses of the past are either not attendant to the subtleties of the historical genres, or seek to banish them wholesale. Yet this book has demonstrated the importance, imaginative complexity and historiographic scope of popular culture's interface with history. The various modes of historical understanding outlined in this book present a set of knowledges that are engaged with. Used, as it has been throughout the argument, it is worth reflecting at the conclusion on that verb 'engage'. The individuals or subjects who come to history through the mediums outlined in this book are participatory, involved, active, part of, employed, and connected.

The historian as a figure has become increasingly high profile – in culture and fiction – and their authority has often been questioned. They are an active part of the meaning of historical engagement, both at the level of presenter or guide to information, and as signifier of gravitas and particular sets of cultural tropes relating to investigation of the past. Certainly the academic historian has tended to be critiqued in popular culture, and regularly audiences and users have circumvented the expert and the direction of the professional in seeking their own personalised historical experience. The academy no longer has a monopoly on historical knowledge, and the leeching of authority suggests that an entirely new way of thinking about history and formulating approaches to it – as Samuel's 'social form of knowledge' – might be necessary.[1] Hayden White has argued that:

> postmodernist experimentation in the representation of historical reality may very well get us beyond the distinction – always kind of scandalous – between the professional historian, on the one hand, and the amateur, dilettante or 'practical' student of history, on the other. No one owns the past, and no one has a monopoly on how to study it, or, for that matter,

how to study the relation between past and present. As [Elizabeth Deeds] Ermarth says, we are all historians today.[2]

Most every type of pastness in this book demonstrates a way of experimenting – whether consciously or not – with 'the representation of historical reality' and thence an undermining of authoritative, legitimised History in favour of multiple histories. This book has illustrated the dynamic between the opening up of 'access' – either through the material enfranchisement of the user or in the ways that traditional forms (from museum exhibits through to documentary style) have been articulated – and the perpetuation of particular types of authority figure. It is clear that history has become one of a set of heritage experiences and referentials. This packaging and commodifying of the past have been critiqued as the 'nostalgia mode', where nostalgia without purpose becomes an empty trope within an overly mediated society.[3] Yet simultaneously the importance of the past – the importance of authenticity, empathy, reality, historical truth – has never been higher.

The competing ways in which 'history' might work in one or more texts or mediums – and thence in tandem with multiple other experiences and discourses of pastness – demonstrate the contradictory multifariousness of contemporary experience. This book is large, but has not considered in depth many historical issues and formats such as vintage fashion, historical painting, what if? novels, 'found' magazines and items, outbound tourism and historical holidays. The fact that history pervades contemporary culture demonstrates the keen importance for the scholar in understanding the ways that it is manifested and in which it is conceptualised. The historical imagination is made up of multiple vying types of pastness – and these all somehow sit together. Users of history engage with it in so many different ways – reading, listening, eating, experiencing, watching, playing, smelling (in the instance of the Jorvik museum) – that its prevalence communicates crucial issues not simply relating to historiography but to the make-up and meanings of popular culture in general.[4] The contemporary historical imaginary is fed by a multiplexity of consumption practices, often diverging and converging simultaneously – at once closing down experiences while opening up new possibilities and potentialities. The past is fantasy, lifestyle choice, part of the cultural economy, something which confers cultural capital, something to win or to desire, a means of embodying difference and a way of reflecting on contemporary life. It is engaged with on a personal, group and family level; it can be experienced in a range of ways at the same time. The historical 'genres' demonstrate the complexity of approaches to history. The past can be narrative, nostalgia, something to be worn, experienced or eaten; it can be a game, a deadly serious combat, or diversion. The ways in which contemporary culture engages with the past are hybrid and complex, and in this teeming diversity lies the challenge and the concern for historians.

Mike Pickering and Emma Keightley argue that nostalgia in culture 'can only be properly conceptualized as a contradictory phenomenon … it is not a singular or fixed condition'.[5] This complexity and innate undecidability allow nostalgia to be a liminal term or sensibility. They see the concept of nostalgia as something which might ultimately allow a critique of culture due to its slipperiness/ prevalence, in its ability to open up multiple spaces for reflection and dissidence. Similarly, in the historical's ability to contain complication, difference, ideology, interrogation, artifice, virtuality, escape and experience, that is, in its sheer multiplying variance in popular culture, might be seen its true value as a discourse. Often it seems that historians wish to mark history out, to control and boundarise it; but it is in the transformations and transgressions of the historical that culture's desires, innermost workings, and underlying assumptions might be seen.

Notes

Introduction

1 K. Jenkins, *Refiguring History*, London: Routledge, 2003, p. 38.
2 Ibid., pp. 39, 38.
3 Ibid., p. 35.
4 On this point, see H. White, 'Afterword: manifesto time', in K. Jenkins, S. Morgan and A. Munslow (eds) *Manifestos for History*, London: Routledge, 2007, pp. 220–32.
5 *History in Practice*, London: Arnold, 2000, p. 153.
6 Ibid., p. 153.
7 I owe this term to Alun Munslow.
8 *Theatres of Memory*, London: Verso, 1994, p. 13.
9 Ibid., p. 8.
10 'History happens', in V. Sobchack (ed.) *The Persistence of History*, London: Routledge, 1996, pp. 1–16 (p. 7).
11 For good discussions of public history, see H. Kean, P. Martin and S.J. Morgan (eds) *Seeing History: Public History in Britain Now*, London: Francis Boutle, 2000, and Jordanova, *History in Practice*, pp. 126–49.
12 S. McCracken, *Pulp*, Manchester: Manchester University Press, 1998, pp. 21–34.
13 See P. Joyce, 'The gift of the past: towards a critical history', in Jenkins *et al.*, *Manifestos for History*, pp. 88–97; and the various anti-heritage points raised in D. Lowenthal, *The Past is a Foreign Country*, Cambridge: Cambridge University Press, 1985; D. Brett, *The Construction of Heritage*, Cork: Cork University Press, 1996; P. Wright, *On Living in an Old Country*, London: Verso, 1985; P.J. Fowler, *The Past in Contemporary Society*, London: Routledge, 1992; and R. Hewison, *The Heritage Industry: Britain in a Climate of Decline*, London: Methuen, 1987.
14 'Fabricating heritage', *History & Memory* 10(1) (1995), available at www.iupjournals. org/history/ham10-1.html (accessed 18 February 2008).
15 'The past of the future', in Jenkins *et al.*, *Manifestos for History*, pp. 205–19 (p. 211), see also his *The Heritage Crusade and the Spoils of History*, Cambridge: Cambridge University Press, 1998, and 'The heritage crusade and its contradictions', in M. Page and R. Mason (eds) *Giving Preservation a History*, London: Routledge, 2004, pp. 19–45.
16 'The gift of the past', p. 97.
17 Ibid.
18 Ibid., p. 96.
19 John Fiske articulates this sense of the potentiality of the cultural product:

> If a particular commodity is to be made part of popular culture, it must offer opportunities for resisting or evasive uses or readings, and these opportunities must be accepted. The production of these is beyond the control of the producers of

the financial commodity: it lies instead in the popular creativity of the users of that commodity in the cultural economy.

('The commodities of culture', in M. J. Lee (ed.) *The Consumer Society Reader*, Oxford: Blackwell, 2000, p. 288)

20 *History in Practice*, p. 149. This is echoed by William D. Rubinstein in his discussion of the varieties of 'amateur' history: 'It would do the academic historian no harm at all to become better acquainted with this vast world, of which, too often, she or he knows so little', 'History and "amateur" history', in P. Lambert and P. Schofield (eds) *Making History*, London: Routledge, 2004, pp. 269–80 (p. 280). See the more historiographic discussion of the uses of popular culture to the historian in G. Williams, 'Popular culture and the historians', in the same volume, pp. 257–69. Robert A. Rosenstone argues that historians need to eschew the 'single way of conveying their [the remains of the past] meaning to our culture … This is a call for opening our eyes and our imaginations to other ways of telling, showing, representing, making meaning out of the stories of humanity's past', in 'Space for the bird to fly', in Jenkins *et al.*, *Manifestos for History*, pp. 11–18 (p. 18).

21 'Backward looks: mediating the past', *Media, Culture & Society* 28(3) (2006), 466–72 (p. 466).

22 Ibid., p. 470.

23 Ibid., p. 470.

24 *The Presence of the Past*, New York: Columbia University Press, 1998.

25 'Introduction', in *The Presence of the Past*, available at www.chnm.gmu.edu/survey/intro.html (accessed 6 December 2007). The survey they circulated to 1,453 people nationwide is available at: www.chnm.gmu.edu/survey/question.html.

26 'Two World Wars and One World Cup' and 'Ten German Bombers' are standard songs at England football games, and a Dutch company controversially sold replica German WWII helmets to Dutch and English fans during the 2006 World Cup in Germany. Football crowds are an interesting example of a community with a clear sense generally orally perpetuated of local and specific history that is constantly accessible, important to their contemporary definition and identity, and resolutely integrated into their supporting practice. Newspaper coverage of 2006 was less jingoistic, see Luke Harding, 'The tabloid war is over: Germany and the World Cup 2006', Anglo-German Foundation for the Study of Industrial Society special report, www.agf.org.uk/pubs/pdfs/1519web.pdf (accessed 26 November 2007).

27 There is even a celebratory clothing label, *BlitzSpirit*, www.blitzspirit.co.uk/aboutus.php.

28 See R. Holmes (ed.) *The World at War*, London: Ebury Press, 2007, pp. 95–115 and 131–49.

29 See J. Huizinga, *Homo Ludens: A Study of the Play-Element in Culture*, Boston: Beacon Press, 1955, and C. Rojek, *Decentring Leisure*, London: Sage, 1995, pp. 184–6.

30 See the educational philosopher J.E. McPeck's 'Critical thinking and the "Trivial Pursuit" theory of knowledge', in K.S. Walters (ed.) *Rethinking Reason*, New York: SUNY Press, 1994, pp. 101–18.

31 J. Mittell, *Genre and Television*, London: Routledge, 2004, p. 32.

32 J. Culpeper, 'Impoliteness and entertainment in the television quiz show: *The Weakest Link*', *Journal of Politeness Research*, 1 (2005), 35–72.

33 B. Guffey, *Retro: The Culture of Revival*, London: Reaktion, 2006, p. 17.

34 R. Goldman, *Reading Ads Socially*, London: Routledge, 1992; R. Grafton Small and S. Linstead, 'Advertisements as artefacts: everyday understanding and the creative consumer', *International Journal of Advertising*, 8(3) (1989), 205–18.

35 S. O'Donohoe, 'Raiding the postmodern pantry: advertising intertextuality and the young adult audience', *European Journal of Marketing*, 31(3/4) (1997), 234–53 (p. 245).

36 C. Byrne, 'Ridley Scott's Hovis advert is voted all-time favourite', *The Independent*, 2 May 2006, www.news.independent.co.uk/media/article361342.ece (accessed 16 August 2007).

37   *Theatres of Memory*, p. 93. See also M. Pickering and E. Keightley, 'The modalities of nostalgia', *Current Sociology*, 54(6) (2006), 919–41 (p. 935).

38   www.youtube.com/watch?v=CFLBvLxLJMI (accessed 16 August 2007).

39   See S. Brown, 'Retro-marketing: yesterday's tomorrows, today!', *Marketing Intelligence and Planning*, 17(7) (1999), 363–76.

40   *American Graffiti*, 1973, George Lucas; *Grease!*, 1978, Randal Kleiser; *Happy Days* TV series, 1974–84.

41   *Theatres of Memory*, p. 95.

42   See G. Withalm, 'Commercial intertextuality', in S. Petrilli and P. Calefato (eds) *Logica, dialogica, ideologica*, Milan: Mimesis, 2003, pp. 425–35 and 'Recycling Dorothy, dinosaurs, and dead actors: digi-textuality in the TV-commercials of the 1990s', *Semiotische Berichte* 27(1–4) (2003), 297–315.

43   The Heineken advert took its technique from the 1982 film *Dead Men Don't Wear Plaid* (Carl Reiner) which pioneered the intercutting of archive footage from older films; other films which use this technique are Woody Allen's *Zelig* (1983) and *Forrest Gump*, 1994, Robert Zemeckis. The splicing of old and new to create a commercially viable product – a kind of nostalgia-branding, or a way of holding the past and the present in a strange state of tension or suspension – reached the cultural mainstream with Natalie Cole's 1991 single 'Unforgettable'. This recording intercut Natalie Cole's voice with her father, Nat 'King' Cole's, creating a hybrid artefact which is both past and present. The family connection amplified this semiotic dissonance, with questions of influence, creation and pastiche resonating.

44   Gloria Withalm adds to this list the Coca Cola adverts of 1991–2 which featured Paula Abdul and Elton John playing and dancing with Gene Kelly, James Cagney, Humphrey Bogart and Louis Armstrong, and the Coors Light series from 1997's use of John Wayne, 'Recycling Dorothy', pp. 303–4; she also points out that this inter-cutting is in general an American trope.

45   See B. Cronin and E. Davenport, 'E-rogenous zones: positioning pornography in the digital economy', *The Information Society*, 17(1) (2001), 33–48 and J. Coopersmith, 'Does your mother know what you really do? The changing nature and image of computer-based pornography', *History and Technology*, 22(1) (2006), 1–25. Cronin, Davenport and Coopersmith all argue that the tropes, technologies and economic models of porno-graphy are not simply important to understand but fundamentally influential in the evolution of the internet.

46   Consider, for instance, the websites *Sins of Time* 'Historic Erotica from a kinder, gen-tler era', www.sinsoftime.com/, *Historica Erotica* www.historicerotica.com/. The boom in sales of vintage pornography is recorded by K. Riordan, 'The joy of texts', *Time Out*, 27 February 2008, pp. 38–9.

47   *Pornography: The Secret History of Civilisation*, 1999. See J. Hoff, 'Why is there no history of pornography?', in S. Gubar (ed.) *For Adult Users Only: The Dilemma of Violent Pornography*, Bloomington, IN: Indiana University Press, 1989, pp. 17–47.

48   On Small and this genre, see E. Murphy Selinger, 'Rereading the Romance', *Contemporary Literature*, 48(2) (2007), 307–24.

49   For this, see J. Radway, *Reading the Romance: Women, Patriarchy and Pop Literature*, Chapel Hill, NC: University of North Carolina Press, 1984; H. Wood, 'What Reading the Romance did for us', *European Journal of Cultural Studies*, 7(2) (2004), 147–54; and the critique of Radway by I. Ang, 'Feminist desire and female pleasure: on Janice Radway's *Reading the Romance*', *Camera Obscura*, 16 (1988), 179–90.

50   P. Gregory, 'Born a writer: forged as a historian', *History Workshop Journal*, 59 (2005), 237–42.

51   History Freak, 'Not even particularly interesting', posted 11 February 2005, www.amazon.com/review/RB4OA11262UQA/ref=cm_cr_rdp_perm (accessed 24 February 2008).

52   Heteroglossia is a term first theorised by Mikhail Bakhtin, see *The Dialogic Imagination*, ed. M. Holquist, trans. C. Emerson and M. Holquist, Austin, TX: University of Texas Press, 1981.

Part I The popular historian

1 *History in Practice*, London: Arnold, 2000, p. 155.
2 J. Moran, 'Cultural Studies and academic stardom', *International Journal of Cultural Studies*, 1(1) (1998), 67–82.
3 See E.W. Said, 'The public role of writers and intellectuals', in H. Small (ed.) *The Public Intellectual*, Oxford: Blackwell, 2002, pp. 19–40.

1 The public historian, the historian in public

1 See S. Collini, *Absent Minds: Intellectuals in Britain*, Oxford: Oxford University Press, 2007.
2 Y. Alighai-Brown, 'History is everywhere – but whose history is it?', *The Independent*, 22 July 2002, p. 13; M. Dodd, 'The new rock'n'roll', *The New Statesman*, 10 December 2001, www.newstatesman.com/200112100032 (accessed 29 October 2007).
3 *Empire: How Britain Made the Modern World*, London: Allen Lane, 2003, pp. xiii–xvi. See J. Wilson, 'Niall Ferguson's imperial passion', *History Workshop Journal* 56 (2003), 175–83.
4 A useful study of how 'an expert body of knowledge is mediated, shaped and transformed through television for mass audiences', particularly concerned with the material experiences of professional historians involved in programme making, is E. Bell and A. Gray, 'History on television: charisma, narrative and knowledge', *European Journal of Cultural Studies*, 10(1) (2007), 113–33 (p. 113).
5 J. Langer, 'Television's "personality system"', in P. David Marshal (ed.) *The Celebrity Culture Reader*, London: Routledge, 2006, pp. 181–96.
6 R.A. Posner, *Public Intellectuals*, Boston: Harvard University Press, 2001.
7 www.nytimes.com/2007/06/18/arts/television/18stan.html?partner=rssnyt&emc=rss; www.query.nytimes.com/gst/fullpage.html?res=9C03E6DA1439F937A15752C1A96 49C8B63&n=Top/Reference/Times%20Topics/People/S/Schama,%20Simon; www. query.nytimes.com/gst/fullpage.html?res=9C03E6DA1439F937A15752C1A9649C8B 63&scp=1&sq=simon+schama+bizarre; www.number10.gov.uk/output/Page11941. asp; www.gawker.com/news/media/tina-brown/topic-a-with-tina-brown-grammy-wha-gr ammy-who-032934.php, my italics (all accessed 4 December 2007).
8 A. Billen, 'The man who made history sexy', *The Times*, 20 May 2003, www.entertain ment.timesonline.co.uk/tol/arts_and_entertainment/books/article1133953.ece (accessed 4 December 2007).
9 D. Starkey, 'Diary', *The Spectator*, 1 March 1997, www.findarticles.com/p/articles/ mi_qa3724/is_199703/ai_n8747043 (accessed 16 November 2007).
10 A. Martin, 'The Queen is a philistine who lacks education', 22 December 2007, www. dailymail.co.uk/pages/live/articles/news/news.html?in_article_id=504137&in_page_ id=1770 (accessed 1 February 2008).
11 For instance, an article on the deal in *The Independent* had a 'head-to-head' comparison of the two historians, Ian Burrell, *Media*, 'Schama's pounds 3m BBC deal', 21 May 2003, www.findarticles.com/p/articles/mi_qn4158/is_20030521/ai_n12684998 (accessed 16 November 2007).
12 A coda to this discussion is the fact that in *Prospect UK* magazine's 2005 poll of Global Intellectuals some 20,000 reader votes cast included very few historians – Niall Ferguson, Francis Fukuyama, Eric Hobsbawn, Timothy Garton Ash; the list is instead dominated by authors, economists and scientists.
13 *Historians of Genius: Edward Gibbon*, BBC4, 2004, 30 February 2004, 21.30 hrs.
14 J. Thompson, 'History just isn't what it used to be', *The Independent*, 22 February 2004, www.findarticles.com/p/articles/mi_qn4159/is_20040222/ai_n12752224 (accessed 16 November 2007).
15 This position was clarified in a letter to the *Independent on Sunday* complaining that he had been misrepresented in an initial article, 29 February 2004, www.findarticles. com/p/articles/mi_qn4159/is_20040229/ai_n12750904 (accessed 16 November, 2007).

16 *Absolute Power: History Man*, BBC2, 2003, 10 November, 21:00 hrs.

17 www.tomandnev.co.uk/drscript1.htm (accessed 24 October 2007).

18 T. Timpson, 'Return the Marbles? Forget it', 19 January 2006, www.news.bbc.co.uk/1/hi/magazine/4624334.stm (accessed 2 November 2007); 'Author spotlight: Dorothy King', www.randomhouse.ca/author/results.pperl?authorid=59405 (accessed 2 November 2007); D. Smith, 'Hands off our Marbles', *The Observer*, 8 January 2006, www.observer.guardian.co.uk/review/story/0,6903,1681545,00.html (accessed 2 November 2007)

19 'The way of the PhDiva', *The Guardian*, 25 May 2005, www.education.guardian.co.uk/higher/columnist/story/0,9826,1491066,00.html (accessed 2 November 2007).

20 H. Deedes, 'Tristram is in the hunt for a plum Labour seat', *Independent*, 27 April 2007, www.news.independent.co.uk/people/pandora/article2488858.ece (accessed 5 November 2007).

21 www.whitehouse.gov/mrscheney/ (accessed 14 November 2007). On Bush's predilection for particular historical exemplars, see the chapter 'Dead Precedents' in Jacob Weisberg, *The Bush Tragedy*, London: Bloomsbury, 2008, pp. 223–42.

22 *A History of Britain*: Episode 15, *The Two Winstons*, BBC1, 2002, 18 June, 21:00 hrs.

23 *An Utterly Impartial History of Britain: Or, 2000 Years of Upper Class Idiots In Charge*, London: Doubleday, 2007.

24 *Bumper Book of British Battleaxes*, London: Robson, 1998.

25 Hague has written biographies of William Wilberforce and William Pitt the Younger while Major has written a history of cricket.

26 *The English*, London: Penguin, 1999, p. viii. He followed this with *On Royalty*, London: Vintage, 2006.

27 *England, Our England*, London: Hodder & Stoughton, 2007, back cover.

28 See, for instance, Stefan Berger, 'History and national identity', *History and Policy*, www.historyandpolicy.org/papers/policy-paper-66.html (accessed 13 December 2007).

29 Michael Portillo and Lucy Moore in *Great Britons*: Episode 11, *The Greatest of them All*, BBC2, 2002, 24 November, 21:00 hrs.

30 *Great Britons*: Episode 2, *Darwin*, BBC2, 2002, 25 October, 21:00 hrs.

31 *Great Britons*: Episode 7, *Elizabeth*, BBC2 2002, 12 November, 21:00 hrs.

32 *Great Britons*: Episode 8, *Newton*, BBC2, 2002, 15 November, 21:00 hrs.

33 Ibid.

34 *Great Britons*: Episode 3, *Diana*, BBC2, 2002, 29 October, 21:00 hrs.

35 Ibid.

36 M. Reynolds, 'Who is Jára Cimrman?', *Prague Post*, 27 January 2005, www.praguepost.com/P03/2005/Art/0127/news3.php (accessed 17 August 2006). The Finns similarly added 'humorous' nominees, including Matti Nykänen, scandal-dogged gold medalist-turned porn star, and Väinö Myllyrinne, the tallest Finn ever.

37 There is also a European-wide poll, 'Europe's 100', which seeks to find a consensus about the 'most influential' Europeans, www.euro100.org.

38 *My Trade: A Short History of Journalism*, London: Macmillan, 2004.

39 R. Harris, *Selling Hitler: The Story of the Hitler Diaries*, London: Faber & Faber, 1986.

40 See D.D. Guttenplan, *The Holocaust on Trial: History, Justice and the David Irving Libel Case*, London: Granta, 2001, and R. Evans, *Lying about Hitler*, London: Basic Books, 2001, pp. 1–40.

41 *The Irving Judgement: David Irving v. Penguin Books and Professor Deborah Lipstadt*, London: Penguin, 2000, p. 1.

42 Ibid., pp. 27–109.

43 Ibid., p. 348.

44 *The Irving Judgement*, p. 2.

45 Evans, *Lying about Hitler*, p. 37.

46 R. Ingrams, 'Irving was the author of his own downfall', *The Independent*, 25 February 2006, www.comment.independent.co.uk/commentators/article347567.ece (accessed 13 November 2007).

47 M. Greif, 'The banality of Irving', *The American Prospect*, 30 November 2002, www.prospect.org/cs/articles?article=the_banality_of_irving (accessed 13 November 2007).

48 *The Irving Judgement*, p. 293.

49 Ibid.

50 Guttenplan, *The Holocaust on Trial*, p. 277.

51 In addition to this, he has also had to pay various libel damages, see Evans, *Lying about Hitler*, pp. 13–14.

52 www.fpp.co.uk (accessed 14 November 2007); *The Holocaust on Trial*, p. 224.

53 *Lying about Hitler*, p. 35.

54 S. Moss, 'History's verdict on Holocaust upheld', *The Guardian*, 12 April 2000, www.guardian.co.uk/irving/article/0,181050,00.html (accessed 14 November 2007).

2 Popular history in print

1 D.P. Ryan, *The Complete Idiot's Guide to Ancient Eygpt*, London: Alpha, 2002; K.D. Dickson, *World War II for Dummies*, New York: Wiley, 2001; C. Lee, *This Sceptred Isle – Twentieth Century*, London: BBC Worldwide with Penguin Books, 1999, p. viii; A. Venning, *Following the Drum: The Lives of Army Wives and Daughters*, London: Headline, 2005.

2 Historical writing does not gain as much cultural capital through prizes as fiction, but there are still a large number – from the populist Costa Prize (formerly the Whitbread) which has a biography strand, to the James Tait Black Memorial Prize for Biography, the Samuel Johnson Prize for Non-fiction, the Duff Cooper Prize, and the annual Pulitzer Prize for history of the United States, see J. Moran, 'The reign of hype: the contemporary literary star system', in P. David Marshall (ed.) *The Celebrity Culture Reader*, pp. 324–44 and also his *Star Authors: Literary Celebrity in America*, London: Pluto Press, 2000.

3 L. Jardine, *The Curious Life of Robert Hooke*, London: HarperCollins, 2004; W. Dalrymple, *The Last Mughal*, London: Bloomsbury, 2002.

4 J. Thompson, 'History just isn't what it used to be', *The Independent*, 22 February 2004, www.findarticles.com/p/articles/mi_qn4159/is_20040222/ai_n12752224 (accessed 16 November 2007).

5 This selection demonstrates the range and complexity of subject and treatment that popular history encompasses: Alison Weir writes biographies of key female figures from the past including Elizabeth I, Queen Isabella and Katherine Swynford; Terry Jones, formerly of Monty Python, writes reassessments of medieval and ancient periods, arguing for the popular view to take into account the sophistication of medieval life or the cultural achievements of the Barbarians; A.N. Wilson is a literary journalist who writes historical biography; Rebecca Fraser has produced people's histories of nation; Alan Haynes writes about spying and sex in Elizabethan England. There is also a creative element to this work, aside from the narrative style and storytelling ability associated with these publications. Weir and Wilson also write historical fiction; Jones has written updated versions of ancient tales

6 D. Miller, 'The Sobel effect', *Metascience*, 11 (2002), 185–200.

7 *Longitude*, London: Fourth Estate, 1995, p. 8.

8 J. Cartwright and B. Baker, *Literature and Science*, Santa Barbara, CA: ABC Clio, p. 302.

9 Ibid., p. 304.

10 Thompson, 'History just isn't what it used to be'.

11 Demonstrated by the very title of *Speaking for Themselves: The Personal Letters of Winston and Clementine Churchill*, London: Black Swan, 1999.

12 T. Benn, *Office Without Power: Diaries 1968–72*, London: Hutchinson, 1988, p. xiii.

13 'I awoke this morning and decided to pick a fight with Willie Whitelaw. I am sick of him', 19 May 1980; 'That great big booby Geoffrey Dickens', 23 March 1981, Ion Trewin (ed.) *Diaries: Into Politics*, London: Weidenfeld & Nicolson, 2000. He also pays a female blackmailer £5000, 9 July 1980, pp. 159, 220, 169.

14 *Diaries 1987–1992*, London: Little, Brown, 2002, p. vii.

15 *The Blunkett Tapes*, London: Bloomsbury, 2006, pp. 682, 856.

16 For instance, the Russian Lt. Col. Sherovski's account in *The World at War* of the autopsy on Hitler, proving that he was monorchic, is propaganda.

17 *The World at War*, London: Ebury Press, 2007.

18 *Their Darkest Hour*, London: Random House, 2007.

19 T. Holman, 'Bookselling by numbers', *The Bookseller*, 27 January 2005, p. 3.

20 *Being Jordan*, London: John Blake, 2005, p. 4.

21 *Diana: Her True Story*, London: Michael O'Mara, 1992.

22 See J. McGuigan, 'British identity and "the people's princess"', *Sociological Review*, 48(1) (2000), 1–18; J. Thomas, *Diana's Mourning: A People's History*, Cardiff: University of Wales Press, 2002.

23 *The Way We Were: Remembering Diana*, London: HarperCollins, 2006, p. 11.

24 Ibid., p. 253.

25 *Shadows of a Princess*, London: HarperCollins, 2000, p. vii.

26 Ibid., p. 167.

27 Inspector Ken Wharfe with Robert Jobson, *Closely Guarded Secret*, London: Michael O'Mara, 2002.

28 *Georgiana, Duchess of Devonshire*, London: HarperCollins, 1998, p. xvi. Similar popular biographies of famous eighteenth-century women were published following the success of Foreman's biography, including Paula Byrne's *Perdita: The Life of Mary Robinson*, London: Harper Perennial, 2004, which similarly emphasised the proto-'celebrity' status of her subject, 'the Madonna of the eighteenth century', p. 2.

29 *Georgiana*, p. xiv.

30 K. Hawkey, 'Theorizing content: tools from cultural history', *Journal of Curriculum Studies*, 39(1) (2007), 63–76.

31 T. Deary, *The Rotten Romans*, London: Scholastic, 1994, p. 5.

32 M. Scanlon and D. Buckingham, 'Popular histories: "education" and "entertainment" in information books for children', *The Curriculum Journal*, 13(2) (2002), 141–61.

33 T. Deary, *Rotten Rulers*, London: Scholastic, 2005, p. 65.

34 E. MacCallum-Stewart, '"If they ask us why we died": children's literature and the First World War, 1970–2005', *The Lion and the Unicorn*, 31 (2007), 176–88. See also K. Agnew and G. Fox, *Children at War: From the First World War to the Gulf*, London: Continuum, 2001.

35 Deary, *Rotten Romans*, p. 14.

36 W.C. Sellar and R.J. Yeatman, *1066 and All That*, London: Methuen, 1930.

37 See the set of papers critical of the initial 1987 Educational Reform Bill which set up the system now in place collected in D. Lawton and C. Chitty (eds) *The National Curriculum*, London: Institute of Education, 1988.

38 www.nchs.ucla.edu/standards1.html (accessed 21 November 2007).

39 T. Haydn, 'History', in J. White (ed.) *Rethinking the School Curriculum*, London: RoutledgeFalmer, 2004, pp. 87–103 (p. 87).

40 Ibid., pp. 89–91.

41 In opposition to this trend, Grant Bage argues for the continuing importance of storytelling in history education, *Narrative Matters: Teaching and Learning History through Story*, London: Falmer Press, 1999.

42 K. Andreetti, *Teaching History from Primary Evidence*, London: David Fulton, 1993, p. 8; J. Blyth, *History in Primary Schools*, Milton Keynes: Open University Press, 1990, pp. 27–8.

43 P. Lee, www.history.ac.uk/whyhistorymatters/2007-02-12-5-PeterLeeLouder.mp3 (accessed 12 December 2007).

44 *History: Programme of Study for Key Stage 3*, London: Qualifications and Curriculum Authority, 2007, p. 111.

45 www.curriculum.qca.org.uk/subjects/history/index.aspx (accessed 2 December 2007).

46 *History*, p. 117.

47 G. Bage, *Thinking History 4–14*, London: Routledge, 2000, p. 152.

48 K. Barrow, D. Hall, K. Redmond and K. Reed (eds) *Key Stage 3 History: Complete Revision and Practice*, Newcastle-upon-Tyne: Coordination Group Publications, 2005, p. 1.

49 A. Shepperson (ed.) *GCSE History: Complete Revision and Practice*, Newcastle-upon-Tyne: CGP, 2003, p. 2.

50 H. Cooper, 'Historical thinking and cognitive development in the teaching of history', in H. Bourdillon (ed.) *Teaching History*, London: Routledge in association with the Open University, 1994, pp. 101–21 (pp. 109–11).

51 Deary, *Rotten Rulers*, p. 129.

52 Ibid., p. 174.

53 Nick Arnold's *Horrible Science* series 1996– has 31 titles and a magazine; Anita Ganeri's *Horrible Geography* has 14 titles; *Murderous Maths* by Kjartan Poskitt has 16 titles.

54 Scanlon and Buckingham, 'Popular histories', p. 159.

55 Cited at www.harpercollins.co.uk/books/default.aspx?id=11632 (accessed 4 December 2007).

56 'Esprit de corps', *The Spectator*, 8 December 2001, www.spectator.co.uk/search/ 19799/part_2/esprit-de-corps.thtml (accessed 4 December 2007).

57 *The Literary Review*, cited at www.harpercollins.co.uk/books/default.aspx?id=11632 (accessed 4 December 2007).

58 'Tommy', *The Independent on Sunday*, 6 July 2004, www.arts.independent.co.uk/books/ reviews/article46030.ece (accessed 4 December 2007).

59 This notion of empathy as key to historical writing is common; the confusingly named Richard Holmes, romantic biographer, argues that 'Empathy is the most powerful, the most necessary, and the most deceptive, of all biographical emotions', www.conte mporarywriters.com/authors/?p=auth119 (accessed 4 December 2007), see also C. E. Rollyson, 'Biography theory and method', *Biography*, 25(2) (2002), 363–8.

60 A. Irwin, 'Fighting a war in all but name', *The Spectator*, 22 May 2006, www.spectator.co. uk/search/22309/fighting-a-war-in-all-but-name.thtml (accessed 4 December 2007).

61 J. Hartley and S. Turvey, *Reading Groups*, Oxford: Oxford University Press, 2001, p. 4.

62 See J. Radway, *Reading the Romance: Women, Patriarchy and Pop Literature*, Chapel Hill, NC: University of North Carolina Press, 1984; and S. McCracken, *Pulp*, Manchester: Manchester University Press, 1998.

63 Hundreds of reading guides at www.readinggroups.co.uk/Guides/default.aspx (accessed 11 October 2007).

64 Again, this differs from such subscription groups as the History Book Club, which sends a new book monthly to members, www.historybookclub.com (accessed 11 October 2007).

65 For instance, www.romanhistorybooksandmore.freeservers.com/, a group for the discussion of Roman history, meets in a dedicated chatroom at set times according to US timezones despite the fact that many of the contributors are not American.

66 For an overview of the selling of books, and in particular the commodification of writing, see C. Squires, *Marketing Literature*, Basingstoke: Palgrave, 2007.

67 J. Wind and V. Mahajan, *Convergence Marketing: Strategies for Reaching the New Hybrid Consumer*, London: Financial Times/Prentice Hall, 2001.

68 K. O'Sullivan, 'The art of biography', 13 October 2006, www.amazon.co.uk/review/ R2CLPQYJU6W1B0/ref=cm_cr_rdp_perm (accessed 12 October 2007).

69 'john sutherland IS SHOCKED BY THE STATE OF book-Reviewing on the web', *The Telegraph*, 19 November 2006, www.telegraph.co.uk/arts/main.jhtml?xml=/arts/ 2006/11/19/bolists12.xml (accessed 12 October 2007).

70 Ibid.

71 www.blog.susan-hill.com/blog/_archives/2006/11/13/2496064.html (accessed 12 October 2007).

72 Ibid.

73 Ibid.

74 www.reviewcentre.com/products1358.html (accessed 26 November 2007).
75 There are specialist history book websites which use similar formats, such as www. historydirect.co.uk.

3 The historian in popular culture

1 www.paramountpictures.co.uk/romzom/ (accessed 25 October 2007).
2 The sketch was also used by two of the Mary Whitehouse team in *Newman and Baddiel in Pieces* (BBC2, 1993).
3 This mainly pedagogical rather than discipline specific strand draws on the nostalgia of James Hilton's (1934) *Goodbye, Mr. Chips*; other examples might include Michelle Pfeiffer changing students' lives in *Dangerous Minds*, 1995, John N. Smith.
4 See J. Cartwright and B. Baker, *Literature and Science*, Santa Barbara, CA: ABC Clio, pp. 301–4.
5 For instance, Ian Carter estimates that 71 per cent of British university novels published 1945–88 are set at Oxford or Cambridge, *Ancient Cultures of Conceit: British University Fiction in the Post-war Years*, London: Routledge, 1990, p. 15.
6 *Raiders of the Lost Ark*, 1981, Stephen Spielberg. This is followed by *Indiana Jones and the Temple of Doom*, 1984, Stephen Spielberg, *Indiana Jones and the Last Crusade*, 1989, Stephen Spielberg, and *Indiana Jones and the Kingdom of the Crystal Skull*, 2008, Stephen Spielberg. The franchise has continued on television with the *Young Indiana Jones Chronicles*, 1992–93, and *The Adventures of Young Indiana Jones*, 1999.
7 *Death Comes as the End* (1944); *The Man in the Brown Suit* (1926); *Murder in Mesopotamia* (1936); *They Came to Baghdad* (1951).
8 See Carter, *Ancient Cultures*, E. Showalter, *Faculty Towers*, Philadelphia, PA: University of Pennsylvania Press, 2005, and L. Blaxter, C. Hughes and M. Tight, 'Telling it how it is: accounts of academic life', *Higher Education Quarterly*, 52(3) (1998), 300–15.
9 *A Very Peculiar Practice* was the first series written by Andrew Davies, see Chapter 12 on Television Drama.
10 A.S. Byatt, *Possession*, London: Vintage, 1991, p. 238.
11 E. Kostova, *The Historian*, London: TimeWarner, 2005, p. 644.
12 Ibid., p. 644.
13 Ibid.
14 *Archangel*, London, Cresset Editions 2000, p. 55.
15 Ibid.
16 E. O'Gorman, 'Detective fiction and historical narrative', *Greece and Rome*, 46(1) (1999), 19–26.
17 *The Da Vinci Code*, London: Corgi, 2003.
18 *Digital Fortress*, London: Corgi, 2000, p. 21.
19 *False Impression*, London: St. Martin's Press, 2006.
20 A sequel, *National Treasure: Book of Secrets*, 2007, Jon Turteltaub investigates the assassination of Lincoln.
21 The idea that a child of Christ is still living is also considered in Garth Ennis and Steve Dillon's graphic novel sequence *Preacher*, 1995–2000. In this scenario the 'Grail' are a shadowy and influential semi-militarised organisation protecting the heir of Christ. *National Treasure* also posits a semi-secret organisation dedicated to concealing secret hoards; *The Mummy* includes the Medjai, an ancestral group dedicated to protecting the world from the mummy; and in Kostova's *The Historian* a special Order still survives to protect Turkey from Dracula. The trope of an ancient, patrilineal, shadowy group with secret knowledge takes much from the legends of the Templars and the Masons, and therefore intersects clearly with theories of historical conspiracy and unspoken special interests, but it also argues a cultural interest in tradition. These groups are nearly always dying out, unable to prevent the foolish moderns from waking the creature, and ineffectual in their attempts to combat it. The Templars and

the bloodline of Christ theories were popularised by M. Baigent, R. Leigh and H. Lincoln, *The Holy Blood and the Holy Grail*, London: Jonathan Cape, 1982, whose authors sued Dan Brown for plagiarism and lost in 2006.

22 Brown, *Da Vinci Code*, p. 326.

23 Ibid., p. 405.

24 Ibid., p. 15. The alleged veracity of the novel extends to a playful mock 'Official' website for Robert Langdon, www.randomhouse.com/doubleday/davinci/robertlangdon/ (accessed 2 November 2007).

25 www.danbrown.com/novels/davinci_code/faqs.html (accessed 2 November 2007).

26 Ibid.

27 See G. Ward, *Christ and Culture*, Oxford: Blackwell, 2005.

28 P. Knight, *Conspiracy Culture*, London: Routledge, 2000.

29 See, for instance, S. Berry, *The Templar Legacy*, London: Hodder & Stoughton, 2006, although Berry is a conspiracy author who has also addressed the Romanovs and Israel, R. Young, *Brethren* trilogy London: Hodder & Stoughton, 2006– and J. Rollins, *Map of Bones*, London: Orion, 2005.

30 D. Polan, 'The professors of history', in V. Sobchack (ed.), *The Persistence of History*, London: Routledge, 1996, pp. 235–56 (p. 251).

31 J. Gregory and S. Miller, *Science in Public: Communication, Culture and Credibility*, London: Plenum, 1998; R.K. Sherwin, *When Law Goes Pop: The Vanishing Line Between Law and Popular Culture*, Chicago: University of Chicago Press, 2000.

Part II Enfranchisement, ownership and consumption

1 'History happens', in V. Sobchack (ed.), *The Persistence of History*, London: Routledge, 1996, pp. 1–16 (p. 7).

2 See W.D. Rubinstein, 'History and "amateur" history', in P. Lambert and P. Schofield (eds.) *Making History*, London: Routledge, 2004, pp. 269–80.

3 D.L. Gillespie, A. Leffler and E. Lerner, '"If it weren't for my hobby, I'd have a life": dog sports, serious leisure, and boundary negotiations', *Leisure Studies*, 21(3/4) (2002), 285–304 (p. 286).

4 C. Rojek, *Leisure Theory*, Basingstoke: Palgrave Macmillan, 2005, p. 178, see also R. Stebbins, *Amateurs, Professionals and Serious Leisure*, Montreal: McGill-Queens University Press, 1992.

5 Ibid.

4 The everyday historical: local history, metal detecting, antiques

1 W.G. Hoskins' *The Making of the English Landscape*, London: Longman, 1955; P. Riden, *Local History: A Handbook for Beginners*, Cardiff: Morton Priory Press, 1998, pp. 7–16. See also H.P.R. Finberg, *The Local Historian and His Theme*, Welwyn: University College Leicester, 1952, and the discussion of the developing historiography of local history in S.J. Davies, 'The development of local history writing', in M. Dewe (ed.) *Local Studies Collections: A Manual*, Aldershot: Gower, 1991, pp. 28–55.

2 W.G. Hoskins, *Local History in England*, London: Longman, 1972, p. 8.

3 Ibid., p. 14.

4 *The Local Historian and His Theme*, p. 9.

5 *Local History in England*, p. 15.

6 Ibid., p. 4.

7 Ibid., p. 4.

8 Ibid., p. 5.

9 *The Local Historian and His Theme*, p. 11.

10 See J. Sharpe, 'History from below', and G. Levi, 'On microhistory', in P. Burke (ed.) *New Perspectives on Historical Writing*, Cambridge: Polity, 2001, pp. 25–43 and 97–120.

11 T.K. Hareven, 'The impact of family history and the life course on social history', in R. Wall, T.K. Hareven and J. Ehmer (eds) *Family History Revisited*, London: Associated University Presses, 2001, pp. 21–40 (p. 21).

12 *On Doing Local History*, Lanham, MD: Rowman Altamira, 2003, p. 62.

13 S. Friar, *The Sutton Companion to Local History*, Stroud: Sutton, 2004; J. Griffin and T. Lawes, *Exploring Local History*, Reading: Hodder and Stoughton, 1997; D. Iredale and J. Barrett, *Discovering Local History*, Buckinghamshire: Shire, 1999.

14 *Sources for Local History*, Cambridge: Cambridge University Press, 1981, p. 1.

15 D. Iredale and J. Barrett, *Discovering Your Old House*, Buckinghamshire: Shire, 1994, p. 3.

16 J.R. Ravensdale, *History on Your Doorstep*, ed. B. Brooks, London: BBC, 1982.

17 See also M. Aston, *Interpreting the Landscape: Landscape Archaeology in Local Studies*, London: BT Batsford, 1985.

18 Tempus publish the books of the National Trust, lending them a national institutional cache.

19 'Publications of 2004', *The Local Historian*, 35(1) (2004), 55–8 (p. 57).

20 C. Dobinson and S. Denison, with contributions by H. Cool and K. Sussams, *Metal Detection and Archaeology in England*, London: English Heritage and Council for British Archaeology, 1995.

21 R. Bland, 'A pragmatic approach to the problem of portable antiquities: the experience of England and Wales', *Antiquity*, 79(304) (2005), 440–7.

22 www.finds.org.uk/index.php (accessed 30 May 2007).

23 www.opsi.gov.uk/ACTS/acts1996/1996024.htm (accessed 30 May 2007).

24 Figures from Don Henson, Education Officer, Council for British Archaeology.

25 www.treasurenet.com/westeast/ (accessed 30 May 2007).

26 www.channel4.com/history/microsites/B/bigdig/behind/behind.html (accessed 30 May 2007).

27 www.channel4.com/history/microsites/T/timeteam/schools_intro.html (accessed 30 May 2007).

28 www.bbc.co.uk/history/familyhistory/get_started/boesinghe_01.shtml (accessed 30 July 2007).

29 C. Eddie Palmer and C.J. Forsyth, 'Antiques, auctions, and action: interpreting and creating economic value', *Journal of Popular Culture*, 39(2) (2006), 234–59 (p. 239).

30 F. Deblauwe, 'Iraq: looting of national treasures', *Washington Post*, 21 April 2003, www.washingtonpost.com/wp-srv/liveonline/03/special/iraq/sp_iraq-deblauwe042103.htm (accessed 1 March 2007) and N. Brodie, J. Doole and P. Watson, 'Stealing history', www.savingantiquities.org/pdf/Stealinghistory.pdf (accessed 3 March 2007).

31 O. Ashenfelter and K. Graddy, 'Auctions and the price of art', *Journal of Economic Literature*, 41(3) (2003), 763–87.

32 *Theatres of Memory*, London: Verso, 1994, pp. 83–118.

33 S.M. Pearce, *Collecting in Contemporary Practice*, London: Sage, 1998, pp. 1, 46.

34 Ibid., p. 48.

35 There is also a Children's Roadshow each Christmas for toys and memorabilia.

36 R. Bishop, 'Dreams in the line: a day at the *Antiques Roadshow*', *The Journal of Popular Culture*, 35(1) (2001), 195–209.

37 It is consistently in BBC1's top 15 viewed shows according to BARB information.

38 BARB statistics used by Angela Piccini and Don Henson, *Survey of Heritage Television Programming 2005–06* report for English Heritage, thanks to Don Henson for a copy of this document.

39 *Flog It!* was the highest contributor with 17 per cent share; *Cash in the Attic* 14 per cent and *Bargain Hunt* 13 per cent show a consistently high contribution for this kind of show. The highest non-antique-related programme was *Coast* with 4 per cent; the multi-million costing and critically acclaimed series *Rome* had 3 per cent. Piccini and Henson choose not to consider antique shows, as their brief is to consider the

representation of more traditional 'heritage' on television, and their decision to cut these shows from analysis demonstrates how such pulp programming is barely thought of when 'history' in the public imagination is discussed.

40 Palmer and Forsyth, 'Antiques, auctions, and action', p. 239.
41 P. Klemperer, 'Auction theory: a guide to the literature', *Journal of Economic Surveys*, 13 (3) (1999), 227–86 (pp. 228, 273–4), and see also E.S. Maskin, J.G. Riley, 'Auction theory with private values', *The American Economic Review*, 75(2) (1985), 150–5.
42 T. Wonnacott, 'Interview', www.bbc.co.uk/antiques/tv_and_radio/bargainhunt_timwo nnacott.shtml (accessed 3 May 2007).
43 Llewelyn-Bowen, quoted in D. Philips, 'Transformation scenes: the television interior makeover', *International Journal of Cultural Studies* 8(2) (2005), 213–29 (p. 217).

5 Genealogy: hobby, politics, science

1 E.A. Wrigley, 'Population history', in Peter Burke (ed.) *History and Historians in the Twentieth Century*, Oxford: Oxford University Press, 2002, pp. 141–64; B. Reay, *Microhistories*, Cambridge: Cambridge University Press, 1996.
2 M. Saar, 'Genealogy and subjectivity', *European Journal of Philosophy*, 10(2) (2002), 231–45.
3 R. Bishop, '"The essential force of the clan": developing a collecting-inspired ideology of genealogy through textual analysis', *The Journal of Popular Culture*, 38(6) (2005), 990–1010.
4 Lowenthal notes that this surge in popularity was evident by 1984, *The Past is a Foreign Country*, Cambridge: Cambridge University Press, 1985, p. 38.
5 S. Colwell, *The Family Records Centre: A User's Guide*, Kew: Public Record Office, 2002, p. 1.
6 Ibid., p. 1.
7 *The Past is a Foreign Country*, p. 38.
8 N. Barratt, *The Family History Project*, Kew: National Archives and the History Channel, 2004, p. xi.
9 Ibid., p. xi.
10 A. Bevan, *Tracing Your Ancestors in the National Archives*, Kew: Public Record Office, 2006, p. 20. See also S. Colwell, *The National Archives*, Kew: National Archives, 2006.
11 See also the section on family stories, heirlooms and photographs in S. Fowler, *The Joys of Family History*, Kew: Public Record Office, 2001, pp. 10–15, for instance.
12 P. Christian, *The Genealogist's Internet*, Kew: National Archives, 2005, p. ix, pp. 5–6 and 'Computers in Genealogy', www.ancestry.com/learn/library/article.aspx?article=7356 (accessed 6 March 2007),
13 M. Olson, 'Genealogy newsgroups', www.homepages.rootsweb.com/~socgen/Newshist.htm (accessed 6 March 2007).
14 Christian, *The Genealogist's Internet*, p. 228.
15 It was unlooked for: in 1991, Richard Harvey suggested that new technology might have some small impact in service to genealogists in the future, mainly 'handling correspondence enquiries by means of word processing, and databases', 'Genealogy and family history', in Michael Dewe (ed.) *Local Studies Collections*, pp. 173–93 (p. 191).
16 'P2P leisure exchange: net banditry and the policing of intellectual property', *Leisure Studies*, 24(4) (2005), 357–69 (p. 367).
17 C. Needham, 'The citizen as consumer: e-government in the UK and US', in R.K. Gibson, A. Römmell and S.J. Ward (eds) *Electronic Democracy*, London: Routledge, 2004, pp. 43–70 (p. 43).
18 N. Katherine Hayles, *How We Became Posthuman: Virtual Bodies in Cybernetics, Literature, and Informatics*, Chicago: University of Chicago Press, 1999, p. 19. See pp. 1–25 and 192–222 for a discussion of the erasure of 'embodiment' in globalised culture, see also p. 4. She theorises the posthuman as 'an informational-material entity', p. 11.
19 *Tracing Your Ancestors in the National Archives*, Kew: National Archives, 2006, p. 1.
20 Ibid., p. 13.

21 *The Family Records Centre*, p. 1.
22 Information from C. Sumpner *et al.*, 'Who Do You Think You Are? 360 audience feedback', report for the National Archives and the BBC, many thanks to Lucy Fulton of the National Archives for a copy of this report.
23 This is noticed by the participants: 'It's a detective story', *Who Do You Think You Are? 4:7*, BBC1, 2007, 19 September, BBC1, 21:00 hrs.
24 *Who Do You Think You Are? 1:7*, BBC2, 2004, 23 November, 21:00 hrs.
25 *Who Do You Think You Are? 1:1*, BBC2, 2004, 12 October, 21:00 hrs.
26 *Who Do You Think You Are? 1:8*, BBC2, 2004, 30 November, 21:00 hrs.
27 Ibid.
28 *Who Do You Think You Are? 1:7*, BBC2, 2004, 23 November, 21:00 hrs.
29 *Who Do You Think You Are? 1:10*, BBC2, 2004, 14 December, 21:00 hrs.
30 This particular episode was personalised further by a follow-up documentary in which David Baddiel explored the possibility of restitution for his family and considered the issues associated with such compensation, *Baddiel and the Missing Nazi Billions*, BBC1, 2007, 15 November, 22:40 hrs.
31 I owe part of this discussion to A. Holdsworth, 'Moving pictures: family history, memory and photography in *Who Do You Think You Are?* and *Not Forgotten*', unpublished conference paper.
32 *Who Do You Think You Are? 1:10*, BBC2, 2004, 14 December, 21:00 hrs.
33 Ibid.
34 *Who Do You Think You Are? 1:8*, BBC2, 2004, 30 November, 21:00 hrs.
35 A. Lavender, 'Pleasure, performance, and the *Big Brother* experience', *Contemporary Theatre Review*, 13(2) (2002), 15–23.
36 G. Turner, *Understanding Celebrity*, London: Sage, 2004, pp. 4–5, 23–5.
37 Ibid., p. 5, p. 6, citing Chris Rojek.
38 I owe this point to Eithne Quinn.
39 www.walltowall.co.uk/catalogue_detail.aspx?w2wprogram=164 (accessed 7 February 2007).
40 *You Don't Know You're Born 3*, ITV, 2007, 6 February, 21:00 hrs.
41 Ibid.
42 Ibid.
43 Haley admitted in court that some 100 words of the material were taken from Harold Courlander's *The African*, and his genealogical research has been challenged by Gary B. Mills and Elizabeth Shown Mills, www.en.wikipedia.org/wiki/Roots:_The_Saga_of_a n_American_Family#_note-5 (accessed 13 March 2007). See also R. M. Current, 'Fiction as history: a review essay', *The Journal of Southern History*, 52(1) (1986), 77–90.
44 *Roots*, London: Vintage, 1991, p. 662.
45 Ibid., p. 669.
46 Ibid., p. 670.
47 Ibid., p. 681.
48 Ibid., p. 681.
49 Ibid., p. 681.
50 'Obama told of family's slave-owning history in deep South', *The Observer*, 4 March 2007, p. 3; the genealogical account is at www.wargs.com/political/obama.html.
51 Ibid.
52 R. Tutton, '"They want to know where they came from": population genetics, identity and family genealogy', *New Genetics and Society*, 23(1) (2004), 105–20 (p. 106).
53 See J. Van Dijck, *Imagenation: Popular Images of Genetics*, Basingstoke: Macmillan, 1998, and J. Roof, *The Poetics of DNA*, Minneapolis, MN: University of Minnesota Press, 2007.
54 Tutton, 'Population genetics', pp. 106–7.
55 C. Nash, 'Genetic kinship', *Cultural Studies*, 18(1) (2004), 1–33 (p. 2).
56 J. Johnson and M. Thomas, 'Summary: the science of genealogy by genetics', *Developing World Bioethics*, 3(2) (2003), 103–8.

57 D.A. Bolnick '"Showing who they really are": commercial ventures in genetic gen-ealogy', www.shrn.stanford.edu/workshops/revisitingrace/Bolnick2003.doc (accessed 15 March 2007).

58 M.D. Shriver and R.A. Kittles, 'Genetic ancestry and the search for personalised genetic histories', *Nature Reviews Genetics*, 5 (2004), 611–18 (p. 611).

59 Shriver and Kittles, 'Genetic ancestry', p. 621.

60 www.oxfordancestors.com/links.html (accessed 16 March 2007).

61 C. Elliot and P. Brodwin, 'Identity and genetic ancestry tracing', *British Medical Journal*, 325 (2002), 1469–71, and Nash, 'Genetic kinship'.

62 Tutton, 'Population genetics', pp. 109–12.

63 www.oxfordancestors.com/your-maternal.html (accessed 16 March 2007).

64 www.smgproductions.tv/content/default.asp?page=s2_3_22 (accessed 15 March 2007).

65 www.pbs.org/wnet/aalives/about.html# (accessed 4 April 2007).

66 J. Marks, '"We're going to tell these people who they really are": science and relat-edness', in S. Franklin and S. McKinnon (eds) *Relative Values: Reconfiguring Kinship Studies*, Durham, NC: Duke University Press, 2001, pp. 355–83.

6 Digital history

1 L. Grossman, 'You – Yes, You – are TIME's Person of the Year', 17 December 2006, www.time.com/time/magazine/article/0,9171,1570810,00.html (accessed 19 January 2007).

2 The 'digital divide', however, means that any discussion of the internet and Web 2.0 must take into account the fact that this is largely a Western and middle-class phe-nomenon, see, for instance, J. Chakraborty and M. M. Bosman, 'Measuring the digi-tal divide in the United States: race, income and personal computer ownership', *The Professional Geographer*, 27 (2005), 395–410, and M. Castells, *The Rise of the Network Society*, Oxford: Blackwell, 2000.

3 The Free Software Foundation has played a crucial role in ensuring user/programmer rights to study, copy and modify programs, www.fsf.org/.

4 See, for instance, Castells, *The Rise of the Network Society*.

5 *History in Practice*, London: Arnold, 2000, p. 189.

6 D. J. Cohen and R. Rosenzweig, 'Web of lies? Historical knowledge on the Internet', *First Monday*, 10(12) (2005), www.firstmonday.org/issues/issue10_12/cohen/index.html (accessed 15 January 2007).

7 A. Appadurai, 'Disjuncture and difference in the global cultural economy', in J. Xavier Inda and R. Rosaldo (eds) *The Anthropology of Globalization*, Oxford: Blackwell, 2002, pp. 46–64 (p. 50).

8 See D.J. Cohen, 'History and the second decade of the web', *Rethinking History*, 8(2) (2004), 293–301 and, for an applied reading, S. Ho, 'Blogging as popular history making, blogs as public history: the Singapore case study', *Public History Review*, 14 (2007), 64–79.

9 'Disjuncture and difference in the global cultural economy', p. 50.

10 M. Featherstone, 'Archiving cultures', *The British Journal of Sociology*, 51(1) (2000) 161–84 (p. 161).

11 Ibid, p. 177.

12 See M. Bakardjieva, *Internet Society*, London: Sage, 2005.

13 'The analysis of culture', in J. Storey (ed.) *Cultural Theory and Popular Culture*, London: Pearson Education, 2006, pp. 56–64 (p. 57).

14 W.H. Dutton, 'The Internet and social transformation: reconfiguring access', in W.H. Dutton, B. Kahin, R. O'Callaghan, and A.W. Wyckoff (eds) *Transforming Enterprise*, Cambridge, MA: MIT Press, 2005, pp. 375–89 (p. 383).

15 So, for instance, the rate of museums signing up to sites such as MySpace or starting blogs is exponential, see www.museumblogs.org/.

16 www.anders.com/lectures/lars_brownworth/12_byzantine_rulers/ (accessed 6 February 2007).

17 www.news.bbc.co.uk/1/hi/magazine/decades/1990s/default.stm (accessed 22 June 2007).

18 www.bbc.co.uk/ww2peopleswar/ (accessed 22 June 2007).

19 H. Zinn, *A People's History of the United States*, London: HarperPerenial, 2005, and edited with A. Arnove, *Voices of a People's History of the United States*, New York: Seven Stories Press, 2004.

20 See T. Hunt, 'Reality, identity and empathy: the changing face of social history television', *Journal of Social History*, 39(3) (2006), 843–58, and R. Rosenzweig, 'Historians and audiences', *Journal of Social History*, 39(3) (2006), 859–65.

21 www.911digitalarchive.org

22 See A. Hoskins, 'Television and the collapse of memory', *Time and Society*, 13(1) (2004), 109–27.

23 Cohen and Rosenzweig, 'Web of lies?'.

24 R. Rosenzweig, 'Scarcity or abundance? Preserving the past in a digital era', *The American Historical Review*, 108(3) (2003), www.historycooperative.org/journals/ahr/108.3/rosenzweig.html (accessed 15 January 2007) and R. Anderson, 'Author disincentives and open access', *Serials Review*, 30(4) (2004), 288–91.

25 Rosenzweig, 'Scarcity or abundance?'. See also J. Gomez, *Print is Dead*, Basingstoke: Palgrave Macmillan, 2007.

26 See Cohen, 'History and the second decade of the web' and 'From Babel to knowledge: data-mining large collections', www.chnm.gmu.edu/resources/essays/d/40 (accessed 15 January 2007).

27 T. Brabazon, *The University of Google: Education in the PostInformation Age*, Aldershot: Ashgate, 2007. See also her *Digital Hemlock: Internet Education and the Poisoning of Teaching*, Sydney: University of New South Wales Press, 2002.

28 As discussed in, for instance, T. Jordan, *Cyberpower*, London: Routledge, 1999.

29 W. J. Turkel, 'Searching for history' (12/10/2006), *Digital History Hacks: Methodology for the Infinite Archive* (weblog accessed 15 January 2007).

30 *The Search: How Google and Its Rivals Rewrote the Rules of Business and Transformed Our Culture*, Boston and London: Nicholas Brearley, 2005.

31 Cohen, 'From Babel to knowledge'.

32 L. Manovich, *The Language of New Media*, Cambridge, MA: MIT Press, 2001, p. 86.

33 K.D. Squire and C.A. Steinkuhler, 'Meet the gamers: games as sites for new information literacies', *Library Journal*, 2005, www.libraryjournal.com/article/CA516033.html (accessed 15 January 2007).

34 *Information Architecture*, Sebastopol, CA: O'Reilly, 2002, p. 23.

35 www.gutenberg-e.org.

36 R. Rosenzweig, 'Should historical scholarship be free?', www.chnm.gmu.edu/resources/essays/d/2 (accessed 21 February 2007).

37 'The commodities of culture', in M.J. Lee (ed.) *The Consumer Society Reader*, Oxford: Blackwell, pp. 282–88 (p. 283).

38 'P2P leisure exchange', p. 367.

39 *The Language of New Media*, p. 55.

40 J. Stratton, 'Cyberspace and the globalization of culture', in D. Bell and B.M. Kennedy (eds) *The Cybercultures Reader*, London: Routledge, 2000, pp. 721–31 (p. 729); in the same volume, S.P. Wilbur argues that this idealism is in some ways misplaced 'An archaeology of cyberspaces: virtuality, community, identity', pp. 45–55.

41 M. Dery, *Escape Velocity*, New York: Grove Press, 1996, p. 6.

42 R. Rosenzweig, 'Can history be open source? Wikipedia and the future of the past', www.chnm.gmu.edu/resources/essays/d/42 (accessed 9 February 2007).

43 Ibid.

44 Some 27,000 people made more than five edits during December 2005, for instance, www.en.wikipedia.org/wiki/Wikipedia#Policies_and_guidelines (accessed 21 February

2007). Entries have often been hacked and amended for various reasons, from the scoring of political points to comic situationism, see www.theregister.co.uk/2007/02/02/colbert_wikipedia_reality/.

45 www.en.wikipedia.org/w/index.php?title=Wikipedia:Neutral_point_of_view&oldid=102236018 (accessed 21 February 2007).

46 www.en.wikipedia.org/wiki/Wikipedia:Verifiability (accessed 21 February 2007).

47 See P. Jackson, *Maps of Meaning: An Introduction to Cultural Geography*, London: Routledge, 1995. The use of 3D satellite maps to discipline and order space is clear, for instance, in news dispatches in which the topography of the region is represented before focusing in on a specific location.

48 W. Kienreich, M. Granitzer and M. Lux, 'Geospatial anchoring of encyclopedia articles', *Tenth International Conference on Information Visualisation*, 4(6) (2006), 211–15.

49 I owe this point to Tim Derby.

50 J.W. Crampton and J. Krygier, 'An introduction to critical cartography', *ACME*, 4(1) (2006), 11–33 (p. 19).

51 It is key here that Google Earth came to prominence during the Hurricane Katrina disaster in New Orleans when imagery of the flooding was hacked and used by news agencies around the world as well as individual users and communities to demonstrate the extent of the damage and therefore undermine the US government line that all was well. Other dissident uses include *Nature*'s mapping of avian flu – www.nature.com/nature/googleearth/avianflu1.kml or the unspun presentation of conflict zones like Basra or Baghdad (the Former Republican Palace in Baghdad is one of GE's featured locations).

52 Similar historical maps can be found at www.npemap.org.uk, a site serving images of the New Popular Edition maps of the UK from the 1940s.

53 www.googleearthhacks.com/dlcat40/Sightseeing:-Historical-Placemarks.htm.

54 Rojek, 'P2P leisure exchange', p. 363.

55 Habermas, *The Structural Transformation of the Public Sphere: An Inquiry into a Category of Bourgeois Culture*, trans. Thomas Burger and Frederick Lawrence, Cambridge: Polity Press, 1992, p. xi.

56 E. Rennie, *Community Media*, Oxford: Rowman and Littlefield, 2006, p. 3.

57 www.brightonourstory.co.uk/index2.htm; www.clayheritage.org/; www.historyatthecidermuseum.org.uk/; www.igca.mysite.wanadoo-members.co.uk/.

58 L.J. Servon, *Bridging the Digital Divide*, Oxford: Blackwell, 2002.

59 *Comma* is the software most generally used, a simple database programme sold by Commanet; some 200 or more local archives use it.

60 www.nationalarchives.gov.uk/documents/finalreport.pdf (accessed 22 February 2007).

61 Ibid.

62 www.commanet.org/English/Default.htm (accessed 22 February 2007).

Part III Performing and playing history

1 V. Agnew, 'What is re-enactment?', *Criticism*, 46(3) (2004), 327–39.

2 Raphael Samuel, *Theatres of Memory*, London: Verso, 1994, p. 175.

3 Ibid., p. 188.

7 Historical re-enactment

1 See J. de Groot, 'Empathy and enfranchisement: popular histories', *Rethinking History*, 10(3) (2006), 391–413.

2 J. Thompson, *War Games: Inside the World of Twentieth Century War Reenactors*, Washington, DC: Smithsonian Books, 2004. Thompson finds 97.8 per cent white and 96.8 per cent male in her survey, p. 79.

3 V. Agnew, 'What is re-enactment?', *Criticism*, 46(3) (2004), 327–39 (p. 328).

4 Ibid., p. 330. See also I. McCalman, 'The Little Shop of Horrors: reenacting extreme history', *Criticism*, 46(3) (2004), 477–86.

5 'Introduction: making history go', in Della Pollock (ed.) *Exceptional Spaces: Essays in Performance and History*, Chapel Hill, NC: University of North Carolina Press, 1998, pp. 1–48 (p. 7).

6 Thompson, *War Games*, pp. 169–71.

7 www.sealedknot.org/index.asp?Page=about.htm (accessed 5 May 2005).

8 www.sealedknot.org/index.asp?Page=cav.htm (accessed 5 May 2005).

9 *The Civil War Reenactors' Encyclopedia*, London: Salamander, 2002, p. 29.

10 For instance, Thompson lists around 6,000 regular enactors from these periods in the USA.

11 Thompson, *War Games*, p. xvi.

12 Re-enactment is a live political issue in Ireland, as witnessed by the annual re-enacting of the Battle of the Boyne.

13 www.drhg.pwp.blueyonder.co.uk/Wars_Info.htm (accessed 5 May 2005).

14 Ibid.

15 Thompson, *War Games*, p. 153.

16 Ibid., p. xvii.

17 J. Anderson, *Time Machines: The World of Living History*, Nashville, TN: American Association of State and Local History, 1984, p. 191.

18 Thompson, *War Games*, p. 162.

19 See, for instance, www.authentic-campaigner.com, and www.fcsutler.com.

20 *A Cock and Bull Story*, 2005, Michael Winterbottom.

21 'Heritage: an interpretation', in D. Uzzell (ed.) *Heritage International*, London and New York: Belhaven Press, 1989, pp. 15–23 (p. 21).

22 T. Stearn, 'What's wrong with television history?', *History Today*, 52(12) (2002), 26–27 (p. 27).

23 *Great Britons*: Episode 1, BBC2, 2002, 22 October, 21:00 hrs.

24 J. Hallam and M. Mashment, *Realism and Popular Cinema*, Manchester: Manchester University Press, 2000, p. 19.

25 The Blue Plaque scheme is administered by English Heritage. The criteria for approval include the stipulation that the commemorated figure must 'Have made an important positive contribution to human welfare or happiness', www.english-heritage.org.uk/server/show/nav.1498 (accessed 26 January 2006).

26 P. Snow and D. Snow, *Battlefield Britain*, London: BBC Books, 2004, p. 11.

27 *Wellington*, London: HarperCollins, 1996, p. xviii.

28 Similarly, Holmes' episode of *Great Britons*, which was on Oliver Cromwell, emphasises the importance of the Fens to his subject's biography, with lingering shots of bleak flatness; to understand Cromwell's motivations, values – and therefore his significance to the nation – you have to understand the place he was from, *Great Britons: Episode 4*, BBC2, 2002, 1 November, 21:00 hrs.

29 Snow and Snow, *Battlefield Britain*, p. 51.

30 Dir: David McNab, 120 mins, first broadcast in the USA on the Discovery Channel.

31 P. Ward, 'The future of documentary? "Conditional tense" documentary and the historical record', in G.D. Rhodes and J. Parris Springer (eds) *Docufictions*, Jefferson, NC: McFarland & Company, Inc, 2006, pp. 270–84.

32 *The Making of Virtual History*, www.discoverychannel.co.uk/virtualhistory/_pages/making_of/back_to_life.shtml (accessed 30 January 2006).

33 Ibid.

34 Simon Roberts, quoted in ibid.

35 www.bbc.co.uk/arts/romantics/intro.shtml (accessed 26 January 2006).

36 See S.F. Roth, *Past into Present: Effective Techniques for First-Person Historical Interpretation*, Chapel Hill, NC: University of North Carolina Press, 1998, and K.F. Stover, 'Is it real history yet?: An update on living history museums', *Journal of American Culture*, 12 (2) (1989), 13–17.

37 B. Goodacre and G. Baldwin, *Living the Past*, London: Middlesex University Press, 2002, p. 51.

38 David Lowenthal has criticised living history and first-person interpretation for problematising the audience's relationship to the past, see *The Past is a Foreign Country*, Cambridge: Cambridge University Press, 1985, p. 298.

39 *Theatres of Memory*, p. 195.

40 J. Tivers, 'Performing heritage: the use of live "actors" in heritage presentations', *Leisure Studies*, 21: 3/4, 2002, 187–200 (p. 198).

41 Tivers, 'Performing heritage', p. 194.

42 See T. Bennett, *The Birth of the Museum*, London: Routledge, 1995.

43 *Theatres of Memory*, London: Verso, 1994, p. 175.

44 T. Bennett, 'Museums and the people', in Robert Lumley (ed.) *The Museum Time Machine: Putting Cultures on Display*, London: Routledge, 1988, pp. 63–85 (p. 63).

45 www.beamish.org.uk/about.html (accessed 4 October 2007).

46 Ibid.

47 www.ironbridge.org.uk/downloads/STRATEGIC%20PLAN%202007–10%20FINAL. pdf (accessed 8 October 2007).

48 'Putting your house in order: representations of women and domestic life', in Lumley, *The Museum Time Machine*, pp. 102–28.

49 R. Handler and E. Gable, *The New History in an Old Museum: Creating the Past at Colonial Williamsburg*, Durham, NC: Duke University Press, 1997.

50 T. Bridal, *Exploring Museum Theatre*, Walnut Creek, CA: AltaMira Press, 2004, p. 5.

51 www.imtal.org/keyQuestions.php (accessed 4 October, 2007).

52 A. Jackson, 'Inter-acting with the past – the use of participatory theatre at museums and heritage sites', *Research in Drama Education*, 5(2) (2000), pp. 199–215.

53 A. Jackson and H. Rees Leahy, '"Seeing it for real?" – Authenticity, theatre and learning in museums', *Research in Drama Education*, 10(3) (2005), pp. 303–25.

54 www.sca.org/officers/chatelain/ForwardIntothePast.pdf (accessed 3 October 2007).

55 www.sca.org/docs/govdocs.pdf (accessed 3 October 2007).

56 www.grandcouncil.sca.org/oct05detail4.php (accessed 3 October 2007).

57 Ibid.

58 See M. Alexander, *Medievalism: The Middle Ages in Modern England*, New Haven, CT: Yale University Press, 2007.

59 www.renaissancefestival.com/ (accessed 3 October 2007); see S. Blazer, 'The Renaissance pleasure faire', *The Drama Review*, 1976, pp. 31–7, who emphasises the randomness of the experience: 'At no time during the course of the long day is an attempt made to lead the spectator to any specific gathering place', pp. 36–7.

60 www.renfair.com/bristol/ (accessed 8 October 2007).

61 www.projo.com/lifebeat/content/wk-faire_08-30-07_AK6TPA5.19db2cf.html (accessed 3 October 2007).

62 Ibid.

63 www.renfaireworld.com/?SC=wiki (accessed 3 October 2007).

64 www.lumleycastle.com/events/elizabethanbanquets.htm (accessed 1 October 2007).

65 O. Redon, F. Sabban and S. Serventi, *The Medieval Kitchen*, Chicago: University of Chicago Press, 2000, p. 51.

66 M. Black, *The Medieval Cookbook*, London: Thames & Hudson, 1996, p. 23.

67 *Take a Thousand Eggs or More*, Pottstown, PA: Cindy Renfrow, 1997.

68 H. Knibb, '"Present but not visible": searching for women's history in museum collections', *Gender and History*, 6(3) (1994), 352–69 (p. 356).

69 A similarly embodied health series is Channel 4's *The Diets That Time Forgot* (2008), which asks the volunteer participants to live according to particular models of weight loss.

70 *Bringing Up Baby*: Episode 1, Channel 4, 25 September 2007, 21:00 hrs.

8 Recycling culture and re-enactment

1 J. Butt, *Playing with History: The Historical Approach to Musical Performance*, Cambridge: Cambridge University Press, 2002.
2 Ibid., pp. 54–5.
3 The Globe has been site of discussions of authenticity and research for centuries, see G. Egan, 'Reconstructions of the Globe: a retrospective', *Shakespeare Survey*, 52 (1999), 1–16.
4 There are 13 replica Globes around the world, from Tokyo and Prague to Rome; there are seven in the USA.
5 Although as scholars have pointed out, the Globe is built using various assumptions that can be challenged, see Egan, 'Reconstructions', pp. 12–14.
6 G. Holderness, 'Bardolatry; or, the cultural materialist's guide to Stratford-upon-Avon', in G. Holderness (ed.) *The Shakespeare Myth*, Manchester: Manchester University Press, 1988, pp. 2–16 (p. 11). See also J. Drakakis, 'Theatre, ideology, and institution: Shakespeare and the roadsweepers', in the same volume, pp. 24–41.
7 Although Shakespeare is not the only author to have an attraction associated with him – Dickens World in Kent expects some 300,000 visitors a year, for instance – the Globe is unique in its active celebration and recreation of the works. That said, it is unclear just how different performing plays to a tourist audience is from a theme park experience presenting live, animatronic and architecturally embodied versions of novels.
8 See S. Homan, *Access All Eras: Tribute Bands and Global Pop Culture*, Maidenhead: Open University Press, 2006.
9 A. Moore, 'Authenticity as authentification', *Popular Music*, 21(2) (2002), 209–23.
10 That said, original artists have done this repeatedly over the past 20 years, as might be demonstrated by Madonna's self-conscious invocation of Marilyn Monroe in *Diamonds are a Girl's Best Friend* for the 1985 *Material Girl* video.
11 www.completebeatles.com/ (accessed 2 October 2007).
12 www.zepagain.com/jimmy_page1.html (accessed 1 October 2007); www.intothebleach.co.uk/quotes.html# (accessed 1 October 2007).
13 The hit was 'I'd like to teach the world to sing', a New Seekers' song that in a 1994 lawsuit Oasis were themselves judged to have plagiarised for their song 'Shakermaker'.
14 A similar phenomenon is the live replaying in its entirety of a seminal album by a band, including Love's *Forever Changes*, the Zombies' *Odyssey & Oracle* and Brian Wilson's *Smile*.
15 The film *Be Kind Rewind*, 2008, Michael Gondry, similarly centres on the re-enacting of classic films in a DIY style.
16 www.yokesandchains.com/ (accessed 1 October 2007).
17 www.iainandjane.com/work/index.shtml (accessed 1 October 2007).
18 www.shaze.info/sla.html (accessed 1 October 2007).
19 www.sensesofcinema.com/contents/02/21/karmakar.html (accessed 1 October 2007).
20 www.wacoreenactment.org; www.milgramreenactment.org (accessed 1 October 2007).
21 H. Sumpter, 'Back to the future', *Time Out*, 14–20 March 2007, pp. 26–8 (p. 28).
22 K. Kitamura, 'Re-creating chaos: Jeremy Deller's *The Battle of Orgreave*', available at www.anu.edu.au/hrc/research_platforms/Re-Enactment/Papers/kitamura_katie.pdf (accessed 16 October 2007).
23 L. Buck, 'Leaving Los Angeles', *Art Forum*, 2002, www.findarticles.com/p/articles/mi_m0268/is_5_40/ai_82469489/pg_1 (accessed 28 September 2007).
24 'Postmodernism and consumer culture', in J. Belton (ed.) *Movies and Mass Culture*, London: Athlone Press, 1996, pp. 185–202 (p. 188).
25 Email to author, 11 October 2006.
26 Email to author, 12 December 2004.

27 www.darkplaces.co.uk (accessed 5 May 2006).

28 www.abandoned-britain.com/about1.htm (accessed 5 May 2006).

29 http://www.abandonedpast.co.uk/index.cfm?sid=6605&pid=101184 (accessed 5 May 2006).

30 'Nicholas Royle: interview', www.bookmunch.co.uk/view.php?id=1394 (accessed 5 May 2006).

9 History games

1 See B. Rejack, 'Toward a virtual re-enactment of history: video games and the recreation of the past', *Rethinking History*, 11(3) (2007), 411–25.

2 *Medal of Honor* is more 'authentic' than the German government is happy with due to the reproduction of swastikas in the gaming landscape. In Germany, the swastika is only allowed to be reproduced in historical materials; this led to the game being placed on the index of youth-endangering media in 2000.

3 B. Atkins, *More than a Game*, Manchester: Manchester University Press, 2003, p. 93.

4 For the debate on narrative, ergodic and ludic interpretations of such games, see G. Frasca, 'Simulation versus narrative: introduction to ludology', in M.J.P Wolfe and B. Perron (eds) *The Video Game Theory Reader*, London: Routledge, 2003, pp. 221–37, and J. Newman, 'The myth of the ergodic videogame: some thoughts on player-character relationships in videogames', *Game Studies*, 2(1) (2002), www.gamestudies.org/0102/newman.

5 *Medal of Honor: Rising Sun* Instruction manual, Redwood City, CA: EA Games, 2003, p. 9.

6 www.callofduty.com (accessed 5 May 2005).

7 Ibid.

8 Ibid.

9 Ibid.

10 www.eagames.com/official/battlefield/1942/us/home.jsp

11 www.brothersinarmsgame.com/uk/features.php (accessed 5 May 2005).

12 Indeed, Sony applied to copyright the phrase 'Shock and Awe' on the day the United States invaded Iraq, and the application was subsequently withdrawn.

13 www.conflict.com/conflictDesertStorm2/default.htm (accessed 5 May 2005).

14 A.R. Galloway, 'Social realism in gaming', *Game Studies*, 4(1) (2004), at www.gamestudies.org/0401/galloway/

15 U. Schultze and J. Rennecker provide a useful overview, *Reframing Online Games*, Boston: Sprinter, 2007. See also the essays in H. Corneliussen and J. Walker Rettberg (eds) *Digital Culture, Play and Identity: A World of Warcraft Reader*, Boston: MIT Press, 2008.

16 C. R. Ondrejka, 'Aviators, moguls, fashionistas and barons: economics and ownership in Second Life', available at *Social Science Research Network*, www.ssrn.com/abstract=614663.

17 Websites such as IGE and Gaming Open Market have traded Linden$ from *Second Life* and currencies from other virtual worlds since 2003, and both trade thousands of dollars per month. See H. Yamaguchi, 'An analysis of virtual currencies in online games', 2004, available at *Social Science Research Network*, www.ssrn.com/abstract=544422 and T. Malaby, 'Parlaying value: capital in and beyond virtual worlds', *Games and Culture*, 1(2) (2006), 141–62.

18 'Constructions and reconstructions of self in virtual reality: playing in the MUDs', www. web.mit.edu/sturkle/www/constructions.html (accessed 7 September 2007).

19 These role-playing games differ in orientation and form from MMOFPS like *World War II Online* which is a battlefield simulation with first-person interface akin to *Medal of Honor*, although with simulated experience-led development such as the gaining of higher rank.

20 www.roma-victor.com/sotw/ (accessed 29 August 2007).

21 G. Fine highlights the importance of community in creating, sharing, enjoying and developing game scenarios in *Shared Fantasy: Role Playing Games as Social Worlds*, Chicago: University of Chicago Press, 1983.

22 See S. Turkle, *Life on the Screen: Identity in the Age of the Internet*, New York: Simon and Schuster, 1995.

23 T.L. Taylor, 'Multiple pleasures: women and online gaming', *Convergence*, 9(1) (2003), pp. 21–46.

24 This is not my joke, it is Kenneth Chen's, 'Civilisation and its disk contents: two essays on civilisation and *Civilisation*', *Radical Society*, 30(2) (2003), 95–107.

25 *Civilization* is turn-based, where the player interacts with other users in a structured way; *Age of Empires* is in real-time, in which everything is in play simultaneously.

26 The positivism of the games has been criticised by M. Kapell, 'Civilization and its discontents: American monomythic structure as historical simulacrum', *Popular Culture Review*, 13(2) (2002), 129–36.

27 Kevin Schut, 'Strategic simulations and our past: the bias of computer games in the presentation of history', *Games and Culture*, 2 (2007), 213–35 (pp. 213, 222).

28 The game's straightforward and ideological concept of culture has been criticised, see discussion in Chen, '*Civilisation* and its disk contents'.

29 N. Ferguson, 'How to win a war', 16 October 2006, *New York Magazine*, www.nymag.com/news/features/22787/ (accessed 7 September 2007).

30 T. Friedman, '*Civilization* and its discontents: simulation, subjectivity and space', in G. M. Smith (ed.) *On a Silver Platter: CD-ROMs and the Promises of a New Technology*, New York: New York University Press, 1999, pp. 132–50.

31 Ferguson, 'How to win a war'.

32 *Everything Bad is Good for You*, London: Penguin, 2005, p. 62.

33 www.microsoft.com/games/empires/behind_bruce.htm (accessed 29 August 2007).

34 Ibid.

35 www.firaxis.com/community/teachers-spk.php (accessed 29 August 2007) and see also www.insidehighered.com/news/2005/11/28/civ (accessed 29 August 2007), K. Squire and H. Jenkins, 'Harnessing the power of games in education', *Insight*, 3 (2003), 5–33, and W. Wright, 'Dream machines', *Wired*, 14(4) (2006), 110–12.

36 *Little Wars* at www.gutenberg.org/dirs/etext03/ltwrs11.txt (accessed 7 September 2007).

37 Some 1,300 people compete in the Boardgame Players Association World Boardgaming Championships every year, for instance.

38 *We the People* card game Rules of Play, Avalon Hill, 1993, 1.0.

39 See B. Whitehill, 'American games: a historical perspective', *Journal of Board Game Studies*, 2 available at www.boardgamestudies.info/studies/issue2/contents.shtml (accessed 6 December 2007).

40 P. Shaw, 'Abjection sustained: Goya, the Chapman Brothers, and the *Disasters of War*', *Art History*, 26(4) (2003), 479–504 (p. 490).

Part IV History on television

1 See A. Hill, *Restyling Factual TV*, London: Routledge, 2007.

2 J. Corner, 'Backward looks: mediating the past', p. 470.

3 J. Dovey, *Freakshow: First Person Media and Factual Television*, London: Pluto Press, 2000, p. 11.

4 *Reality TV: Audiences and Popular Factual Television*, London: Routledge, 2005, p. 24. Hill argues that the audience itself is sceptical of authority and therefore open to such evolution.

5 S. Schama, 'Television and the trouble with history', in David Cannadine (ed.) *History and the Media*, Basingstoke: Palgrave Macmillan, 2004, pp. 20–34 (p. 28).

6 M. Andrejevic, *Reality TV: The Work of Being Watched*, Oxford: Rowman and Littlefield, 2004, p. 13 the second phrase is Andrejevic quoting Howard Rheingold.

7 Ibid, p. 13.

8 Ibid, p. 13.

10 Contemporary historical documentary

1 J. Ellis, 'Documentary and truth on television: the crisis of 1999', in A. Rosenthal and J. Corner (eds) *New Challenges for Documentary*, Manchester: Manchester University Press, 2005, pp. 342–59 (p. 342).

2 See M. Renov, 'The truth about non-fiction', in M. Renov (ed.) *Theorizing Documentary*, London: Routledge, 1993, pp. 1–12, and B. Nichols, 'The voice of documentary', in Rosenthal and Corner, *New Challenges for Documentary*, pp. 17–34.

3 *An Introduction to Television Documentary*, Manchester: Manchester University Press, 1997, p. 4.

4 Ibid., p. 12.

5 B. Nichols, *Blurred Boundaries: Questions of Meaning in Contemporary Culture*, Bloomington, IN: Indiana University Press, 1994, p. 118.

6 T. Elsaesser, 'Subject positions, speaking positions: from *Holocaust*, *Our Hitler* and *Heimat* to *Shoah* and *Schindler's List*', in V. Sobchack (ed.), *The Persistence of History*, London: Routledge, 1996, pp. 145–86 (p. 178).

7 Paul Smith (ed.) *The Historian and Film*, Cambridge: Cambridge University Press, 1976.

8 'The colour of war: a poacher among the gamekeepers?', in G. Roberts and P. M. Taylor, *The Historian, Television and Television History*, Luton: University of Luton Press, 2001, pp. 45–53.

9 S. Badsey, '*Blackadder Goes Forth* and the "Two western fronts" debate', in Roberts and Taylor, *The Historian*, pp. 113–25.

10 Stearn, 'What's wrong with television history?', p. 26.

11 I. Kershaw, 'The past on the box: strengths and weaknesses', in D. Cannadine (ed.), *History and the Media*, Basingstoke: Macmillan, 2004, pp. 118–24 (p. 121).

12 J. Kuehl, 'History on the public screen II', in Smith, *The Historian and Film*, pp. 177–85 (pp. 178–9).

13 'All our yesterdays', in Cannadine, *History and the Media*, pp. 34–50 (p. 35).

14 'Against the ivory tower: an apologia for "popular" historical documentaries', in Rosenthal and Corner, *New Challenges for Documentary*, pp. 409–19 (p. 411).

15 'What is history? – now?' in D. Cannadine, *What is History Now?*, Basingstoke: Palgrave Macmillan, 2002, pp. 1–19 (p. 15).

16 Ibid., p. 16.

17 'Tempus fugit' interview, in *A History of Britain* DVD box set, 2002, disc 6, no credits.

18 T. Hunt, 'How does television enhance history?' in Cannadine, *History and the Media*, pp. 88–103 (p. 95).

19 Ibid., p. 96.

20 T. Downing, 'Bringing the past to the small screen', in ibid., pp. 7–20 (pp. 15, 16).

21 Ibid., p. 17.

22 Ibid., p. 17.

23 H. White, *Tropics of Discourse*, Baltimore, MD: Johns Hopkins University Press, 1978.

24 B. Chase, 'History and poststructuralism: Hayden White and Frederic Jameson', in B. Schwarz (ed.) *The Expansion of England*, London: Routledge, 1996, pp. 61–91 (p. 67).

25 K. Jenkins, *Refiguring History*, London: Routledge, 2003, pp. 46, 49.

26 *Everything Bad Is Good for You*.

27 On these series, see E. Hanna, 'A small screen alternative to stone and bronze: *The Great War* series and British television', *European Journal of Cultural Studies*, 10(1) (2007), 89–111.

28 J. Isaacs, 'All our yesterdays', p. 38, N. Frankland, *History at War*, London: Giles de la Mare, 1998, p. 183, and J.A. Ramsden, '*The Great War*: The Making of the Series', *Historical Journal of Film, Radio and Television*, 22(1) (2002), 7–19.

29 J. Chapman, '*The World at War*: television, documentary, history', in Roberts and Taylor, *The Historian*, pp. 127–43.

30 'Tempus fugit'.

31 K. Burk, *Troublemaker: The Life and History of A.J.P. Taylor*, New Haven, CT: Yale University Press, 2000, pp. 388–97.

32 Burk, *Troublemaker*, pp. 394, 395.

33 S. Schama, 'Television and the trouble with history', in Cannadine, *History and the Media*, p. 27.

34 Quoted in J. Champion, 'Seeing the past: Simon Schama's *A History of Britain* and public history', *History Workshop Journal*, 56 (2003), 153–74 (p. 159).

35 *A History of Britain*: Episode 1 *Beginnings*, BBC1, 2000, 30 September, 21:00 hrs.

36 Champion, 'Seeing the past', p. 169.

37 *A History of Britain*: Episode 9 *Revolutions*, BBC1, 2001, 15 May, 21:00 hrs.

38 'Channel 4 Review of 2004' at www.channel4.com/about_c4/spp/c4review_04.doc (accessed 10 July 2005).

39 *Elizabeth*: Episode 1, Channel 4, 2000, 4 May, 21:00 hrs.

40 Figures from the Broadcasters' Audience Research Board (BARB) available at www.barb.co.uk (accessed 10 July 2005). Even when repeated on BBC2 from 9–10am in December 2004–January 2005, the programme held up well, with 400–700,000 viewers, www.viewingfigures.com (accessed 10 July 2005). This is around the entire daily audience for the UKTV History Channel.

41 Figures for week ending 26/06/05 from BARB. These figures are near enough exactly the same as those for both 2004 and 2003, demonstrating a constant market: the History Channel 0.2 per cent in 2003, 0.2 per cent in 2004; UKTV History 0.3 per cent in 2003, 0.4 per cent in 2004.

42 Such comparative study is rare but useful, see, for instance, A. Dhoest, 'Identifying with the nation: viewer memories of Flemish TV fiction', and S. de Leeuw, 'Dutch documentary film as a site of memory: changing perspectives in the 1990s', *European Journal of Cultural Studies*, 10(1) (2007), 55–73, 75–87.

43 I. Veyrat-Masson, 'French television looks at the past', in Roberts and Taylor, *The Historian*, pp. 157–60, and *Quand la télévision explore le temps: L'histoire au petit écran 1953–2000*, Paris: Fayard, 2000.

44 Veyrat-Masson, 'French television looks at the past', p. 157.

45 Ibid., p. 159.

46 H. Dauncey, 'French Reality TV: more than just a matter of taste?', *European Journal of Communication*, 11(1) (1996), 83–106.

47 *The Holocaust in American Film*, Philadelphia, PA: Jewish Publication Society, 1987, p. 193. Episodes of the programme were seen by between 32 and 41 per cent of the available audience, J. Kuehl, 'Truth claims', in A. Rosenthal (ed.) *New Challenges for Documentary*, Los Angeles: University of California Press, 1988, pp. 103–10.

48 *The Holocaust in American Film*, pp. 192–3.

49 T. Ebbrecht, 'Docudramatizing history on TV: German and British docudrama and historical event television in the memorial year 2005', *European Journal of Cultural Studies*, 10(1) (2007), 35–53 (p. 49).

50 Ibid., p. 50.

51 D. Harlan, 'Ken Burns and the coming crisis of academic history', *Rethinking History*, 7 (2) (2003), 169–92 (p. 169).

52 *The American Civil War* (DVD), 2002, viewing notes in accompanying booklet, p. 7.

53 G. Edgerton, *Ken Burns's America*, Basingstoke: Palgrave, 2001.

54 See S.F. Wise and D.J. Bercuson (eds) *The Valour and the Horror Revisited*, Montreal and Kingston: McGill-Queen's University Press, 1994, for a discussion by historians of the original source materials and the ensuing controversy.

55 Despite this, the series has not been rebroadcast, www.waramps.ca/news/valour/96-04-03.html (accessed 15 November 2007).

11 Reality History

 1 J. Corner, 'Performing the real', *Television and New Media*, 3(3) (2002), 255–70 (p. 263). See also L.H. Edwards, 'Chasing the real: reality television and documentary forms',

in G. Rhodes and J. Parris Springer, *Docufictions*, Jefferson, NC: MacFarland and Co., 2005, pp. 253–70, and J. Corner's 'Archive aesthetics and the historical imaginary: *Wisconsin Death Trip*', *Screen*, 47(3) (2006), 291–306.

2 A. Biressi and H. Nunn, *Reality TV: Realism and Revelation*, London and New York: Wallflower Press, 2005, p. 2.

3 B. Nichols, *Blurred Boundaries*, Bloomington, IN: Indiana University Press, 1994, p. 47.

4 L. Williams, 'Mirrors without memories: truth, history, and the new documentary', in A. Rosenthal and J. Corner (eds), *New Challenges for Documentary*, Manchester: Manchester University Press, 2005, pp. 59–75 (p. 60).

5 Corner, 'Performing the real', p. 267.

6 Ibid., pp. 265, 263.

7 www.advanced-television.com/2002/sep16_23.html (accessed 16 May 2006).

8 'The voice of documentary', in Rosenthal and Corner, *New Challenges for Documentary*, p. 28.

9 The special edition of *Film & History*, 37(1) (2007) begins to redress this, with useful articles on the British, American and Australian Reality History shows.

10 One practitioner who cleaves to the new possibilities of the format is T. Hunt, see 'Reality, identity and empathy', which argues that the models of empathy and ordinary involvement in history that the programmes offer are an important development of the historiography of social history.

11 J. Dovey, *Freakshow: First Person Media and Factual Television*, London: Pluto Press, 2000, p. 7.

12 Ibid., p. 86.

13 M. Andrejevic, *Reality TV: The Work of Being Watched*, Oxford: Rowman and Littlefield, 2004, p. 2.

14 Ibid., p. 13.

15 Biressi and Nunn, *Reality TV*, p. 2.

16 E. Tincknell and P. Raghuram, '*Big Brother*: reconfiguring the "active" audience of cultural studies?' in S. Holmes and D. Jermyn (eds) *Understanding Reality Television*, London: Routledge, 2004, pp. 252–70 (p. 264).

17 G. Palmer, '*Big Brother*: an experiment in governance', *Television and New Media*, 3(3) (2002), 295–310 (p. 297).

18 J. Lewis, 'The meaning of real life' in L. Oullette and S. Murray (eds) *Reality TV: Remaking Television Culture*, New York: New York University Press, 2004, pp. 288–302 (pp. 290, 294).

19 R. Kilborn, *Staging the Real*, Vancouver: University of British Columbia Press, 2003, p. 15.

20 Schama, 'Television and the trouble with history', in D. Cannadine, *History and the Media*, Basingstoke: Macmillan, 2004, p. 9.

21 Ibid.

22 www.endemoluk.com/news/display.jsp?dyn=newsarticle.20031007134350 (accessed 4 February 2008).

23 www.bbc.co.uk/dna/ww2/A2584208 (accessed 4 February 2008).

24 www.bbc.co.uk/history/programmes/trench/chat_230302.shtml (accessed 4 February 2008).

25 www.bbc.co.uk/history/programmes/archive.shtml (accessed 5 February 2008).

26 S. Waisbord, 'McTV: understanding the global popularity of TV formats', *Television and New Media*, 5(4) (2004), 359–83 (p. 360). Some countries have resisted, see, for instance, H. Dauncey, 'French Reality TV: more than just a matter of taste?', *European Journal of Communication*, 11(1) (1996), 83–106.

27 L.H. Edwards discusses this perpetuating of myth, 'The endless end of frontier mythology: PBS's *Frontier House* 2002', *Film & Television*, 37(1) (2007), 29–34.

28 www.abc.net.au/tv/outbackhouse (accessed 17 August 2006). See the discussion of Australian history in M. Arrow, '"That history should not have ever been how it was": *The Colony*, *Outback House*, and Australian history', *Film & History*, 37(1) (2007), 54–66.

29 www.historytelevision.ca/ontv/titledetails.aspx?titleid=22029 (accessed 17 August 2006).

30 www.pbs.org/wnet/colonialhouse/meet/meet_tuminaro_craig.html (accessed 18 August 2006).
31 www.pbs.org/wnet/colonialhouse/meet/meet_tisdale_danny.html (accessed 18 August 2006).
32 http://www.abc.net.au/tv/outbackhouse/txt/s1376105.htm (accessed 18 August, 2006). See V. Agnew, 'History's affective turn: historical re-enactment and its work in the present', *Rethinking History*, 11(3) (2007), 299–312.
33 *RealityTV*, p. 14.
34 www.smh.com.au/news/TV – Radio/Settlers-life-unsettles-ABC-viewers/2005/06/14/1118645809421.html (accessed 17 August 2006).
35 J. Gardiner, 'The Edwardian Country House', *History Today*, 52(7) (2002), 18–21 (p. 21).
36 A. Scharz, '"Not this year!" re-enacting contested pasts aboard *The Ship*', *Rethinking History*, 11(3) (2007), 427–46.
37 See J. Finkelstein, *The Art of Self Invention: Image, Identity and the Makeover in Popular Visual Culture*, London: IB Tauris, 2007.
38 *The Trench Episode 1*, BBC2, 2002, 15 March, 21:00 hrs.
39 Gardiner, 'The Edwardian Country House', p. 21.
40 *Reality TV*, p. 2.
41 *The Trench Episode 1*, BBC2, 2002, 15 March, 21:00 hrs.
42 For a discussion of the legitimacy of the witness, see G. Carr, 'Rules of engagement: public history and the drama of legitimation', *The Canadian Historical Review*, 86(2) (2005), 317–54.
43 For a full discussion of audience concepts of 'authenticity' and acting up in Reality programmes see Hill, *Reality TV*, pp. 57–79.
44 See the discussion of Reality history and ideology in J. Bignell, *Big Brother: Reality TV in the Twenty-first Century*, Basingstoke: Palgrave Macmillan, 2005, pp. 80–85
45 *The 1940s House*: Episode 1, Channel 4, 2002, 2 January, 20:30 hrs.
46 Ibid.
47 www.pbs.org/wnet/colonialhouse/about_rules.html (accessed 18 August 2006).
48 Later shows such as *Frontier House* eschewed such a set of historical rules for more contemporary, game-show type regulations, see www.pbs.org/wnet/frontierhouse/project/rules.html.
49 *The 1940s House*: Episode 1, Channel 4, 2002, 2 January, 20:30 hrs.
50 D. Scott Diffrient discusses this privation in 'History as mystery and beauty as duty in the *1940s House* 1999', *Film & Television*, 37(1) (2007), 43–53.
51 *The 1940s House*: Episode 1, Channel 4, 2002, 2 January, 20:30 hrs.
52 J. Gardiner, *The 1940s House*, London: Channel 4 Books/Macmillan, 2000, p. 40.
53 *The 1940s House*: Episode 1, Channel 4, 2002, 2 January, 20:30 hrs.
54 *The 1940s House:* Episode 3, Channel 4, 2002, 11 January, 21:00 hrs.
55 Biressi and Nunn, *Reality TV*, p. 99.
56 Ibid., p. 107.
57 www.pbs.org/wnet/colonialhouse/meet/meet_samuels_clare.html (accessed 18 August 2006).
58 *The 1940s House*: Episode 1, Channel 4, 2002, 2 January, 20:30 hrs.
59 *The 1940s House*: Episode 5, Channel 4, 2002, 25 January, 21:00 hrs.
60 Similarly, *Pioneer Quest* was followed by *Pioneer Quest: Survivors of the Real West*, Telefilm CA, 2002.
61 *The 1940s House*: Episode 5, Channel 4, 2002, 25 January, 21:00 hrs.
62 'Es ist, als ob ich jetzt immer einen Zusatztank in mir hätte, der bis zum Rand mit Energie gefüllt ist, und aus dem ich Kraft tanken kann, wann immer es nötig ist', www.swr.de/schwarzwaldhaus1902/familie/reya.html (accessed 17 August 2006).
63 *Outback House*: Episode 2, Sky 3, 2007, 29 March, 19:00 hrs.
64 '*The Trench*: live chat', available at www.bbc.co.uk/history/3d/trench.shtml (accessed 5 May 2005).

65 Ibid.
66 Ibid.
67 Ibid.
68 Chris Wilson, 'Two weeks in the trench', available at www.bbc.co.uk/history/program mes/trench/volunteers_chris_wilson.shtml (accessed 10 July 2005).
69 *The Edwardian Country House*: Episode 6, Channel 4, 2002, 28 May, 21:00 hrs.
70 *The Edwardian Country House*: Episode 5, Channel 4, 2002, 21 May, 21:00 hrs.
71 *The Edwardian Country House*: Episode 3, Channel 4, 2002, 7 May, 21:00 hrs.
72 *The Edwardian Country House*: Episode 6, Channel 4, 2002, 28 May, 21:00 hrs.
73 *The Edwardian Country House*: Episode 3, Channel 4, 2002, 7 May, 21:00 hrs.
74 Ibid.
75 Ibid.
76 *Outback House*: Episode 2, Sky 3, 2007, 29 March, 19:00 hrs.
77 See M. Rymsza-Pawlowska, '*Frontier House*: Reality television and the historical experience', *Film & History*, 37(1) (2007), 35–42.
78 Gardiner, 'The Edwardian Country House', p. 21.

Part V The 'historical' as cultural genre

1 Jordanova in V. Sobchack (ed.), *History in Practice*, London: Arnold, 2000, p. 166.
2 See N. Perry's chapter on *The Singing Detective* 1986 and its 'refusal of a visually and musically accomplished integration' which allows for both nostalgic recognition and subversion in *Hyperreality and Global Culture*, London: Routledge, 1998, pp. 24–35 (p. 34).
3 C. Rojek, 'After popular culture: hyperreality and leisure', *Leisure Studies*, 12(4) (1993), 277–89.
4 In F. Jameson, *The Historical Novel*, trans. Hannah and Stanley Mitchell, London: Merlin, 1962, p. 63.
5 J. Ellis, 'Documentary and truth on television: the crisis of 1999', in A. Rosenthal and J. Corner (eds), *New Challenges for Documentary*, Manchester: Manchester Univesity Press, 2005, pp. 342–59 (p. 353).
6 Ibid.
7 D. Paget, *No Other Way to Tell It: Dramadoc/Docudrama on Television*, Manchester: Manchester University Press, 1998, p. 126.

12 Historical television

1 E. Seiter, *Television and New Media Audiences*, Oxford: Clarendon Press, 2002, p. 4.
2 C. Monk, 'The heritage-film debate revisited', in C. Monk and A. Sargeant (eds) *British Historical Cinema*, London: Routledge, 2002, pp. 176–98 (pp. 177, 178).
3 See, for instance, E. Braun, '"What truth is there in this story?": the dramatisation of Northern Ireland', in J. Bignell, S. Lacey and M. Macmurraugh-Kavanagh (eds), *British Television Drama*, Basingstoke: Palgrave, 2000, pp. 110–21 (p. 111).
4 See S. Cardwell, *Adaptation Revisited*, Manchester: Manchester University Press, 2002, for an applied discussion of this concept.
5 L. Cooke, *British Television Drama: A History*, London: BFI, 2003, p. 166.
6 *Television Drama: Realism, Modernism, and British Culture*, Oxford: Oxford University Press, 2000, pp. 208–9.
7 D. Kompare, 'Publishing flow: dvd box sets and the reconception of television', *Television & New Media*, 7(4) (2006), 335–60.
8 J. Caughie, *Television Drama*, Oxford: Oxford University Press, 2000, p. 208.
9 See A. Home, *Into the Box of Delights: A History of Children's Television*, London: BBC Books, 1993.
10 For instance, 2002's *The Forsyte Saga* was an attempt at wrestling the 'quality' drama from the BBC, see I. Kleinecke, 'Representations of the Victorian Age: interior space

and the detail of domestic life in two adaptations of Galsworthy's *The Forsyte Saga*', *Screen*, 47(2) (2006), 139–63 (pp. 149–50).

11 C. Brunsdon, 'Problems with quality', *Screen*, 31(1) (1990), 67–90 (p. 86).

12 The exceptions to this are *Pride and Prejudice* which has been updated into *Bridget Jones's Diary*, 2001, Sharon Maguire, and *Emma* which is the basis for *Clueless*, 1995, Amy Heckerling; both films use the Austen novels as broad narrative frameworks rather than overtly refer to them. Andrew Davies, costume drama TV script writer, wrote the screenplay for *Bridget Jones's Diary*.

13 Cardwell, *Adaptation Revisited*, p. 114.

14 Ibid.

15 R. Nelson, 'They do "like it up 'em": *Dad's Army* and myths of Old England', in J. Bignell and S. Lacey (eds) *Popular Television Drama*, Manchester: Manchester University Press, 2005, pp. 51–68 (pp. 54–5).

16 S. Cardwell, *Andrew Davies*, Manchester: Manchester University Press, 2004.

17 *Middlemarch* (1994), [DVD], Episode 1.

18 "Beholding in a magic panorama": television and the illustration of *Middlemarch*', in E. Sheen and R. Giddings (eds) *The Classic Novel: From Page to Screen*, Manchester: Manchester University Press, 2000, pp. 71–92 (p. 74).

19 *Middlemarch* (1994), [DVD], Episode 1.

20 *Middlemarch* (1994), [DVD], Episode 6.

21 *Middlemarch* (1994), [DVD], Episode 1.

22 *Middlemarch* (1994), [DVD], Episode 6.

23 On this, see E. Sheen, '"Where the garment gapes": faithfulness and promiscuity in the 1995 *Pride and Prejudice*', in Sheen and Giddings, *The Classic Novel*, pp. 14–30 and Cardwell, *Adaptation Revisited*, pp. 133–59.

24 See G. Preston, '*Sense and Sensibility*: Ang Lee's sensitive screen interpretation of Jane Austen', and K. Bowles, 'Commodifying Austen: the Janeite culture of the Internet and commercialization through product and television series spinoffs', in G. MacDonald and A. MacDonald (eds) *Jane Austen on Screen*, Cambridge: Cambridge University Press, 2003, pp. 12–15 and 15–22.

25 M. Crang, 'Placing Jane Austen, displacing England: touring between book, history and nation', in S. Pucci and J. Thompson (eds) *Jane Austen and Co.: Remaking the Past in Contemporary Culture*, New York: State University of New York Press, 2003, pp. 111–32, and A. Higson, 'English heritage, English literature, English film: selling Jane Austen to movie audiences in the 1990s', in E. Voigts-Virchow (ed.) *Janespotting and Beyond: British Heritage Retrovisions since the Mid-1990s*, Stuttgart: Gunter Narr Verlag, 2004, pp. 35–51.

26 S. Fraiman, 'Jane Austen and Edward Said: gender, culture, and imperialism', *Critical Inquiry*, 21(4) (1995), 805–21.

27 C.M. Dole, 'Austen, class, and the American market', and A. Collins, 'Jane Austen, film, and the pitfalls of postmodern nostalgia', in L. Troost and S. Greenfield (eds) *Jane Austen in Hollywood*, Kentucky: University Press of Kentucky, 1998, pp. 58–78 and pp. 79–89.

28 L. Troost and S. Greenfield, 'The mouse that roared: Patricia Rozema's *Mansfield Park*', in ibid., pp. 188–204.

29 H. Margolis, 'Janeite culture: what does the name "Jane Austen" authorize?', in MacDonald and Macdonald, *Jane Austen on Screen*, pp. 22–43 p. 28.

30 See L. Hopkins, 'Mr. Darcy's Body: Privileging the Female Gaze' in Troost and Greenfield, *Jane Austen in Hollywood*, pp. 111–21.

31 A later BBC series, 'The Century That Made Us', attempted to revise perceptions with programmes on the Scottish Enlightenment and Culloden yet there were still docudramas on Beau Brummell and shows considering the Harlot's Handbook.

32 See J. Pidduck, 'Of windows and country walks: frames of space and movement in 1990s Austen adaptations', *Screen*, 39(4) (1998), 381–400.

33 H. Wheatley, 'Haunted houses, hidden rooms: women, domesticity and the female Gothic adaptation on television', in Bignell and Lacey, *Popular Television Drama*, pp. 149–65.

34 2007's *Oliver Twist* followed the same half-hour pattern but was broadcast on five subsequent evenings, further emphasising the soap-like quality of the programme.

35 The classic works on this are S.M. Gilbert and S. Gubar, *The Madwoman in the Attic: The Woman Writer and the Nineteenth-Century Literary Imagination*, New Haven, CT: Yale University Press, 1979, and Gayatri Chakravorty Spivak, 'Three women's texts and a critique of imperialism', *Critical Inquiry*, 12(1) (1985), 243–61.

36 There are precedents – John Fowles' *The French Lieutenant's Woman* was filmed in the 1980s, and the historical novel as a genre has often provided material for television and film. The difference here is the self-consciousness of the original novel and its presentation within the discourse of the 'classic serial'. The BBC continued in this vein with its production of Phillip Pullman's piece of sensationalist Victoriana *The Ruby in the Smoke* in 2006.

37 *Tipping the Velvet* was followed in 2005 by an adaptation of Waters' novel *Fingersmith* with similar production values and marketing.

38 *Tipping the Velvet* (2002) [DVD], Episode 1.

39 The Broadcasting Standards Authority rejected 35 complaints about the series, news. bbc.co.uk/1/hi/entertainment/tv_and_radio/2712133.stm (accessed 2 July 2007).

40 P. Swaab, 'The Line of Beauty', *Film Quarterly*, 60(3) (2007), 10–15.

41 It is certainly a costume drama, due to its being adapted rather than a dramatic meditation on the recent past such as Alan Bleasdale's *GBH*, Channel 4, 1991, and Peter Flannery's *Our Friends in the North*, BBC1, 1996.

42 P. Wright, *On Living in an Old Country*, London: Verso, 1986, p. 42.

43 Ibid., p. 47.

44 A. Hollinghurst, *The Line of Beauty*, London: Picador, 2005, p. 214.

45 Ibid., p. 140.

46 Wright, *On Living in an Old Country*, pp. 33–8; R. Hewison, *The Heritage Industry*, London: Methuen, 1987, p. 52.

47 This authenticity is as important as that for the country house series; where they have 'making-of' tie-in books, so does Sharpe: M. Adkin, *The Sharpe Companion*, London: HarperCollins, 2000.

48 *Sharpe's Rifles*, ITV, 1993, 5 May, 19:00 hrs.

49 In *Sharpe's Rifles* and *Hornblower: Mutiny* (2001) [DVD] and *Loyalty* (2003) [DVD].

50 *Sharpe's Rifles*, ITV, 1993, 5 May, 19:00 hrs.

51 Cooke, *British Television Drama*, p. 163.

52 T. Mordue, '*Heartbeat* country: conflicting values, coinciding visions', *Environment and Planning*, 31(4) (1999), 629–46.

53 R. Nelson, *TV Drama in Transition*, Basingstoke: Macmillan, 1997, pp. 75–78.

54 A. Higson, *Waving the Flag: Constructing a National Cinema in Britain*, Oxford: Clarendon Press, 1995, p. 47.

55 www.hbo.com/rome/watch/season2/episode22.html (accessed 17 August 2007).

56 Ibid.

57 The series was 'authentic' to the point of being filmed at Cinecitta in Rome; the producers emphasised how important it was to cast Roman extras, and how the Italian 'light' impacted upon the look of the series.

58 www.hbo.com/deadwood/ (accessed 10 September 2007).

59 D. Lavery, '*Deadwood*, David Milch, and television creativity', in D. Lavery (ed.) *Reading Deadwood: A Western to Swear By*, London: IB Tauris, 2006, pp. 1–11 (p. 3).

60 H. Havrilesky, 'The man behind *Deadwood*', 5 March 2005, www.dir.salon.com/story/ent/feature/2005/03/05/milch/index.html?pn=2 (accessed 22 August 2007).

61 See the essays in D. Lavery (ed.) *This Thing of Ours: Investigating the Sopranos*, New York: Columbia University Press, 2002.

62 www.channel4.com/history/microsites/C/city-of-vice/producer_interviews_extended.html (accessed 23 January 2008).

63 *The Last Days of Newgate*, London: Weidenfeld and Nicolson, 2006.

64 www.channel4.com/history/microsites/C/city-of-vice/producer_interviews.html (accessed 23 January 2008).

65 www.imdb.com/title/tt0086659/quotes (accessed 12 September 2007).

66 Ibid.

67 J. Butler, *Gender Trouble*, London: Routledge, 1990, p. 137.

68 See S. Badsey, 'The Great War since The Great War', *Historical Journal of Film, Radio and Television*, 22(1) (2002), 37–45.

69 Badsey, '*Blackadder Goes Forth* and the "Two western fronts" debate', in G. Roberts and P.M. Taylor, *The Historian, Television and Television History*, Luton: University of Luton Press, 2001.

70 See, for instance, M. Dobson and N.J. Watson, *England's Elizabeth: An Afterlife in Fame and Fantasy*, Oxford: Oxford University Press, 2002, and S. Doran and T.S. Freeman (eds) *The Myth of Elizabeth*, Basingstoke and New York: Palgrave Macmillan, 2003.

71 On the ethics of time travel in television drama, see K. McKinney Wiggins, 'Epic heroes, ethical issues, and time paradoxes in *Quantum Leap*', *Journal of Popular Film and Television*, 21(3) (1993), 111–20.

72 *Life on Mars*, Episode 3, BBC1, 2006, 23 January, 21:00 hrs; Episode 5, BBC1, 2006, 6 February, 21:00 hrs. Similarly the sequel *Ashes to Ashes* explores the devastation of community by economic development, *Ashes to Ashes*: Episode 3, BBC1, 2008, 21 February, 21:00 hrs.

73 'Mars drama could spark bullying', 12 April 2007, www.news.bbc.co.uk/1/hi/entertainment/6549163.stm (accessed 11 September 2007).

74 R. King, 'Life on Mars writers on another planet', *Manchester Evening News*, 21 February 2006, p. 15.

75 *Ashes to Ashes*, Episode 1, BBC1, 2008, 7 February, 21:00 hrs.

76 *Ashes to Ashes*, Episode 2, BBC1, 2008, 14 February, 21:00 hrs.

77 Ibid.

78 *Ashes to Ashes*, Episode 3, BBC1, 2008, 21 February, 21:00 hrs.

79 This is reflected by the use of David Bowie's 1980 'Ashes to Ashes' song and iconic video as an intertext. The song is itself an extremely self-conscious and weary reflection on the central character of Bowie's 1969 'Space Oddity'. See S. Waldrep, *The Aesthetics of Self-Invention: Oscar Wilde to David Bowie*, Minneapolis: University of Minnesota Press, 2004, p. 124.

13 Historical film

1 I. Vanderschelden, 'Strategies for a "transnational"/French popular cinema', *Modern and Contemporary France*, 15(1) (2007), 36–50.

2 See, for instance, the essays in R. Rosenstone (ed.) *Revisioning History: Film and the Construction of a New Past*, Princeton, NJ: Princeton University Press, 1995; R. Brent Toplin, *History by Hollywood: The Use and Abuse of the American Past*, Urbana, IL: University of Illinois Press, 1996; and Brent Toplin, *Reel History*, Lawrence, KS: University of Kansas Press, 2002; C. Monk and A. Sargeant, *British Historical Cinema*, London: Routledge, 2002; A. Rosenstone, *Visions of the Past*, Cambridge, MA: Harvard University Press, 1995; Andrew Higson, *English Heritage, English Cinema: Costume Drama since 1980*, Oxford: Oxford University Press, 2003.

3 See S. Hake, *German National Cinema*, London: Routledge, 2007.

4 S. Žižek, '*The Dreams of Others*', www.inthesetimes.com/article/3183/the_dreams_of_others/ (accessed 3 January 2008). Žižek argues that the *Ostalgie* of the two films is more desperate in *Goodbye Lenin!*, and that both films sidestep dealing with the true horror of the GDR. Another post-1989 film which idealises Stasi officers is *Die Stille nach dem Schuss/The Legend of Rita* (Volker Schlöndorff 2000), suggesting a necessary romanticising of the traumatic past.

5 Quoted by A. Funder, 'Tyranny of terror', 5 May 2007, www.books.guardian.co.uk/review/story/0,2072454,00.html (accessed 11 February 2008).

6 Yimou was also cinematographer on Kaige's *Huan tu di/Yellow Earth* (1984, based in 1938), and the first 'independent-minded cultural critique of the entire socialist experiment in China', J. Silbergeld, *China into Film*, London: Reaktion Books, 1999, p. 16.

7 *Raise the Red Lantern, Farewell My Concubine* and *Ju Dou* were all banned from distribution in China at least temporarily, Silbergeld, *China into Film*, p. 55.

8 In *Contemporary Spanish Cinema*, Manchester: Manchester University Press, 1998, B. Jordan and R. Morgan-Tamosunas point out the key element of nostalgia and 'recuperating a historical past that had been denied, distorted or suppressed' in Spanish film-making post-1976, p. 11, and see further J. Hopewell, *Out of the Past: Spanish Cinema After Franco*, London: BFI Books, 1986.

9 See S. Hayward, *French National Cinema*, London: Routledge, 2005, particularly pp. 293–332.

10 See P. Powrie, *French Cinema in the 1980s: Nostalgia and the Crisis of Masculinity*, Oxford: Oxford University Press, 1997, pp. 13–28.

11 C. James Grindley, 'Arms and the man: the curious inaccuracy of medieval arms and armor in contemporary film', *Film and History*, 36(1) (2006), 14–19.

12 A. Higson, *Waving the Flag: Constructing a National Cinema in Britain*, Oxford: Clarendon Press, 1995, pp. 26–7. For an excellent analysis and deconstruction of the politics of this heritage debate, see C. Monk, 'The heritage-film debate revisited', in C. Monk and A. Sargeant (eds) *British Historical Cinema*, London: Routledge, 2002, pp. 177, 178.

13 I. Baucom, 'Mournful histories: narratives of postimperial melancholy', *Modern Fiction Studies*, 42(2) (1996), pp. 259–88.

14 Hewison, *The Heritage Industry*, A. Higson, 'Re-presenting the national past: nostalgia and pastiche in the heritage film', in Lester Friedman (ed.) *British Cinema and Thatcherism: Fires Were Started*, Minneapolis: Univesity of Minnesota Press, 1993, pp. 109–29, P. Wright, *On Living in an Old Country*, London: Verso, 1986.

15 A. Higson, 'The heritage film and British cinema', in A. Higson (ed.) *Dissolving Views: Key Views on British Cinema*, London: Cassell, 1996, pp. 232–48 (pp. 232–33).

16 Higson, *Waving the Flag*, pp. 26–7.

17 See R. Samuel, *Theatres of Memory*, London: Verso, 1994, p. 242; P. Wright, *A Journey Through Ruins*, London: Radius, 1992, pp. 45–67 for full argument and also *On Living in an Old Country*.

18 *The Heritage Industry*, p. 51.

19 J. Pidduck, 'Travels with Sally Potter's *Orlando*: gender, narrative, movement', *Screen*, 38(2) (1997), pp. 172–89.

20 J. Hill, *British Cinema in the 1980s*, Oxford: Clarendon Press, 1999.

21 Cardwell, *Adaptation Revisited*, pp. 108–33.

22 On *Maurice*, see T. Waugh, *The Fruit Machine: Twenty Years of Writing on Queer Cinema*, Durham, NC: Duke University Press, 2000, and W. Rohan Quince, '"To thine own self be true … ": adapting E.M. Forster's *Maurice* to the screen', *Literature/Film Quarterly*, 17(2) (1989), 108–12; On *Howard's End*, see Lizzie Franke, '*Howard's End*', *Sight and Sound*, 2(1) (1992), 52–3.

23 Along with *Gandhi*, the TV series of *The Jewel in the Crown*, 1982, and *Heat and Dust*, 1981, David Lean's film has been seen as late, interrogative if nostalgic, blooming of the 'imperial film'.

24 'Of windows and country walks: frames of space and movement in 1990s Austen adaptations', *Screen*, 39(4) (1998), 381–400, see also her *Contemporary Costume Drama*, London: BFI, 2004.

25 See H.K. Bhabha, 'Anxious nations, nervous states', in J. Copjec (ed.) *Supposing the Subject*, London: Verso, 1994, pp. 201–17.

26 The fact that one of their first films together was *Shakespeare Wallah*, 1965, which dramatises cultural conflict deploying literary texts demonstrates this complexity.

27 K. McKechnie, 'Taking liberties with the monarch: the royal bio-pic in the 1990s', in Monk and Sargeant, *British Historical Cinema*, pp. 217–36.

28 See, for instance, M. Dobson and N.J. Watson, *England's Elizabeth: An Afterlife in Fame and Fantasy*, Oxford: Oxford University Press, 2002, and S. Doran and T.S. Freeman (eds) *The Myth of Elizabeth*, Basingstoke and New York: Palgrave Macmillan, 2003, and S. Massai (ed.) *World-wide Shakespeares: Local Appropriations in Film and Performance*, London: Routledge, 2005.

29 This self-conscious costume motif is similarly apparent in the opening shot of *The Madness of King George* which lingers over the King's being dressed for his official opening of Parliament and, indeed, Lear-like, the King's constantly throwing his clothes away is evidence of his irrationality and madness.

30 R. Dudley Edwards, 'Why does Ken Loach loathe his country so much?', 30 May 2006, www.dailymail.co.uk/pages/live/articles/news/news.html?in_article_id=388256&in_page_id=1770&in_a_source=(accessed 1 October 2007).

31 T. Luckhurst, 'Director in a class of his own', *The Times*, 31 May 2006, www.timesonline.co.uk/tol/comment/thunderer/article669926.ece; it is unclear whether the writer of this article had seen the film at the time (accessed 1 October 2007); G. Montbiot, 'If we knew more about Ireland', *The Guardian*, 6 June 2006, www.guardian.co.uk/commentisfree/story/0,1791178,00.html (accessed 1 October 2007).

32 *The Wind that Shakes the Barley*, 2006, Ken Loach.

14 Imagined histories: novels, plays and comics

1 *Enough is Enough; or, the Emergency Government*, London: Picador, 2006, pp. 367–70.

2 Historical popular fiction has always sold well, see H. Hughes, *The Historical Romance*, London: Routledge, 1993, and D. Wallace, *The Women's Historical Novel*, Basingstoke: Palgrave Macmillan, 2004.

3 P. Gregory, 'Born a writer: forged as a historian', *History Workshop Journal*, 59 (2005), 237–42 (p. 242).

4 P. Gregory, *The Other Boleyn Girl*, London: HarperCollins, 2002, p. 359.

5 Ibid., p. 365.

6 Ibid., p. 276.

7 Ibid., p. 525.

8 Ibid., p. 276.

9 P. Gregory, *The Queen's Fool*, London: HarperCollins, 2004, p. 438.

10 Ibid., p. 452.

11 Ibid., p. 488.

12 S. Dunn, *The Queen of Subtleties*, London: HarperPerennial, 2005.

13 K. Hughes, 'Hal's kitchen', *The Guardian*, 12 June 2004, www.guardian.co.uk/review/story/0,12084,1236078,00.html (accessed 18 June 2006).

14 J. Jamison, 'A disappointment', posted 8 October 2004, www.amazon.com/review/R3MQEPK44XDTZ2/ref=cm_cr_rdp_perm (accessed 3 March 2005).

15 T. Lehner, 'An appallingly bad book', posted 24 February 2004, www.amazon.com/review/R2FPHX9VPI638U/ref=cm_cr_rdp_perm (accessed 3 March 2005).

16 Christine, 'A silly waste of time', posted 21 October 2004, www.amazon.com/review/R3JJ31NFUMHXVP/ref=cm_cr_rdp_perm (accessed 3 March 2005).

17 J. Jamison, 'A disappointment'.

18 Review cited at www.philippagregory.com/reviews/the-other-boleyn-girl/newsday.php, ellipsis original (accessed 9 April 2008). I am grateful to an anonymous student for citing this quote in an essay.

19 *Astraea*, London: Vintage, 2002, p. 4.

20 Ibid., p. 5.

21 Ibid.

22 Ibid.

23 L. Doan and S. Waters, 'Making up lost time: contemporary lesbian writing and the invention of history', in D. Alderson and L. Anderson (eds) *Territories of Desire in Queer*

Culture: Refiguring the Contemporary Boundaries, Manchester: Manchester University Press, 2000, pp. 12–29.

24 Email to author, 31 October 2006.

25 The long-running cartoon *Hägar the Horrible*, 1973–, and pseudo-historical fantasy *Conan the Barbarian* (created by R.E. Howard in 1932; in comics from 1970 onwards) notwithstanding.

26 J.A. Hughes, '"Who watches the watchmen?": ideology and "real world" superheroes', *Journal of Popular Culture*, 39(4) (2006), 546–57.

27 A. Moore and K. O'Neill, *The League of Extraordinary Gentlemen* Volume 1, LaJolla, CA: America's Best Comics, 2000. In a similar counterfactual-fictional vein, E. Lavallee and G. Bond's *Revere* pits the War of Independence hero against redcoats *and* werewolves, San Diego, CA: Alias Comics, 2006.

28 A. Moore and E. Campbell, *From Hell*, London: Knockabout Comics, 1999, p. 33.

29 *King: A Comics Biography of Martin Luther King, Jr.*, Seattle, WA: Fantagraphics Books, 2005.

30 www.komikwerks.com/comic_title.php?ti=86 (accessed 23 November 2007).

31 See J. Witek, *Comic Books as History*, Jackson, TN: University Press of Mississippi, 1989, pp. 75–96.

32 G. Groth, 'Critique revisited: an interview with Jack Jackson', *The Comics Journal*, 213, www.tcj.com/237/i_jackson.html (accessed 19 September 2007).

33 *Maus I: My Father Bleeds History*, London: Penguin, 1987; *Maus II: A Survivor's Tale*, London: Penguin, 1992.

34 Explained by the epigraph of the first book: '"The Jews are undoubtedly a race, but they are not human". Adolf Hitler', *Maus* I, p. 4.

35 *Maus* II, pp. 98–9, *Maus* I, p. 159.

36 Witek, *Comic Books*, p. 117.

37 *Maus* II, pp. 70, 84. M. Hirsch, 'Surviving images: Holocaust photographs and the work of postmemory', *Yale Journal of Criticism*, 14(1) (2001), 5–37 and 'Family pictures: *Maus*, mourning and post-memory', *Discourse*, 15(2) (1992–93), 3–29 discusses in depth the reuse of images and photographs.

38 *Maus* II, p. 69.

39 Hirsch, 'Surviving images' p. 9, see also her *Family Frames: Photography, Narrative and Postmemory*, Cambridge, MA: Harvard University Press, 1997.

40 Hirsch, 'Surviving images', pp. 9, 31.

41 M. Orvell, 'Writing posthistorically: Krazy Kat, Maus, and the contemporary fiction cartoon', *American Literary History*, 4(1) (1992), 110–28 (p. 110).

42 Nicholas Hytner said of this last production: 'As the war [in Iraq] finished and as scepticism returned and we were looking at it with cooler heads, that which is propagandistic about the play and that within the play which is hagiographic about the king felt very familiar', www.nationaltheatre.org.uk/Nicholas%20Hytner%20on%20Henry%20V+16746.twl (accessed 7 December 2007).

43 The original 1980 production had been privately prosecuted for an 'act of gross indecency' by the moral campaigner Mary Whitehouse.

44 R. H. Palmer, *The Contemporary British History Play*, London: Greenwood Press, 1998.

45 S. Watt, *Postmodern/Drama*, Ann Arbor, MI: University of Michigan Press, 1998. See also M. Vanden Heuvel, '"Is postmodernism?": Stoppard among/against the postmoderns', in K.E. Kelly (ed.) *The Cambridge Companion to Tom Stoppard*, Cambridge: Cambridge University Press, 2001, pp. 213–29.

46 Barry, *The Steward of Christendom*, 1995, Royal Court, 1995; Friel, *Dancing At Lughnasa* 1990, National Theatre; McGuinness, *Observe the Sons of Ulster Marching Towards the Somme*, 1985, revived 1996 London, Barbican. See M. Llewellyn-Jones, *Contemporary Irish Drama and Cultural Identity*, London: Intellect Books, 2002; while it covers prose, A. Arrowsmith, 'Photographic memories: nostalgia and Irish diaspora writing', *Textual Practice*, 19(2) (2005), 297–322 has interesting things to say about heritage-nostalgia Irishness as it is manifested in diasporic writing and contemporary culture.

47 *Mother Clap's Molly House*, London: Methuen, 2001, pp. 85–6.
48 Ibid., p. 56.
49 G. Saunders: *'Love Me or Kill Me'. Sarah Kane and the Theatre of Extremes*, Manchester: Manchester University Press, 2002.
50 The play transferred to the Duchess Theatre in London from 1999 to 2001 and was performed on Broadway from 2000 to 2001.
51 See V. Stewart, 'A theatre of uncertainties: science and history in Michael Frayn's *Copenhagen*,' *New Theatre Quarterly*, 15(4) (1999), 301–7.
52 See the essays in Matthias Dörries (ed.) *Michael Frayn's Copenhagen in Debate*, Berkeley, CA: University of California Press, 2005, and D.C. Cassidy, 'A historical perspective on *Copenhagen*', *Physics Today*, 53(7) (2000), 28–32.
53 'Dark matter: the controversy surrounding Michael Frayn's *Copenhagen*' *Archipelago*, 8(3) (2004), 80–103.
54 Michael Frayn, *Copenhagen*, London: Methuen, 2003, pp. 71–2.
55 Ibid., p. 88.

Part VI Artefact and interpretation

1 www.culture.gov.uk/global/press_notices/archive_2006/dcms032_06.htm (accessed 1 June 2006).
2 Obviously, though, museums still only appeal to a relatively small and self-selecting section of the population, despite their attempts at engaging with key access issues, see E. Hooper-Greenhill, *Museums and their Visitors*, London: Routledge, 1994.
3 See, for instance, K. Moore, *Museums and Popular Culture*, London: Leicester University Press, 1997.
4 Moore, *Museums and Popular Culture*, p. 8. See P. Vergo (ed.) *The New Museology*, London: Reaktion Books, 1989; T. Bennett, *The Birth of the Museum*, London: Routledge, 1995; Sharon MacDonald (ed.) *The Politics of Display: Museums, Science, Culture*, London: Routledge, 1998; and E. Hooper-Greenhill, *Museums and the Shaping of Knowledge*, London and New York: Routledge, 1992.
5 'Introduction', in Vergo, *The New Museology*, pp. 1–6 (p. 3).
6 'ICOM Code of Professional Ethics', in G. Edson and D. Dean, *The Handbook for Museums*, London: Routledge, 1994, pp. 238–55 (p. 239).
7 'Museums, artefacts, and meanings', in Vergo, *The New Museology*, pp. 6–22 (p. 9).
8 See, for instance, P.H. Welsh, 'Re-configuring museums', *Museum Management and Curatorship*, 20 (2005), 103–30, on the complex relationship between theory and practice.
9 *Museums and their Visitors*, p. 20.
10 From the late 1980s onwards, there was a proliferation of training programmes producing museum professionals, K. Hudson, 'The museum refuses to stand still', in B. Messias Carbonell (ed.) *Museum Studies*, Oxford: Blackwell, 2004, pp. 85–92.

15 Museums and physical encounters with the past

1 www.culture.gov.uk/global/press_notices/archive_2005/lammy_ma_speech.htm
2 Ibid.
3 Ibid.
4 This led to a massive surge in visits – nearly 6 million more visits to the formerly charging national museums in 2004, compared to the year before admission charges were abolished; visits went up *c*.75 per cent per year nationally.
5 *Understanding the Future: Museums and 21st Century Life*, London: HMSO 2005, p. 3.
6 Ibid.
7 D. Prudames, 'Visitors at heart of new Renaissance chapter', *Renaissance News*, Autumn 2005, p. 11.

8 www.mla.gov.uk/webdav/harmonise?Page/@id=73&Document/@id=18357&Section (@stateId_eq_left_hand_root)/@id=4302 (accessed 18 January 2006).

9 Ibid.

10 'Popularity of museums and galleries', www.mori.com/polls/2004/mla.shtml (accessed 5 May 2006).

11 K. Moore, *Museums and Popular Culture*, London: Leicester University Press, 1997, p. 5.

12 T. Bennett, 'Museums and the people', in Lumley, *The Museum Time Machine*, pp. 63–86 (p. 63).

13 Ibid., p. 64.

14 Ibid., p. 84.

15 J. Corner and S. Harvey, 'Mediating tradition and modernity: the heritage/enterprise couplet', in J. Corner and S. Harvey (eds) *Enterprise and Heritage*, New York: Routledge, 1991, pp. 45–75 (p. 49).

16 *The Historic Environment: A Force for Our Future*, 2001, at www.culture.gov.uk/NR/rdonly res/EB6ED76A-E1C6–4DB0-BFF7–7086D1CEFB9A/0/historic_environment_review _part1.pdf, p. 7.

17 Ibid., p. 9.

18 Ibid.

19 www.visitwales.co.uk/57660/08.AA.AA.html/?profile=NDpMT05fV1RCMjY2MzEz ODk6TE9OX1dUQjE3OTTg0NjExOkVOR0xJU0g6R0I6OjExMzY4MjAyMTE6Ojo (accessed 9 January 2006).

20 www.visitscotland.com/aboutscotland/history/ (accessed 9 January 2006).

21 *The Historic Environment*, p. 17.

22 Ibid., p. 4.

23 Ibid., p. 7.

24 *Imagined Communities: Reflections on the Origin and Spread of Nationalism*, London: Verso, 1991.

25 A. Leon Harney, 'Money changers in the temple? Museums and the financial mission', in K. Moore (ed.) *Museum Management*, London: Routledge, 1994, pp. 132–47.

26 E. Hooper-Greenhill, *Museum and Gallery Education*, Leicester: Leicester University Press, 1994, p. 67.

27 S. Kirby, 'Policy and politics: charges, sponsorship, and bias', in Lumley, *The Museum Time Machine*, pp. 89–102.

28 *Marketing the Museum*, London: Routledge, 1997, p. 37. See also E. Hooper-Greenhill, *Museums and their Visitors*, London: Routledge, 1994, M.A. Fopp, *Managing Museums and Galleries*, London: Routledge, 1997, and P. Lewis, 'Museums and Marketing', in Moore, *Museum Management*, pp. 216–32.

29 This is an enormous shift in culture if one considers the state of the profession just under 20 years ago as delineated in E. Hooper-Greenhill, 'Counting visitors or visitors who count?' in Lumley, *The Museum Time Machine*, pp. 213–30. 'The quality of the experience is beginning to matter' she suggests, while noting that to most museum staff 'visitors are faceless ciphers' and that 'evaluation of the work of the museum is measured by weight of bodies rather than by depth of experience', ibid., pp. 215, 213. This contrasts with the 1999 publication of S. Runyard and Y. French, *The Marketing and Public Relations Handbook for Museums, Galleries and Heritage Foundations*, London: The Stationery Office, 1999.

30 'Mediating tradition', p. 73.

31 The Friends of the British Museum, for instance, have been instrumental in 'saving' objects for the Museum – and therefore the 'nation'. Their support impacts upon collections, too, as Friends' donations both financial and material to the museum account for some £3.5 million since the foundation of the organisation in 1968.

32 Information from FAME financial information database.

33 Cited in G. Edson, *Museum Ethics*, London: Routledge, 1997, p. 242. It seems that this passage has been taken out of the code of ethics ratified by ICOM in 2004, replaced

with the more general 'Income-generating activities should not compromise the standards of the institution or its public', www.icom.museum/ethics.html (accessed 4 March 2008).

34 C. Duncan, 'Museums and department stores: close encounters' in J. Collins (ed.) *High-Pop: Making Culture into Popular Entertainment*, Oxford: Blackwell, 2002, pp. 129–55 (p. 129).

35 See N. McLaughlin, 'Where art and commerce meet', *Marketing*, 24(1), Jan. 9 1986, 20–23, M. Kennedy, 'Shopping and looking', *Museums Journal*, 104(4) (2004), 28–29, B. Hodgdon, *The Shakespeare Trade*, Philadelphia, PA: University of Pennsylvania Press, 1998, pp. 232–4, and A. Kraus, 'Extending exhibits: integrating the museum store', *Museum News*, 82 (2003), 36–9.

36 Even site-specific institutions are involved in this virtualised or distanced commercialisation. The National Heritage Act of 2002 broadened the power of English Heritage, allowing them to become involved in underwater archaeology but more importantly to trade in overseas countries.

37 See, for instance, www.themuseumstorecompany.com, which sells reproductions and real pieces under the trademark 'Own a piece of history … Give a piece of history'.

38 Cited in I. van Aalst and I. Boogaarts, 'From museum to mass entertainment: the evolution of the role of museums in cities', *European Urban and Regional Studies*, 9(3) (2002), 195–209 (p. 209).

39 Ibid., p. 196.

40 K. Hetherington, 'Museums and the visually impaired: the spatial politics of access', *Sociological Review*, 48(3) (2000), 444–62 (p. 450), and Foundation de France/ICOM, *Museums Without Barriers: A New Deal for Disabled People*, London and New York: Routledge, 1991.

41 See Hetherington, 'Museums and the visually impaired'.

42 O. Richwald, 'Museum shop is a real curiosity', *Northern Echo*, October 3 2005, p. 7. It also won several national awards.

43 www.hartlepool.gov.uk/news/archivednews/curiosityshoptoopenitsdoors (accessed 12 December 2005).

44 P. Wright, *On Living in an Old Country*, London: Verso, 1986, p. 14, the concept here arises in his discussion of Agnes Heller's work and *Theory of History* in particular.

45 A. Barry, 'On interactivity', in S. Macdonald (ed.) *The Politics of Display: Museums, Science, Culture*, London: Routledge, 1998, pp. 98–118.

46 Barry, 'On interactivity', p. 102, italics original. See also H. Hein, *The Exploratorium*, Washington, DC: Smithsonian, 1990.

47 R. Parry, 'Including technology', in J. Dodd and R. Sandell (eds) *Including Museums: Perspectives on Museums, Galleries and Social Inclusion*, Leicester: RCMG, 2001, pp. 110–14, and his *Re-coding the Museum*, London: Routledge, 2007.

48 R. Parry and N. Arbach, 'The localized learner: acknowledging distance and situatedness in on-line museum learning', in J. Trant and D. Bearman (eds) *Museums and the Web 2005: Proceedings*, Toronto: Archives & Museum Informatics, published 31 March 2005 at www.archimuse.com/mw2005/papers/parry/parry.html (accessed 1 June 2006).

49 This has obvious educational benefits as well as challenges, see S. J. Knell, 'The shape of things to come: museums in the technological landscape', *Museum and Society*, 1(3) (2003), 113–21 and S. Brown, 'Do richer media mean better learning? a framework for evaluating learning experiences in museum web site design', *International Journal of Heritage Studies*, 12(5) (2006), 412–27.

50 Parry and Arbach, 'The localized learner' and Parry, *Re-coding the Museum*.

51 See, for instance, work on using specifically web-based platforms and techniques to deal with a variety of learning styles, D.T. Schaller, S. Allison-Bunnell and M. Borun, 'Learning styles and online interactives', in Trant and Bearman *Museums and the Web*, available at www.archimuse.com/mw2005/papers/schaller/schaller.html (accessed 1 June 2006).

Conclusions

1 I owe this phrasing to Martin L. Davies.
2 K. Jenkins, S. Morgan and A. Munslow (eds) *Manifestos for History*, London: Routledge, 2007, p. 231.
3 Ibid., citing the work of Paul Grainge, p. 932.
4 C. Rojek, *Decentring Leisure*, London: Sage, 2004, p. 9. See M.L. Davies, *Historics: Why History Dominates Contemporary Society*, Abingdon: Routledge, 2006.
5 Pickering and Keightley, 'The Modalities of Nostalgia', p. 937.

Index